Ghosts

Ghosts

Edited by Peter Brookesmith

BLACK CAT

Acknowledgements
Pictures were supplied by Aldus Archives, American International Pictures, Ancient Monuments of Scotland, Anglia TV, Aerofilms, BBC Hulton Picture Library, Janet and Colin Bord, Boston Athenaeum, Bridgeman Art Library, British Tourist Authority, Richard Burgess, City of Manchester Art Gallery, Bill Clegg, Clyde Surveys, Bruce Coleman, A. Cornell, Country Life, Anne Court, J. Cutten, Arnold Desser, Devon Library Service, Ian Duncan, East Lothian Library, Eastman Photography, Robert Estall, Mary Evans Picture Library, Joan Forman, Werner Forman Archive, Fortean Picture Library, Roy Fulton, R.H. Gibhours, Colin Godman, Andrew Green, Martin Green, Maurice Grosse, Elmer Gruber, Sonia Halliday, Jim Hancock, Melvin Harris, Hodder and Stoughton, Toby Hogarth, Michael Holford, Mike Hooks, Robert Hunt Library, Institut fur Grenzgebiete der Psychologie, Maurice Johanasburg, Keystone, Kobal, McEwan Library, Mansell Collection, Medical Illustration Service, Graham Morris, Jeannie Morrison, National Gallery of Scotland, National Portrait Gallery, Peter Newark's Western Americana, Newsday, Picturepoint, Pitkin Pictorial, Guy Lyon Playfair, Popperfoto, Psychic News, RAF Museum, Rex, Mike Reynolds, Kate Robertson, J. Rundle, Scottish National Portrait Gallery, Sheffield Newspapers, Ronald Sheridan, Spectrum, J. Strang, Suddeutscher Verlag, Syndication International, John Topham, D.C. Thomson, David Towersey, Nigel Tranter, Turner's Photography, UPI, Blair Urquhart, J. Whitelaw, Graham Whitlock.

Consultants
Professor A.J. Ellison
Dr J. Allen Hynek
Brian Inglis
Colin Wilson
Editorial Director
Brian Innes
Editor
Peter Brookesmith

Deputy Editor
Lynn Picknett
Executive Editor
Lesley Riley
Sub Editors
Mitzi Bales
Chris Cooper
Jenny Dawson
Hildi Hawkins

Picture Researchers
Anne Horton
Paul Snelgrove
Frances Vargo
Editorial Manager
Clare Byatt
Art Editor
Stephen Westcott

Designer
Richard Burgess
Art Buyer
Jean Morley
Production Co-ordinator
Nicky Bowden
Volume Editor
Lorrie Mack

The publishers would like to thank the following authors for contributing to this book:
Paul Begg 67–70; Joan Forman 185–193; Colin Godman 144–150; Colin Godman and Lindsay St Claire 156–163; Michael Goss 63–66; Andrew Green 9–25; Anita Gregory 116–118; Elmar Gruber 164–166; Elmar Gruber and Susan Fassberg 152–155; Melvin Harris 76–77, 84–86, 168–173; Guy Lyon Playfair 39–50, 107–115; Archie Roy 140–143; Frank Smyth 27–38, 71–74, 78–83, 87–106, 120–139, 174–183, 194–204; Colin Wilson 51–62.

© 1980, 1981, 1982, 1983, 1984 Orbis Publishing Ltd

First published in Great Britain by
Orbis Publishing Limited, London 1984
Reprinted 1992 under the Black Cat imprint

Printed and bound in Czechoslovakia by Aventinum
50837/01

ISBN 0 7481 0310 4

Contents

A GUIDE TO POLTERGEISTS 8

Bumps, thumps, rattles and pranks 9
Sex and the mischievous spirit 14
Paradoxes of the poltergeist 18
Is exorcism really necessary? 22

A GUIDE TO GHOSTS 26

A short history of hauntings 27
Ghosts without souls? 31
Understanding ghosts 35
In search of apparitions 39
Ghosts true and false 44
A ghost hunter's guide 47

GHOSTS AND LEGEND 50

Spirit guides at Glastonbury 51
A career in ruins 56
A very strange place 59
Taken for a ride? 63
Phantom of the high seas 67
Out of the Celtic twilight 71

HAUNTED ENGLAND 75

No judge of the truth 76
The ghost and the gossips 78
Poltergeist on trial 81
The ghost with wet boots 84
Mayfair's haunted house 87
Borley: a haunting tale 91
Borley: the tension mounts 96
Borley in ruins? 100
No end to Borley 103

Enfield: the trouble begins 107
Enfield: whatever next? 112
Enfield on trial 116

HAUNTED SCOTLAND 119

Turning in his grave 120
The horror of Glamis 124
Dead men tell no tales 128
The curse of Fyvie Castle 132
Burning with guilt 136
A sense of something strange 140
The case of the crippled phantom 144
A desirable residence? 148

HAUNTED EUROPE 151

A pinch and a punch 152
Beware – PK at work 156
A spirit of anger 160
Faces from another world? 164

HAUNTED AMERICA 167

Amityville – horror or hoax? 168
Amityville unlimited 171
The Bell Witch strikes 174
Spook lights over America 180

PHANTOM PHENOMENA 184

Old soldiers never die 185
Ghosts on the march 190
The skulls that screamed 194
A large measure of spirits 198
Ghosts of the air 202

Introduction

What is a ghost? I suspect that most of us – if we think about the subject at all – imagine transparent wraiths haunting ruined castles or, equally traditionally, a headless horseman riding soundlessly down a country lane, both at midnight. Those who admit to a belief in ghosts generally assume that such spectres are spirits of the dead, bound to the scene of ancient passions and crimes by some mysterious law.

On the whole such creatures do not inspire the intelligent man or woman with a belief in the paranormal, hence the frequency of the motion 'This house does not believe in ghosts' among school and university debating societies. But, as Professor Henry Habberley Price of Oxford University insisted in the 1950s, the question 'Do you believe in ghosts?' is ridiculous unless one can define 'ghosts'. He pointed out that nobody could seriously deny that 'hundreds of people in their right minds have seen or heard somebody who was not there'; in other words, an apparition. But if apparitions, or ghosts, can be seen or heard, in what sense are they 'not there'? Do they have an objective existence – can anybody see them – or are they 'merely' hallucinations, existing only in the eye of the beholder?

Even if apparitions are hallucinations, they often appear to have a paranormal component. Goethe once 'saw' his friend Frederick walking along a road, somewhat ludicrously attired in his, Goethe's, dressing gown, bedroom slippers and nightcap. This must have been an hallucination, because Frederick was at that very moment sitting in Goethe's house. But the poet did not know this – nor could he have known that Frederick had changed into Goethe's nightclothes after being drenched to the skin on his way there.

There are scores of such well-attested accounts of apparitions, often witnessed by two or more people simultaneously. Sometimes, as in Goethe's case, these spectres are of the living. Such curious doubles, traditionally known as *doppelgängers*, appear in two places at once. Sometimes images are of the dying, or of those experiencing profound emotional distress, and these are called crisis apparitions.

Then too there are the cases of friends who promise each other that whoever dies first will appear to the other – and who have indeed returned as apparitions. A college friend of Lord Chancellor Brougham kept just such a promise, suddenly appearing while the Chancellor was in the bath! Brougham later discovered that his friend had died at that very moment, but being a sceptical Scot, he attributed this to 'coincidence'. Even without their pledge, however, the appearance of the friend at the moment of his death cannot be dismissed so lightly. Supposing – as seems likely from the evidence – the dead man was redeeming his pledge? How was he able to seem indistinguishable from his live self? For make no mistake, as William James asserted, 'Every hallucination is a perception, as good and true a sensation as if there were a real object there. The object happens not to *be* there – that is all.'

The experiencing of ghosts need not be exclusively visual however; they may be heard, felt, or even smelled, although not by all of the people or all of the time. Certain 'sensitives' are more likely to be aware of ghostly presences than the vast majority of people. But there is one type of 'ghost' that makes itself felt in no uncertain fashion – the poltergeist (noisy spirit).

Poltergeists seem, as the Enfield investigation revealed, to delight in defying natural laws. They can make solid objects materialise out of thin air, or dematerialise. They can throw objects in ways that make nonsense of gravity – around corners, for example. One of their greatest delights is to wreak havoc with the investigators' recording and monitoring equipment; not only is this infuriating and expensive, but naturally plays into the hands of the sceptics, since they can then take the line that, since no proof can be supplied, the phenomena do not exist. As the investigators of the Rosenheim poltergeist reported, the havoc caused appeared to be under the control of some kind of intelligence that exhibited 'a tendency to evade investigation'.

Nevertheless there is plenty of strong evidence for poltergeist infestation, because the investigators have time on their side; the phenomena tend to continue for weeks or even months, leaving a trail of destruction and chaos behind them. The Rosenheim case in particular was investigated over a period of time – by the police, the telephone company, the electricity board, engineers from Siemens and two of Germany's most eminent physicists, all trying to find a natural explanation for the mayhem in the lawyer's office – before Professor Hans Bender (West Germany's leading parapsychologist) discovered the 'focus'. This was a young secretary working in the office, who was subconsciously 'exteriorising' her inner tensions. She was not physically capable of causing the chaos at her workplace, but she is one of those people who seem able to mobilise psychic forces as an expression of her frustrations.

In fact, no human being could have caused some of the strange happenings at Rosenheim, such as the sudden, massive 'surges' in the electricity supply and the extraordinarily large number of telephone calls that were recorded by the telephone company; these were not only not being dialled, but were being made faster than was physically possible. As the physicists were compelled to admit, 'the events defied explanation in terms of current physical theories', facing them 'with the unexpected situation that theoretical physics may be led to the discovery of new principles through the study of human faculties.'

But this raises the question: is every ghost the product of a similar kind of psychic 'exteriorisation'? Do we – especially those of us capable of receiving and transmitting the psychic current – create phantoms? Is this what happens when we experience apparitions of the dying, hundreds of which have been reported? It is theoretically possible to account for them by ESP; perhaps we pick up some emanation from the dying person by telepathy and our subconscious minds translate this into the form of an apparition.

Nevertheless there is also evidence that the dead do return, with or without help from the living. The Italian psychical researcher Ernesto Bozzano tells of one such case in which there seemed no doubt that the extraordinary mayhem in an empty, locked and sealed flat was the work of a friend of his – who had committed suicide there.

If, then, we accept survival of death as a fact, elaborate alternative theories are unnecessary; the spirit of the dying or dead person may actually present itself to us. As in the story of Lord Chancellor Brougham and his friend, many ghosts appear at the very moment of their death – as if performing a kind of leave-taking. There are many other point-of-death phenomena, such as the wailing of the banshee, clocks that stop at that fatal second, or bells that toll without human agency. Death seems to set up powerful psychic currents.

Of course there are many with a feel for the dramatic who create ghost stories or masquerade as poltergeists to impress the gullible. But to dismiss all the – very considerable – evidence for the reality of ghosts because some have turned out to be fakes is as facile as saying that because there are thieves and forgers no one has come by his credit card honestly.

Ghosts do exist. There is very little, however, that we can claim to understand about them, but we should not give up hope. Investigations into all aspects of hauntings are difficult and tedious, as was that of Guy Lyon Playfair and Maurice Grosse into the Enfield poltergeist, but they add significantly to perhaps the most fascinating aspect of human knowledge.

Brian Inglis

A guide to poltergeists

Bumps, thumps, rattles and pranks

Poltergeists, unlike ghosts, 'haunt' by causing commotions, making noises, throwing things around. These odd disturbances have been the subject of detailed investigation

MYSTERIOUS BANGS, loud crashes, objectionable smells, furniture that moves about on its own, sudden cold spells, inexplicable voices, objects that appear and disappear, the uncontrolled levitation of victims – these are all symptoms of what is often called poltergeist activity. (The word poltergeist is derived from two German words – a folklore term, *polter*, meaning 'noisy' and the word for 'spirit', *geist*.) The development of psychical research and parapsychology during the last 100 years has introduced into the language a more cumbersome phrase to describe the same phenomena – recurrent spontaneous psychokinesis (RSPK).

Such disturbances have been recorded since at least the 12th century. At one time they were believed to be caused by an evil force, a creature of Satan, though the identity of the force remained a mystery. Writing in the 13th century, Gerald of Wales noted that a 'spirit' was heard to converse with a group of men in an alarmingly aggressive fashion; 300 years later, in 1599, one of the first authentic examinations of this type of incident was undertaken by Martin del Rio. He described 18 kinds of demon, including one that specialised in causing disturbances:

> The 16th type are spectres which in certain times and places or homes are wont to occasion various commotions and annoyances. I shall pass over examples since the thing is exceedingly well known. . . . Some disturb slumbers with clattering of pots and hurling of stones and others pull away a mattress and turn one out of bed.

Although there are still some people today

Living ghosts

An unusual feature of some RSPK cases is the materialisation of 'phantoms' – invisible manifestations of living people or animals.

In one famous case a boy of four was lying asleep in a bedroom in a Sussex public house where his father was landlord. His mother was resting on a bed in the opposite corner of the room. The child was obviously having a disturbing dream, and suddenly his body twitched three times. Each time his mother felt 'something invisible' fall on to her bed. When the child woke up he asked a strange question: 'What has happened to the cat?' The family did not have a cat – but the former landlord, who had also had a four-year-old son, had shared the room with a black cat that vanished when they left the public house. A coincidence? Perhaps – but a parapsychologist who heard of the case has suggested that a force generated by the dreaming child was powerful enough to simulate the imaginary and invisible cat.

This explanation could account for the phantom footsteps heard on another occasion. In this case steps were heard in a room that was known to be quite empty, and it was later discovered that a child asleep in an adjoining bedroom had been dreaming about one of his relations, whom he imagined to be striding through the property.

But it seems that such phantoms can be summoned up by design as well as by accident. In the course of a fascinating experiment conducted in the 1950s a researcher was asked to try to dream about visiting a certain room in a house he knew in Brighton, which was a long way away. Two witnesses, who had not been told of the details of the experiment, were stationed in the room. In due course they watched the dreamer – in fact, a phantom who resembled the dreamer in every detail – open the door of the room, as instructed, walk around for a moment or two and then leave. Throughout the experiment the dreamer himself had not left his bed.

Previous page top: Mama, Papa and the maid stand aghast as the nursery is bombarded by flying pots and pans. The child, however, sleeps on through this barrage of objects

Previous page bottom and below: scenes during the poltergeist 'haunting' in a council house at Enfield, north London, between August 1977 and September 1978. Twelve-year-old Janet seemed to be the epicentre (focus) of the disturbances, often being dragged out of bed by an invisible force Even when she took to sleeping on the floor she was still forcibly moved and was often found asleep on top of the large radio When Janet was seized by the force it was very difficult to hold her down, as researcher Maurice Grosse discovered

who maintain that RSPK can be attributed to the activity of 'elementals', it is more generally accepted that 'hauntings' of this kind have a 'natural', not a 'supernatural', origin. Yet we still do not understand them.

The most spectacular case of RSPK ever recorded lasted for an 11-month period, from August 1977 to September 1978. During this time a woman and her four children, who were living in a council house in Enfield, on the northern outskirts of London, experienced practically every type of poltergeist phenomenon that has been identified. No fewer than 1500 separate incidents were recorded between August and March, and this astonishing barrage of disturbances mystified all those who were involved in the investigations, including social workers, a speech therapist, photographers, psychologists, priests and two investigators, Guy Lyon Playfair and Maurice Grosse.

As is normal in such cases, the 'haunting' started in a comparatively quiet fashion. A 'sort of shuffling sound' seemed to come from the floor of a bedroom, which was like the noise made by someone shambling across a room in slippers, according to the mother of the family. Then knocking started, and this continued for nearly 11 months.

A voice, deep, gruff and crude, was tape-recorded on many occasions. After several attempts had been made to identify it, the voice itself claimed to belong to a 72-year-old man from Durants Park, a nearby road. A listener to a local radio phone-in programme heard a recording of the voice and identified it as that of her uncle, Bill Haylock, whom she described as 'a gypsy type'. But every attempt to prove the validity of the claims failed – a fairly common experience in cases of this kind.

There were many other inexplicable incidents. On one occasion a toy brick suddenly appeared, 'flew' across the room and

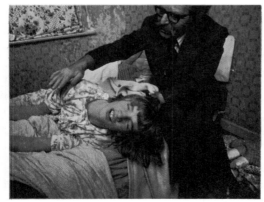

hit a photographer on the head. Paper and pieces of cloth caught fire spontaneously, and a box of matches that was lying in a drawer burst into flames, which extinguished themselves without igniting the rest of the contents of the drawer. A message, patched together from lengths of sticky tape, was found on the lavatory door. Cutlery, a metal teapot lid and a brass pipe were all seen to bend and twist of their own accord. Three pieces of stone were found scattered about the house, which were later discovered to be fragments of a single stone that had been split.

The strength of the force at work in the house can be gauged from some of the more impressive incidents. Part of a gas fire was wrenched away from the fireplace, and its grille was thrown across the sitting-room. Large pieces of furniture, among them a chest of drawers, a heavy sofa and a double bed, were tossed around the house.

Janet, the 12-year-old daughter, seems to have been the focus (the epicentre) of all this activity. It was from her that the deep voice appeared to emanate. It was she who experienced levitation (witnesses on two occasions said that she seemed to be suspended in mid-air). She and her sister Rose were thrown out of bed so often that in the end they decided to sleep on the floor – but that

Above: 'The drummer of Tidworth' – a poltergeist outbreak recorded in 1666 by the Reverend Joseph Glanvill. 'A strange scratching sound', or sometimes a drumming noise, was often heard in the bedroom occupied by two young girls

did not put an end to the poltergeist's activities, for Janet was often found, fast asleep, on top of a radio in her bedroom.

Although the family was very frightened at first, as time wore on the children and their mother were mystified rather than alarmed. Their reaction was typical of the attitude adopted by many of those who experience RSPK in Britain, as poltergeists generally cause little actual damage or physical injury. As one investigator has pointed out: 'RSPK is really a series of nuisance incidents, rather like the actions of a frustrated adolescent or a child-like personality.' This is not entirely true of American cases, however; experts such as W. G. Roll have acknowledged that many victims of poltergeist activity in the United States do suffer physical injury, albeit minor.

The Enfield case was certainly remarkable for the extent and duration of the phenomena

that the family experienced, and a study is included in this volume. Many of its features however are common to other 'hauntings'.

Mysterious knocking and rappings, for example, are often the first indications of the presence of a poltergeist (though some people notice first that objects are moved from their usual places). An early classic British case of RSPK, which became known as the Drummer of Tidworth, was recorded in 1666 by the Reverend Joseph Glanvill, who lived in a house on the site of the present Zouch Manor in Wiltshire. Two girls occupied a bedroom from which a 'strange drumming sound' seemed to emerge. The noise was traced to a point 'behind the bolster'; sceptics argued that the girls were the cause. But eventually the girls were cleared of suspicion. Their hands were always outside the bedclothes, and as for the noise, the Reverend Glanvill reported that he

Far left: Maurice Grosse with some souvenirs from his investigation of the Enfield case. Among them are household objects that were burnt or broken mysteriously

Above left: boxes of matches that were set alight and then extinguished by London poltergeists

A guide to poltergeists

could find 'no trick, contrivance or common cause' to explain it. In the absence of concrete evidence, a legend arose to account for the weird drumming sound.

In America in 1848 a celebrated case, known as the Fox case, appeared to confirm that raps were an early indication of poltergeist activity. It was this case that later prompted the founding of the Spiritualist movement, as hysterical and imaginative witnesses assumed that spirits were trying to communicate through the two girls who were apparently (but unconsciously) responsible for the sounds that were heard.

In 1960 a similar case was investigated in Alloa, in Scotland, where a girl of 11 heard a curious 'thunking' noise, rather like a ball bouncing (or a drumming?), that seemed to come from the head of her bed. An unusual aspect of what later developed into an extremely interesting example of RSPK was that the girl herself was so calm about the experience that investigators were able to record the incidents in a rational and detailed manner. Like the Reverend Glanvill 300 years earlier, the Reverend Lund, one of the investigators involved with the case, found that the violent vibrations were indeed coming from the head of the girl's bed, and he ruled out the possibility of fraud.

In a case in Battersea, in south London, in the 1950s, however, the poltergeist announced its arrival by placing an unidentified key on the bed of a 14-year-old girl, Shirley Hitching. This incident remained as puzzling as Shirley's ability to produce raps, several paces from her body, in answer to questions that she asked her 'polty'. Perhaps to prevent hysteria and mental stress, she and her parents, like many other victims, invented a personality for the poltergeist, whom they called Donald. They decided that he was the spirit of a 14-year-old illegitimate son of Charles II of France named Louis Capet. Donald was irrepressible. He decorated the walls and ceiling of Shirley's bedroom with graffiti and pictures of film stars, and he wrote letters (or so it was

Top: Harry Hanks, a psychic, gives his views on the Battersea poltergeist to an interviewer after a seance

Above: Shirley Hitching, the 14-year-old who was the focus for the 'haunting'

Right: blocks of paving stones – too large for a man to pick up – were hurled with great violence at a coalman's house in Paris in 1846. The missiles continued to smash the house even when it was guarded by police and soldiers. After bombarding the house for several weeks the poltergeist abruptly ceased its activities

claimed) to a number of dignitaries, including Lord Brabazon.

Alien voices are a common feature of RSPK. Various theories have been advanced to explain the phenomenon, among which perhaps one of the most plausible is that of a 19th-century French doctor, Gilles de la Tourette. He identified certain symptoms of trauma and severe stress and classified them as forms of copropraxia (the delight in, and inappropriate use of, obscene language) and echolalia (the meaningless repetition of speech patterns). He observed that some of his patients made 'obscene gestures and explosive utterances', and many of the noises and barking sounds that he described were identical to those produced by 12-year-old Janet in Enfield who, like the Frenchman's patients, was under great stress (caused by, among other things, her parents' separation).

Spontaneous combustion too is often associated with poltergeist activity. In one case in Sussex a leading exorcist who was called in to deal with an alarming series of incidents was sitting chatting quietly to a five-year-old boy. Suddenly he noticed that a fire had started in one corner of the room. Within minutes all the wallpaper and the curtains were alight – but they were burning from the ceiling downwards. The flames stopped at an invisible line drawn all round the room. Objects on the windowsill remained untouched. The researcher realised that the fire was limited to the area beyond the child's reach, and the boy himself seemed only a little disturbed by the flames, which quickly extinguished themselves.

Stones play a part in many RSPK cases. A particularly rare instance occurred in Ceylon earlier this century. A man who had often

Are ghosts 'real' only in the eye of the beholder? Or are they perhaps part of an objective phenomenon that is nevertheless created – like poltergeists – by the human mind? In 1972 eight members of the Toronto, Canada, Society for Psychical Research decided to create a ghost. They invented a totally fictitious character called Philip, giving him a distinct personality and agreeing on the details of his non-existent 'life'. They made him the ghost of a 17th-century English aristocrat – a cavalier – whose torrid love affair with a gypsy called Margo ended when his wife denounced his mistress as a witch. She was burnt at the stake and Philip, enduring agonies of remorse, took to wandering the battlements and finally hurled himself to his death. The setting for this drama was Diddington Manor in Warwickshire – a real manor house, which still stands today, but the

Philip the phantom phantom

rest of the details were studiedly imaginary. Having 'created' Philip, the group held a seance once a week to try to get in touch with their brainchild. After a year, he began to answer back, giving one rap (on the table around which the group sat) for 'yes' and two for 'no'. They questioned him closely about his 'life' and, although most of his replies accorded exactly with his manufactured lifehistory, occasionally he seemed to take an independent line – almost as if he 'had a mind of his own'! Philip became a celebrity. The group demonstrated a typical 'Philip' seance on Canadian and American television with spectacular results (a heavy table turning over completely and floating in mid-air, for example). Inspired by the success of the Philip experiment, other groups are now creating their own 'ghost thoughtforms', and are trying to contact them.

been alerted by scratching and rapping sounds had always associated them with his two sons, aged 5 and 14. One afternoon the two boys went out for a walk with a friend. A little later the boys' father realised that it had been unwise to let the children wander about on their own, and he hurried after them. He was still some way away from them when he happened to turn around. He saw a stone, about the size of a small tennis ball, rapidly approaching him in mid-air. He put up his hand to catch it, but the stone swerved away from him at an angle of about 45 degrees, resumed its former route and flew on towards the boys. When the father caught up with the youngsters he learned that the stone had hit his elder son on the back, gently but firmly. Was the blow a punishment? Had the boy been bullying his younger brother? Impossible to tell – but it certainly seemed as though some form of intelligence had been controlling the path of the stone, for the father's attempt to catch it had proved useless: he merely deflected it.

This type of unseen control was once observed by the author, when he was investigating reported phenomena at a military establishment in Folkestone, in Kent, in 1974. Accompanied by two other researchers (and an armed guard, on whose presence the authorities had insisted), he was about to descend the main staircase of the building when he heard the sound of tinkling glass behind him. Turning instantly, he saw a light bulb rocking to and fro gently on the floor of the landing. The two other researchers also heard the noise, and one bent to pick up the bulb. The glass was warm to the touch. There were no cracks in the glass, and the filament was intact. The mystery – and it has remained unresolved to this day – was where did the bulb come from? If it had been fixed in one of the light sockets on the

Below: scene of poltergeist activity in Folkestone, Kent, in 1974. Observers discovered a light bulb on the landing of this staircase. it was warm and unbroken – yet had apparently travelled 26 feet (just under 8 metres) by means of some invisible agency

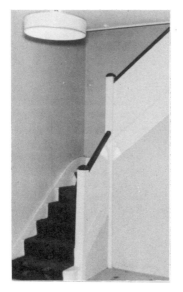

first floor, it would have had to travel in an S bend about 26 feet (just under 8 metres) from the ceiling of an empty room, around a half-open door and down on to the landing. Leaving aside the question of how it undertook this strange journey on its own, how was the bulb able to make such a soft landing that it suffered no damage? And what 'tinkled'?

It was in this same building that a large laundry basket, too heavy for three people to lift, was found to have moved from the ground floor to the airing cupboard close to where the light bulb was seen – and this happened when the building was quite empty. On another occasion, when the table in the large dining-room had been laid for an official function, two sets of cutlery vanished.

In the circumstances it can only be assumed that people who were in the building at different times were unconsciously responsible for the incidents. One of them may have been a particularly sensitive researcher who accompanied the author; the other was perhaps one of the female assistants who helped to prepare for the function on the day that the cutlery disappeared.

This is speculation, of course; we still have a great deal to learn about the sources of 'commotions and annoyances'. But one thing is certain: poltergeist activity is too common to be ignored or explained away as the product of fevered minds. The phenomena experienced by victims of RSPK are not illusions triggered by mental breakdown. On the other hand, neither should such experiences be taken too seriously. Perhaps just the right blend of scepticism and acceptance was displayed by an insurance company in 1942, when it paid out £400 against an £800 claim for damage caused by a poltergeist.

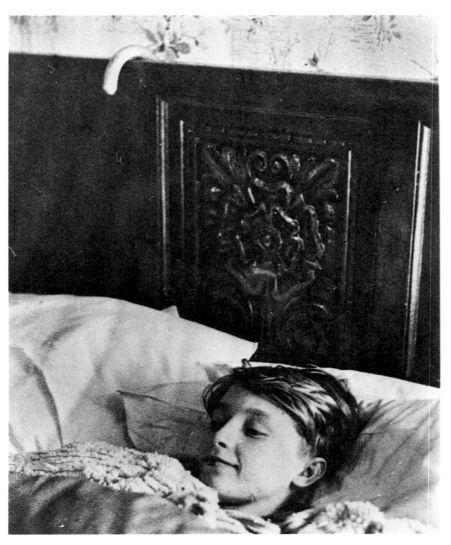

It was long held that at the centre of any poltergeist activity would be found a disturbed adolescent girl. But sexual tension in young or old, male or female, may result in an outbreak of the 'mischievous spirit'

AS MORE AND MORE CASES of poltergeist activity are subjected to rigorous investigation by parapsychologists, a clearer picture is emerging, not only of the possible causes of such phenomena, but also of those who are generally the victims. There are, of course, cases that evade classification, but research into recurrent spontaneous psychokinesis (RSPK) appears to support some broad conclusions.

The sexual drive, or libido, seems to be at the root of much paranormal experience. In the 1840s, when the case of the Fox sisters stirred up a great deal of interest in the United States and elsewhere, it was widely assumed that the girls' experiences were associated with the fact that they had reached puberty. Other cases that were examined at that time appeared to confirm the assumption that girls on the threshold of sexual maturity were to be blamed for all mysterious incidents; only young women, it was thought, could summon up reserves of energy that could move tables, produce strange sounds and cause objects to appear and disappear.

Certainly, many cases today involve girls at about the age of puberty. In the classic case of the Enfield family, which experienced intense and protracted disturbances

Sex and the mischievous spirit

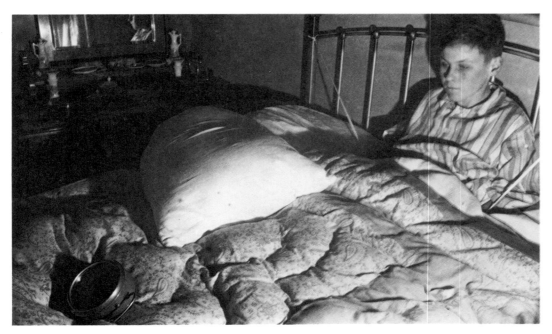

Above: while this 10-year-old boy was being filmed, the walking-stick hanging from his bed head jerked and jumped about of its own accord

Left: 12-year-old Alan Rhodes had his hands taped to the bedclothes to guard against trickery when his poltergeist was investigated by researcher Harry Price in 1945. Even so, the alarm clock managed to jump onto his bed, and was later joined by a trinket case from the dressing table

over a two-year period in 1977/78, Janet, the 12-year-old daughter, was clearly the epicentre. Shirley Hitchings of Battersea, in south London, another famous victim of poltergeist activity, was 14 years old. One middle-aged mother with a 12-year-old daughter recently told a parapsychologist that her family had experienced a number of incidents of RSPK during the course of a few weeks, both in the kitchen and in her daughter's bedroom.

Bumps, crashes and· saucepans flying about – you know, the usual type of thing. But when Sheila started her menses, it all stopped, of course. It was all a bit of a nuisance at the time, but we are all right now.

Apart from the onset of puberty, other common features have been observed in young victims of RSPK. Janet and her sister in Enfield, for example, were obsessed with Starsky and Hutch, the heroes of the television serial; Shirley Hitchings adored James

Above: Eleanora Zugun, whose face shows the marks that mysteriously appeared whenever she felt insulted

Dean, the film star; and another girl was infatuated with Dr Who, the character in the science fiction series. It has been suggested that this passion, this concentration of emotion on fictional characters, served to ensure that the power or force deployed by the girls was unconstrained by the influences of normal, day-to-day life. This isolation from the normal was even more apparent in the case of a young Romanian peasant girl, Eleanora Zugun, who was able, between the ages of 12 and 15, to produce marks on her body whenever she felt that her personal 'devil' was being insulted. At the slightest word or gesture that she interpreted as offensive, scratches and bites appeared on the girl's face and arms.

Although young girls are often the focus of RSPK, however, it has been observed that they are rarely the sole agents of the disturbances. In the Fox case, for instance, two sisters out of three were involved, and at Enfield both Janet and her sister were at the

Above: rappings disturb the Fox family. This early case helped to establish the assumption that poltergeist activity was particularly associated with young girls

Right: scratches on the arm of a 19-year-old girl from Rotherhithe, England. They erupted spontaneously, apparently as a result of emotional disturbances

centre of many of the incidents. (Another member of the family, Janet's brother, was attending a school for the mentally subnormal; subnormality is often – though by no means always – associated with poltergeist activity.)

In some cases girls are not involved at all, though a hundred years ago male victims of RSPK were often ignored or discounted, so entrenched was the view that pubescent girls were the source of poltergeist activity. The experiences of one sensitive, D. D. Home, did provoke more serious examination of paranormal incidents associated with men, but the investigators were content to conclude that Mr Home was a homosexual and to leave the matter there.

In recent years male sensitives, young boys and men alike, have received a more sympathetic hearing. One 10-year-old boy was filmed as he lay in bed, awake, while a walking-stick moved of its own accord, in erratic jerks, behind the head of his bed. Like many young epicentres, he was of an extremely nervous disposition and, again in common with other victims, he was anaemic. Then there was a fascinating case involving two boys in Glasgow between August 1974 and May 1975. The boys were 15 and 11 years old, and they lived with their parents in a tenement flat. A series of 'peculiar sounds' was heard, followed by communicative raps; it turned out that the boys, without knowing it, were linked telepathically with an old man who lived in a flat on the ground floor and who was afflicted by a malignant tumour. As the old man's condition deteriorated, the raps became more frequent. They ceased, suddenly, when the old man died. And perhaps the most celebrated case of all is that of Matthew Manning, who at the age of 11 was able to produce genuine phenomena at will. Disturbances occurred both at his Cambridge home and at school: beds moved;

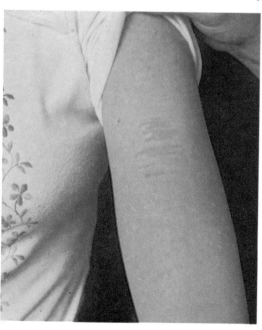

A guide to poltergeists

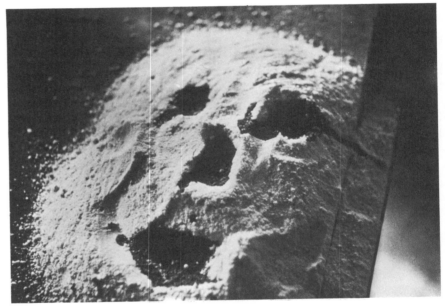

Left: the Harper family from Enfield, whose home was visited by some of the most elaborate and remarkable poltergeist activity on record

Below: a 'face' formed by sulphate of ammonia, used as fertiliser at a garden centre in Bromley. This was one of several manifestations that occurred during 1976: the epicentre was a 50-year-old man

Bottom: Anne-Marie Schneider, whose poltergeist sent her employer's telephone bill soaring by constantly dialling the speaking clock. Once she was married, however, the activity seemed to cease

stones appeared inexplicably; sudden cold spots were discovered. His brother and sister seemed to be unaffected by the experiences.

But it would be inaccurate to assume that RSPK is linked exclusively with puberty. A survey carried out in the 1950s indicated that seven was the age at which most children were particularly sensitive and receptive, and this finding has been confirmed by subsequent studies – although children as young as four or five have been identified as epicentres. Most are quite unaware that they are responsible for the disturbances that are experienced. Their powers vary: some, like Shirley Hitchings, have to 'screw up their eyes as if concentrating' in order to produce intelligent raps; many of the children who are able to bend metal (in the manner of Uri Geller) have only to gaze at the object for a moment or two, and then glance away, for the metal to move, bend or twist.

And at the other end of the age range adults long past the age of puberty experience poltergeist activity, although in many cases there does appear to be an unequivocal link between sexuality and RSPK. The majority of mediums who provoke – or claim to provoke – physical phenomena are women in their middle years, the years of the menopause, when the metabolism is disturbed, as it is at puberty. (In this connection it is interesting to note that Janet's mother at Enfield was at that age, a fact that may have contributed to the intensity of the poltergeist activity in the household.) Among mediums of both sexes there are those who admit to sexual frustration and who acknowledge that seances provide a form of sexual satisfaction.

Sexual maladjustment may indeed contribute to, or heighten, sensitivity; some recent cases suggest that RSPK may be related to frustration and distress. One involved a man of 48, who was living with his elderly

uncle in a large house in York. Whenever the younger man entered his study the room appeared to react to his presence: his desk moved; chairs shuffled across the floor; the curtains blew into the room even on airless days; the windows opened and shut very rapidly. The incidents persisted for nearly three years, increasing in frequency and intensity all the time, until mental exhaustion forced the man to seek medical assistance. He was found to be sexually impotent and was given treatment. Within a week the phenomena ceased.

Another case was that of a family of four who lived in Somerset. For some months the household was disrupted by paranormal incidents of all kinds, and the two teenage children were assumed to be the cause. But when the case was investigated it appeared to be the father, and not the children, who was the source of the disturbance. He was a professional man of 49, who had become increasingly concerned about his promotion at work, had developed insomnia and had become sexually impotent. His anxiety had pushed him towards the brink of breakdown. When he had been given the help and encouragement that he needed, the family experienced no further disruption.

A particularly strange case of this kind was documented in Bavaria, in Germany, in 1967. A number of inexplicable incidents were observed by employees at the office of a lawyer, accompanied by an alarming increase in the size of the telephone bill. The electricity and telephone companies were alerted and requested to check all equipment in the building, and Professor Hans Bender undertook the investigation of the case. A survey of the numbers dialled from the office revealed that one particular number was constantly being activated, though no one was dialling it: the number was that of the speaking clock, 0119. Eventually Professor Bender traced

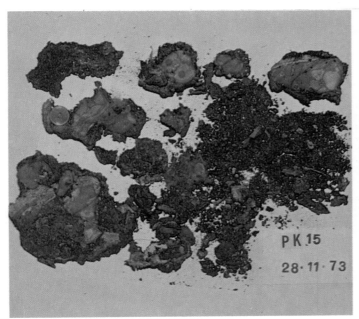

Above: two cases of spontaneous combustion, both centring on girls in Brazil. One, which plagued a family in São Paulo for six years, set fire to clothes inside a closed wardrobe and reduced them to ashes (left), while the other, occurring in Suzano in 1970, was content to burn the wardrobe (right). When the police were called, they too became the victims of mysterious fires!

Left: council house tenants Mrs Mary Sharman and her two sons, who were victims of poltergeist disturbances for 12 years. The trouble stopped when the family moved house

the incidents to the source – a 19-year-old girl called Anne-Marie. He concluded that she was dissatisfied with her working conditions and was generally unhappy, for she seemed to have a remarkable effect on the machines in the office, which she admitted she disliked, and on other electrical equipment. Overhead lamps would swing to and fro whenever she passed underneath them, and the fluid in photo-copying machines would spill on to the floor. The only plausible explanation for the steep rise in the telephone bill was that Anne-Marie was bored with her job and was mentally clock-watching, stimulating a response from the speaking clock. A full case history is included in Chapter 6, Haunted Europe.

Sexual maladjustment is not the only source of tension or distress, however; RSPK may be related to many other conditions. Migraine and temporal lobe epilepsy are common among middle-aged epicentres and sensitives, for example; there is evidence to suggest that there is some link between these disorders and 'psychic' faculties. And it has been observed that the parents of many young epicentres hold conflicting religious views, which appear to trigger distress in their children that in turn leads to outbreaks of RSPK.

But perhaps the most significant finding of recent research is that 86 per cent of all poltergeist activity is experienced by families that have recently moved into council houses. It is not hard to find an explanation for this. Any move is bound to be disturbing, and the strangeness of a new house may be compounded by the pressures of a new job for one or both parents, a new school for the children, the loss of friends and so on. In these circumstances, it is hardly surprising that tension generated by the members of the family, both individually and as a group, should provoke incidents and noises that cannot be readily explained away, or that ultimately many families, frightened and distraught, should demand to be rehoused.

Establishing the cause of poltergeist activity can be a very complex undertaking, calling for patience and understanding, and for an informed and sympathetic attitude – the approach, in fact, of a detective. Any attempt to provide a definitive categorisation of actual and potential poltergeist epicentres would need to be based on a thorough psychological and medical examination of all victims who can be identified, but such examinations are hardly ever conducted. Investigators have, on the whole, been too anxious to record incidents or to eliminate the possibility of fraud to concern themselves with the state of victims and their families.

Paradoxes of the poltergeist

What is the power behind poltergeist activity? Are its origins physical? Does it stem from the subconscious mind? Or could it be caused by some kind of 'cosmic force', as yet unexplored?

Below: a saucepan, scissors and a telegraph form leap into the air in a cottage in the French Alps. 'We can't explain what we saw,' said the photographer and his colleague; 'we can only guarantee that none of the pictures is faked'

IN 1952 RESEARCHERS investigating poltergeist activity, or psychokinesis, witnessed a remarkable incident. The heavy oak table around which they were sitting suddenly tilted slightly and rose – of its own accord – a little way off the floor. It then moved forward over the floor, pushing ahead of it two of the men, both of whom were tall and well-built, until they fell into the fireplace behind them. They were unharmed, for the fireplace was empty, but all present were puzzled. No external cause could be found to account for the phenomenon, yet the temperature in the room had dropped dramatically, and one of the group (who was later discovered to be a sensitive) appeared to be in a coma or trance.

What is the force that was at work in that room in 1952, the effects of which have been observed on countless other occasions, before and since? Are its origins simply physical?

Could atmospheric conditions explain it, for example? Or are they physiological – related to the metabolism of the people who witness or provoke such incidents? Or is the force produced by a combination of physiological and psychological causes?

Certain physiological reactions to psychokinesis have been observed, recorded and measured. First, it has been noted that loss of weight is associated with the phenomenon. Laboratory trials conducted with sensitives who were concentrating on causing objects to move under controlled conditions suggested that weight loss is commonly experienced – which confirmed the claim of one medium, Eusapia Palladino (1854–1918), that she 'shed' 20 pounds (9 kilograms) during a seance. And experiments in Ireland with a table weighing 30 pounds (13.6 kilograms), which was wired up to equipment designed to monitor movement and weight, showed that when it was levitated (sometimes for as long as 30 minutes) it lost 15 pounds (6.8 kilograms). Unfortunately a thorough examination of

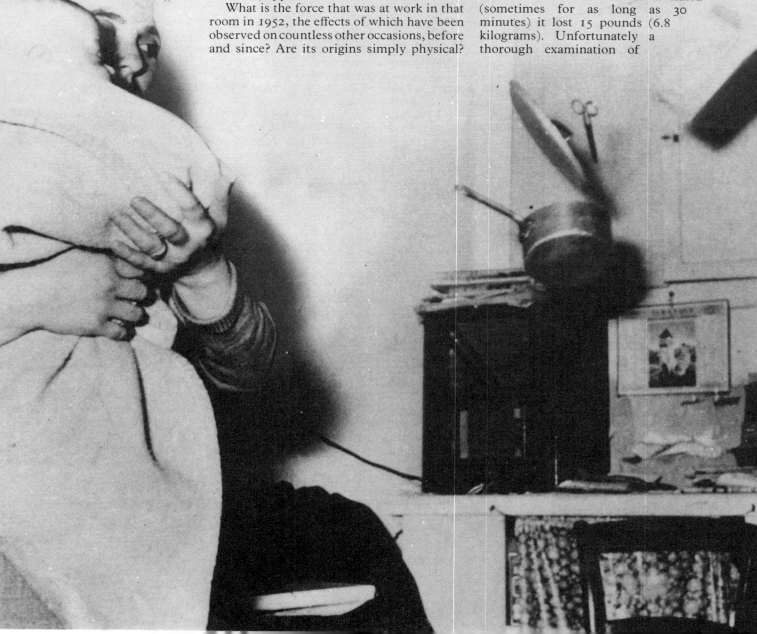

relationship between psychokinesis and hyper-ventilation, the deep and rapid breathing popular among mediums about to enter a state of trance. This procedure is acknowledged to be one method of raising levels of brain activity above 'normal'.

Finally, the mystery surrounding the curious substance known as ectoplasm cannot be divorced from a discussion of the physiological aspects of poltergeist activity, although the existence of this inexplicable product is questioned much more seriously today than it was when the Spiritualist movement was born. One reason for the association of the two is that many mediums specialising in 'physical demonstrations' claimed that table rapping, levitation and the movement of objects were all achieved through 'ectoplasmic rods' or 'pods'. In the 1920s one researcher testified to watching 'a mass of visible psychokinesis' approach a screen of fine gauze, travel through it, reform on the other side and congeal into a shape that resembled a hand. The sceptic would argue that only two examples of ectoplasm have ever been produced by those who assert that the substance is often 'created' by sensitives (one is a fragment of butter muslin, the other a piece of chewed-up lavatory paper), but there are hundreds of photographs of the product, and many people claim that the factual evidence of its existence cannot be rejected out of hand. (It is interesting that the slightly fetid smell associated with ectoplasm is often akin to that noticed during poltergeist activity.)

The psychological causes or effects of poltergeist activity are less easy to measure, though many victims display the same symptoms and have similar experiences. For example, many victims see apparitions, some of which are replicas of living people and some thought to be hallucinatory images – although they could be apparitions of unrecognised people. At the time when the Enfield case (see page 10) was being investigated, the 'ghost' of Maurice Grosse,

weight loss among epicentres during episodes of poltergeist activity is difficult, if not impossible to arrange, as no warning is given before the levitation of objects occurs.

Second, it seems that the rapid drop in temperature that was noticed by the researchers who met in 1952 is common in cases of both psychokinesis and spontaneous phenomena of other kinds. Records testify to a drop in temperature of as much as $8°F$ ($4.4°C$) in 10 seconds. This sudden loss of heat apparently releases a great deal of energy, which could account not only for the blue sparks that some witnesses claim to see but also for the malfunction of electrical equipment that is often observed. Reports of lights, cookers and televisions turning themselves on or off are not uncommon. (A frustrating consequence of this aspect of psychokinesis is that recording and monitoring apparatus is often also affected.)

The generation of highly concentrated electrical charges is another measurable by-product of psychokinesis. During some experiments conducted in Folkestone, Kent, in 1973 it was established that a group of seven people, sitting at a table with hands joined, were able to generate a considerable electrical charge that lasted for three seconds. As was the case with the experiments that featured Philip, the Imaginary Ghost (see page 13), this group was able to produce recordable and apparently intelligent raps originating from the table, despite the fact that the 'entity' responsible was fictional.

Fourth, there seems at times to be a direct

Above: Eusapia Palladino, a famous Italian medium, raises a table about 10 inches (25 centimetres) from the floor. During a demonstration of this sort, she claimed that she lost as much as 20 pounds (9 kilograms) in weight

Below: one of the seances in which 'Philip', the imaginary phantom, caused a table to levitate in front of television cameras

Substance of the spirit?

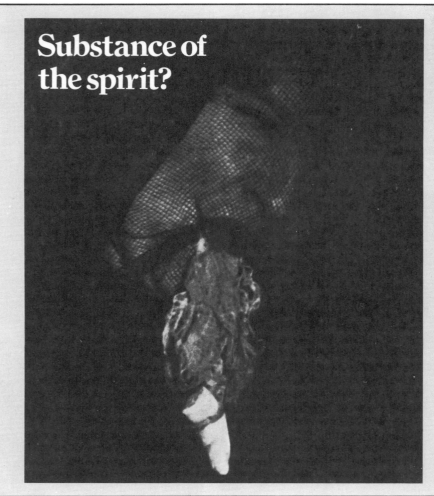

Ectoplasm was originally a biological term, meaning the outer layer of the cell protoplasm; in 1905 the French physiologist and psychical researcher Charles Richet also gave the name to 'a kind of liquid paste or jelly [that] emerges from the mouth or breast . . . [and] organises itself by degrees, acquiring the shape of a face or limb.'

In the cases described by Juliette Bisson in her book *Phénomènes dits de matérialisation*, the most stringent precautions produced no evidence of fraud, and the investigators were unable to determine the nature of the substance. However, in the many instances of ectoplasmic materialisation that have been recorded since 1905, the phenomenon is almost always suspect.

Mediums insist that ectoplasm is a living substance, which is destroyed by exposure to light; interestingly, since the availability of infra-red film, there have been very few claims for the production of ectoplasm.

. In photographs obtained during the 1920s and 30s, the 'ectoplasm' bears a close resemblance to butter muslin – indeed, one of the only two specimens of ectoplasm ever obtained was of this material; the other was of chewed lavatory paper. The fetid smell often associated with ectoplasm also indicates that it could have emerged from concealment in one of the body orifices.

one of the researchers, was seen in the house at least twice, and dozens of other reports confirm that the experience is not uncommon, though by no means all claims have been substantiated by evidence. It seems that it is often necessary for the victim to create a visible form for the invisible agent of the disturbances to assume, in order to be able to cope with the phenomenon. In other words, the 'ghost' provides an excuse for the disturbance, and responsibility for damage can be placed on its phantom shoulders. In some instances an apparition is seen *before* a psychokinetic incident takes place, as though it were the catalyst or agent. As poltergeist activity frequently erupts when tension or trauma is experienced, the appearance of a 'ghost' may be a symptom of stress. Few adults of average intelligence are frightened by such incidents, but for children or people of a nervous disposition the shock caused by the appearance of a mysterious figure could trigger a series of inexplicable events for which the 'ghost' is blamed.

Neurosis is another psychological condition associated with psychokinesis. Professor A. R. G. Owen has suggested that 'poltergeistry' is a conversion neurosis – that in certain people acute anxiety may be converted into noise and movement of objects;

Below: the Russian housewife Nina Kulagina, who has been able to exert considerable psychokinetic force. During one test her pulse rate was found to have increased to as much as 240 beats per minute, and she lost 4 pounds (1.8 kilograms) in weight

but, if that is the case, why does poltergeist activity cease? 'Maybe', Professor Owen suggests, 'the activity eventually ends because it is not a disease but the cure.' And sleepwalking, another symptom of deep anxiety, is also associated with victims of poltergeist activity. One curious fact is that the activity often continues while the victim is asleep, which supports the theory that the mind is the source of the power. Mary Carrick, an Irish girl living in America in 1898, was 'pursued' by raps on the walls of rooms in which she worked, and quite heavy objects would move in her presence. She would often carry out housework while still asleep, while the knockings continued unabated. More recent cases in Britain testify to the same phenomenon: when Shirley Hitchings was asleep taps and scratchings could be heard near her bed and similar sounds were heard when Janet and her sister were in bed asleep in Enfield.

A series of laboratory tests conducted on a housewife in the Soviet Union in the 1970s revealed the extent to which physiological and psychological factors collaborate to produce psychokinetic forces. Among other things, Nina Kulagina was able to separate the yolk of an egg from the white, and then reassemble the egg, without touching the

appears to have its origins in certain psychological conditions, to which physiological symptoms bear witness. Yet the power seems, to some extent, to have an existence that is independent of those who generate it. A concentration of energy, once it is consciously created, appears to linger in selected areas. In 1973, for example, it was discovered that a compass needle deflected by psychokinetic force would continue to oscillate if placed in the area in which a sensitive had originally projected the power, despite the fact that she was no longer present. And one researcher, William Roll, claims that areas affected by poltergeist activity can be clearly defined: 'If a disturbance has taken place in a given area, another disturbance is likely to occur in that area.'

Does this apparent independence of psychokinetic power suggest the existence of a 'cosmic force' that is channelled through certain people and is responsible for the generation and direction of the power? The idea that a 'cosmic force' lies behind the

container in which it had been placed. She was also able to arrest the heartbeat of a frog by suppressing an electric current (she was not told that the wires carrying the current were connected to a living creature). In other tests small electrodes were attached to her head and recording apparatus to her heart and wrists so that electrical pulses generated during psychokinetic incidents could be monitored.

The tests proved that the electrical activity of her brain rose to a very high level, and her pulse rate increased to an incredible 240 beats a minute (a pulse rate of about 70 is considered normal). The magnetic field around Nina also increased significantly, and when all the electrical and electromagnetic forces reached their peak, they merged in a single, fluctuating rhythm. At this point she was able to move objects at some distance from her without touching them in any way. During each successful trial in which her psychokinetic power was evident Nina lost 4 pounds (1.8 kilograms).

The continuous monitoring of the woman's physical condition provided proof that she was in a state of considerable nervous tension. An electroencephalograph registered intense brain activity; she experienced slight dizziness; and her sleep pattern was disturbed. The sugar content of her blood increased, and her pulse rate became erratic. (Practically identical symptoms have been observed in people suffering from a mild form of epilepsy and in women who are going through the menopause.) Further indications of the physiological changes that take place when an epicentre generates psychokinetic power were the serious hormonal imbalance that scientists observed in Nina and the fact that her limbs ached and felt weak.

So the generation of psychokinetic power

Above: levitation of a table during a seance by the English medium Jack Webber

Right: the Polish medium Stanislawa Tomczyk demonstrates the levitation of small objects in full daylight. After her marriage in 1919 to the Hon. Francis Fielding she gave up all practices of this kind, and indeed claimed that her 'act' had been fraudulent – but she was never able to explain how it was done

inexplicable incidents that are categorised as poltergeist activity is at least four centuries old; Paracelsus is believed to have proposed this explanation in the 16th century, and Mesmer, the celebrated hypnotist, promoted the belief in the 19th century. Today experts in the field of parapsychology are extremely reluctant to concede any ground to the theory; it is generally acknowledged that psychokinesis is a form of 'thought force', whose origins are natural rather than supernatural. As Scott Rogo puts it in a paper in the *Journal* of the Society for Psychical Research in June 1980: 'Psychokinesis is a phenomenon of vast contradictions. It seems to be both a mental and a physical force at one and the same time.' At present an explanation for the phenomenon lies beyond the boundaries of scientific theory; general acceptance and a deeper understanding of the force will depend on strictly controlled investigation of psychokinesis in all its forms.

The 'casting out of devils' has been part of Christianity since its earliest days. Although its efficacy may be questioned, the ritual of exorcism can bring great comfort to poltergeist victims and their families

AMONG THOSE VICTIMS of poltergeist activity who plead for, or even demand, an exorcism – and to judge from figures quoted by leading British exorcists there are many hundreds – few have any idea of what is involved. Even fewer victims should be considered suitable for such a rite. There is agreement among those who have been concerned with poltergeists that only about 2 per cent of all reported cases genuinely involve inexplicable phenomena – that is, psychokinetic effects for which no cause can be found in the lives of those affected. While there is as yet no explanation for the means whereby mattresses are slashed, the contents of drawers or wardrobes spontaneously combust, or people and things levitate uncontrollably, the source of most poltergeist activity can usually be traced to some form of emotional disturbance in an individual within the afflicted household.

The real question, then, is whether the rite of exorcism is appropriate for the *person* involved – even in cases where the effects themselves may be explicable in emotional terms, and even regardless of the individual's religious commitment. For some atheists, the rite may be comforting and effective; for some believers, who have unwittingly engaged fanatics or incompetents to perform the rite, the results can be as terrifying as the work of the 'demon' itself.

What most victims require above all are

Is exorcism really necessary?

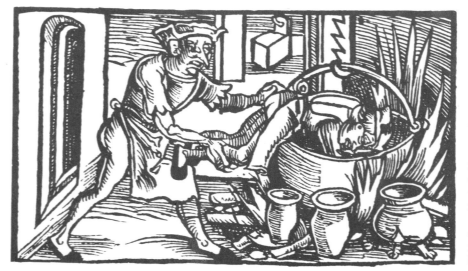

sympathy, concern and a willingness on the part of investigators to become involved with the problem. It is very common for victims to wonder if they are going mad; a warm and sympathetic investigator, who is prepared to accept the possibility that incidents of RSPK are perfectly authentic, can do a great deal to alleviate the acute mental distress that is often provoked by poltergeist activity.

Despite increasing knowledge and awareness of the diverse causes of apparently inexplicable phenomena, some advisers and doctors still feel unable to deal with patients who fall victim to RSPK and refer them instead to religious exorcists.

'Exorcism' takes many forms. If the main object of intervention by a clergyman is to relieve an undefined 'feeling', this can often be achieved through a religious service or

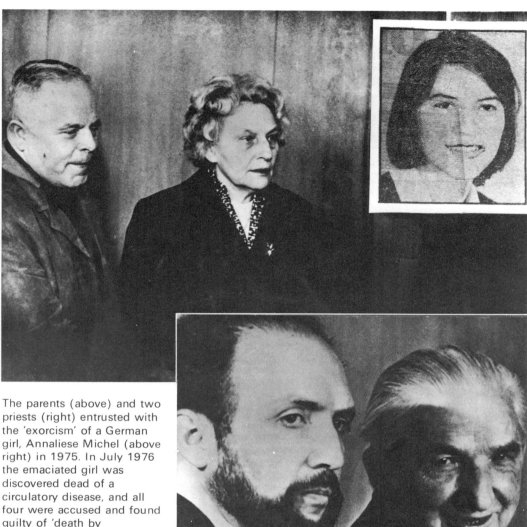

The parents (above) and two priests (right) entrusted with the 'exorcism' of a German girl, Annaliese Michel (above right) in 1975. In July 1976 the emaciated girl was discovered dead of a circulatory disease, and all four were accused and found guilty of 'death by negligence'

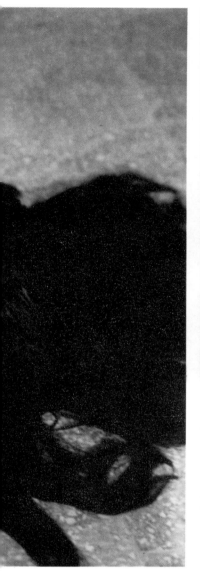

Above: after a violent spiritual struggle, this Italian woman lies peacefully at the end of a ceremony of exorcism

Left: medieval thinkers regarded the poltergeist as a physical manifestation of the devil. In this woodcut of 1515, 'The poltergeist in the kitchen', a cook is being pushed face-first into his cauldron of boiling water

blessing, or by encouraging the victim to accept that the 'atmosphere' of the affected room or house is not malign. It may take time to convince the victim, but if the 'exorcist' is caring and patient, this approach can eliminate symptoms of poltergeist activity.

A full 'exorcism' cannot be authorised until a thorough examination of the circumstances of the victim has been undertaken. Normally this process involves obtaining a report from the family doctor, an assessment from the local clergyman and, often, the views of a social worker. Indicating the more balanced approach now being adopted by some responsible members of the Churches, Father Peter Ball, Bishop of Lewes, has said that he would not consider giving his approval to the holding of an exorcism unless a medical expert were present, or had examined the victim and had agreed that such a service might assist. And it should be stressed that a theatrical performance complete with bell, book and candle is usually inappropriate nowadays.

Many victims of RSPK obtain relief as a result of the introduction of a religious ceremony into their households, though it is by no means certain that the effects of such ceremonies are lasting. Unfortunately, just as many people endure even greater suffering in the wake of a request for an exorcism, as there is still a body of fanatics, both clerics and laymen, who have little or no knowledge of psychology or parapsychology and whose ridiculous and scaremongering activities serve merely to increase the distress of those whom they claim to be able to help.

In Hastings, Sussex, in 1979, for example, a canon so harrassed a disturbed victim, who was suffering from the effects of the menopause and a drug problem, that she was admitted to a clinic for three months' treatment. The woman's condition could well have been far more serious if her husband had not stopped the canon in the middle of his 'treatment' and told him to leave. And in 1977 a family in the Midlands was subjected to a horrifying sequence of 'cures'. First, their house was blessed by an archbishop and a local vicar. Then a religious group visited the victimised family (who were suffering from hallucinations) and held a two-hour 'stomping session'. Within a few months two seances had been held in the house, and numerous 'spiritualist' mediums had called upon the family, each providing a different (and usually nonsensical) explanation for the imagined phenomena. One claimed that the house was haunted by the evil spirit of a tall Negro; another informed the family that the incidents were to be attributed to the influence of a ginger-haired dwarf girl. The family was able to return to normal only after a parapsychologist had spent a few hours with the mentally disturbed wife and made arrangements for a local doctor to visit.

'I was told to bury a snail underneath an oak tree at midnight, then to walk around the tree reciting the Lord's Prayer three times,' one victim of poltergeist activity told an investigator. This remarkable piece of advice was offered to her not in 1777, as one might have imagined, but in 1977. The woman later sought and received treatment for a psychological ailment, and the phenomena that had been distressing her ceased.

But psychological treatment is not always the correct method for dealing with incidents of RSPK. Often a simpler 'cure' will help. A woman in Hampshire who claimed that she was 'anti-religious' was disturbed enough by a minor outbreak of inexplicable incidents to consider calling upon the services of her local vicar. Initially, however, she confided in her mother-in-law, a spiritualist, who recommended that she should attend a 'rescue seance' to try to remove the 'troubled spirit'; this procedure has occasionally been known to help, though it is potentially dangerous if conducted by people without experience.

The solemn rite

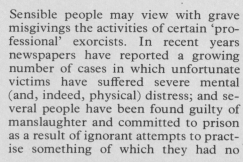

Below: an exorcism in the Italian church of St Vicinius, in Sarsina. The iron ring is a relic of the saint, who wore it about his neck, with heavy weights attached, as a penance

Sensible people may view with grave misgivings the activities of certain 'professional' exorcists. In recent years newspapers have reported a growing number of cases in which unfortunate victims have suffered severe mental (and, indeed, physical) distress; and several people have been found guilty of manslaughter and committed to prison as a result of ignorant attempts to practise something of which they had no

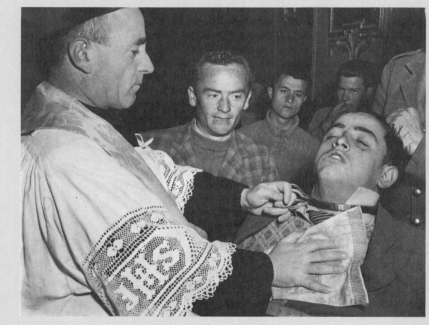

Left: English medium Donald Page performing an 'exorcism' on a woman patient. Whatever explanations may be put forward for the ritual and its outcome, there is no doubt that a considerable amount of physical energy is expended by the medium

The suggestion made the victim somewhat apprehensive; instead she took her problem to a parapsychologist. On his advice, she used a 'magic sign' to enable her to cope with the disturbance, and in two weeks the household had returned to normal. Needless to say, there was nothing 'magic' about the sign that she used: it was simply a device, an aid – and a successful one.

One young man in Richmond, Surrey, accidentally discovered his own method of disposing of an 'evil spirit', which offered – not to him, perhaps, but to a scientific observer – evidence that the phenomena he was experiencing were basically psychological in nature. After three months of suffering from 'cracking and popping noises and strange lights on the landing', he was determined to confront and eliminate the poltergeist. One morning, exhausted and irritated, he walked out of his room on to the landing and swore at the 'thing'. From then on he experienced no further incidents.

Is it true to say that all that is needed to eradicate disturbance caused by poltergeists is a symbol or a symbolic gesture? In some cases a symbol may certainly help; the

understanding or experience. Even within the ranks of the Anglican and Roman Catholic Churches there is some disquiet concerning the principles and practices involved.

In both Churches, the ritual of exorcism is based upon the belief that a person or a place may be 'possessed' by an evil spirit or spirits, and that the appropriate words and ceremonies can be used to 'command' the evil spirit to leave. The form of the ritual is very simple, and it appears that the most important element is the strength of personality of the exorcist himself.

Since about AD 250 a ceremony of exorcism has been a part of the baptismal service in the Roman Catholic Church. This does not mean that candidates are considered to be 'possessed'; it is regarded rather as a ceremony to remove the effects of original sin.

The exorcism of those considered to be possessed by evil spirits is rigorously controlled in Roman Catholic canon law, and was established in the *Rituale* of Pope Urban VIII; a similar ceremony of exorcism has been retained within the canon of the Anglican Church, but it is seldom performed in its original form.

In the earliest days of Christianity exorcism was a ceremony that could be practised by anybody. Any major exorcism now requires the authorisation of a bishop before it may be performed, but many parish priests (and also certain specialist practitioners recognised within the body of the Church) have been

known to carry out private exorcisms on their own responsibility.

The form of words in the ritual varies considerably. The Rev. J. Christopher Neil-Smith, for instance, begins with the traditional words: 'I rebuke thee! I rebuke thee! I rebuke thee! I abjure thee and summon thee forth from this man. . . .' On the other hand, Dom Robert Petitpierre, an Anglican monk and Church of England authority on all psychic matters, has written: 'An exorcism, in fact, is no more than surrendering to God and saying "Please Lord, clean up the mess".'

Above: the Rev. Neil-Smith, of Hampstead, London, is one of the most active of Anglican exorcists. At one time he claimed to have performed over 2000 exorcisms within a period of four years

distress may be reduced to an acceptable level, depending on the state of the victim and on his or her confidence in the 'power' or 'force' of the symbol.

Although the number of cases of RSPK reported each year in Britain appears to be increasing – and there are many possible reasons for this, including the stresses of modern life, the tranquillisers and anti-depressants that are prescribed to alleviate the symptoms of stress, and a greater willingness among victims to admit to their experiences – the success rate of exorcism is declining. A mere 20 per cent of exorcisms are now considered to be successful, and then only after repeated visits by authorised exorcists. As the waning of religious belief makes way for the scientific study of phenomena hitherto regarded as supernatural, the days of the exorcist may be numbered, though the title may continue to be accorded to parapsychologists and other experts in the field who are proving more and more successful in dealing with the paranormal.

Right: the New Testament tells how Christ himself expelled demons by a 'word of power', and said that this act was a sign of the coming of God's Kingdom. The evil spirits were believed to issue from the body's orifices, and this decorated initial, from a 12th-century manuscript in Winchester Cathedral library, shows a 'little blue devil' emerging from the mouth of the possessed man

A guide
to ghosts

A short history of hauntings

Above: Nathaniel Hawthorne (1804–1864), the American novelist and short-story writer. His account of the ghost of Dr Harris, which haunted the reading room of Boston's Athenaeum Library (left), is remarkable for its straightforward presentation of the facts

Ghosts seem to take many different forms, appear in the most unlikely places, and haunt all kinds of people. But what exactly are these apparitions? And what causes them? A survey of famous phantoms from the past may offer some answers

BEFORE HIS NOVEL *The scarlet letter* made him famous, the American novelist and short-story writer Nathaniel Hawthorne was an official at the Boston Customs House. At this time, in the 1830s, he went every day to the Athenaeum Library to research and write for a few hours. One of the other regulars there was the Reverend Doctor Harris, an octogenarian clergyman who for years had sat in 'his' chair by the fireplace, reading the *Boston Post*.

Hawthorne had never spoken to him, as conversation was strictly forbidden in the reading room, but Dr Harris was almost a fitment of the place, so that Hawthorne felt sure he would have missed him if Dr Harris had not been there. The novelist was, therefore, surprised one evening when a friend told him the old man had died some time previously. He was even more amazed when, the following day, he found the clergyman in his normal chair, reading the newspaper. For weeks Hawthorne continued to see Dr Harris, looking perfectly solid and lifelike.

One of the things that puzzled Hawthorne

was the fact that many of the other regulars had been close friends of Dr Harris, though Hawthorne had not. So why did they not see him? Or *did* they see him, but suffer from the same reluctance as Hawthorne to acknowledge his 'presence'? Another factor that puzzled Hawthorne in retrospect was his own unwillingness to touch the figure, or perhaps snatch the newspaper from its hands: 'Perhaps I was loth to destroy the illusion, and to rob myself of so good a ghost story, which might have been explained in some very commonplace way.'

After a while the old gentleman appeared to be watching Hawthorne as if expecting him to 'fall into conversation'.

But, if so, the ghost had shown the bad judgement common among the spiritual brotherhood, both as regarding the place of interview and the person whom he had selected as recipient of his communications. In the reading room of the Athenaeum, conversation is strictly forbidden, and I couldn't have addressed the apparition without drawing the instant notice and indignant frowns of the slumberous old gentlemen around me. And what an absurd figure I would have made, solemnly . . . addressing what must have appeared in the eyes of all the rest of the company an empty chair.

'Besides,' concluded Hawthorne in a last appeal to the social proprieties, 'I had never been introduced to Dr Harris.' After some months, Hawthorne entered the Athenaeum to find the haunted chair empty, and he never saw Dr Harris again.

The only drawback to this story as a piece of psychical evidence is that it rests on the testimony of an author who wrote many short stories concerning the supernatural. Hawthorne was a friend of Edgar Allan Poe and Herman Melville, both of whom dealt with the realms of the unknown. On the other hand, he became interested in ghostly phenomena after moving into a house in Massachusetts reputed for years to be haunted. Of this place he wrote: 'I have often, while sitting in the parlour in the daytime, had a perception that somebody was passing the windows – but on looking towards them, nobody is there.'

First class evidence

In neither case – that of his house nor that of Dr Harris – does he appear to have tried to embellish the facts at all, and yet he is acknowledged as a great story writer, accustomed to giving his tales a beginning and a satisfactory end. As a ghost story of fiction, the Dr Harris tale is flat and relatively uninteresting; but as a piece of evidence for an apparition it is first class.

So what was it that Hawthorne saw? To many people the ready answer would be that he saw the earthbound spirit of Dr Harris, somehow trapped in the place that he had been accustomed to 'haunt' in life. Others would say that the ghost was a projection of Hawthorne's memory of the old man, echoing Hamlet's mother's comments on her son's visions: 'This is the very coinage of your brain.' More recently, psychical researchers would suggest that the apparently solid person by the fire was a sort of spiritual 'recording', left by the dead man on his environment, which was somehow received by Hawthorne's mind in much the same way as a television set receives a transmission.

One thing is certain: Nathaniel Hawthorne was far from being alone in seeing a 'ghost' – or what serious parapsychologists and psychical researchers prefer to term an 'apparition'. Since earliest times all civilisations have recorded 'ghosts' – some as a mere generality, a part of folklore, while others have produced specific instances. The difficulty, for the modern observer, is sifting the likely from the less likely instances.

About 500 years earlier, at the beginning of what are loosely known as the 'Dark Ages', a Benedictine monk named Brother John

Below: Edgar Allan Poe (1809–1849), master writer of the macabre short story. He was a friend of Nathaniel Hawthorne, and it is possible that he could have participated in the 'creation' of the ghost of Dr Harris at the Athenaeum Library

Below: 'Marley's ghost appears to Scrooge' from Dickens's *A Christmas carol*. Doomed to walk the earth to atone for his ill-spent life, 'Marley' warns that Scrooge too will be condemned unless he mends his ways

Goby took on a case of psychical research and recorded all the facts with commendable care. Again, although to modern eyes the incident seems bizarre enough at first to be dismissed out of hand, the Goby case was so rare for its time to be worthy of study.

In December 1323, a merchant of Alais, in the south of France, died. His name was Guy de Torno, and within days of his death he was reputed to have returned to haunt his widow in the form of a 'spirit voice'. News of this persistent 'ghost' spread to the town of Avignon, 40 miles (65 kilometres) away, where Pope John XXII then had his residence. (This was during the Great Schism, when two popes, one in Avignon and one in Rome, vied for power.) Pope John was impressed, and appointed Brother John Goby, Prior of the Benedictine Abbey of Alais, to investigate.

Accompanied by three of his fellow Benedictines and about 100 of the town's most respected citizens, Brother John went to the widow's house on Christmas Day and began his investigations. First he examined the house and gardens for any hidden tricks or freak sound effects. Then he posted a guard around the premises to keep out sightseers. The focus of the ghostly manifestations was the bedroom. Goby asked the widow to lie on the bed, along with a 'worthy and elderly woman' while the four monks sat at each corner.

The monks then recited the Office for the Dead, and soon became aware of a sweeping sound in the air, like the brushing of a stiff

broom. The widow cried out in terror. Goby asked aloud if the noise was made by the dead man, and a thin voice answered: 'Yes, I am he.'

At this point some of the townspeople were admitted to the room as witnesses, and stood in a circle round the bed. The voice assured them that it was not an emissary of the Devil – the usual assumption in medieval times – but the earthbound ghost of Guy de Torno, condemned to haunt its old home because of the sins it had committed there. It said that it had every hope of getting to heaven once its period of purgatory was over. It also told Brother John that it knew he was carrying the Sacrament in a pyx – a silver box in which the Host is carried – concealed under his robes. This was a fact known only to Goby. The spirit added that its prime sin had been adultery, which carried the penalty of excommunication from the Sacrament in those days. The spirit then 'sighed and departed'.

Brother John wrote out his report and despatched it to the Pope at Avignon. The incident's abiding interest to psychical research lies in the objectivity with which the investigation was carried out. Of course it was not perfect and does leave a number of questions unanswered. The 'sweeping' noise and the 'sigh' might well have been a result of the Mistral, the mournful wind that blows across that part of France in the winter. The 'voice' itself may have been produced by ventriloquism on the part of the widow –

IOANNES·PP·XXI·GALVS

Above: Pope John XXII, who directed a Benedictine prior, Brother John Goby, to investigate the 'ghost of Alais' in 1323

Below: Prince Rupert leads his cavalry into the first major battle of the English Civil War at Edgehill in 1642. For months afterwards, people claimed to have seen a ghostly re-enactment of the battle; among those reported to have taken part was Prince Rupert himself – but he was still alive

consciously or unconsciously – particularly if she suspected her husband of infidelity and wanted to discredit his memory. Against this, however, has to be weighed the fact that, had she been discovered in such trickery, she stood a very real chance of being accused of witchcraft and suffering death at the stake.

Another impressive investigation, this time of a 'mass apparition', was conducted in 1644 by a number of level-headed army officers and remains an enigma: either they were all lying, or something untoward did indeed happen. On 23 October 1642, Royalist troops under Prince Rupert of the Rhine, nephew of King Charles I, and Parliamentarians under Robert Devereux, third Earl of Essex fought the first serious battle of the English Civil War at Edgehill, Warwickshire. After the indecisive clash the bodies of some 2000 men lay on the unseasonably frozen slopes of Edgehill.

A month after the battle, a number of local shepherds saw what they at first thought was another fight at the same spot: the thundering cavalry, rolling gunsmoke, flashing steel. And they also heard the neighing of horses, the screams of the wounded and the steady beat of drums. It was only when the whole tableau suddenly vanished that they took fright and ran to tell the authorities in the nearby town. On Christmas Eve the phantom battle was enacted again, and was so convincing that a London printer, Thomas Jackson, interviewed several witnesses and published an acount of the phenomenon in

pamphlet form on 4 January 1643.

This was drawn to the attention of the King, who was so intrigued that despite his hard-pressed military position he appointed half a dozen army officers to investigate on his behalf. They were led by Colonel Sir Lewis Kirk, former governor of the garrison at Oxford, and a young cavalry captain named Dudley who had ridden at Edgehill.

On their return the officers brought detailed confirmation of the news. Not only had they interviewed the shepherds and recorded their accounts, but on two occasions they had seen the battle themselves, recognising not only a number of the men who had died on the field, but also Prince Rupert, who was still very much alive. Whether or not anyone took notice of it at the time, this last fact carried with it the intriguing suggestion that the phenomenon was a sort of action replay rather than haunting by revenant spirits.

Although Sir Lewis and his colleagues were justifiably startled, they drew no conclusions, merely reporting the facts of what they had seen. There was no obvious reason for them to lie: their evidence might have pleased the King or upset him. As it chanced he took the incident as a good omen – wrongly, as it turned out, for six years later he was beheaded.

The ghostly man in grey

A recent example of an apparition witnessed on innumerable occasions by literally dozens of people is that provided by the so-called 'man in grey' who is recorded as appearing at the Theatre Royal in Drury Lane, London, from the early 18th century until the late 1970s. The accounts are remarkably consistent, although the 'stagey' look of the ghost and the fact that it appears in a theatre has convinced more than one witness that they were seeing an actor dressed for a part.

The figure is that of a man of above average height with a strong, handsome face. He wears a three-cornered hat, powdered wig, long grey cloak, sword and riding boots, and emerges from a wall on the left hand side of the upper circle, walks around behind the seats, and vanishes into the opposite wall. He has never been known to speak or pay any attention to witnesses, and although he seems perfectly solid, if his way is barred by a living person he dissolves and then reappears on the other side of them.

The identity of the 'man in grey' has never been satisfactorily proven, but a possible clue turned up in the late 1840s, when workmen were making alterations to the wall from which he appears. In a bricked-up alcove they found the seated skeleton of a man, with a rusty dagger between his ribs. A few tattered remnants of cloth clung to the figure but crumbled to dust when touched. At the obligatory inquest it was suggested that the man may have been a victim of Christopher Ricks, the 'bad man of old Drury' who had

Top: this is not, as it may seem, final evidence for the existence of ghosts, but a carefully staged visitation photographed for the British Tourist Authority at London's Theatre Royal, Drury Lane. The ghostly apparition is the so-called 'man in grey', a spectre said to have haunted the theatre for over 200 years. Even in reality it obligingly appeared for the critic and historian W. J. McQueen Pope (above) when he was conducting sightseers round the theatre

managed the theatre in the time of Queen Anne and was notorious for his violence. Ricks made constant alterations to the theatre's structure, and could easily have disposed of a body without too much difficulty. However, there was no solid evidence, and after an open verdict was returned the body was given a pauper's funeral at a nearby graveyard.

However, the 'man in grey' continued to be seen throughout the Victorian era and on into the 20th century. W. J. McQueen Pope, theatre critic and historian, saw the ghost many times and made ardent but fruitless attempts to establish its identity. An interesting point was that the ghost appeared regularly in the period between the mid 1930s and Pope's death in 1960, while he was conducting sightseers around the Theatre Royal. On every occasion, the visitors saw the ghost too, many of them signing testimonials to this effect.

This fact raises a salient question in the minds of psychical researchers: did Pope serve as an unconscious catalyst for the apparition? We know that people differ in their ability both to perceive psychic phenomena and to project apparitions to others. If Pope was gifted in both respects, was the vision of his visitors somehow stimulated by him? Did he, in some way, summon up the 'man in grey'?

Certainly he did not invent the ghost, and its last recorded sighting, by an American who thought he was seeing an actor during an afternoon matinée, took place in 1977, 17 years after Pope's death. But it is certain that the spectre appeared most frequently during Pope's association with the Theatre Royal.

The Pope puzzle presents just one more baffling aspect of the complex phenomenon known to parapsychology as 'apparitions'.

Ghosts without souls?

If ghosts are spirits of the dead, as many believe, how can we account for the 'soulless' apparitions – those of animals and inanimate objects – that have been seen?

Above: the tale of this phantom ship was reported by the American minister and author Dr Cotton Mather in his book *Wonders of the invisible world* (1702). The ship set sail from America but never reached its destination in England, and nothing was ever heard of it again. Some months later, however, spectators at the port from which it sailed saw what seemed to be the self-same ship appear in a cloud; then it keeled over and simply disappeared

IN THE MIDDLE of the 1930s a large red London bus bearing a number 7 route number harassed motorists in the North Kensington area of London. The junction of St Mark's Road and Cambridge Gardens in that area had long been considered a dangerous corner – it was 'blind' from both roads – and had caused numerous accidents.

The decision of the local authority to straighten out the bend was partially influenced by the testimony of late night motorists, who claimed that they had crashed at the junction while swerving to avoid a speeding double decker bus that hurtled down St Mark's Road in the small hours, long after regular buses ceased service.

A typical report to the Kensington police read: 'I was turning the corner and saw a bus tearing towards me. The lights of the top and bottom decks and the headlights were full on but I could see no sign of crew or passengers. I yanked my steering wheel hard over, and mounted the pavement, scraping the roadside wall. The bus just vanished.'

After one fatal accident, during which a driver had swerved and hit the wall head on, an eyewitness told the coroner's inquest that he had seen the mystery bus hurtling towards the car seconds before the driver spun off the road. When the coroner expressed what was perhaps natural cynicism, dozens of local residents wrote to his office and to the local newspapers offering to testify that they had seen the 'ghost bus'. Among the most impressive of these witnesses was a local transport official who claimed that he had seen the

31

vehicle draw up to the bus depot in the early hours of the morning, stand with engine purring for a moment, and then disappear.

The mystery was never solved, but it is perhaps significant that the 'ghost' bus was not seen after the danger of the sharp corner was removed, and it was suggested that the vision was 'projected' onto the spot to dramatise the inherent danger of the intersection. If so, by whom? And if, as was also suggested, it was in the minds of the motorists themselves – a sort of natural projection of their fears at the corner – how did they manage to superimpose it on the vision of the passers-by, not to mention that of the bus depot official who saw it from an entirely different angle?

In fact, the phantom motor bus of Kensington epitomises a problem that for centuries has faced those who believe that ghosts are revenant spirits. If a ghost is the 'soul' of a dead person returned to earth, how do we account for phantom buses – and of course their lineal ancestors phantom coaches, which feature so heavily in folklore?

Come to that, why do returning spirits not appear in the nude – for with very few reliably recorded exceptions, none do? As Lyall Watson succinctly puts it in his book *Supernature*: 'While I am prepared in principle to concede the possibility of an astral body, I cannot bring myself to believe in astral shoes and shirts and hats.'

'Ghostly' lore is strewn with stories of inanimate objects suddenly becoming apparent to the sense of observers, from the 'phantom' accordion accredited to Daniel Dunglas Home, the 19th-century Spiritualist, to Macbeth's dagger. In the latter case William Shakespeare, writing in an age steeped in superstition, seems to have been as aware of the anomaly of 'spirit objects' as he was of almost every other field of human

Above: most ghosts appear fully clothed or are dressed in a shroudlike garment, as was the ghost that terrorised the residents of Hammersmith, London, in the early 1800s

Below: the junction of St Mark's Road and Cambridge Gardens in Kensington, London, became renowned in the 1930s for the mysterious double decker bus that travelled at great speed in that area in the middle of the night – when no buses were in service

experience: '. . . art thou, O fateful dagger, sensible to feeling as to sight, or art thou but a dagger of the mind, a false creation, proceeding from the heat oppressed brain?'

One of the most convincing stories of totally 'soulless' apparitions is recorded in the day book of the Tower of London – a place that according to popular belief is saturated with ghosts. The man who made the entry was Edmund Lenthal Swifte, who in 1814 was appointed Keeper of the Crown Jewels and continued in the office until 1842, a total of 28 years. The account of what he saw on a Sunday evening in October 1817 is best left to him.

I was at supper with my wife, our little boy, and my wife's sister in the sitting room of the Jewel House, which is said to have been the 'doleful prison' of Anne Boleyn and of the ten bishops whom Oliver Cromwell piously accommodated there. The doors were all closed, heavy and dark curtains were let down over the windows, and the only light in the room was that of two candles on the table. I sat at the foot of the table, my son on my right, my wife fronting the chimney piece, and her sister on the opposite side. I had offered a glass of wine and water to my wife, when on putting it to her lips she paused, and exclaimed, 'Good God! What is that?'

I looked up, and saw a cylindrical figure, like a glass tube, something about the thickness of my arm, and hovering between the ceiling and table; its contents appeared to be a dense fluid, white and pale azure . . . incessantly rolling and mingling within the cylinder. This lasted about two minutes, when it began to move before my sister-in-law, following the oblong shape of the table, before my son and myself. Passing behind my wife it paused for a moment over her right shoulder (observe there was no mirror opposite in which she could then behold it.) Instantly she crouched down, and with both hands covering her shoulder, shrieked out, 'Oh Christ! It has seized me!'

Even now as I write I feel the horror of that moment. I caught up my chair striking at the 'appearance' with a blow that hit the wainscot behind her. It then crossed the upper end of the table and disappeared in the recess of the opposite window.

There was no recurrence of this curious manifestation, but some years later it did help Swifte's judgement of a soldier in the Tower who actually died from fright of what he had seen outside Swifte's 'front door'.

The soldier had been on sentry-go outside the Jewel House when, at around midnight, he had heard a guttural snarl behind him and turned to see a huge black bear, reared up on

its hind legs, fangs bared, eyes red with rage, and talons groping towards him. The soldier rammed his bayonet into the belly of the animal, but the weapon passed clean through and the apparition disappeared.

A patrol found the soldier a few moments later, senseless. The bayonet, with a heavy 'Tower issue' musket attached, was embedded in the solid wood of the door. The soldier was taken, still insensible, to the guardroom, where a doctor pronounced that he was neither drunk nor asleep, and the following morning Swifte interviewed him; over and over the soldier repeated his bizarre tale until, three days later, he died.

For about 300 years, until the middle of the 17th century, the Tower housed a royal menagerie, and among the animals recorded as having been kept were a number of bears. Although no account of an autopsy on the soldier survives, the fact that he died three days after his experience could indicate that he was ill without knowing it, and that the apparition was an hallucination caused by his illness. On the other hand, animal ghosts make more sense as 'revenant spirits' than their human counterparts, for the reason already given; they at least 'appear' exactly as in life. The fact that Man has lost most of his 'primitive' instincts while animals retain theirs may also have an as-yet unexplained bearing on their 'paranormal' role.

A phantom pig

Stories of phantom dogs are common to the United States, Europe, and many parts of Africa. Ghostly horses, cattle, and even sheep have their part in folklore, and although, like all folk tales, the accounts of their appearances have undoubtedly become distorted in the telling over centuries, some are eerily convincing. In 1908 the British Society for Psychical Research (SPR) made exhaustive enquiries into the appearance of what appeared to be a phantom pig in the

Above: the Jewel House in the Tower of London where Edmund Swifte and his family were troubled by a cylindrical form filled with blue and white fluid

Below: phantom horses, complete with riders, are a common form of haunting, and are usually associated with a particular place. Possibly they are a kind of recording of a highly emotional or dramatic event, which is 'replayed' in certain circumstances

village of Hoe Benham, near Newbury, Berkshire.

On 2 November 1907, two young men named Oswald Pittman and Reginald Waud were painting in the garden of their house, Laburnum Villa. At 10 a.m. Pittman got up to speak to the milkman and saw his friend Miss Clarissa Miles coming up the lane; she was due to join the men for a painting session. Accompanying her like a pet dog was a large white pig with an unusually long snout. When Pittman told Waud about it, Waud asked him to tell Miss Miles to keep the animal outside and close the garden gate securely – Waud was a keen gardener and did not want it among his plants. However, when Miss Miles arrived she was alone, and denied all knowledge of the animal. If it had been following her, she pointed out, she would surely have heard it grunting and pattering. However, she and Pittman went back up the lane and asked several children if they had seen a pig that day; none of them had done so. The following morning the milkman, pressed by a bewildered Pittman, signed a statement to the effect that he had not seen a pig, and he pointed out that in any case the area was under a swine fever curfew, and any stray animal would be destroyed.

Pittman and Waud went to London for a few months and while there reported the odd incident to a member of the SPR. When they returned to Hoe Benham in February, however, the story of Pittman's apparition had become widespread, and shedding their natural reserve the villagers inundated them with stories of previous 'phantoms'. Local theory had it that they all stemmed from the suicide of a farmer named Tommy King whose farm, which was demolished in 1892,

had bordered the lane. Investigation of the parish records showed there had been two Tommy Kings, one dying in 1741 and the other in 1753, but there was no indication of which one was the suicide. An old man named John Barrett testified that when he was a boy in 1850 he had been returning with seven or eight men in a hay cart along the lane when 'a white thing' appeared in the air. All the men had seen it, and the horses obviously had too, for they went wild.

'This thing kept a-bobbin' and a-bobbin' and the horses kept a-snortin' and a-snortin'' until the wagon reached the neighbourhood of King's Farm, when the shape vanished. In 1873, at the same spot, Barrett had seen a creature 'like a sheep' pawing the ground in the lane. He took a blow at it with his stick, but it disappeared before the stick landed.

Another man, Albert Thorne, said that in the autumn of 1904 he heard 'a noise like a whizzin' of leaves, and saw summat like a calf knuckled down' about 2½ feet (75 centimetres) high and 5 feet (1.5 metres) long, with glowing eyes. As he watched, it faded away. Yet another witness, unnamed, said that, in bright moonlight in January 1905, he had

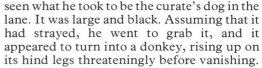

Okehampton Castle in Devon, England. A 17th-century phantom coach, constructed of the bones of the four husbands of the 'Wicked Lady Howard' – all of whom she is said to have murdered – travels the road that runs across the moor from Tavistock to Okehampton. The ashen, sheeted spectre of Lady Howard rides inside the coach and a skeleton hound runs before it. According to legend, each night the hound must pick a blade of grass from Okehampton Park to take back to Lady Howard's family home at Tavistock – a penance that must be endured until every blade of grass is picked

seen what he took to be the curate's dog in the lane. It was large and black. Assuming that it had strayed, he went to grab it, and it appeared to turn into a donkey, rising up on its hind legs threateningly before vanishing.

Pittman, Waud, and Miss Miles reported one more experience. While walking in the lane, Miss Miles was suddenly overcome by an irrational fear, and told her companions that she felt the presence of an evil being, charged with malice towards them. She also felt that she was suffocating. As they reached the spot where Pittman had seen the pig, all three heard an 'unearthly scream', although no one else was about. Waud, who had been sceptical from the beginning, was finally convinced that the ghostly animal existed by this cry from nowhere.

Animal investigators

The sensitivity of animals, particularly cats and dogs, to paranormal phenomena is almost a truism. Dr Robert Morris of Kentucky, a parapsychologist who used animals as 'controls' in his experiments in the 1960s, reported his investigation of a haunted house in one room of which a tragedy had occurred. He used a dog, cat, rat, and rattlesnake.

The dog upon being taken about two or three feet [less than a metre] into the room immediately snarled at its owner and backed out of the door. No amount of cajoling could prevent the dog from struggling to get out and it refused to re-enter. The cat was brought into the room carried in its owner's arms. When the cat got a similar distance into the room, it immediately leaped upon the owner's shoulders, dug in, then leaped to the ground, orienting itself towards a chair. It spent several minutes hissing and spitting and staring at the unoccupied chair in a corner of the room until it was finally removed . . .

[The rattlesnake] immediately assumed an attack posture focusing on the same chair that had been of interest to the cat. After a couple of minutes it slowly moved its head toward a window, then moved back and then receded into its alert posture about five minutes later . . .

The rat was the only creature not to react at all, but all four animals were tested in a separate room some time later, and there behaved normally.

In the misty world of apparitions, no one, not even the most dedicated psychical researcher, knows quite what is the motivation behind them. What we do know is that they are not confined to human beings; the 'ghosts' of both animals and inanimate objects have been lucidly recorded over the years, even including the 'soul' of a London Transport bus.

Understanding ghosts

The troubled spirits of the dead, phantom animals, spectral coaches – all these have been called 'ghosts'. But are they all the same? We can learn a great deal from what hauntings have in common – and how they differ

THE PERENNIAL QUESTION as to whether ghosts exist must, in view of various surveys carried out by such bodies as the British Society for Psychical Research (SPR) over the last 100 years or so, be answered in the affirmative. To reject the testimony of the many hundreds of respectable people who claim to have experienced apparitions as wishful thinking, self-delusion or downright lying would be sheer wilfulness.

The question facing modern parapsychologists and psychophysical researchers is: *how* do ghosts exist? Are they revenant spirits? Are they the result of telepathy? Are they produced by mass hallucination or self-hypnosis? Advances in psychology over the last few decades have brought us nearer to understanding some aspects of apparitions, but the definitive truth still eludes us.

The most common form of 'ghost' appears to be the 'crisis apparition', which occurs when a person under great stress – sometimes on the point of death – appears to someone close to them as a 'vision' or, occasionally, as a disembodied voice.

The majority of crisis apparition cases have tragic overtones. For instance, soldiers have appeared to their mothers or wives at the exact time of their own deaths on far-away battlefields. But not all do so.

Victoria Branden, in her book *Understanding ghosts*, quotes the case of a friend who

This photograph of the library at Combermere Abbey in Cheshire was taken on 5 December 1891 by Sybell Corbet, who had been staying at the house. When she developed the plate, she was startled to see the shape of an elderly gentleman sitting in a chair on the left of the picture. The figure was later identified as that of Lord Combermere himself: but at the time the photograph was taken, he was being buried a few miles away

was evacuated from England to Canada during the Second World War because of a health problem, leaving her husband behind in the Services. One evening, the children were busy with their homework, while their mother was ironing in what she admitted to Mrs Branden was 'a rather dreamlike state'.

Suddenly she saw the door of the room open, and her uniformed husband came in. Before she could recover from her astonishment, he vanished. She put down the iron and sat, near to fainting, in a chair. The children clustered around her anxiously and when she told them what had happened they said that they had not seen anything and the door certainly had not opened. The mother and the elder child had, however, read of crisis apparitions and became convinced that the vision meant that the husband had been killed or injured. They made a note of the time and circumstances, but agonisingly, that was all they could do.

Some days later, to what must have been their enormous relief, news came: the husband had been unexpectedly chosen to go on a training programme to Canada, at a camp very near to his family. This meant, of course, that he could live with them while abroad. When the couple were finally reunited the husband said that the news had come as a happy shock. He could not remember consciously 'projecting' any thought to his wife, but they worked out that he had probably opened his commanding officer's door after hearing the news at about the same time as the wife had 'seen' her door open.

An interesting point about this incident is that the wife was 'rather dreamlike' at the time, with her mind in an open and receptive state. The children, who saw nothing, were concentrating hard on their homework.

Exactly how telepathic information is communicated remains a mystery, particularly so in the case where an apparition

appears solid and living. However, scientists point out that perception is a much more complex business than at first appears: vivid dreams, for instance, often appear perfectly solid and physical, and in such cases the percipient is not receiving information through his eyes. A hypnotist may tell a subject that when he or she awakes only the hypnotist will be in the room – even though other people may be present. When the subject comes around he will not see the others present until the hypnotist removes the suggestion. Something like this may happen in cases of telepathy, although it seems remarkable that the agent – or person 'sending' the hallucination – can achieve at a distance, and in many cases while he is unconscious, what the hypnotist can only manage by giving specific instructions.

Evidence points to the fact that the agent's mind plays a smaller part in crisis apparitions than does that of the percipient. If we look at recorded cases it becomes apparent that the agent rarely appears as he is at the moment of 'transmission' – the percipient does not see a mangled body in a motor car, or a dying wounded soldier in a trench, but what appears to be a normal image of the agent that, moreover, relates to the percipient's surroundings.

This point is stressed by G. N. M. Tyrrell in his book *Apparitions*. He points out that apparitions in crisis cases have been guilty of such unghostlike phenomena as casting shadows or appearing reflected in a mirror.

[They] adapt themselves almost miraculously to the physical conditions of the percipient's surroundings, of which the agent as a rule can know little or nothing. These facts reveal the apparition to be a piece of stage machinery which the percipient must have a large hand in creating and some of the details

Below: cases of crisis apparitions are most common in times of war, when a mother may see her son at the moment of his death on a battlefield. It seems that the shock of death causes some kind of telepathic communication between son and mother. But rarely does the mother have a vision of a dying soldier; in most cases she sees her son as he appeared in normal, everyday life

for which he must supply – that is to say, an apparition cannot be merely a direct expression of the agent's *idea*; it must be a drama worked out with that idea as its *motif*.

But telepathy can only partly explain cases of collective apparitions, where a group of people witness the same thing. And it is hard to see how it could play any part in the case of, for instance, the phantom London Transport bus already mentioned, for by definition the telepathic agent must be a sentient being. One of the most famous cases of a collective apparition was reported to the SPR in the late 19th century by Charles Lett, the son-in-law of a Captain Towns of Sydney. One day at about 9 p.m. some six weeks after the Captain's death, his daughter, Mrs Lett, and a Miss Berthon entered a bedroom at his home. The gas light was burning:

And they were amazed to see, reflected

Left: when Mr Bootman, a bank manager pursuing his hobby of photographing church architecture, took this picture at Eastry, Kent, in 1956, his wife and a cleaning woman were the only other people present. But the ghostly form of a vicar somehow appeared on the film. Some years later Mr Bootman showed the photograph to a Women's Institute group and was told that a similar phantom had been seen in the same church in the 1940s. This may well be an example of what is called a 'place-centred' ghost: the vicar's strong attachment to the church could have led to a 'record' of his image being imprinted upon it

in the polished surface of the wardrobe, the image of Captain Towns. It was . . . like an ordinary medallion portrait, but life-size. The face appeared wan and pale . . . and he wore a kind of grey flannel jacket, in which he had been accustomed to sleep. Surprised and half alarmed at what they saw, their first idea was that a portrait had been hung in the room and that what they saw was its reflection – but there was no picture of the kind. Whilst they were looking and wondering, my wife's sister, Miss Towns, came into the room and before any of the others had time to speak she exclaimed: 'Good gracious! Do you see Papa!'

One of the housemaids passing by was called into the room. Immediately she cried: 'Oh miss! The Master!' The captain's own servant, the butler, and the nurse were also called in and immediately recognised him. Finally Mrs Towns was sent for and, seeing the apparition, she advanced towards it with her arm extended as if to touch it, and as she passed her hand over the panel of the wardrobe the figure gradually faded away, and never again appeared.

Those parapsychologists who lean to the telepathic origin of all apparitions would probably say that the vision was seen first by either Mrs Letts or Miss Berthon, who then passed it on by thought transference to each arrival. But the question remains: where did the vision come from in the first place?

One of the early SPR pioneers, F. W. H. Myers, author of the book *Human personality and its survival of bodily death*, suggested that it was the revenant spirit or 'essence' of Captain Towns taking a last look at his old home six weeks after death. Myers said that an apparition 'may be a manifestation of persistent personal energy' and quoted several cases to illustrate his point.

In one a travelling salesman, Mr F.G., arrived at a hotel in Boston, Massachusetts,

The ghost that grew and grew

One of the main problems facing the objective psychical researcher is that of sheer human gullibility. People like a good ghost story and tend to embellish the narrative, so that after a few re-tellings the stark facts of the case become wrapped up in a cocoon of invention.

In the summer of 1970 the author of this series, Frank Smyth, who was at that time an associate editor of the magazine *Man, Myth and Magic*, tried an experiment to examine the form taken by this gullibility. He *invented* a ghost, complete with location, background and 'witnesses' and published the story in the magazine.

The invention was completely random. One Sunday morning Smyth had gone down to London's dockland to meet John Philby, son of super-spy 'Kim' Philby. Philby's building company was renovating a site at Ratcliffe Wharf, and Smyth decided that the deserted dock was sufficiently eerie to provide a location for his ghost. Hard by Ratcliffe Wharf is the semi-derelict church of St Anne, and this, plus the fact that it was a Sunday morning, decided Smyth to make his 'ghost' that of a clergyman. Alongside the wharf runs Ratcliffe Highway, once – at least until the late 19th century – a thoroughfare of brothels, grog shops, and cheap boarding houses. The proximity of this old road suggested to Smyth that his vicar had been the owner of a sailor's rooming house, and that he had robbed 'homeward-bounders' (seamen newly paid off from ships in the Thames), had killed them in their lodgings, and disposed of their bodies in the river. Thus the background was set up.

Philby, himself a former war correspondent, and Smyth then decided that witnesses were important. They and one of Philby's employees lent their names to the fiction that they had seen the ghost – the figure of an old white haired man with a walking stick. They also agreed that if anyone, either researcher or interested enquirer, asked about the 'phenomenon' they would immediately confess that it was invented.

Smyth then wrote the story as a 'factual' article in *Man, Myth and Magic*. No one ever queried the credentials of the 'Phantom Vicar of Ratcliffe Wharf' but over the next twelve months or so eight books purporting to tell the stories of genuine ghosts appeared, each featuring the phantom vicar. Only one, by a London *Sunday Times* feature writer, treated the subject with some scepticism; the others not only recounted the tale without comment but one, by a well-known writer on the supernatural, actually embellished it.

In 1973 Smyth wrote an article telling of his experiment for the *Sunday Times*, and subsequently appeared in a BBC-2 film produced from Bristol entitled *A leap in the dark*. This film, too, told the story of the invention, but it also featured a number of people who claimed actually to have *seen* the phantom vicar. One man said that he had witnessed an old man in 18th-century clerical garb walking in the roadway outside the 'Town of Ramsgate' pub, near St Katherine's Dock – a good half mile from Ratcliffe Wharf. The writer Jilly Cooper told of interviewing a police superintendent who, on retirement from the River Branch of the Metropolitan force, had said that as a young man he had been unwilling to enter Ratcliffe Wharf for fear of the ghostly priest. A Thames waterman claimed that he had seen the shadowy form of the vicar standing on Ratcliffe Wharf some months before the story appeared in the magazine. After the television programme many other letters were sent to the BBC's Bristol office, most of them apparently sincere, telling of sightings.

There is absolutely no foundation for the Ratcliffe Wharf story. Nowhere in the record of Wapping – or indeed any other part of London's dockland – does there feature any tale of a ghostly cleric. One psychical researcher suggested that Smyth's ghost may have existed, and somehow made itself felt to him. The fact is that apparently reasonable people still claim to see the apparition in the area – despite its widespread refutation.

one afternoon and sat working in his room. He suddenly became aware of a presence and looked up to see his sister, who had died nine years previously. As he sprang delightedly to his feet and called her name she vanished, and yet he had time to take in every detail. 'She appeared as if alive,' he said, but added that there was a small red scratch on her right cheek.

Disturbed, Mr F.G. made an unscheduled stop at his parents' home and told them of his experience. When he mentioned the scratch, his mother was overcome with emotion, and said that she had made the scratch on the dead body of her daughter accidentally, as she was preparing it for burial. Two weeks later, the mother died.

Myers wrote that the figure was 'not the corpse with the dull mark on which the mother's regretful thoughts might dwell, but . . . the girl in health and happiness, with the symbolic *red* mark worn simply as a test of identity.' He suggested that the apparition

most likely explanation of, for instance, the en masse haunting at Edgehill. It also ties in with the telepathy theories; if a person can send an image of himself telepathically to a percipient, may he not also be able to send a sort of 'free floating' image that hangs, as it were, in the atmosphere to be picked up by anyone sensitive enough to receive it?

Such a concept would also explain the occasionally convincing 'photographs' of apparitions; in such cases the photographic film may be more sensitive to the surroundings than its operator; conversely, where a photographer sees a ghost and his camera fails to do so, he may be hypersensitive.

If such phantom recordings are possible, it may be that they are not necessarily fixed for ever. Andrew Green, in his book *Ghost hunting*, quotes an interesting case of a woman in red shoes, red dress and a black head-dress reported to haunt a mansion in 18th-century England. In the early 19th century it was reported that the apparition

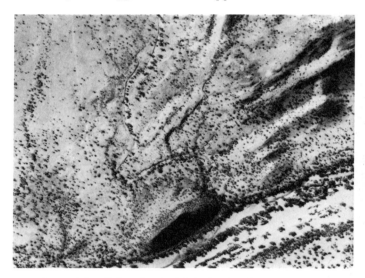

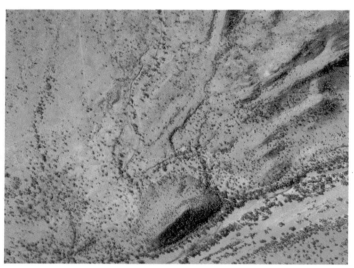

was the spirit of the dead girl inducing her brother to go home and see their mother before she died.

Where an apparition persistently 'haunts' a place or a house – or sometimes even a person – believers in an afterlife assert that the spirit is trapped in its earthly environment, perhaps because of some unfulfilled task, or for the purpose of punishment. Unfortunately, unlike the ghosts of well-rounded fiction, these 'haunting' apparitions do not seem to make much sense in their actions; like Nathaniel Hawthorne's seated image of Dr Harris, they carry on in a mundane fashion, either wandering about or simply staring out of windows.

By and large parapsychologists as a whole, however, tend to theorise that in certain cases a kind of psychic record may be imprinted on a location, perhaps because of some violence or strong emotion generated there. In these cases, the apparition would not be a sentient spirit, a 'mind', but merely a projection like a cinema film. This certainly seems to be the

Ghost photographs often show images unseen by the human eye, as film is inherently more sensitive to certain light frequencies. The difference is rather like that between a picture shot with a standard film (left) and one taken with infra-red equipment (right). The infra-red photograph shows this tract of Australian desert more clearly and with much sharper detail, and provides information not otherwise available

was that of a lady in pink shoes, pink dress, and a grey head-dress. She was not witnessed again until the mid 19th century, when the figure had dwindled down to 'a lady in a white gown and with grey hair'. Just before the Second World War, all that was reported was 'the sound of a woman walking along the corridor and the swish of her dress'. In 1971, shortly before the demolition of the property involved, workmen felt 'a presence in one of the old corridors'.

All these explanations may account for the mysterious sightings of apparently solid, living beings where no such beings should be. Or perhaps none of them do. Modern scientific research – into, for instance, the baffling field of quantum physics – constantly produces new slants on old phenomena. Ghosts – whether human or non-human – may yet prove to belong to a sphere of reality so far undreamed of in our philosophy.

In search of apparitions

No two ghosts are alike — and a good ghost hunter will approach each haunting differently. Serious researchers have developed special techniques for gathering and documenting the kind of evidence they seek

'FEAR CAME UPON ME, and trembling, which made all my bones to shake. Then a spirit passed before my face; the hair of my flesh stood up. It stood still, but I could not discern the form thereof.'

This is how the experience of seeing a ghost is described in the Book of Job 4: 14–16. The word 'ghost' comes from an ancient root meaning 'to be scared', and to many, including Job, encounters with ghosts have been literally hair-raising. Fortunately, some people, far from being frightened, are willing to seek out ghosts and actively investigate them.

The existence of ghosts has been accepted without question in almost all cultures throughout history. Only with the growth of

The screaming skull of Bettiscombe Manor in Dorset is said to be that of a West Indian slave who swore his spirit would not rest until he was buried in his homeland. After his burial blood-chilling cries shook the house until he was exhumed, and his body sent for burial in the West Indies. If it is ever disturbed again, will the ghost return to the Manor? This case is thoroughly investigated in Chapter 8

the scientific outlook in the West in the last few centuries have their existence and nature been disputed. But serious attempts to find out what they are and to study their behaviour are surprisingly few. And many people still respond to the idea of ghosts with an irrational blend of fear, ridicule and laughter. We reject what we do not understand, rather than face the possibility that there are indeed more things in heaven and earth than are dreamed of, let alone taken seriously, by the scientific establishment.

Ghosts are even rejected by people who have seen them. 'I saw it, but I still don't believe it!' is a commonly reported reaction, for the human mind instinctively rejects information it cannot assimilate and interpret. Clearly, better evidence, and more of it, is needed before the ghost can find its way into the physics and biology textbooks.

What, to begin with, is a ghost? Dictionaries define it as the supposed disembodied spirit, or soul, of a dead person. This

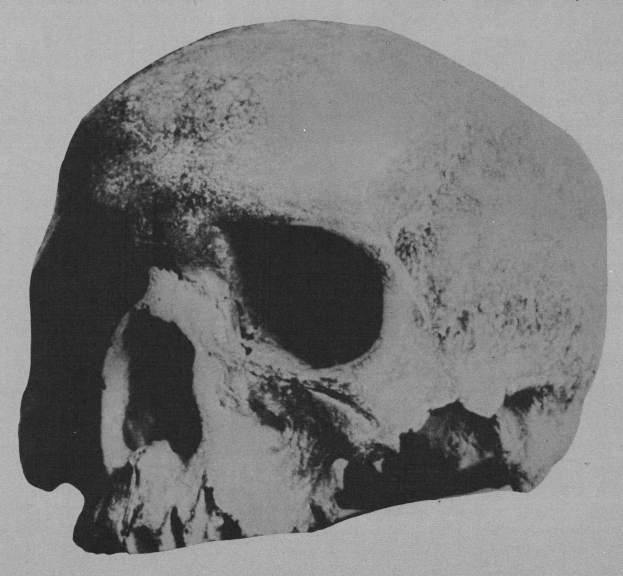

far as you could discover, was not due to any external physical cause?

Almost 10 per cent of the 17,000 people who replied said 'yes'. Later surveys in several other countries confirm this picture.

Isolated appearances of a ghost may be undramatic, but when repeated over a long period become worthy of study. An example is the ghost reported in 1892 by a medical student, Miss R. C. Morton. She wrote:

I saw the figure of a tall lady dressed in black, standing at the head of the stairs. After a few moments she descended the stairs, and I followed for a short distance, feeling curious what it could be. I had only a small piece of candle, and it suddenly burnt itself out; and being unable to see more, I went to my room.

This ghost lent itself to study. Over the following seven years six people besides Miss Morton saw the ghost, which closely resembled a known former occupant of the house, while about 20 people heard sounds apparently made by it. Sightings followed a regular pattern: the figure would walk downstairs (the resourceful Miss Morton sometimes tied threads across them, but they remained unbroken), enter the drawing-room and stand in the window. Then it would leave the room by the door, walk along the passage and disappear.

Cornering a phantom

Miss Morton, who must have been an exceptionally courageous young woman, made frequent attempts to converse with the ghost, but although it seemed aware of her presence, it never replied. She also tried to touch it, but it always got out of the way. 'On cornering her, as I did once or twice,' she wrote, 'she disappeared.' Miss Morton even tried to 'pounce on it', with the same result.

Once she saw the figure at the usual window and asked her father if he too could

explanation of the nature of ghosts will not be assumed here, however, for apparitions of living people are frequent. The word 'ghost' has also acquired the sense of a vestige of something, as in 'the ghost of a smile'. Frederic W. H. Myers, a leader of Victorian psychical research, echoed this meaning in his characterisation of a ghost as 'a manifestation of persistent personal energy' – a conclusion he had reached after careful study of a mass of evidence.

A great deal of evidence is available, for seeing or hearing ghostly presences is a very common experience. In 1889 the British Society for Psychical Research, of which Myers was a founder member, embarked upon a large-scale survey of experiences of apparitions, asking the question:

Have you ever, when believing yourself to be completely awake, had a vivid impression of seeing or being touched by a living being or inanimate object, or of hearing a voice; which impression, so

Above: the Brown Lady of Raynham Hall in Norfolk. This ill-defined form was seen by the photographer as well as captured on film

Right: the form of a kneeling monk is said to appear in this picture, taken by a local solicitor in St Nicholas's Church, Arundel, in 1940

The amazing Gladys Hayter

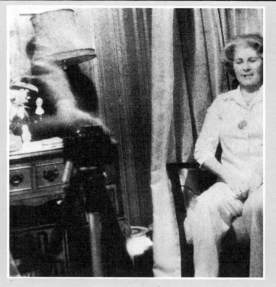

While Gladys Hayter sits in trance, a phantom hand appears, unseen in the darkness but captured in this infra-red photograph

An East London psychic, Gladys Hayter, apparently has the ability to cause phantoms to materialise and living people and inanimate objects to de-materialise and change position, under the gaze of the camera. In 1970 Mrs Hayter, who already practised psychic healing, began photographing strange phenomena with a simple Instamatic camera. Glowing streaks of 'ectoplasm' often appear, emerging from her body. Sometimes her image does not appear in the picture, even though, as she insists, she has not moved. In fact, she claims she is unable to move when in trance during one of these sessions. The picture shown here is one of a number taken by a local photographer, using infra-red film in the near-darkness. The camera on the tripod is Mrs Hayter's.

see it, but he could not. When he walked to the window, the phantom promptly walked round him.

The family's cat took no notice at all of the ghost. The dogs, however, frequently reacted as if they had seen somebody. One would run to the foot of the stairs, wag its tail and jump up as if waiting to be patted, but then back away with its tail between its legs and hide under a sofa. Another dog was often found 'in a state of terror' for no obvious reason. This sensitivity of some animals to supernatural presences has prompted their use as 'ghost-detectors'.

In any investigation, it helps to know something of the likely course of events. While the nature of ghosts is still mysterious, their behaviour has been studied in great detail. G. N. M. Tyrell, in his book *Apparitions*, published in 1943, identified four main groups by their pattern of activity.

Below: the kneeling figure in this photograph of the altar of St Mary's Church Woodford, was not seen by the photographer at the time the picture was taken

The first of Tyrell's groups consists of apparitions that haunt certain places. These, of which Miss Morton's ghost is a typical example, are what are now termed 'place-centred', rather than 'person-centred'. On the whole they do not arouse fear and they sometimes come to be treated as part of the family. They rarely do any harm.

The second category consists of post-mortem apparitions, taking place some time after the death of the person seen, and not related to any particular place or event.

Thirdly, there are crisis cases, in which the apparition is of someone who is undergoing some profound experience at the time (often unknown to the percipient), such as an accident or illness or, of course, death.

Experimental apparitions

The last of Tyrell's categories is the least-known type of apparition, but perhaps the most intriguing of all – the experimentally induced apparition. The ghost in these cases is not of a dead or dying person but of someone alive and well who has deliberately attempted to make his or her image visible to someone else. Tyrell found records of 16 successful attempts of this type, and wondered why such an evidently repeatable experiment had been ignored by researchers. It remains a neglected area of study and, although there has been considerable recent study of 'out-of-the-body' experiences, reports of self-induced visibility at a distance remain very rare.

Those ghosts for which evidence is most compelling, and that critical researchers have concluded are genuine, usually show a number of features. Such a ghost obeys the laws of perspective, looking different to different observers; it appears solid; it is visible when viewed in a mirror; and it makes sounds appropriate to its movements – footsteps can be heard, for example. It generally gives the impression of being as real as a

Right: two ghostly forms appear behind the figure of an English lady, Miss Townsend, in the Basilica at Domrémy, in France. The apparitions were unseen by Miss Townsend's companion, Lady Palmer, when she took this photograph during a visit in 1925

Below: another haunting of a holy place. The church in this case is at Newby, in North Yorkshire. Its vicar, the Reverend K. F. Lord, was amazed to find this form on his developed photograph of the altar

living person, if only for a limited period. A sensation of sudden cold may be felt.

The feeling of coldness is also a commonly reported feature of poltergeist cases, but poltergeists are unlike conventional ghosts: they cause physical objects to move, yet they are not seen doing so. Apparitions have been reported in association with poltergeist activity, but we have yet to see one pick up an object and throw it.

When a ghost is seen by only one person, the suspicion arises of hallucination, error or deception – whether practised by the percipient or someone else. But ghosts are often seen by more than one person at the same time, though not necessarily by everybody present. This is often sufficient to rule out the possibility of deception or mistake, but the true nature of the apparition remains unknown. It is not necessarily a disembodied spirit – it could be an 'intersubjective' phenomenon, the joint creation of the percipients' minds.

An apparition may provide some plain evidence of its non-physical nature. It may pass through walls; sometimes it appears and disappears through phantom doors that open and close while 'real' doors stay closed; it may become transparent and fade away.

Nevertheless, these elusive wraiths can apparently be recorded on photographic film. There are many alleged photographs of ghosts, but few are convincing. Fraud has been so prevalent in the field of psychic photography that attention has been diverted

The ancient manor house at Sandford Orcas, set in an attractive part of Dorset, is the very type of an English haunted house – and it seems to have more than its fair share of ghosts. They include a lady in green; another in red, noted for her punctual appearances at 11.50 a.m. on the stairs; a monk; an Elizabethan lady; a local man who hanged himself in the gatehouse; and Sir Hubert Medlycott, whose family still owns the house. A ghost dog is sometimes seen, and the sound of a phantom spinet can occasionally be heard. The ghost of a footman, 7 feet (2 metres) tall, adds to the problems of the house, for it reputedly takes an improper interest in virgins. It is not, however, often seen nowadays. There are allegedly 14 ghosts in all at the manor – offering a tempting field for the energetic ghost investigator.

Scene of many hauntings

from the rare examples that may well be the real thing. One impressive case took place at Raynham Hall, Norfolk, home of the Marquis of Townshend, in 1936. A professional photographer and his assistant were taking photographs of the house. While photographing the staircase, the assistant reported seeing a ghostly figure coming down the stairs. The picture taken at that time, which has been pronounced genuine by photographic experts, does indeed show a misty form. The house has a long history of haunting by a lady in brown, who was seen simultaneously by two witnesses in 1835. Later she was seen by the author Captain Marryat, who ungallantly fired a shotgun at her. Despite this unwelcoming action, she was seen again in 1926 by Lord Townshend and two other witnesses.

Ghostly worshippers

Convincing pictures of ghosts have been taken in churches. In 1940, a local solicitor snapped an unmistakably human form in front of the altar of St Nicholas's church, in Arundel, Sussex. More solid in appearance than the brown lady of Raynham Hall, it was still partly transparent. Some have interpreted it as the figure of a kneeling priest. A similar figure appeared in a photo taken in St Mary's, Woodford, in Northamptonshire, by Gordon Carroll in 1966. Two ghostly priests turned up in the picture of Lady Palmer taken by her friend Miss Townsend in the Basilica of Domrémy, in France.

The prize for technical quality in a ghost photograph must go to the Reverend K. F. Lord of Newby, in Yorkshire, who recorded the presence of a very clear, if somewhat stagey, hollow-eyed spook before his altar.

These are examples of 'place-centred' ghosts. Photographic evidence for 'person-centred' apparitions is more ample. The family photograph albums of the London medium Gladys Hayter contain dozens of colour pictures of inexplicable lights, shadows and – apparently – partly dematerialised living human beings. In 1979 she took a shot of a child in a car, a picture that seems entirely normal except for the fact that, as she has testified, no child was in the car when the picture was taken.

There are no photographs, however, as persuasive as the best eyewitness accounts. Cumulatively, the weight of evidence, of all kinds, suggests that ghosts exist. But, despite a century of intensive research, what they are, and the conditions under which they manifest themselves, are questions that are still awaiting definitive answers. Ghost hunters still face mysteries in plenty.

A serious ghost investigation is long and arduous, and some publicity-conscious authors find it profitable not to be too critical of the cases they retail. As with most areas of study, there are good and bad researchers

'THE MOST HAUNTED HOUSE in England' was a local inhabitant's description of Borley Rectory, on the Essex-Suffolk border, when he gave directions to a motorist in 1929. The driver was Harry Price, self-styled ghost-hunter and the most energetic and controversial psychical researcher of the century. He found his way to Borley, where he found – or claimed to have found – the ingredients for a series of books, radio broadcasts and newspaper articles that he was to produce for the rest of his life. The case apparently had everything: ringing bells, strange lights, footsteps, flying stones, a skull wrapped in brown paper, mysterious writing on walls, and, of course, a ghost. Local legend had it that the rectory was built on the site of a monastery, from which a monk had unsuccessfully tried to elope with a young lady from a nearby nunnery. Both had been caught and executed, but the nun and the monk (minus his head) and the coach they used were said to be still around. Borley Rectory, Harry Price claimed, was 'the best-authenticated case of haunting in the annals of psychical research.'

This would be welcome news indeed, for

A brick flung through the air at the site of the ruined Borley Rectory is captured on film by a *Life* magazine photographer. Harry Price, who was present at the time, later cited this picture as photographic evidence of poltergeist activity at Borley – without mentioning the workman who was demolishing a nearby wall when the picture was taken

surprisingly, although ghosts have been seen over the centuries, very few have ever been investigated thoroughly in order to learn their true nature. But had Price authenticated the Borley hauntings?

Not in the opinion of a team of members of the Society for Psychical Research (SPR), who tore the case to pieces in a devastating report published in 1956. Not only, they claimed, was there no proper evidence for any paranormal occurrences at Borley, but some of the reported phenomena had very probably been caused by Price himself. They quoted one outright accusation of fraud, made by a *Daily Mail* reporter, Charles Sutton, after Price's death:

Many things happened the night I spent in the famous Borley Rectory with Harry Price and one of his colleagues, including one uncomfortable moment when a large pebble hit me on the head.

After much noisy 'phenomena' I seized Harry and found his pockets full of bricks and pebbles. This was one 'phenomenon' he could not explain, so I rushed to the nearest village to 'phone the *Daily Mail* with my story, but after a conference with the lawyer my story was killed.

Even some of Price's fellow investigators concluded that he was more interested in a good story than in the truth of the case. A

Ghosts true and false

typical example of this was given by a *Life* magazine reporter, Cynthia Ledsham, who visited Borley with Price and a photographer in 1944. The rectory, which had burned down in 1939, was being demolished. The photographer took a distant shot of the ruins, which showed a brick flying through the air. Price later claimed that this could be 'the first photograph ever taken of a Poltergeist projectile in flight'. However, the reporter later admitted to the SPR investigators that while the picture was being taken a workman was dismantling a wall nearby, throwing bricks at regular intervals. She accused Price of 'the most bare-faced hocus pocus'.

Price's account of the haunting was demolished as surely as the building itself. The rectory had not been built on the site of a monastery after all. The 'nun' who had been spotted by a newspaper reporter 'flitting about in the gloom' was in fact the maid, a lively girl who later admitted to having carried out a spot of poltergeist activity herself. One former occupant of the rectory declared it to have been haunted by no more than 'rats and local superstition'. Another, the source of a great deal of the anecdotal material (which Price himself privately admitted to not believing), turned out to have lived previously near Amherst in Nova Scotia, scene of a well-publicised 19th-century haunting with many remarkable similarities to the alleged happenings at Borley. And so the indictment continues through 180 pages of a special issue of the SPR's *Proceedings* wholly devoted to an exposé of Price's bold claims.

In Trevor H. Hall's *Search for Harry Price* (1948), the 'ghost-hunter extraordinary' is depicted as a publicity-seeking charlatan and an unscrupulous liar. Although argument was still raging in 1980 in the pages of the SPR's *Journal* over both the facts of the Borley case and the integrity of its investigator-publicist, it cannot be claimed that Price made any useful contribution at all to our understanding of ghosts, or that there is any reason to believe a word of what he wrote about Borley Rectory.

One moral of this lamentable episode, which is covered at much greater length in Chapter 4, Haunted England, seems to be that it is all too easy, as well as profitable, to offer the public what it wants – shock, horror and occult thrills. It is much more difficult and costly to do the painstaking work of a good investigator. The late Jay Anson, who scripted the film based on the novel *The exorcist*, made an estimated £3 million from his book *The Amityville horror*, but he had no first-hand experience of this case whatsoever. A researcher who followed up the case, Dr Stephen Kaplan, dismissed the book as 'mostly fiction'. Another writer who investigated the story, Melvin Harris, has written that 'there is plenty of evidence which shows unambiguously that the Amityville story is a gross fabrication'.

How, then, should ghosts be hunted? In an ideal world, funds, personnel and equipment would be available for an enquiry as thoroughly conducted as a police murder

Overleaf: wreckage scattered over Florida swampland after the crash of Eastern Airlines' flight 401 on 29 December 1972, with two of the crew who died. The ghosts of the pilot, Bob Loft (centre), and the second officer, Don Repo (below), were later seen on other Eastern Airlines Tri-Star flights (inset)

A television special

In 1964 Anglia Television filmed a documentary at an allegedly haunted 16th-century manor house, Morley Old Hall in Norfolk. Anthony D. Cornell (below left) demonstrated how a ghost-hunter worked. After a night's investigation, he was interviewed in the room where the ghost was said to have appeared. He concluded there was little evidence for the haunting.

Five people contacted the television company to say that they had seen a 'hooded monk' standing between Cornell and the interviewer, Michael Robson. Although Robson could see nothing when he re-ran the film, he decided to broadcast it again. Viewers were asked to write in if they saw anything odd.

Twenty-seven viewers wrote in. Fifteen said they had seen a monk or priest; one said it was a lady in a mantilla; one said it was a hooded skull.

When some of the relevant frames were enlarged, certain markings were at last seen that corresponded with drawings sent in by viewers. They proved to be due to dampness on the stonework.

As Anthony Cornell commented, the case was of interest to psychical researchers. The dim lighting of the television screen and the 'atmosphere' engendered by the rest of the film favoured 'spectral' appearances. Secondly, an impressive number of witnesses sited the 'figure' exactly at the spot where a physical cause was later found. Lastly, although the markings were vague, many of the witnesses were in substantial agreement about the 'figure' they saw.

hunt, or as research into subatomic particles or the mating habits of cockroaches. But they are not available, and the work is left to individual investigators, many of whom understandably make a living by writing about their experiences. The best to be hoped for is that such individuals will record as much first-hand evidence as they can, as soon as possible after the event.

While the perfect ghost investigation has yet to be recorded, at least two cases of the 1970s were researched and written up in considerable detail. One consisted of a series of apparitions on board several jumbo jets of an American airline.

Airborne apparitions

An Eastern Airlines Tri-Star, flight 401, crashed in December 1972 in a Florida swamp, killing 101 people. The ghosts of the pilot, Bob Loft, and his flight engineer, Don Repo, were seen on more than twenty occasions by crew members of other Eastern Tri-Stars, especially those that had been fitted with salvaged parts of the crashed plane. The apparitions were invariably described as wholly lifelike. They were reported both by men and women who had known Loft and Repo and by others who had not, but who recognised them later from photographs. The haunting became well-known among

people in the airline community, and an account of it even appeared in the newsletter of the US Flight Safety Foundation, in 1974.

An author, John G. Fuller, made thorough investigations of the case with the help of several airline personnel. They produced a mass of compelling testimony, including claims that log books recording apparitions had been withdrawn and crew members reporting them had been threatened with a visit to the company psychiatrist. Moreover, a seance was eventually held in the presence of Repo's widow at which evidence was produced that satisfied her of her husband's continuing existence. This would be a near-perfect case if the airline had co-operated but, perhaps understandably, it did not.

It is to be hoped that future ghosts will be as visible and informative as Loft and Repo, and that future hunters will be as determined as the investigators of this famous case. Ghost-hunting, says Andrew Green, himself an expert in the art, 'enlarges the field of knowledge, which is in itself a valid reason for any pursuit.' But for the dedicated ghost-hunter, the sheer fascination of the chase is a sufficient spur.

A ghost hunter's guide

Resourcefulness and skill are required to carry out an investigation of ghostly apparitions. The method used to test the authenticity of a haunting is of primary importance to a good ghost hunter

FINDING A GHOST worthy of investigation is not too difficult. It is rather like looking for a flat: just as home hunters can go to an agency, look in the papers, and 'ask around', so ghost hunters can seek information from official organisations, from the specialised press and from friends and work-mates.

The first step for the would-be ghost hunter is to join the Society for Psychical Research (SPR). It was founded in 1882 'to examine without prejudice or prepossession and in a scientific spirit those faculties of man, real or supposed, which appear to be inexplicable on any generally recognised hypothesis.' The SPR *Journal* is published

Above: the ghost hunter's dream come true – a meeting face-to-face with an apparition. However, this eminent investigator, the physicist Sir William Crookes, is generally thought to have been duped. The medium responsible for the 'materialisation' – Florence Cook, here apparently recumbent on the floor – bore a remarkable physical resemblance to the 'spirit', Katie King

regularly; its *Proceedings*, containing full reports and more technical articles, appears irregularly. It holds regular meetings and annual international conferences; and it offers its members, of which there are more than a thousand, the use of its unique library. It holds no corporate views, and its membership includes men and women with or without qualifications or religious convictions. Although ghosts are only one of many areas of research that come within its scope, the majority of Britain's serious ghost hunters have been, or are, members. The SPR has often provided new members with ghost cases of their own, but it cannot, obviously, guarantee to do this.

The weekly newspaper *Psychic News* is also an excellent source of new case material. Any good public library will have a number of books by such experienced ghost hunters as Andrew Green, Peter Underwood, Joan Forman and Andrew Mackenzie, many of which give the addresses of places with a well-established history of haunting. *Ghost-hunting, a practical guide* (1973) by Andrew Green is a particularly clear and concise work for beginners seeking a general introduction to the subject. The SPR's *Notes for investigators of spontaneous cases* are also recommended.

Finally, one can attempt to find a case by word-of-mouth contact. Since about one person in ten has had some kind of paranormal experience, it is more than likely that in an average office or factory there is somebody who has seen a ghost or knows someone who has.

Preliminary assessment

When a case has been found, the first thing to do is to make sure that there is enough firm evidence to make it worth investigating. The criteria for assessing evidence are much the same as in a criminal enquiry, and a study of police methods is useful to the ghost hunter. The following notes may sound somewhat obvious, but it is amazing how often they have not been observed in the past.

Witnesses' descriptions must be recorded, in writing or, preferably, on tape. The place and date, both of the incident described and of the statement, should be included. Written statements should be signed.

Second-hand accounts are almost never of value. First-hand accounts of a single event by a single witness are virtually impossible to verify and, though they are worth recording, they are seldom worth following up, since further occurrences are unlikely.

If there are several witnesses, they should be interviewed separately. Questioning should be deferred until the statements have been obtained, in order not to put ideas into the witnesses' heads. Questioning will almost certainly be necessary, however, to make up deficiencies in the statements. The aim should be to arrive at as full an account as possible of the circumstances of the incident:

47

A guide to ghosts

Above: Joan Forman has written valuable guides to the haunted places of East Anglia and southern England

Above right: the Society for Psychical Research plots cases of hauntings on this map, and maintains copious files concerning them

Below right: photographic evidence of a haunting, obtained by a budding ghost hunter. Andrew Green, then a 15-year-old boy, walked around this empty and reputedly haunted house in 1944. When he left, he took this photograph. When it was developed he was amazed to see the figure at the upper window. A murder and no fewer than 20 suicides took place here. It has been suggested that the figure is an apparition of Ann Hinchfield, who jumped from the tower in 1886, when she was 12 years old

Below: Andrew Green, today a noted researcher and author on parapsychology

time and place, the witnesses' activities and states of mind immediately before and during it, the physical layout of the scene, the positions of other people, independent confirming evidence – broken or displaced objects, for example – and any similar experiences that the witnesses may have had.

The occasional trick question can be useful. For example: 'Mrs Smith says the ghost was wearing a green hat. Are you *sure* it was bare-headed?' If the witness suddenly 'remembers' the green hat (which Mrs Smith did not mention) the hunter is dealing with an unreliable witness.

The witnesses should be interviewed on more than one occasion. Their stories may develop from one telling to the next; if so, it is necessary to judge whether this is really due to an increased recall, or to continuing inventiveness.

On the basis of these preliminary enquiries, which should be routine for any ghost report, the ghost hunter must judge whether a serious follow-up investigation is justified. Ideally, detailed and consistent reports will be provided by several witnesses, of good local reputations and no apparent motives for deceit (such as a council tenant's desire for a better house).

If more thorough research is undertaken, possible natural causes for the reported incident must first be sought. Ghostly noises are often made by such everyday agencies as the wind, water pipes, windows or ornaments vibrating in resonance with passing traffic, animals and so on. In one case a family was haunted by no more than rats, pushing apples stored in a loft down a cavity wall.

A superficial search for such a cause has a good chance of finding such a mundane explanation, but the variety of possible misleading occurrences is so great that little can

usefully be said here as guidance. The investigator must be sceptical of the easy paranormal explanations that suggest themselves, and imaginative in devising commonplace (but possibly far from obvious) causes that can be tested; he or she must aim to be a Sherlock Holmes of psychic detection, in fact.

A thorough investigation of the phenomena needs equipment (see box), patience and an acceptance of the likelihood of disappointment. If the occurrences are person-centred, there are great difficulties. It is rarely practicable to keep someone under continuous observation for long periods – let alone restrain their movements while apparent ghost activity is under way. There is

The well-equipped investigator

If the frequency of appearances is sufficient to justify lying in wait for a ghost, there is no end of material that might be useful to the investigator. The area being observed can be sealed off from human access by putting masking tape along the edges of doors and windows. Threads stretched across the ghost's route and scattered chalk powder will reveal a human presence. Fluorescent powder can also be scattered in suitable places – if it is picked up on the person of some occupant of the house, it will reveal itself when ultra-violet light is shone on it. Capacitance switches can be purchased, which will actuate cameras and tape recorders at the approach of a human being or animal. Tape recordings should be made in stereo if possible, and if an area can be surveyed with more than one tripod-mounted camera, so much the better. The 'fastest' (most sensitive) films available are black and white, and these can also be 'pushed' considerably in developing, in order to bring out more detail. If, however, it is planned to use flash, there is no reason why colour film should not be used. Since the space to be covered is usually confined, a short-focus (wide-angle) lens is valuable. A motor-drive attachment permits a sequence of photographs to be taken rapidly. Such obvious items as notebooks, pens, torch, luminous watch and a simple tool-kit should also not be omitted from the equipment list.

also the problem that people's feelings will be ruffled if they come to believe that they are being suspected of fraud.

On the other hand, ghostly phenomena, like some other paranormal events, may happen more predictably in the presence of certain people, and offer the opportunity of detailed study. Many mediums have claimed that it is possible to materialise a spirit. Past studies of such events, such as those carried out by the eminent physicist William Crookes in 1874, are still surrounded by controversy. Yet there remains a substantial body of evidence that certain mediums, such as the late Alec Harris, are able to cause such phenomena. It is a sad fact of the history of ghost hunting that few people have ever made a serious attempt to examine this subject properly. There are great opportunities for the ghost hunter here.

Setting up a team

Establishing the genuineness of a case is very much a matter of personal judgement, and since this is highly fallible, it is always a good idea for more than one person to study a given case. Unless the investigator is a qualified psychologist, physicist and chartered surveyor combined, he will need help from specialists. Furthermore, if an investigation team can be set up, it may be possible to keep the site under constant observation.

Ghost hunters will naturally want to see reported apparitions for themselves. They will almost certainly be disappointed. Perhaps ghosts will appear to order when we know more about the conditions they require; in the meantime, the more evidence that can be recorded about such conditions, the better for paranormal research.

Whatever the results of an investigation – whether it is called off at an early stage, ends inconclusively, or ends in a finding of fraud, misinterpretation or the genuinely paranormal – a report should be filed with the SPR. In addition to its intrinsic interest it may gain significance in the future should it be

The late Alec Harris, one of those mediums who can reputedly materialise spirits – an ability that may be related to some 'ordinary' hauntings

studied in relation to other cases, or should developments take place in the same case.

Where ghostly activities genuinely seem to be taking place, the question of getting rid of them may arise. If the ghost is not doing any harm, there is no need to do anything. In fact, it can be very good for trade in a pub or hotel (one of the motives for deceit that the ghost hunter must bear in mind).

But not all ghosts are harmless. The witnesses can be extremely frightened, and the phenomena can disrupt family life – or even, as in some recent cases, factory and office life. How can they be got rid of? There is no easy answer, but certain methods have been tried, with uneven success.

The best-known of these is exorcism. At the risk of oversimplifying this emotive and controversial subject, it can be said that it may be effective if the victim believes it will be. But it can also have frightening and dangerous side-effects, and in at least four well-reported cases of the 1970s, involving both Roman Catholics and Protestants, its use resulted in death.

A somewhat safer and less sensational way to combat an invisible agency is prayer. Canon J. D. Pearce-Higgins, former Vice-Provost of Southwark Cathedral, claims to have 'cleared' more than a hundred houses of 'unwanted visitors', by first identifying the entities with the help of a medium, and then persuading them to depart.

Ghosts will doubtless continue to provide entertainment in the newspapers and on the screen, and ghost hunters will continue to be regarded by some as harmless cranks. Yet the subject is a serious one, of tremendous potential significance. Once fully understood, it will vastly extend our knowledge both of the human mind and of matter. But it will not be understood unless far more people take it more seriously and investigate it more thoroughly. And the more amateur ghost hunters there are, collecting more and better evidence and forcing it upon the attention of scientists, the sooner this will happen.

Ghosts
and legend

Spirit guides at Glastonbury

Many of the more impressive fragments of the ruins at Glastonbury were uncovered in excavations that began in 1909. The extraordinary feature of this discovery was the unearthing of the treasures by 'psychic archaeology'

GLASTONBURY IS UNDOUBTEDLY one of the most ancient sacred sites in Britain. Standing high above the surrounding countryside, it is an obvious landmark, and archaeological evidence suggests that it has been a place of religious significance since the time of the Druids. But there are other kinds of evidence that suggest the Tor was a holy place long before the Celts came to Britain in the seventh or sixth century BC. A modern investigator, Stephen Jenkins, who studied Buddhism in Tibet, one day asked his guru about Shambala, the legendary sacred place of the ancient Hindus. He was astonished to be told that it was located in Britain at the place now called Glastonbury.

Nestled in the valley beneath the Tor is

Glastonbury Abbey, which was founded in the fifth century by St Patrick before he went on to convert Ireland. According to Giraldus Cambrensis, it was the burial place of King Arthur – and the discovery in 1191 of a coffin containing the skeletons of a man and woman, bearing the inscription 'Here lies Arthur, the Once and Future King', seemed to confirm it. Because of its association with Arthur, the abbey became one of the richest and most powerful in England. In 1539, Henry VIII's commissioners executed its last abbot, Richard Whyting, on top of the Tor. The abbey was destroyed. And for almost four centuries it remained a neglected ruin.

In 1907 the abbey ruins were bought by the Church of England for £36,000. Yet,

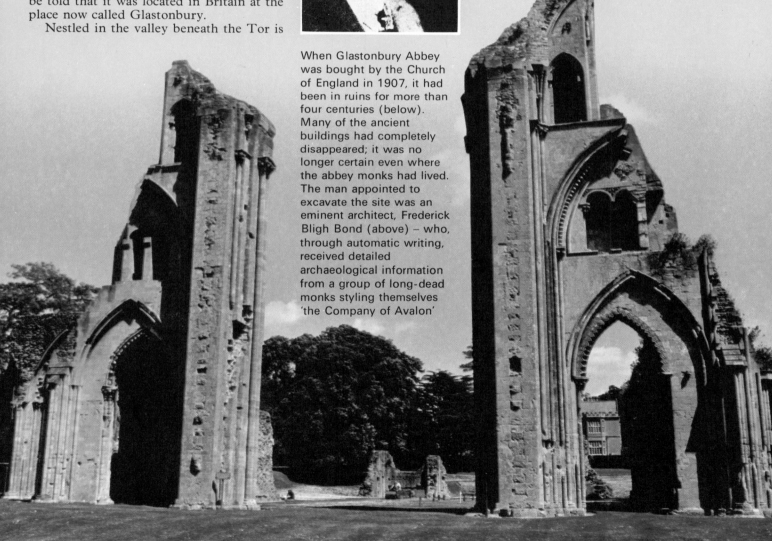

When Glastonbury Abbey was bought by the Church of England in 1907, it had been in ruins for more than four centuries (below). Many of the ancient buildings had completely disappeared; it was no longer certain even where the abbey monks had lived. The man appointed to excavate the site was an eminent architect, Frederick Bligh Bond (above) – who, through automatic writing, received detailed archaeological information from a group of long-dead monks styling themselves 'the Company of Avalon'

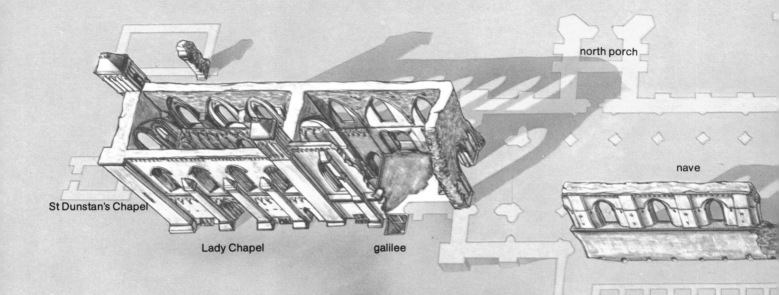

St Dunstan's Chapel

Lady Chapel

galilee

north porch

nave

cloister

vault under refectory

amazingly enough, the Church had no idea what it had bought. Time and vandalism had done their work so well that no one was even certain where the monks had lived. Obviously, the site had to be carefully excavated. And the man chosen to do the job was a 43-year-old architect named Frederick Bligh Bond.

Bond certainly seemed an admirable man for the job. He was one of England's leading experts on Gothic architecture and the restoration of old churches. But the Church of England might have been slightly less enthusiastic if it had known something about Bond's background – for Bond had psychic and occult leanings. As a child he had been a dreamer and a bookworm, and when he had to go into the world and make a living, his first reactions were shock and disgust. Then he came across a book called *The night side of nature* by Katherine Crowe – one of the great Victorian bestsellers, full of discussions of psychic powers and occult mysteries. Bond became a lifelong devotee of psychic studies. When he became apprenticed to the architect Charles Hansen – who specialised in Gothic architecture – he had a chance to turn his romantic love of the medieval period to practical account. By 1907 he was one of England's most successful and respectable architects. But his association with Glastonbury Abbey was to put an end to all that.

In the late 15th century the last Abbot of Glastonbury but one, Richard Bere, had started a cult of Joseph of Arimathea – Christ's uncle – who, according to legend, had visited Glastonbury with the child Jesus, and returned there later with the cup used at the Last Supper – the Holy Grail. Abbot Bere was said to have built two chapels, called the Loretto Chapel and the Edgar Chapel. But these were apparently destroyed

The plan (above) indicates the extant ruins of Glastonbury Abbey, together with the positions of foundations that have been excavated or have been known to exist in the past. Frederick Bligh Bond's great find was the Edgar Chapel, which was known from records to have existed but was completely lost. For some years, it was believed that he had also succeeded in locating the Loretto Chapel. Although there is undoubtedly a building on the site, this is not believed to have been a sacristy. The aerial view (right) shows the extent to which the abbey ruins have been excavated

by Henry VIII's vandals, and by the 19th century no one even knew where they were situated. Finding them was one of the tasks assigned to Bond.

There was one minor problem – there was no money to organise a full-scale dig. Bond therefore had to rely on luck and 'educated guesses'. Worse still, he had a rival architect called Caroe, who had been appointed to 'preserve' the ruins, and who obviously hoped to stumble upon the right answers before Bond did and take the credit for the discovery. Bond needed results quickly. And he decided upon a bold solution. He would ask the 'spirits'.

This was not, of course, quite the way that he expressed it. He said merely that he was going to undertake a 'psychological experiment'. At this time, everyone who was interested in psychical research was aware of the extraordinary case of spirit contact that has become known as the 'cross-correspond-

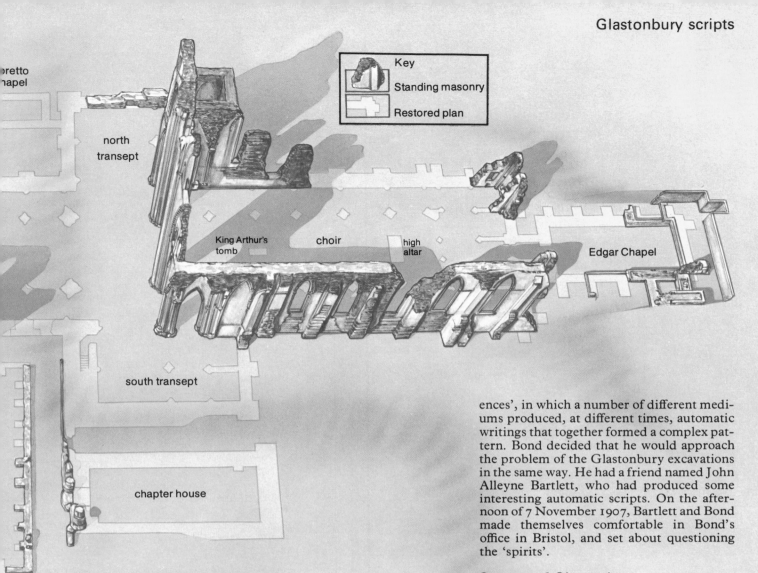

Key

Standing masonry

Restored plan

oretto
hapel

north
transept

King Arthur's
tomb

choir

high
altar

Edgar Chapel

south transept

chapter house

ences', in which a number of different mediums produced, at different times, automatic writings that together formed a complex pattern. Bond decided that he would approach the problem of the Glastonbury excavations in the same way. He had a friend named John Alleyne Bartlett, who had produced some interesting automatic scripts. On the afternoon of 7 November 1907, Bartlett and Bond made themselves comfortable in Bond's office in Bristol, and set about questioning the 'spirits'.

Secrets of Glastonbury
Their method was simple. Bond sat down opposite Bartlett at a plain wooden table, resting his fingers lightly on Bartlett's hand; Bartlett held a pencil above a sheet of paper. Then Bond cleared his throat and asked: 'Can you tell us anything about Glastonbury?' Bartlett's hand began to write. When the men deciphered the small, irregular writing, they saw that it said: 'All knowledge is eternal and is available to mental sympathy. I was not in sympathy with the monks – I cannot find a monk yet.'

This looked promising. Bond suggested that he knew a few living monks who might form a sympathetic link. At this, the pencil began to move again, tracing an outline that they soon recognised as the abbey, but with a long rectangle stuck on its eastern end. It was signed 'Gulielmus Monachus' – William the Monk. The rectangle looked too large to be a chapel, so Bond asked for a more careful drawing. The pencil obliged, with another precise drawing of a chapel, and also showed two smaller chapels to the north. Bond asked who had built it, and received the answer – in Latin – 'Abbot Bere', and the statement that this was the Edgar Chapel. It was added to, said the writer, by Abbot Whyting, in whose

handwritings. But was it all pure fantasy?

Finally, in 1908, the money for excavation became available. Digging started in 1909. And, to Bond's amazement and delight, it was soon abundantly clear that the monks had been telling him the truth.

Understandably, the first thing he wanted to know was whether there really was a large chapel at the east end of the abbey church. Johannes Bryant had also told him that he would find the remains of two towers at the west end. In May 1909, the workmen began to dig trenches at the east end of the ruined church. When Bond's rival Caroe came and looked at the work, he must have been mystified by the apparently random arrangement of the trenches. Any scepticism he felt must have changed to astonishment as the workmen quickly came upon an immense and unsuspected wall running north and south for 31 feet (10 metres). Moreover, excavation at the other end of the ruined church quickly revealed the outline of two unsuspected towers. To Bond's superiors, it must have seemed like a run of incredible luck, combined with intelligent deduction. As to Bond, he must have wondered many times whether he should reveal the secret of his ghostly 'communicators'. Yet common sense told him that he should be cautious. His employer was the Church of England – and the Church has never been very sympathetic to Spiritualism. Of course, it believes in life after death, since this is part of Christian dogma; but from the beginning, the Church has shown itself hostile and sceptical about the notion of communication with the dead. So how could Bond explain

reign it was destroyed. When they asked the name of the writer, it wrote: 'Ego Johannes Bryant, monk and lapidator.' (Lapidator means 'stonemason'.)

The two men were excited, yet at the same time disappointed. Someone who seemed to know what he was talking about was answering the questions, but the answers looked too good to be true. Did these 'facts' about the Edgar Chapel come from their own minds?

Four days later, they tried again. Their 'communicator' began by saying that he was becoming tired towards the end of the last session, but that the monks were now very eager to communicate. 'They say the times are now ripe and the curse is departing.' Then another hand wrote: 'Benedicite. Go unto Glaston soon. . . .' And later, the hand added: 'Ye names of builded things are very hard in Latin tongue. . . . My son, thou canst not understand. Wee wold speak in the Englyshe tongue. . . .' To the question, 'Tell us more about yourself,' it replied: 'I died in 1533.' He was, he said, curator of the chapel in the time of Henry VII.

From then on, Bond and Bartlett held regular sessions, and the monks of Glastonbury poured out information. There were several different monks, and several different

Above: the foundations of the Edgar Chapel, in a photograph taken shortly after they were restored by Bond. The site of the chapel was identified by one of Bond's ghostly informants, a monk named Johannes Bryant. In one respect, however, it seems that Johannes was mistaken. The angled walls at the far end of the chapel are no longer to be seen: Johannes claimed that they were built as an apse by Abbot Bere, but experts now believe that they are actually a water channel and part of an ancient abbey wall, and they have been removed

Right: the tomb of Arthur, 'the once and future king', seen through the peaceful ruins of the abbey nave

that his communicators called themselves the Company of Avalon – the old name for Glastonbury – and, worse still, described themselves as 'watchers from the other side'? Wisely, he decided to keep his amazing secret. At least, for the time being.

Meanwhile, discovery followed discovery, and Bond's reputation was greatly enhanced. His monkish correspondents proved to be phenomenally accurate. They told him there was a door in the east wall, leading into the street. This seemed unlikely, since eastern doorways in churches are unusual; yet digging revealed the doorway in the middle of the east wall. They told him the chapel would be 90 feet (28 metres) long, which seemed enormous; excavation showed it to be 87 feet (27 metres), and the wall and plinth added another 3 feet (1 metre). They even told him he would find the remains of azure-coloured windows – which again seemed unlikely, since most stained glass of that period used white and gold. But they duly found their fragments of blue stained glass in the Edgar Chapel. A communicator who seemed to be Abbot Bere said the roof was painted in gold and crimson; digging revealed arch mouldings with gold and crimson paint still on them.

In 1918, 10 years after the start of the triumphant excavations, Bond decided to publish the full story behind the discovery. No doubt he assumed that his success would justify his method. But this assumption proved to be a tragic mistake.

Above: the Lady Chapel, one of the best-preserved parts of the abbey, was consecrated in 1189. It is also known as St Joseph's Chapel, after St Joseph of Arimathea, Christ's uncle, who, according to legend, brought the child Jesus to Glastonbury

Right: Bond and Bartlett were told by one of their ghostly communicators of the location of the unfinished Loretto Chapel. When the site was excavated in 1920, the foundations of a building were found, but it is now believed that they are not, in fact, remains of the Loretto Chapel. The foundations in the photograph have since been covered over with turf

A career in ruins

The success of the excavations at Glastonbury convinced the man in charge that he could safely reveal the paranormal source of his information, but he was tragically wrong

IT MUST BE FRANKLY CONFESSED that, as a human being, Frederick Bligh Bond, discoverer of phenomenal architectural remains at Glastonbury, left something to be desired. Even his admiring biographer William Kenawell admits that he was paranoid, and tended to suspect plots and conspiracies everywhere. But at Glastonbury his suspicions were not entirely unjustified, for his two chief associates, W. D. Caroe and Dean J. A. Robinson, who found him eccentric and disorganised, would have been glad to see the back of him.

But the extraordinary success of the excavations at Glastonbury Abbey placed him in a very strong position. His 'enemies' had no suspicion that this success was due largely to the advice of dead monks. Moreover, the invisible communicators who called themselves the 'Company of Avalon' were not merely concerned to help him dig up the past; they declared that their aim was to restore Glastonbury as a centre of religious power and significance. A man who carried around a secret like that was bound to behave a little oddly.

And Bond had more than one secret to keep to himself. The long-dead monks who

The tranquillity of the ruins at Glastonbury conceals the abbey's turbulent and chequered past. Once the richest and most powerful church in all England, it was destroyed by Henry VIII and remained neglected and crumbling for four centuries until its former glory was all but extinguished.

guided John Bartlett's pencil were able to provide him with all kinds of historical titbits. In 1908, he was digging along the south side of the nave, hoping to find evidence for the two towers that the 'communicators' had described, when he came upon a giant skeleton. It was that of an old man, nearly 7 feet (2 metres) tall, and he had been buried without a coffin. Stranger still, there was another skull between his legs. It was the kind of mystery that gives archaeologists sleepless nights. Had the old man been murdered? That seemed unlikely, since a stone pillow had been carefully placed underneath his head.

Bond, of course, had easy access to a solution. He merely had to sit down beside his friend Bartlett, ask the dead monks to explain the matter, and wait for Bartlett's pencil to trace out a reply. In this case, the reply was precise and fascinating. The skeleton, said the monk who called himself Gulielmus (William), was that of Radulphus Cancellarius – Radulphus the treasurer – who had slain someone called Eawulf in fair fight. Eawulf had caused considerable damage to Radulphus with his axe, and had broken several of his bones. However, Radulphus lived on for many years, and died at the age of 103. He asked to be buried right outside the church he loved so much. Oddly enough, his old enemy Eawulf had been buried in the same spot, and when the monks buried Radulphus, they were startled when

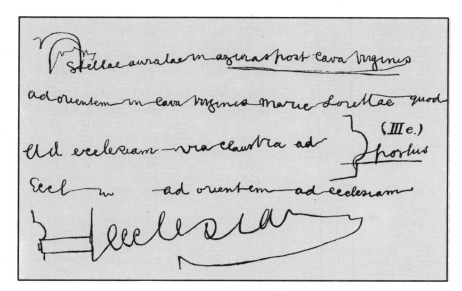

The monk said that the Saxon monks had their reward, for 'a Saxon again was Abbot for a time.' That proved to be accurate. Thurstan was removed by William the Conqueror, and in his place was appointed Herlewin – a Saxon name.

But did Eawulf exist? Bond, who was nothing if not thorough, searched the records, but without success. History had nothing to say about Earl Eawulf of Edgarley.

Then, in an ancient chronicle by someone called Fabius Ethelwerd, and dated AD 866, there was a sentence that read: 'During this year died Eanulf, nobleman of the province of Somerset.' It went on to say that his body now rested 'in the monastery at Glastingabyrig' – Glastonbury. This showed that a nobleman with a very similar name – only an 'n' instead of a 'w' – was associated with the abbey and Somerset. But *was* 'Eanulf' really

they disturbed the bones of Eawulf. So they put them into the same grave.

And who were these men? It seemed that Radulphus (or Ralph) was a Norman who came to England with William the Conqueror – Gulielmus mentioned the date 1087 – and Eawulf was a Saxon earl. This had been in the time of a Norman abbot, Thurstan.

Now history tells us that, when Norman monks took over Glastonbury Abbey, they treated the Saxon monks (who belonged to an Irish order) with considerable brutality. Abbot Thurstan was their chief persecutor. In fact, Thurstan was so brutal that William the Conqueror dismissed him. But history mentions no one called Eawulf. So who was he? The 'communicator' answered this question promptly. Eawulf, it seemed, was the Earl of Edgarley, of royal blood, 'a doughty Saxon he, and one who said that Glaston was builded by the Saxon, and Saxon it should remain.' What happened, apparently, is that Norman soldiers killed some Saxon monks of Glastonbury Abbey. Earl Eawulf of Edgarley – a village a mile (1.6 kilometres) southeast of Glastonbury – retaliated by attacking the Normans. He was killed in a fight with Thurstan's treasurer Radulphus, and buried (without a coffin) outside the abbey church.

Testing the ghostly fathers

It was a fascinating story. But was it true? Here was a good opportunity to test the accuracy of the ghostly monks. No one had ever heard of Earl Eawulf of Edgarley, and neither Bartlett nor Bond had any recollection of having heard of him. So if he really existed, this would prove that the message came from real communicators, not from Bond's or Bartlett's unconscious mind.

Gulielmus claimed that Radulphus had had his bones broken by Eawulf's axe. They examined the skeleton, and found that, in fact, the right forearm *had* been fractured, but had healed. A man defending himself from an axe would fling up his right forearm, and it might well get broken.

Architectural details of the lost Loretto Chapel, supplied by a monk who signed himself *Camillus Thesiger* – probably Camel, the purse-bearer to the Abbot Bere who built the chapel. Camillus told of a 'covered way, or cloister, leading to the church, to the east' (top), of the undervaults, whose ribs are 'carven with fruit and many colours', and drew an unfinished sketch of one of the statues of sitting lions to be found in the Loretto Chapel (above). Unfortunately, although Bond believed that his informants had given him the location of the Loretto Chapel, experts now believe that this is not, in fact, the true site – which remains unknown

another version of 'Eawulf'? Bond continued his search – and found another ancient chronicle, Asser's *Annals of the exploits of Alfred*, dated AD 855, which mentioned 'Eanwulf, Earl of the district of Summurton.' This is definitely the same man who is referred to as 'Eanulf', for both chronicles associate him with a certain Bishop Ealhstan. Somerton is very close to Edgarley.

Of course, *this* Earl Eanwulf is two centuries too early to be the one killed by Radulphus the treasurer. But he was obviously an ancestor; Bond had proved that there *was* an Earl of Edgarley in the Glastonbury area two centuries before the fight between Radulphus and Eawulf. It is one of the most remarkable and convincing proofs of the objective existence of Bond's ghostly communicators.

Perhaps one of the most charming things about this curious tale is the positive character of the 'communicators' that emerges in the writing. For example, Bond thought at first that Radulphus the treasurer was another Radulphus called Fitzstephen, who rebuilt the abbey church after the great fire of 1184. But this, of course, was a century after Radulphus Cancellarius's time. Bond asked

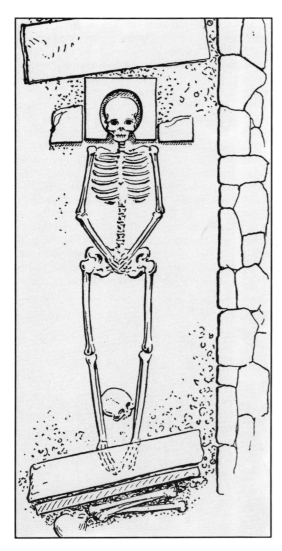

Left: in 1908, while excavating the south wall of the nave, Bond came across this 7-foot (2-metre) skeleton, which had been buried without a coffin, but with a skull between its legs. The reason for this strange method of burial was a complete mystery – until Bond resolved to consult the Company of Avalon

Below: an engraving of the romantic ruins of the abbey church at Glastonbury as they appeared in the early part of the 19th century. When Bond began his excavations, many of the original buildings had completely disappeared; it was all the more extraordinary, then, that he found so many of them through automatic writings

distances be a mystery – the mystery of our Faith, which ye have forgotten.' Now it is believed by some people that many medieval abbeys and cathedrals were built according to some kind of numerical code, enshrining the occult secrets of the ancients. Bond himself became increasingly fascinated by the possibility that Glastonbury Abbey was a code in stone and began the study of gematria, the cabalistic relationship between words and numbers. In 1916, he gave a lecture to the Somerset Archaeological Society entitled: 'The Lady Chapel of Glastonbury Abbey: A study of measures and proportions' about his theory of secret meanings. His audience included his sceptical 'boss', Dean Robinson, who was understandably irritated.

And finally, Bond could bear the secrecy no longer. He decided to tell the whole story – everything that had happened since that first 'sitting' in November 1908. He confessed in a book called *The gate of remembrance*, which came out in 1918. The effect was instantaneous and disastrous. Budgets were cut, a co-director was appointed, Bond found himself obstructed in every possible way and was made the victim of red tape. In 1921 he was reduced to cataloguing and cleaning his earlier finds for £10 a month. In 1922 he received a letter that stated: 'The Council of this Society informs you that you are no longer responsible for the excavations at Glastonbury Abbey and that the Excavation Committee appointed by them is therefore dissolved. . . .'

the communicator to clarify this matter, and got the reply: 'Ne [not] Radulphus of Henry the King' – that is Radulphus Fitzstephen. 'Radulphus the Treasurer was a Norman of the time of Thurstan. . . .' Bond was still a little confused by all these Radulphuses, and asked 'Why do you say that Ralph the treasurer was Ralph of King Henry?' In reply he got an irritable blast: 'Rede!' (In other words, 'Read – use your eyes!') 'I said it not. I said not "Ralph of King Henry" but "Ralph ye Norman."' Then, in an outburst of furious Latin: 'Listen to me, you stupid barbarian! To me, the Emperor, who have been trying to make these things clear to the minds of you Islanders!' It was signed: 'CAESAR'.

It is easy to see that Bond found himself in a very peculiar position. *He* knew the answer to the mystery of the 7-foot (2-metre) skeleton with the second skull between its legs; yet he could not reveal it unless he could also find some documentary evidence to justify it. Understandably, Caroe simply thought Bond was arrogant and dictatorial.

And there was more. Bond had also been told by the 'watchers' that 'Our Abbey was a message in stones. In ye foundations and ye

A very strange place

Were the messages in the Glastonbury scripts really from the spirit world – or did they, as Frederick Bligh Bond himself believed, originate in his own unconscious?

THE STORY OF THE DISMISSAL of Frederick Bligh Bond from the excavations at Glastonbury is one of the seediest tales in the history of British archaeology. The abbey trustees even ordered that all Bond's books should be removed from sale in the abbey book store, including the purely technical *Architectural handbook to Glastonbury Abbey*. The Church of England was alarmed to discover that his highly successful investigations and his remarkable discoveries were the result of 'seances' with long-dead monks, and it went out of its way to prevent Bond carrying out any further excavations.

Bond lived for almost another quarter-century; he spent much of this time in America, and did a great deal of valuable and interesting work in psychical research. But he was a lonely and embittered man, whose heart remained in Glastonbury Abbey. The trustees even banned him from the abbey grounds. In 1937 a group of American friends put up the money for more excavations at Glastonbury, to test some of the information given by the 'watchers' of Glastonbury, and the trustees gave the group permission. But the moment they heard that

agonised over the question for three years. They ended up by stating that the claims of Spiritualism are probably true, and that there is nothing in the idea of 'communication with the dead' that contradicts the ideas of Christianity. But the report ended with a curious footnote: 'The committee do not recommend that any publicity be given to this.' The Archbishop agreed, and suppressed it. The report was not finally published until March 1979.

Depths of the unconscious

Curiously, where the unfortunate Frederick Bligh Bond is concerned, the absurdity is that he did *not* believe he was communicating with the dead. The title of his book, *The gate of remembrance*, tells us what he had finally come to believe: that his own unconscious mind had somehow gained access to a vast store of unconscious memory about Glastonbury. He wrote: 'From the depths of the subconscious mind, [the power of intuition] has evoked these images. . . .'

It was understandable that Bond should take such a view. He was a member of the Society for Psychical Research, and a friend of Sir William Barrett, who had written a classic book on dowsing. And what fascinated Barrett was that a good dowser seems to possess a form of 'second sight' (or, as Barrett preferred to call it, 'cryptesthesia'). A certain female dowser, for example, was not only able to pinpoint the exact location of an underground cistern, but was also able to

Bond was involved they cancelled it. He died, poor and forgotten, in 1945.

The situation is absurd, almost unbelievable. Between 1909 and 1920 this man proved that his unorthodox methods could lead to spectacular results. Almost single-handed, he rediscovered secrets that had been buried for four centuries. But these discoveries – such as the Edgar Chapel – utilised only a small part of the information obtained from the 'communicators'. Other communications – including some he received after leaving Glastonbury – included information about the tomb of King Arthur, secret passageways, the Holy Grail and several stores of buried treasure. There is still enough assorted information to keep archaeologists busy for another 20 years. The most fascinating part of Bond's life-work still remains to be completed. Yet the abbey trustees are apparently determined that it shall not be completed.

Why is the Church of England still so hostile to this whole notion of 'psychic archaeology'? No doubt because to accept it would imply an acceptance of some of the doctrines of 'Spiritualism'. And this is a matter about which the Church seems determined not to give any definite pronouncements. In 1936 the Archbishop of Canterbury, Cosmo Lang, commissioned a special report on Spiritualism, and his committee

Glastonbury is one of England's most ancient and mysterious sacred places – so perhaps it is not surprising that it should have been the site of an early and successful experiment in psychic archaeology. The Tor (previous page, top) is a landmark that is believed by many to be a centre of some kind of spiritual power. Legend has it that the Holy Thorn within the abbey grounds (above) is descended from one planted by St Joseph of Arimathea, who visited Britain with the infant Jesus, his nephew. King Arthur (previous page, bottom) was buried in the nave; he lies sleeping, ready to come to the aid of Britain in its hour of need. The Chalice Well, at the foot of the Tor, is also part of the Arthurian legend; its cover (right), designed by Frederick Bligh Bond, carries the ancient symbol of the *vesica piscis*, which represents the source of life

Where was Avalon?

Avalon, the Isle of Apples, elusive place of enchantments, where the soil yields crops without sowing and whose happy inhabitants enjoy eternal life, is an integral part of the Arthurian tradition. It was to Avalon, so the legend goes, that Arthur was taken after his last battle, and there he lives on, ready one day to come to the aid of the Celtic peoples and restore them to their rightful sovereignty over their land.

That, at least, is the substance of the so-called 'Breton hope' – and as long as Arthur's burial place remained unknown, this hope continued to be nurtured. But in 1191 came the discovery at Glastonbury of a tomb carrying the inscription 'Here lies the famous King Arthur, buried in the Isle of Avalon'. The Breton hope seemed dashed.

Is Glastonbury really Avalon? The group of hills surrounding Glastonbury has been known as 'the Isle of Avalon' since the opening of the alleged tomb of Arthur, and possibly for much longer. And in the early Christian period, when sea level is known to have been much higher than it is today, the hills and the high ground between them would almost have formed an island.

But the proof is not conclusive – and some people still cherish a faint hope that, after all, the magical island dreamed of by the ancients really exists.

Above: Cosmo Lang, Archbishop of Canterbury, who, in 1936, commissioned a report on Spiritualism. The findings were, surprisingly, not unfavourable – but the report ended with the curious recommendation that no publicity be given to the investigation

Left: the Abbot's Kitchen, built 'to make feast on grete feast-days', according to a communicator named Ricardus. Another monk, Ambrosius the cellarer – who, Ricardus remarks pointedly, 'isne a scholar' – tells how one of the monks drank himself unconscious in front of Henry VIII (right), when he was being entertained by the Abbot. The abbey was subsequently destroyed by Henry

Pope Gregory XVI; the coffin was embossed in tin, copper and gold, just as the Abbé Mermet had described.

Mermet was also successful in locating minerals, oil, treasure and sunken ships, as well as an expedition lost at the North Pole. But the discovery of the bones of Saint Victor is relevant here because it is so similar to what Bond and Bartlett did. And if we can accept – like Sir William Barrett – that dowsing is a peculiar faculty of the unconscious mind, then there really seems no reason why Bond and Bartlett should not have used some form of unconscious dowsing to find the Edgar Chapel.

But anyone who reads *The gate of remembrance* will see that this raises an interesting problem. For the various monks who communicated with Bond are all very distinct personalities. There was Ambrosius the cellarer, who told charming stories about the

describe exactly what it looked like, as if her eyes could see through the ground.

But some dowsers have been able to do even stranger things. The Abbé Mermet – a perfectly respectable Catholic – was able to locate all kinds of things simply by dangling a pendulum over a map. So, for example, in 1934 the Marquis de la Chevalerie asked the Abbé if he could help him locate the bones of one of his ancestors. The Abbé dangled his pendulum over a plan of the chapel, and replied that he could find no trace of the ancestor, but that under the altar there were the bones of another man at a depth of 6 feet (2 metres), together with some tin, copper and gold. The Marquis gave orders for excavation, and they discovered a coffin containing the bones of Saint Victor, presented by

alcohol drunk by the monks (and how one of them drank himself unconscious in front of Henry VIII); Peter Lightfoot, the clock-maker, who told how the abbey clock came to be built because the monks of Glastonbury became jealous when they heard about the one in Wells Cathedral; Johannes Bryant, who has beautiful descriptions of nature and of the abbey's mint garden. Then there was Abbot Bere, who described how he decided to build the Loretto Chapel. He was a huge, fat man and, as he was riding along on his mule, he was attacked by 'rude men', and he rolled down a steep slope. He said a hasty prayer to Our Lady, and his cloak caught on a thorn bush, preventing him rolling over the edge – whereupon he made a vow to build the Loretto Chapel to the Virgin. . . . The 'watchers' also told the sad story of the miscalculation that led to the downfall of Glastonbury Abbey. When Abbot Bere died, the King's adviser Cardinal Wolsey appointed Richard Whyting Abbot, and advised him to invite the King to Glastonbury to try to gain his goodwill. It was a disastrous mistake. The King was royally entertained; but when he saw the abbey's treasures and its lands and farms, he licked his lips and calculated how much all this would add to the royal treasury. So after Henry's break with Rome, Thomas Cromwell had no difficulty 'framing' the monks on a number of false charges; and Henry seized the abbey and destroyed it.

As we read stories as circumstantial as this, it becomes very difficult to swallow the theory that they originate from some kind of 'racial memory'. Either the story is an amusing invention of Bond's unconscious mind, or it is a genuine communication from someone who was there at the time.

Yet the Glastonbury scripts contain one clue that implies that the truth may be even more fascinating and complex. At one point the monk Johannes says,

Why cling I to that which is not? It is I, and it is not I, butt parte of me which dwelleth in the past and is bound to that which my carnal soul loved and called 'home' these many years. Yet I, Johannes, amm of many partes and ye better parte doeth other things – *Laus, Laus Deo!* – only that part which remembereth clingeth like memory to what it seeth not. . . .

Multiple personalities

'I, Johannes, amm of many partes. . . .' This is a puzzling statement, yet one that is supported, for example, by the baffling evidence of so-called 'multiple personalities' – people like the heroine of *The three faces of Eve*, who periodically lose their memory and become a completely different person. Perhaps our greatest error is in thinking of ourselves as 'individuals', single and indivisible. Perhaps every one of us contains a whole crowd of different people. And perhaps the ghosts that haunt the scenes of old

Above: the cathedral clock at Wells. The monks told how improvements were carried out at Glastonbury to rival the beauty of Wells, 'new and faire with carven stone'

tragedies are disjointed personality fragments, left behind like a fragment of tape recording.

But in assessing the evidence about the 'watchers', the 'Company of Avalon' that spoke to Bond through automatic writing, we should also bear in mind that Glastonbury is a place of power, a religious site chosen because the ground seems to concentrate some unknown force – possibly something as simple as a vortex in the Earth's magnetic field. If the late T. C. Lethbridge was correct in believing that 'ghosts' are some kind of emotional tape-recording then perhaps Glastonbury is a vast repository of recordings from the past. If so, it seems reasonable to suppose that other ancient sites conceal similar stores of information – and, on this hypothesis, it might be worthwhile for archaeologists to consider trying to develop methods of 'tuning in' to this secret knowledge. Perhaps Bond's real importance is that he was the first man to stumble on a treasure house that will be explored, documented and catalogued by a new generation of researchers.

Taken for a ride?

The story of the hitch-hiker who unaccountably vanishes before he reaches his destination is told throughout the world. Many people have been led to conclude that the tale is merely a piece of modern folklore – but research shows that the story has hidden depths

ROY FULTON met the phantom hitch-hiker on a fog-streaked Friday evening in October 1979. Stopping close to the small Bedfordshire village of Stanbridge on his way home from a darts match, the 26-year-old carpet fitter had no reason to suppose the figure at the roadside, thumb upraised in customary hitchers' manner, was anything other than human; true, the pale young man in the white shirt and dark trousers was uncommunicative, merely pointing wordlessly towards Dunstable when asked where he wanted to go, but Mr Fulton knew from experience that some hitch-hikers are like that. Besides, it crossed his mind that the stranger might be a deaf mute.

They had been travelling at a steady 40 miles per hour (65 km/h) for several minutes when Mr Fulton decided it was time to break the ice:

> I turned round to offer him a cigarette and the bloke had disappeared. I braked, had a quick look in the back to see if he was there. He *wasn't* and I just gripped the wheel and drove like hell.

Not long afterwards, local police were hearing Roy Fulton's extraordinary story of a hitch-hiker who vanished from a moving vehicle. They formed the opinion that Fulton was reliable, 'an ordinary sort of chap' and not the worse for alcohol – he had drunk only a couple of lagers during the darts match – but they also felt there was little they could do about disappearing passengers, and the case was never properly explained. Anne Court, a journalist from the *Dunstable Gazette* who interviewed Fulton a couple of days later, also found him quite credible. And as late as March 1980 Roy Fulton was still insisting that he had given a ride to a phantom hitch-hiker.

Evidently representatives of police and press were favourably impressed with Roy Fulton as a witness, but does their evaluation mean that we should accept the account as fact? Many parapsychologists would argue that it does not; the story is totally uncorroborated by any kind of independent testimony and rests purely on the word of a single person. Even if they grant that the Stanbridge encounter is not a downright fabrication, psychical researchers jib at accepting

Ghosts and legend

the unsupported, subjective evidence of persons who were emotionally involved in the events they describe. With the best will in the world, such witnesses can tell the truth only as they perceive it to be – and this may not be what actually occurred.

There is an even greater objection to Roy Fulton's story. The tale of the phantom hitch-hiker is a ghostly classic, an ancient, oft-repeated piece told and retold in many localities. 'People,' declared folklorist and anthropologist Andrew Lang, who became President of the Society for Psychical Research in 1912, 'will unconsciously localise old legends in new places and assign old occurrences or fables to new persons.' In this way the tales are given new leases of life and are passed from one narrator to another across great distances.

These 'folk ghosts' are the theme of traditional supernatural stories governed by strict narrative conventions. The teller and his audience tacitly agree to suspend disbelief and pretend the tale *may* be true, the 'evidence' for its accuracy being that 'it happened to a friend of a friend' of the narrator. But it does not stand up to cross-examination. If a researcher demands names of witnesses, for example, it usually proves that, like the ghost of the story, these personages have a talent for disappearing without trace. There is nothing for the investigator to check up on, and the account is reduced to hearsay.

Few ghost stories are as well-travelled as that of the phantom hitch-hiker. The tale is told in Korea, Canada, Malaysia, Sweden, Sicily, Pakistan and South Africa; local specimens occur in most English counties. Of course, details as to age, sex and physical appearance of the hitch-hiker fluctuate, as do the number of witnesses and the type of vehicle in which he or she hitches a ride – a

car, a taxi, a motorcycle, a bus, a horsedrawn wagon or carriage and, in one Malayan version, a trishaw. In the most commonly heard form, the hitch-hiker is a young female who, before vanishing inexplicably, gives the driver an address at which he subsequently calls, learning to his horror that the girl has been dead for days, months or years. None of this corroboration took place after the event at Stanbridge, however. The entire episode lacks the artificially neat conclusion and dramatic touches generally found in folklore phantom hitch-hiker stories.

Cultural beliefs can affect how the phantom hitch-hiker is interpreted. In Britain he or she is habitually regarded as the spirit of a dead person, frequently the victim of a tragic road accident, but elsewhere the phantom hitch-hiker is viewed as a prophet, demon, goddess, witch or fairy. For instance, in Hawaii the phantom hitch-hiker is associated with Pele, a basket-carrying old woman who is tutelary goddess of the volcano Mauna Loa. Malaysia has the *langsuyar*, a vampire-like entity that takes the form of an attractive woman and waits on lonely stretches of road; after a brief time in the car, the hitcher flies into the air uttering blood-curdling cries. The basic motif of a vanishing, supernatural, hitch-hiker adapts itself to the cultural assumptions and needs of whatever society it is told in, something that helps to explain its long-standing popularity.

Prophets of doom

Nowhere is the phantom hitch-hiker story more often told than in the USA. There is hardly a state in which the tale is unknown, from the Mexican border up to Alaska or from New York out to California, where it has established itself as one of the most persistent of ghost stories. This ubiquity was confirmed by the folklorists Richard K.

Beardsley and Rosalie Hankey during compilation of two exhaustive papers entitled 'The vanishing hitch-hiker', published in the *California Folklore Quarterly* for October 1942 and January 1943. They identified four main treatments of the motif: besides the dominant address-giving girl ghost and Hawaii's Pele, there were narratives in which the phantom hitch-hiker – sometimes a nun, and almost always an old woman – delivers a prophecy, which is not infrequently of a catastrophe. The other variant is theatrical: a girl is encountered in a dance hall or bar and borrows from the driver an item of clothing that he later finds on her grave.

Later other American folklorists took up the chase, adding innumerable other phantom hitch-hikers to the original 79 featured in Beardsley and Hankey's sample. By the 1970s, there was emerging a discernible trend towards the 'prophetic' phantom hitch-hiker variant; at the same time it was apparent that widely different cultural groups in the USA were adapting the phantom hitch-hiker story as a new vehicle for their religious or cultural doctrines. Thus the ghost was identified sometimes as one of the Three Nephites of Mormon lore, sometimes as a prophet of Christ's second coming (or as Christ himself), and sometimes – according to American parapsychologist D. Scott Rogo – as a Moonie, a member of the Unification Church.

The cumulative impact of these folklore studies suggests that the phantom hitch-hiker is a creation of repeated story-telling, a piece of fiction. But Andrew Lang once pointed out that identical ghost stories occurring in widely separated locations are not necessarily the results of diffusion. Patterns, like poltergeist stone-throwings, he said, were reported in all ages and cultures, *not* because they were relocated tales but because 'events repeat themselves'. They are evidence of a phenomenon that behaves in the

Top: a stretch of road near Uniondale, South Africa, from which phantom hitch-hiker stories have been reported on four separate occasions. Corporal Dawie van Jaarsfeld (above) said that he travelled for 10 miles (16 kilometres) one day in April 1978 with a girl hitch-hiker riding pillion on his motorcycle – and then turned to find her suddenly gone

same way, at any place and at any time. No one could seriously contend that the majority of phantom hitch-hiker tales are not folk fiction – but can the small remainder be seen as a recurring pattern of this kind?

Roy Fulton claimed that his story was a real experience. Newspapers, which are supposed to report real-life events, have carried similar phantom hitch-hiker tales and, while one may be inclined to take media coverage of the paranormal with a pinch of salt, it is still worth pondering whether *all* phantom hitch-hikers are only updated folk motifs given a species of respectability in print.

Occasionally, research into the background of a well-publicised phantom hitch-hiker reveals that a core of fact may lie at the heart of what sounds an unlikely and hackneyed story. Manifestations of the Uniondale phantom hitch-hiker in South Africa have been reported on four occasions, all associated with Maria Roux, who died at the age of 23 in a car crash on 12 April 1968. Admittedly, two of these alleged sightings are of a vague, unsatisfactory kind, and the remaining two are subject to contradictions

Near the knuckle

One of the more macabre folk stories of the 20th century concerns a driver who *fails* to stop for a hitch-hiker. Usually introduced with the words 'Did I tell you what happened to my friend – well, it was his cousin actually . . .', it goes like this:

A motorist is driving down a country road when he sees a lone young man thumbing a lift. As he slows down to pick him up, he is dismayed to see two or three of the hiker's companions emerge from behind bushes or trees at the side of the road.

Perhaps feeling that his generosity is being taken advantage of, or perhaps alarmed that he is about to be set on by a gang, the driver decides not to offer them a lift after all. Now with the car almost at a stop, he doesn't like the look of the

hitch-hikers in any case.

They're standing rather close to the car, but the driver steps on the accelerator and pulls away as quickly as he can. The would-be hitch-hikers seem angry – they are shouting and yelling as he drives off.

Relieved at his narrow escape, he carries along the road for some miles. Then he sees that fuel is running low, and soon stops at a service station to fill up.

The next thing he knows is that the pump attendant, white as a sheet, is reeling back in horror from the car. The driver leaps out of the car to see what is wrong – and freezes to the spot, appalled at what he sees.

Stuck in one of the door handles are four human fingers.

Blue Bell Hill, on the road between Chatham and Maidstone in Kent – the site of yet another phantom hitch-hiker story. Here the hitch-hiker is associated with the spirit of a young girl who was killed at the foot of Blue Bell Hill on the eve of her wedding in November 1965

in the retelling. Yet, when writing up the results of her researches in the July 1979 issue of *Fate* magazine, Cynthia Hind could not rule out the possibility that phantom incidents *had* occurred more or less as stated and (perhaps more remarkable) that there was evidence to support the view that drivers had encountered the dead girl's apparition.

Analogous with the Uniondale tale is Britain's most famous phantom hitch-hiker story, set on Blue Bell Hill between Maidstone and Chatham in Kent. There is little hard evidence for a psychical researcher·to follow up; witnesses' names are absent, dates

Left: Mount St Helens erupts on 18 May 1980. After the event, motorists began to come forward with stories of an old woman to whom they had given lifts – and who had prophesied the eruption

left obscure and other important details unavailable. Yet the wealth of anecdotes from this area, only a fraction of which have appeared in print, are assigned with monotonous regularity to the spirit of a bride-to-be, who was killed in a car crash on the eve of her wedding at the foot of Blue Bell Hill back in November 1965. This accident, like the Uniondale fatality, is an historical fact, but in other phantom hitch-hiker tales the connection between the hitch-hiker and a death on the road on which the phantom appears is no more than conjectural. People are prone to think ghosts must be the products of tragedies – and, as the phantom hitch-hiker is popularly assumed to be a ghost, there is a strong temptation to hunt for likely accidents to account for it.

It is, of course, possible that the phantom hitch-hiker is not always a lie, a folk tale or a 'spirit'. In searching for alternative hypotheses, it is as well to remember that similar stories by far antedate the automobile age. Other reliable evidence tends to suggest that this antiquated motif is still important to us. In the wake of the eruption of Mount St Helens on 18 May 1980, stories began to circulate of an old woman, sometimes described as a nun, who had prophesied this and other events to Washington and Oregon motorists who gave her lifts. It is just possible that the phantom hitch-hiker story is a variation of the ancient myth of the mysterious stranger who comes to warn mankind of impending danger – a myth that also lives on in the stories of people who have allegedly made contact with aliens.

Phantom of the high seas

A ship runs into a terrible storm. But the demented captain, deaf to all entreaties, refuses to seek shelter – and, as punishment, is condemned to sail the seas for eternity. This chapter examines the legend of the Flying Dutchman, and seeks its origins

THE STORY OF THE FLYING DUTCHMAN is one of the most famous and perhaps one of the oldest legends of the sea, having been in circulation for at least 500 years and possibly having its origin well before the birth of Christ. Essentially, the story is this: a man-iacal Dutch sea captain – the term 'Flying Dutchman' actually refers to the captain, not his ship – challenges the wrath of God and as a result is condemned to sail the ocean for eternity, bringing death to all who sight his spectral ship. This tale has been elaborated upon by many writers – but it is more than a piece of fiction, a sinister tale of the sea with which to frighten credulous landlubbers in waterfront bars. The phantom ship has been seen many times – and there have even been reports in the 20th century.

Many authorities have argued that the story of the Flying Dutchman has its origin in a real event, though there is very little agreement about what that event was. The issue is further confused by the fact that there are many versions of the tale – in which the ship's skipper is variously named Van-derdecken, Van Demien, Van Straaten, or Van something else.

Perhaps the best-known version of the Flying Dutchman story tells of a Captain Vanderdecken who was making a voyage around the Cape of Good Hope when his ship was engulfed by a howling storm. The

Above: an engraving showing the first English production, in 1876, of Richard Wagner's opera *Der fliegende Holländer* ('The flying Dutchman'). The work is based on the familiar story of a Dutch sea captain who is condemned to sail the seas forever – in a ghostly ship that brings death to all who look upon her. Wagner's version allows the captain to be redeemed by the love of a faithful woman – but the opera ends with them both dying

passengers were terrified and pleaded with Vanderdecken to find a safe port, or at least shorten sail and attempt to ride out the storm, but the demented skipper laughed at their pleas and, lashing himself to the wheel, began to sing blasphemous songs.

The crew were also alarmed by the behaviour of their captain and tried to take control of the ship, but the attempted mutiny was quelled when Vanderdecken hurled the ringleader overboard, leaving the terrified passengers and crew to throw themselves on the mercy of God. In answer to their prayers, the storm clouds parted and an incandescent light bathed the forecastle revealing a glorious figure who some said was the Holy Ghost, while others claimed he was God.

The figure confronted Vanderdecken and told him that since he delighted in the torment of others he would henceforth be

Ghosts and legend

Previous page, top: the
Flying Dutchman's ship
appears to a group of
shipwrecked sailors, in this
anonymous illustration after
an original by Hermann
Hendrich.
A sighting of a
ghostly ship, identified as the
Flying Dutchman's, was
reported in 1881 by Prince
George, (later to become
George V) and his elder
brother Prince Albert Victor,
Duke of Clarence (right). On
11 June at 4 a.m., so a
record compiled from the
boys' private journals, letters
and notebooks tells, a
strange and ghostly ship, lit
by a weird red glow, crossed
their bows. Thirteen crew
members on the princes' ship
saw the spectral vessel – and
two other ships of the fleet
flashed signals to ask
whether any other vessels
had seen the strange glow

crew. Vanderdecken and the unfortunate
cabin-boy were left to their fate.

This is the time-honoured story of the
Flying Dutchman. It may have a foundation
in fact but there is little agreement about
what that fact may be. One suggestion is that
the tale is derived from the Norse saga of
Stote, a Viking who stole a ring from the gods
and was later found as a skeleton in a robe of
fire seated on the mainmast of a black spectral
ship. Other authorities believe that the story
is more recent and suggest that it dates from
the adventures of Bartholomes Diaz (c.
1450–1500), the Portuguese navigator who
discovered the Cape of Good Hope in 1488
and whose prowess as a skipper assumed a
superhuman quality in his biography by Luis
de Camois.

Playing dice with the Devil

Other researchers have unearthed a tenuous
story about two Dutch merchantmen in the
1500s whose crews sighted the wraith of a
vessel they knew to have been lost in the
Pacific, and that the Flying Dutchman story
evolved from this. Another theory is that the
tale is based on the legend of a German
named von Felkenberg who played dice with
the Devil for his soul and lost. A similar
Dutch legend tells of Captain van Straaten,
and there is also a tale told about Bernard
Fokke.

Fokke, skipper of the *Libera Nos*, was
renowned for making very fast voyages.
Those envious of his supreme navigational
skills claimed that he was in league with the
Devil, something that Fokke's extreme ugli-
ness and violent temper made all to easy to
believe. One day he embarked on a voyage
from which he did not return, and it was
whispered that the Devil had finally collected
his reward.

It is not unlikely that the legend of the
Flying Dutchman was born as the result of
an actual event – though this would doubtless have been more prosaic than the claiming by the Devil of a human soul. There are
many instances of ships being mistakenly
abandoned by their crew in the belief that
they are about to sink and subsequently
staying afloat for days, weeks, months, or
even years, following the whim of the wind
and tide. The most famous of such ships is
the legendary *Mary Celeste*, but she is by
no means the only one. Perhaps one of the
most remarkable stories concerns the wool
clipper *Marlborough*, which vanished in 1890
on a voyage between Australia and England.
It is said that she was found 23 years later off
the coast of Chile. Even if the *Marlborough*
story is an exaggeration, it is easy enough to
imagine the effect on the minds of superstitious sailors in unfamiliar waters of such a
derelict suddenly looming out of the fog.

The Flying Dutchman story has inspired
many works of fiction. The American poet
Henry Wadsworth Longfellow (1807–1882)
wrote of the spectre in *The phantom ship*,

condemned to sail the ocean for eternity,
forever in the grip of a storm, and that he
would bring doom to all who sighted him;
red-hot iron would be his only food, gall his
only drink, and his only company would be
the cabin-boy, who would grow horns from
his head, have the muzzle of a tiger and the
skin of a dogfish – all of which seems very
unfair to the poor cabin-boy, who had hitherto played no independent part in the story
and presumably had been as afraid of Vanderdecken as had the rest of the crew.
However, with these words the vision disappeared and with him all the passengers and

Above: Portuguese explorer
Bartholomes Diaz on his
voyage to discover the Cape
of Good Hope in 1487.
Some authorities have
suggested that the story of
the Flying Dutchman is
based on the character of
Diaz, whose exploits and
fame as a navigator assumed
legendary proportions

in the log of the ship HMS *Baccante*. It isn't. It comes from *The cruise of Her Majesties Ship Baccante*, a record of the princes' voyage aboard that ship compiled from their private journals, letters and notebooks by John H. Dalton. At the time of the sighting the princes were aboard another ship in the fleet, the *Inconstant*, having been transferred there when the *Baccante* developed rudder trouble. The account reads:

June 11th., 1881, – At 4 a.m. the 'Flying Dutchman' crossed our bows. A strange red light as of a phantom ship all aglow in the midst of which light the masts, spars, and sails of a brig 200-yards [180 metres] distant stood out in strong relief as she came up on our port bow. The lookout man on the forecastle reported her as close on the port bow, where also the officer of the watch from the bridge clearly saw her, as did also the quarterdeck midshipman, who was

contained in his *Birds of passage*. Edward Fitzball wrote a melodrama called *The flying Dutchman* and the Frenchman August Jal produced the most widely known version of the tale in his *Scènes de la vie maritime*. The German lyric poet Heinrich Heine (1797–1856), inspired either by Fitzball's melodrama or by an anonymous story *Vanderdecken's message home* in *Blackwood's Edinburgh Magazine*, wrote of the phantom ship in his *Memoiren des Herrn von Schabelwopski*. This in its turn was undoubtedly the inspiration for Wagner's powerful opera *Der fliegende Holländer* ('The flying Dutchman') in which Vanderdecken is allowed ashore once every seven years to find a woman whose love alone can redeem him. Others who have used the theme include Frederick Marryat (*The phantom ship*, 1839) and Sir Walter Scott (*Rokeby*, 1813).

However, the Flying Dutchman is more than mere legend or a piece of fiction. Down the centuries many people have claimed to have seen the phantom. One of the earliest accounts dates from 1702 and the *Magnalia Christi Americana*, an ecclesiastical history of New England by Cotton Mather, a voluminous writer and celebrated Puritan minister. Many of the sightings, however, are difficult if not impossible to substantiate and must therefore be dismissed, albeit reluctantly, as mirages, hallucinations, or visions conjured by over-indulgence in alcohol. One report, though, stands out as exceptional. In 1881 a sighting of the Flying Dutchman's ship was reported by George, Prince of Wales, later King George V, and his elder brother Prince Albert Victor, Duke of Clarence – the same Duke of Clarence who today features among those suspected of being the infamous Jack the Ripper.

The incident is said to have been recorded

The ancient tale of the Flying Dutchman ranks among the most famous legends of the sea. Its fascination is as strong as ever; an updated version appeared in the 1951 movie *Pandora and the Flying Dutchman* (top), with James Mason as the Dutchman and Ava Gardner as the woman he loved before he was condemned to sail the seas for eternity. And 1975 saw a BBC production of the traditional story, with Norman Bailey as the Dutchman (above)

sent forward at once to the forecastle, but on arriving there no vestige or sign whatsoever of material ship was seen either near or right away on the horizon, the night being clear, the sea calm. Thirteen persons altogether saw her, but whether it was van Demien of the 'Flying Dutchman' or what else must remain unknown.

The *Tourmaline* and *Cleopatra*, who were sailing on our starboard bow, flashed to ask whether we had seen the strange red light.

At 10.45 a.m. the ordinary seaman who had this morning reported the 'Flying Dutchman' fell from the top-galant foretopmast crosstrees and was

Ghosts and legend

Left: an illustration by Gregory Robinson for Rudyard Kipling's poem *Seven seas*: 'We saw the Dutchman plunging/Full canvas head to wind'. The story of the Flying Dutchman has inspired many other authors, including Henry Longfellow and Heinrich Heine

Below: Porthcurno Cove, Cornwall, England, the site of hauntings by a well-known phantom ship – the black, square-rigged *Goblin*. The ship heads for shore and then glides for some time over dry land before disappearing

smashed to atoms. At 4.15 p.m. after quarters we hove to with the headyards back, and he was buried at sea. He was a smart royal yardman and one of the most promising young hands in the ship, and everyone feels quite sad at his loss. At the next port we came to the Admiral was also smitten down.

Around 13 people aboard the *Inconstant* plus an unspecified number of people aboard the *Tourmaline* and *Cleopatra* saw the spectre, though whether it was the Flying Dutchman's ship or another spectre must in the princes' words 'remain unknown'. But true to the legend, death followed the sighting.

Nazis face the spectre

One of the most unexpected sources of a report of the Flying Dutchman's ship is that said to have been made by Karl Dönitz, commander-in-chief of the German navy and, briefly, successor to Adolf Hitler. He is said to have seen the spectral ship while on a tour of duty east of Suez and to have claimed later that his men would rather face the combined might of the Allied fleet than know again the terror of seeing the Flying Dutchman's ship.

The Flying Dutchman's ship is far from the only spectre of the sea. In 1949 it was estimated that there were more than 100 'well-established' cases of vessels haunting the north-east coast of the United States alone.

America's most famous ghost ship is probably the *Palatine*, the subject of a famous poem by John Greenleaf Whittier. According to the legend, in 1752 a storm swept the *Palatine* aground on the rocks of Block Island, Rhode Island, and the wreck was set alight by fishermen; one passenger, a woman, was trapped and burned alive. Since then the spectre of the flaming ship has been seen countless times.

It is difficult to dismiss the evidence that

something – the Palatine light, as it is called – has regularly been seen offshore. Further investigation, however, reveals that no such ship was ever wrecked over Block Island. However, detailed research has shown that 14 years earlier, in 1738, the *Princess Augusta*, carrying 350 refugees from the Lower and Upper Palatinate in Germany, *did* meet its end upon the northern shores of Block Island in circumstances similar to those associated with the *Palatine*, and there can be little doubt that this was the basis of the legend. Only one element of the fate of the *Princess Augusta* differs from the legend of the *Palatine* – *Princess Augusta* merely sank, she was not set alight. So, if the spectre seen so often off Block Island is the spectre of *Princess Augusta*, why is the ghost ship seen ablaze?

Another fairly well-known ghost ship is the black, square-rigged *Goblin* reputedly seen many times by residents of Porthcurno Cove near St Leven, Cornwall, England. This spectre is distinguished by the fact that it is seen to head for shore, then glide for some distance over dry land before vanishing!

What, then, are these ghost ships, these spectres of the sea? They are open to much the same question, speculations and theories as may be applied to ghosts in general. But the Flying Dutchman is different from many ghost and folk tales – sightings have been reported many, many times. If the ship does not exist, what exactly did the princes aboard the *Inconstant* see? Since death or disaster is heralded by a sighting of the Flying Dutchman's ship, perhaps it would be wise not to seek too hard for the answer!

Out of the Celtic twilight

The wailing of the banshee to announce death is a well-known part of Irish folklore. But recent cases have shown that this sad mourner is very much alive – and not only in Ireland

ONE NIGHT EARLY in 1979 Irene McCormack of Andover, Hampshire, England, was lying in bed when she heard what she later described as 'the most awful wailing noise'. She was alone in the house at the time and was in a melancholy mood, for her mother was close to death in Winchester Hospital.

When she heard the wailing she nearly fell out of bed. 'I got up, shaking, and went downstairs; the dog was running round and round the living room, whimpering.' He would not settle, so Mrs McCormack took

Above: 'I saw the banshee flying wild in the wind of March' – this romantic interpretation of the banshee, an illustration by Florence Harrison, dates from 1910

him upstairs to the bedroom where, after the wailing had died away, they both lay waiting for daybreak.

With the dawn came a police message for Mrs McCormack: she was to go to the bedside of her mother. When she arrived at the hospital she found her mother in a coma; she stayed with her until her mother died a short time later. When the funeral was over and the household had returned to normal, Mrs McCormack told her husband and children what she had heard. Although she is not Irish, her husband is: he suggested that she had heard the banshee.

'Many of my family laughed at this,' said Mrs McCormack when discussing the incident at a later date. 'They probably thought I was going mad . . . but I hope never to hear anything like that again.'

Pronounced as it is spelt, the word banshee is derived from the Irish Gaelic *bean sidhe*, meaning 'woman of the fairies'. Her mournful cry is said to foretell death. According to tradition she has long red hair and combs it, mermaid-like, as she keens outside the family home of those about to die. She is rarely heard or seen by the doomed person.

The banshee has her origins deep in Irish legend. She wailed for ancient heroes such as King Connor McNessa, Finn McCool, and the great Brian Boru, whose victory over the Vikings in 1014 broke their power in Ireland. More recently, residents of the Cork village of Sam's Cross claimed to have heard the eerie voice of the banshee when Michael Collins, commander-in-chief of the Irish Free State Army, was killed in an ambush in 1922 during the Irish Civil War.

In the late 1960s the Irish psychical researcher Sheila St Clair produced a radio programme for the BBC on the banshee and, even allowing for Irish exaggeration, some of the accounts were chillingly convincing. A baker from Kerry told of an uncomfortable night that he and his colleagues had spent while baking bread ready for the morning delivery.

'It started low at first like, then it mounted up into a crescendo; there was definitely some human element in the voice . . . the door to the bakery where I worked was open too, and the men stopped to listen. Well, it rose as I told you to a crescendo, and you could almost make out one or two Gaelic words in it; then gradually it went away slowly. Well, we talked about it for a few minutes and at last, coming on to morning, about five o'clock, one of the bread servers came in and he says to me, "I'm afraid they'll need you to take out the cart, for I just got word of the death of an aunt of mine." It was at his cart that the banshee had keened.'

On the same programme an elderly man from County Down tried to describe the death cry in more detail. 'It was a mournful sound,' he said. 'It would have put ye in mind of them ould yard cats on the wall, but it wasn't cats, I know it meself; I thought it was a bird in torment or something . . . a mournful cry it was, and then it was going a wee bit further back, and further until it died away altogether.'

Although *bean sidhe* means literally 'fairy woman' most folklorists classify the banshee as a spirit rather than a 'fairy' in the sense of one of the Irish 'little people'. According to mythology, the banshee cries at the deaths of fairy kings, too. Some of the older Irish families – the O'Briens and the O'Neils, for example – traditionally regarded the banshee almost as a personal guardian angel, silently watching over the fortunes of the family, guiding its members away from danger, and then performing the final service of 'keening' for their departing souls.

Guardian spirits

A County Antrim man told Sheila St Clair his interpretation of the banshee's role: an interpretation, incidentally, that may account for the rarity of the noisy spirit nowadays. He claimed that, centuries ago, certain of the more pious clans had been blessed with guardian spirits. Because these celestial beings were not normally able to express themselves in human terms yet became involved with the family in their charge, they were allowed to show their deep feelings only when one of their charges died: the result was the banshee howl. However, said the Antrim man, with the gradual fall from grace of the Irish over the years, only the most God-fearing families were privileged to have a personal banshee today.

This theory may please a businessman from Boston, USA, who wrote to the journalist Frank Smyth some years ago claiming that

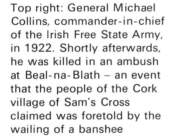

Top right: General Michael Collins, commander-in-chief of the Irish Free State Army, in 1922. Shortly afterwards, he was killed in an ambush at Beal-na-Blath – an event that the people of the Cork village of Sam's Cross claimed was foretold by the wailing of a banshee

Below, far right: a banshee – 'Awful Death warning by the appearance of an Apparition' – in a 19th-century illustration

Below: the funeral of John F. Kennedy. A US businessman and close friend of Kennedy heard the cry of the banshee at the time of the President's assassination

the banshee, like other creatures of European folklore, had crossed the Atlantic. This man, who used the pseudonym James O'Barry, is descended from an Irish family that originally arrived in Massachusetts in 1848. It was as a very small boy that he first heard the banshee.

I was lying in bed one morning when I heard a weird noise, like a demented woman crying. It was spring, and outside the window the birds were singing, the sun was shining, and the sky was blue. I thought for a moment or two that a wind had sprung up, but a glance at the barely stirring trees told me that this was not so. I went down to breakfast and there was my father sitting at the kitchen table with tears in his eyes. I had never seen him weep before. My mother told me that they had just heard, by telephone, that my grandfather had died in New York. Although he was an old man he was as fit as a fiddle, and his death was unexpected.

It was some years before O'Barry learned the legend of the banshee, and then he recalled the wailing noise on the death of his grandfather. In 1946 he heard it, in very different circumstances, for the second time. He was an administrative officer serving with the USAAF in the Far East when one day at 6 a.m. he was awakened by a low howl. He was terrified; but, he says,

That time I was instantly aware of what it was. I sat bolt upright in bed, and the hair on the back of my neck prickled. The noise got louder, rising and falling like an air raid siren. Then it died away, and I realised that I was terribly depressed. I knew my father was dead. A

few days later I had notification that this was so.

O'Barry was to hear the voice again 17 years later, on what he considers the most remarkable occasion of all. He was in Toronto, Canada, by himself, enjoying a combined holiday and business trip.

Again I was in bed, reading the morning papers, when the dreadful noise was suddenly filling my ears. I thought of my wife, my young son, my two brothers, and I thought: 'Good God, don't let it be one of them.' But for some reason I knew it wasn't.

The date was 22 November 1963, the time shortly after noon, and the Irish banshee was bewailing the death of an acquaintance of O'Barry's – President John F. Kennedy.

If the Irish have their banshee, one could reasonably expect their close Celtic cousins, the Scots, to have a version of their own. It is not so, however, although most clans at some time or another have boasted a personal harbinger of death. The nearest thing to the banshee recorded in Scottish folklore is the 'death woman' who sits on westward-running streams on the west coast of Scotland, washing the clothes of those about to die, and the Highland 'red fisherman', a robed and hooded apparition who sits angling for fish. To see him is itself the warning of death.

The Ewans of the Isle of Mull, Argyllshire, preserve a curious legend concerning their own death spirit. In the 16th century Eoghan a' Chin Bhig (Ewan of the Little Head) had a serious quarrel with his father-in-law, The MacLaine. In 1538 both sides collected for a showdown. The evening

The death spirit of the Ewans of the Isle of Mull is a member of the family. In the 16th century the chieftain Eoghan (Ewan) a' Chin Bhig was given the island castle of Loch Scuabain (above) as a wedding gift by his father, The Maclaine of Moy Castle (right). But Ewan, dissatisfied, asked his father for a better castle. A feud resulted, and Ewan was slain in battle. Ever since, the figure of Ewan, a headless horseman, has presaged death in the family

THE BANSHEE.

Awful Death warning by the appearance of an Apparition.

before the battle, Ewan was walking when he met an old woman washing a bundle of blood-stained shirts in a stream. Ewan knew that she was a death woman and that the shirts belonged to those who would die in the morning. Rather boldly he asked if his own shirt was among them, and she said that it was. She told him that if his wife offered him bread and cheese with her own hand he would live and be victorious.

His wife failed to do so. Ewan, demoralised, rode to defeat and at the height of the battle a swinging Lochaber axe cut his head clean from his shoulders. His horse galloped off down Glen More, the headless rider still upright in the saddle. According to the present Ewan of Lochbuie, the dead chief became his own clan's death warning, and his headless body on its galloping horse has been seen three times within living memory before a family death. The vision is also said to herald serious illness in the family.

Another celebrated Scottish death warning involves the phantom drummer of Cortachy Castle, Tayside, seat of the Earls of Airlie. One story says that he was a Leslie, come to intercede for a truce with his clan's enemies the Ogilvies – the family name of

Airlie – and that he was killed before he could deliver his message. A more romantic version is that he was a drummer with a Highland regiment and lover of a 15th-century Lady Airlie. He was caught by the Earl and thrown from a turret window.

Four well-attested accounts from the 19th century indicate that the phantom carried out its warning task efficiently. In the 1840s, the drummer was heard by members of the household before the death of the Countess of Airlie. The Earl married again shortly afterwards, and in 1848 had a house party, the guests including a Miss Margaret Dalrymple. During dinner on her first night, Miss Dalrymple remarked on the curious music she had heard coming from below her window as she dressed – the sound of a fife, followed by drumming. Both her host and hostess paled. After dinner one of the other guests explained the legend.

Ghostly drumming

The following morning Miss Dalrymple's maid, Ann Day, was alone in the bedroom attending to her mistress's clothes. She had heard nothing of the drummer story, so was surprised when she heard a coach draw up in the yard below, accompanied by the sound of drumming. When she realised that the yard was empty though the drumming carried on, she became hysterical. The following day her mistress heard the sound again, and decided she had had enough. Shortly afterwards, Lady Airlie died in Brighton, leaving a note stating that she was sure her own death had been signalled by the drumming.

In 1853 several people heard and reported the drummer again, just before the death of the Earl, and in 1881 two relatives told of hearing the prophetic sound while staying at Cortachy during Lord Airlie's absence in America. Some days later, news of his death reached them.

In the case of both the banshee and the Scottish clans' death warnings there are

Well-authenticated accounts testify to the appearance of the phantom drummer of Cortachy Castle, Tayside (above), whenever one of the Ogilvy family is about to die. Two relatives heard the ghostly drumming before the death of David Ogilvy, 10th Earl of Airlie (above left), in 1881

dozens of instances of people having heard or seen these harbingers of disaster. Laying aside the unlikely possibility that all of them are either lying or exaggerating, can we explain such irrational events in any rational way? Some psychologists, including Carl Jung, have evolved theories of what they term 'collective unconsciousness', a sort of inherited storehouse of memories of mankind's experiences, passed on through an atavistic process from psyche to psyche.

In the case of the banshee, Sheila St Clair says: 'I would suggest that just as we inherit physical characteristics . . . we also inherit memory cells, and that those of us with strong tribal lineages riddled with intermarriage have the banshee as part of an inherited memory. The symbolic form of a weeping woman may well be stamped on our racial consciousness. . . . And just as our other levels of consciousness are not answerable to the limitations of time in our conscious mind, so a particular part of the mind throws up a symbolic hereditary pattern that has in the past been associated with tragedy in the tribe – be it woman, hare, or bird – as a kind of subliminal "four minute warning" so that we may prepare ourselves for that tragedy.'

Haunted England

finished the time was 11.30 p.m. Having put the judgement in an envelope he left it with his butler. This was his regular practice and part of his arrangement with the local newspaper editor and reporters, who all knew that they were welcome to call at the house and make an advance copy of any report they wanted to set up in print.

Just before midnight, the judge retired to bed and within a short while fell asleep. He was soon roused though, by the sound of someone knocking on the door along the corridor – the door leading to the study – but in his fuddled state he assumed it was the butler and took no notice. Then there came a

No judge of the truth

Witnesses of paranormal events are notoriously unreliable, so the SPR was delighted to receive details of a ghost who had visited no less a person than Judge Hornby – surely an impeccable witness. But the case proved to be highly suspect

IN FEBRUARY 1884, the Society for Psychical Research (SPR) received a most remarkable letter from a retired judge. The judge was Sir Edmund Hornby, formerly with the Consular Court at Shanghai. His letter described his encounter and dealings with a very solid-looking phantom. What is more, his account was backed up by the testimony of his wife and mother-in-law.

The judge's story was set in Shanghai some nine years earlier. On the day in question, he had spent a whole evening writing out details of a judgement he was due to give the next morning. He had taken longer than usual for this was quite an important Admiralty case and when he had

tap on the bedroom door. This time he was sure it must be the butler, so he called out 'Come in!'; but when the door opened, in walked the chief journalist and editor of the local newspaper.

The journalist was well-known to the judge and quite unmistakable, since his head seemed to lie sideways on one shoulder, giving him the appearance of being deformed. The judge was not startled by his presence as he simply assumed that the man had come looking for the judgement paper, and he said, 'You've mistaken the room – but the butler has the judgement, so go and get it.' The reporter made no attempt to leave; he just stood where he was, looking sad and deadly pale, then he asked to be told details of the judgement – then and there.

At this, the judge grew angry and ordered him from the room. In fact, he felt like leaping out of bed and throwing him out but there was something so tragic about the man's demeanour that Judge Hornby resisted the impulse, got out of bed and grudgingly dictated a brief summary. He concluded the interview by saying, 'This is the

Above: Abbey Crescent, Torquay, where Judge and Lady Hornby lived in 1884, when the judge – then retired from the Consular Court in Shanghai (left) – first wrote to the SPR about his alleged encounter, and conversation, with a ghost some years before. The SPR was delighted with such an apparently watertight case, but as the file (below) grew, so did doubts about Hornby's story. For example, although his wife backed up his story, their marriage certificate shows they were not married until after the ghostly meeting was alleged to have taken place

last time I will allow a reporter in my house.' The journalist looked at him wistfully and replied, 'This is the *last* time I shall ever see you again – anywhere.' Then he left. With that the judge went back to bed noticing that the time was exactly 1.30 a.m.

Sir Edmund's wife was a heavy sleeper, but she had been vaguely aware of something going on, and on his return to bed she woke up fully and asked what the fuss was all about. He told her what had happened, then they both went to sleep without any further discussion. But the next morning found the judge pondering the events of the previous night. Going over the details again with his wife, he explained: 'The poor fellow looked awfully ill.' Despite this Sir Edmund made it clear that the journalist was due for a reprimand when he saw him next.

When Judge Hornby reached his courtroom and looked for the journalist he could not find him anywhere; at 10 a.m. he discovered why, for the court usher came in to say that the reporter had died some eight and a half hours earlier.

Apparently, he had been writing articles in his room until late at night and at midnight had only one more item to finish and that was the report of the judge's Admiralty case. But he was never to complete the copy for the next day's edition, for at 1.30 a.m. his wife found him dead at his desk.

'In the flesh or the spirit'

As soon as he heard this grim news, Sir Edmund wrote a note to Lady Hornby saying: 'I shall be home at one . . . poor Lang died last night and I am certain that he visited me in the flesh or in the spirit last night, as I told you.' Next, Sir Edmund sent a magistrate to question the journalist's wife and servants, for he needed to know if the man could have possibly left his rooms. But the answers he received showed that the journalist was too ill to have journeyed out. He had been suffering from pains in his chest throughout the course of the evening, before his heart finally gave up beating at 1.30 a.m. – just as the usher had said. The post-mortem report confirmed this.

The judge's story first appeared in print in the *Journal* of the SPR; thus, at first, it was known only to a very small circle. But the SPR's secretary was so excited and delighted with the case that he arranged for it to be published in the *Nineteenth Century* magazine. His excitement was understandable since the story seemed to be unshakeable evidence for the paranormal. Indeed, Edmund Gurney of the SPR had diligently checked out the account with Lady Hornby and her mother and found them 'model witnesses'.

If the story had never appeared in magazine form it probably would have gone unchallenged and been repeated over and over again as an impregnable true event. But as it was, a copy of the magazine reached

Shanghai where it was read by a certain Frederick Balfour – his reaction was one of amusement and amazement. Balfour was a newspaper editor who had known Sir Edmund well. He had also known the dead newspaperman – Hugh Lang – and he promptly wrote to the *Nineteenth Century* challenging the story. It was only then that the truth emerged. It turned out that Hugh Lang had not died at home at 1.30 a.m., but at his office, at 9 a.m. – following a good night's sleep. And there was no inquest, since it was not needed. Apart from that, the death occurred on 19 January 1875, and on that date there was no Lady Hornby! At that time, Sir Edmund was a widower – in fact, he did not re-marry until three months *after* Hugh Lang's death.

Wife, what wife?

Once Balfour's letter appeared, obituaries were checked and Sir Edmund's whole story fell to pieces. He sadly agreed that on the day of Lang's death he was not married – he even added that, at the time, he knew his future wife just well enough 'to bow to and exchange civilities'. So those three vital discussions with Lady Hornby just could not have taken place; thus the evidence to back up the tale simply vanished.

Edmund Gurney himself could offer no explanation – he simply repeated Sir Edmund's words that 'his memory must have played him the most extraordinary trick.' And Gurney blamed himself for failing to check the Shanghai newspapers before accepting the tale as true. The case itself was deleted from the records of the SPR.

Strangely enough, however, in 1969 an attempt was made to argue that 'the story was stopped, not because it was proved untrue, but because it was socially embarrassing.' According to this line of reasoning, the judge had been living with his future wife prior to the date of their marriage – when the story unfortunately revealed this 'shameful liaison', he was obliged to protect the honour of his wife by accepting that the account of the phantom journalist was absurd.

This attempted defence is ingenious but quite unacceptable, since Judge Hornby's account does not stand or fall on the testimonies of his wife and mother-in-law alone. He claimed that the time and place of Lang's death had been confirmed by the court usher, a magistrate, Lang's family and a coroner's inquest – yet all of those claims were found to be false. Perhaps the last words in this puzzling case can be fittingly left to the judge himself, for he wrote:

If ever there was an unconscious or
unintentional liar I am the man. Please
see that on my tombstone is graven
Here lies a liar
Unconscious of truth
Should he become a briar
Its tangled twigs
Will typify his mind.

The ghost and the gossips

The couple who took up lodgings at the home of Richard Parsons seemed ordinary enough. But with their arrival came a series of events that left Parsons fearing for his sanity – and his life

THE 18TH CENTURY, dubbed by the Victorians 'The Age of Reason', was in fact extravagantly credulous. In spite of – or perhaps because of – the influence of rationalists such as Rousseau and Voltaire, the great ruck of citizens, from high courtiers to low commoners, were obsessed with the supernatural, the unnatural and the downright bizarre.

Sir Isaac Newton, discoverer of gravity, President of the Royal Society and Master of the Royal Mint, spent the last quarter of a century before his death in 1727 in the study of alchemy. Ben Franklin, the writer John Wilkes and the satirical poet Charles Churchill donned monks' robes and cavorted at Sir Francis Dashwood's Hell Fire Club on the Thames, acting only half in jest. Nathanael St André, George I's resident anatomist, ruined his reputation by backing the claim of a woman named Mary Tofts, who swore that she had given birth to a litter of rabbits. And an oak tree in an inn yard near Winchester that groaned out prophecies attracted queues of stately carriages until a speaking tube was discovered leading from its trunk to the landlord's quarters.

More seriously, an 18-year-old servant girl named Elizabeth Canning disappeared for a month in 1753 and then reappeared to

In the 18th century, it seems there were no limits to the extent of human credulity. For example, the claim made by Mary Tofts that she had given birth to a litter of rabbits (below) was apparently readily accepted by at least one eminent physician. And, in 1749, crowds of the curious crammed a London theatre to witness for themselves the amazing powers of the mysterious 'bottle conjurer', who – it was promised – would disappear into a wine bottle on stage and sing from inside it. He would also 'play' a common walking stick, reproducing the sound of any instrument then in use, and for an extra gratuity would raise the spirit of any historical character. The 'bottle conjurer' did indeed disappear, but before the performance – and along with the considerable box office takings

claim that she had been held captive in a brothel at Enfield, about 10 miles (15 kilometres) from her home in the City of London. She named her captive as Mother Wells, the 'madam', and her gypsy servant Mary Squires. They had, said Elizabeth, left her in a darkened room with only a loaf of dry bread and a jug of water for sustenance. Nevertheless 'angelic' intervention had kept her alive and fit enough to break out, at the end of the month, and walk home.

Despite the oddity of the story, the great Bow Street magistrate and novelist Henry Fielding believed it and sent Wells and Squires for trial at the Old Bailey. Wells was condemned to death, and Squires to branding and six months' hard labour. Fortunately, the Lord Major of London, Sir Crisp Gascoyne, had sufficient sense of the ridiculous to check the story further; he discovered incontrovertible evidence that the two accused had not been near Enfield at the time,

and they were released and pardoned – though not before pretty Mary Squires had been scarred with the branding iron.

The Canning affair had much in common with one of the greatest talking points of the century, the business of 'Scratching Fanny' – the ghost of Cock Lane. In both cases the credulous clamour of the mob put lives and reputations at stake on the flimsiest of evidence while eminent men looked on. Both cases promoted songs, poems, theatrical burlesques and controversy. But the hindsight of over two centuries and the light of modern psychical research suggest that something paranormal could have happened at Cock Lane, and that 18th-century mass hysteria may for once have clouded a real and striking case of poltergeist activity in the classic mould.

Cock Lane is a short, curving thoroughfare in the City of London on the fringes of Smithfield. In the mid 18th century it was a slightly run down, though respectable, area containing private houses, a tavern called the Wheat Sheaf, tradesmen's shops and a charity school. At what is now No 20 lived Richard Parsons, who drew a stipend as officiating clerk at the nearby church of St Sepulchre, Snow Hill, and had a wife and two young daughters, the eldest, Elizabeth, being about 11 years old when the Cock Lane mystery began.

Top: the modern Cock Lane, in the City of London. Situated on the outskirts of Smithfield (above), the street became the subject of gossip and scandal in the mid 18th century, for one of the houses was said to be haunted – by the ghost of a woman who seemed to be seeking revenge for her own untimely death

Today, Parsons would probably be considered a scandal to the church, for he was a heavy drinker with a tendency to run into debt, particularly with his accommodating friend James Franzen, landlord of the Wheat Sheaf. In 1759, however, his drinking habits were no better and no worse than those of many another minor cleric, and he kept himself solvent by taking in lodgers.

In October of that year, Parsons met a genteel looking couple who introduced themselves as Mr and Mrs William Kent, newly up from Norfolk and looking for lodgings until their house in Clerkenwell was ready for them. Parsons was happy to take them in, particularly because William Kent, after paying his rent in advance, lent Parsons 12 guineas, to be paid back at a guinea a month.

Soon landlord and lodger were on sufficiently friendly terms for William to let Parsons in on his secret: he and his 'wife' Frances, known as Fanny, were not married. Two years previously, William had kept an inn and a post office at the village of Stoke Ferry, Norfolk, and had married Elizabeth Lynes, the daughter of a well-to-do grocer. Unfortunately, Elizabeth was not strong and had a difficult pregnancy, during which her sister Fanny moved in with the Kents to look after her. Elizabeth died in childbirth, and her offspring died a month later. After going through this double tragedy together, William and Fanny had grown very close, but the law at the time forbade marriage between bereaved brothers- and sisters-in-law, so the pair had decided to live in sin. Coming up to London in the summer of 1759 they decided to prove their mutual love and trust by making wills in each other's favour. Fanny had the advantage here, for though, according to later testimony, she had 'a bare hundred pounds', William had 'a considerable fortune'. Apart from half a crown to each of her two brothers and four surviving sisters, Fanny left everything 'she had or might expect' to William 'at his absolute disposal'.

A disturbed relationship

The first intimation that something was odd about the house in Cock Lane came that autumn. Kent was out of town on business, and Fanny's maid, Esther Carlisle, a redhead nicknamed 'Carrots', had been given leave. Fanny was nervous about sleeping alone and asked Richard Parsons's elder daughter Elizabeth to share her four poster bed. During the few nights the pair slept together, both were awakened by a rapping noise, seemingly coming from the wainscot of the bedroom. Elizabeth asked her mother about the noise, and was told that it was probably made by the shoemaker next door, who was in the habit of working late. When the noise began on a Sunday night, however, the family became seriously alarmed, for the cobbler was absent; Parsons, the two women and Elizabeth all heard it.

The noise 'like knuckles rapping' went on night after night, and as the comfort of the household was disturbed, so was the relationship between William Kent and Richard Parsons. Parsons had failed to keep his agreement to repay a guinea a month to his lodger, and Kent, who by now was ready to move into his own house in Clerkenwell, put the matter into the hands of his attorney. The drunken Parsons rather spitefully reacted by broadcasting the news about the Kents' marital status, or lack of it, to all and sundry.

In January the Kents moved to Clerkenwell, but the pleasure of setting up home together was marred by the fact that Fanny,

Sheaf and had no sooner lifted the glass when he heard a thunderous knocking on his front door. When he had steeled himself to open it he found Parsons, white-faced and stammering on the doorstep.

'Give me the largest glass of brandy that you have,' demanded the cleric. 'Oh Franzen! As I was going into my house just now I saw the ghost.'

'And so did I!' replied the landlord. 'And have been greatly frightened ever since. Bless me! What can be the meaning of it? It is very unaccountable.'

Meanwhile there was alarm of a different kind in Clerkenwell, for Fanny Kent was dying. An acquaintance of William's, the Reverend Stephen Aldrich of St John's, Clerkenwell, and the doctor and apothecary sat with her night and day. In the last 50 hours of her life she could take nothing but a little liquid, prepared by the apothecary and administered by the doctor. On the evening of 2 February 1760, Fanny died.

William Kent was distraught with grief and ordered a decent coffin 'both lined and covered' but for fear of prosecution he asked the undertaker not to put a name plate on the lid; the risk was minimal, but nevertheless it was an offence to live together falsely as man and wife. Fanny was laid to rest in the 12th-century vaults of St John's, as her family fumed over the provisions in her will.

The rappings at Cock Lane continued;

six months pregnant, had become seriously ill. William hired a doctor and an apothecary to attend to her, and the doctor diagnosed 'a confluent smallpox of a very virulent nature'.

To the sanctimonious Parsons, Fanny's illness had been sent to 'punish her for her sins'. The knocking on his wainscot had not abated, and he was beginning to form a theory about that too: it was made by the ghost of Fanny's dead sister Elizabeth. His suspicions seemed confirmed when both he and James Franzen had a frightening experience towards the end of January.

Franzen had called at the house to see Parsons and, finding him out, had sat for a while with Mrs Parsons and her two daughters. The persistent knocking frightened him, however, and he got up to leave. As he reached the kitchen door 'he saw pass by him something in white, seemingly in a sheet, which shot by him and up stairs.' The vision gave off a radiance strong enough to illuminate the face of the clock in the charity school across the street.

Franzen, thoroughly alarmed, ran back to fortify himself with brandy at the Wheat

The house in Cock Lane, home of the Parsons family, where every night strange rappings could be heard, apparently coming from the wooden panelling in one of the rooms. Despite investigation, no natural explanation of the sounds could be found – and Richard Parsons, the head of the household, began to fear that some supernatural agency was at work

indeed, two new lodgers there, Catherine Friend and Joyce Weatheral, later testified that they had left the house rather than suffer them further. Frustrated and frightened, Parsons called in a carpenter, Bateman Griffiths, to strip away the wainscot to seek the cause of the trouble; nothing was found and the panelling was replaced. Then Parsons called in the Reverend John Moore, rector of St Bartholomew the Great, West Smithfield, to investigate the supernatural possibilities.

Poltergeist on trial

When investigators were called in to examine the 'ghost' of Cock Lane, they devised a test to establish once and for all who or what lay behind it.

Shops and taverns in the Cock Lane area did a roaring trade as a result of the activity at Richard Parsons's home, which daily drew crowds of sightseers to the street. Only the Parsons family, it seems, failed to profit from the phenomena

RICHARD PARSONS was becoming seriously alarmed by the mysterious noises at his home in Cock Lane. The strange rappings had continued for several months and no natural explanation could be found for them. Then, almost at his wits' end, Parsons asked the Reverend John Moore to investigate, to see if some paranormal agency were the cause.

Moore was a follower of John Wesley, who was himself no stranger to the supernatural. In 1715 Wesley's family home had been troubled by a 'knocking spirit', and his father, the Reverend Samuel Wesley, had 'communicated' with it by knocking back. Moore, told of Parsons's theories as to the origin of the phenomena – he now believed that the ghost of the newly dead Fanny Kent was responsible – began holding seances, using one knock for yes, and two for no, in order to find out the 'spirit's' wishes. The Wesley ghost had centred itself upon Hetty Wesley, John's younger sister, and the Cock Lane ghost now orientated itself upon the person of 11-year-old Elizabeth Parsons.

Moore's most productive sessions were held in Elizabeth's bedroom, after the girl had been put to bed. Sometimes the knocks came from the floorboards, sometimes from the bedstead or the walls. On the rare occasions when the 'spirit' appeared to be pleased, it made a noise like the fluttering of wings; when displeased it made a noise like 'a cat's claws scratching over a cane chair' – and it became known as 'Scratching Fanny'.

A demand for justice

Its message was brutally blunt. It was the ghost of Fanny Kent, murdered by William, who had poisoned her purl – a concoction of bitter herbs in ale popularly used as a restorative – about two hours before she died. Fanny wanted justice.

William Kent, slowly recovering from his bereavement, had set himself up as a stockbroker and busied himself in the City, and it was not until almost a year after Fanny's death, in January 1761, that he heard of the continuing saga of Cock Lane through a series of articles in the *Public Ledger* news sheet. Terrified by the 'ghost's' accusations – which were now, of course, public knowledge – he called on the Reverend Moore. Moore was impressed by Kent's manner and bearing, but assured him that 'there were very strange noises of knockings and scratchings every night, and that there was something behind darker than all the rest.'

As a result of their meeting, Kent went to Cock Lane to sit in on a seance himself. To his horror the knocks accused him personally of having killed Fanny with arsenic, and when he asked, at Moore's instigation, whether he would be hanged, the answer was a single knock.

'Thou art a lying spirit,' he shouted. 'Thou art not the ghost of my Fanny. She would never have said any such thing.'

By this time the ghost of 'Scratching

Fanny' had become a matter of enormous public interest, and crowds on foot and in carriages flocked to watch the comings and goings at the house. Horace Walpole wrote: 'Provisions are sent in like forage, and all the taverns and ale houses in the neighbourhood make fortunes.' To the credit of the Parsons family, however, none of them seems to have made any money from the phenomena.

As the year went on, so the seances continued. On one occasion, one of the sitters, William Legge, Earl of Dartmouth and himself a Methodist, decided to have Elizabeth Parsons moved to the house of a gentleman named Bray, just to see what would happen. The knockings accompanied her, seeming to show that she, and not the actual Cock Lane premises, was the catalyst. But the girl was watched closely, women attendants holding her hands and feet to rule out fraud, and still the noises went on.

The proceedings had taken on the atmosphere of a kangaroo court, with the doctor and apothecary who had attended Fanny Kent in her last illness denying that Kent could have poisoned her – she had drunk only their preparation in the 50 hours before her death – and the knocking contradicting them. The maid servant 'Carrots' Carlisle was implicated also, and indignantly shouted at the 'spirit': 'Then I am sure, Madam, you may be ashamed of yourself, for I never hurt you in my life.'

Elizabeth Parsons herself had begun to have epileptic fits. She claimed to have actually seen the ghost, 'in a shroud and without hands', but claimed that the only aspect of the matter that frightened her was 'what would become of her Daddy . . . if their matter should be supposed to be an imposture.'

William Kent was naturally anxious to clear up the matter; Moore, convinced that the ghost was telling the truth, was also eager for the authorities to act, but the only person in the City of London with the power to order a full investigation was the Lord Mayor, Sir Samuel Fludyer. He 'did not

Above: Dr Samuel Johnson (left) with Oliver Goldsmith (centre). Johnson was one of the 'Committee of Gentlemen' formed by the vicar of St John's, Clerkenwell, and William Legge, Earl of Dartmouth (below), to investigate the Cock Lane affair and William Kent's role in it. The committee's findings – that no supernatural agency was involved – led to the publication of a pamphlet, generally believed to be the work of Oliver Goldsmith, which argued forcefully that Kent was innocent of all charges against him

choose to stir much, for it was somewhat like Canning's affair', which had caused a great deal of trouble for his predecessor, and he refused to order the arrest of either Kent – for suspected murder – or Parsons – for fraud. Instead, he insisted that an independent investigation should be held at the house of the Reverend Stephen Aldrich, vicar of St John's, Clerkenwell.

Aldrich, to make sure that the investigation would be impartial, formed a committee with Lord Dartmouth. They chose Dr John Douglas, an amateur investigator who had exposed a number of frauds, Mrs Oakes, a hospital matron, Dr George Macaulay, a society physician, two or three gentlemen and Dr Samuel Johnson.

Johnson had long been fascinated by ghosts. The idea of total oblivion after death horrified him. He summed up his attitude to his biographer James Boswell: '. . . still it is undecided whether or not there has ever been an instance of the spirit of any person appearing after death. All argument is against it; but all belief is for it.'

But he undertook to assist in the investigation of 'Scratching Fanny' for a typically humanitarian reason. If the affair was a fraud, it was seriously damaging the reputation of William Kent, who seemed an honest and decent man.

The 'Committee of Gentlemen', as the newspapers termed it, decided on a new course of action. They arranged to test Elizabeth Parsons at Aldrich's house, and then, leaving her behind, they would descend to the vault of St John's, where the ghost would knock on Fanny Kent's coffin to 'prove' its objective existence. A preliminary seance was held, and the ghost agreed to these conditions.

The test begins

On the evening of 1 February 1762, Elizabeth was put to bed at Aldrich's house, attended by the matron, Mrs Oakes, and other women. According to Dr Johnson's report, the child said that she could feel the spirit 'like a mouse upon her back [but] no evidence of any preternatural power was exhibited'.

The committee then made its way to St John's, entered the vault, and called upon the spirit to keep its promise by knocking on the coffin. 'But nothing more than silence ensued. . . . It is therefore the opinion of the whole assembly that the child has some art of making or counterfeiting particular noises, and that there is no agency of a higher cause.'

One or two more seances followed, but the affair was nearing its end. On 3 February, a large gathering saw a curtain rod spin violently of its own volition, and heard a knocking of such violence, high up in the chimney, 'that they thought it would have broke it all to pieces'. Finally, Elizabeth was told that she had only one more night, 21 February, to prove her innocence, 'otherwise she and her

Above: St John's Church, Clerkenwell, where Fanny Kent was laid to rest in 1760. Although the investigating committee had, by implication, exonerated William Kent from the charge of Fanny's murder, the case was not closed. When the coffin was opened 90 years later, the corpse was found to be perfectly preserved – which, to modern forensic scientists, would suggest death by arsenic poisoning. So, was Fanny Kent murdered? And, if so, by whom? And why?

Left: John Wesley, whose family also experienced a 'knocking spirit', which centred on Wesley's younger sister – just as that at Cock Lane focused on 11-year-old Elizabeth Parsons. In the 18th century such disturbances were believed to be evil in nature; today they are recognised as classic symptoms of poltergeist activity

father and mother would all be sent to Newgate.'

This final session was held at the house of a gentleman named Missiter in Covent Garden and this time, perhaps not unexpectedly, there were positive results. The child was seen creeping from her bed to pick up a piece of wood with which she subsequently made knocking sounds. But Missiter and his companions agreed that this blatant piece of fraud produced sounds nothing like the ones heard previously: Elizabeth was, naturally, terrified for her freedom.

The tide had turned in Kent's favour. On 5 March a pamphlet entitled 'The mystery revealed', usually attributed to Oliver Goldsmith, put the case for his innocence with force. Later, Charles Churchill published a long poem, *The ghost*, which laughed at the affair – particularly Dr Johnson's part in it – and David Garrick turned the saga of 'Scratching Fanny' to good use by making it the centrepiece of a comic recitation, 'The Farmer's Return', at Drury Lane theatre.

On 9 February a new knocking ghost was advertised as 'likely to perform' in Broad Court, Covent Garden. The magistrate at nearby Bow Street was John Fielding, the half brother of Henry Fielding, and he sent the 'ghost' his compliments 'with an intimation that it would not meet with the lenity

the Cock Lane spirit did, but that it should knock hemp in Bridewell. On which the ghost, very discreetly, omitted the intended exhibition.'

On 10 July, the 'conspirators' were brought for trial at the Court of King's Bench, Guildhall, before Lord Mansfield. The charge was that the Reverend John Moore, Richard Parsons, Mrs Parsons and others had conspired to 'take away the life of William Kent by charging him with the murder of Frances Lynes by giving her poison whereof she died'. James Franzen the landlord, 'Carrots' the servant, the doctor and the apothecary all gave evidence, while several people spoke up for Parsons.

After a trial lasting a day, the accused were found guilty. The Rev. Moore was heavily fined, Parsons was sentenced to two years' imprisonment and three sessions in the pillory, and his wife to one year's jail. Elizabeth Parsons did not stand trial, but was not, apparently, troubled by her 'ghost' again.

Even after leaving prison, Parsons protested his innocence, and his protests have a convincing ring to them. He had gained nothing from the Cock Lane affair but notoriety and punishment. He had had differences with Kent, it was true, but he was, drunkenness apart, a well-liked man of previous good character, with no wish to put another's life at stake. Furthermore hundreds of people – the Duke of York, Horace Walpole, and Lord Hertford included – had heard the knockings from the wainscot, a good distance from Elizabeth's bed.

A twist in the tale

And the manifestations themselves, centring on a young, prepubescent girl who had epileptic tendencies, closely echo modern cases held by parapsychologists to be 'genuine'. Perhaps the 'interpretation' of the Cock Lane rappings was the only fault of Parsons and Moore.

Or perhaps the 'ghost' had a point after all. The coffins were cleared from the vaults of St John's Church in 1860, but 10 years previously an illustrator, J. W. Archer, had visited them to produce illustrations for a book by Charles Mackay entitled *Memoirs of extraordinary popular delusions*, which featured the Cock Lane ghost. By the light of a lantern, the sexton's boy who accompanied Archer had opened the coffin said to be that of 'Scratching Fanny' and shown him the body within. The face was that of a once handsome woman, with a pronounced aquiline nose: 'an uncommon case,' wrote Archer, 'for the cartilage mostly gives way. The remains had become adipocere, and were perfectly preserved.'

There was no sign, as far as he could see, of the smallpox from which Fanny was said to have died. But the preservation of the features – the nose in particular – would unfailingly set a modern forensic scientist looking for traces of arsenic poisoning.

The ghost with wet boots

The Admiral seemed a trifle absent-minded as he ordered his flagship to her doom. Was he also 'absent in spirit' – on a ghostly visit to his London home? A curious collection of tales surrounds the resulting disaster

Left: Vice-Admiral Sir George Tryon, whose naval career was brought to an inglorious end when he ordered a disastrous manoeuvre. Was he the victim of an Arab curse?

Below: the *Camperdown* rams the *Victoria*, as depicted by a French magazine

LA CATASTROPHE DU « VICTORIA »

Mort de l'amiral Tryon et de 359 officiers et marins anglais

ON THE MORNING of 22 June 1893, HMS *Victoria* was the proud and formidable flagship of the British Mediterranean Fleet. By the afternoon, she lay on the sea bed, her hull torn open. Of her crew, 358 were dead – including the Vice-Admiral, Sir George Tryon.

The disaster was one of the most curious episodes in British naval history – for the *Victoria* was rammed by her sister ship HMS *Camperdown* and rammed as a direct result of orders given by Vice-Admiral Tryon himself!

When the fatal orders were given the fleet was in the eastern Mediterranean, steaming in two parallel columns – five ships in one, six in the other. The five were led by HMS *Camperdown*, commanded by Rear-Admiral Markham. The other column was headed by Vice-Admiral Tryon's *Victoria*. They were separated by a mere six cables – a trifle over 1200 yards (1100 metres). Yet they were ordered to turn *inwards* simultaneously and reverse direction before anchoring.

This order was monstrously inept, for the turning circles of the ironclads were huge – 800 yards (730 metres) easily. The warships would be set on a collision course. The danger was at once apparent to Admiral Markham, who queried the signalled orders – but they were repeated. After that, no one argued – indeed, few people ever dared argue with the arrogant Sir George. Instead, Markham acquiesced, blindly trusting that Tryon had some elaborate master plan in mind, and the *Camperdown* swung inwards.

'As if locked in a trance'

The *Victoria* began its turn at the same time, and the two giants steamed towards each other. They charged at each other as if they were foes bent on using the vicious steel rams on their bows. No one took evasive action: Admiral Markham was still confident that his chief would prove to be a tactical genius. Aboard the *Victoria* Captain Bourke was in a turmoil. He spoke to the Vice-Admiral and warned of the imminent danger. Yet Tryon remained dumb, almost as if he were locked in a trance, and the ship relentlessly followed its collision course. The Captain urgently asked for permission to go astern at full speed but Tryon remained silent, as if transfixed. The question was repeated again and again until, finally, the Admiral wearily answered: 'Yes'!

But by then it was far too late to save the

flagship. For even though the *Camperdown* had also reversed her screws, she did not have time to stop: still driving forward, she smashed into the *Victoria*'s bows with her ram. Behind that ram was the weight of the ship's 10,600 tonnes, against which the flagship's armour plate was pathetically weak protection. It was caved in and split open by sheer brute force – and the sea poured in.

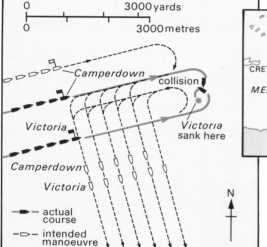

The end was horrific. The men in the engine room were trapped at their posts; many of the sailors who managed to struggle into the sea were chopped to pieces by the furiously revolving propellers. As for Sir George, he made no attempt to save himself.

With Admiral Tryon's death all chance of knowing what he had really had in mind vanished. There are some, though, who claim that he was supernaturally doomed: that his mind was unhinged by the remorseless working out of a curse. The latest among the 'curse' advocates is Mr Richard Winer, well known for his books on the notorious Bermuda Triangle.

Winer, in *From the Devil's Triangle to the Devil's Jaw*, takes 10 pages to tell the story. He spices it with the claim that this curse began to unfold on the shores of the Mediterranean. According to Winer, hundreds of Syrian Arabs had waited and watched for the British fleet to be hit by this curse.

To add strength to his fantastic view, he relates the amazing tale of Sir George Tryon's 'last London appearance'. This took place at a late morning tea party organised by Lady Tryon at her home in Belgravia.

The majority of the guests were wives of the Royal Navy's leading commanders. About noon, Admiral Tryon was seen walking down the stairs and across the drawing room. The Admiral was attired in his full-dress uniform but appeared to be oblivious to the guests in his home.

We then learn that this party was held on that sorrowful 22 June – so that solid-looking Admiral was nothing but a spectre, for at the

The sinking of the *Victoria* took place off Tripoli in what is now Lebanon (below). Admiral Tryon intended that his two columns of ships should turn inwards and then form up in pairs (below left), but there was insufficient space for the manoeuvre

Above: Sir George Tryon was involved in some mishaps of varying degrees of seriousness in the years before his death. Here he shows a notable lack of sea legs as his ship is caught by a squall during naval manoeuvres off Plymouth in 1890. During these exercises he distinguished himself by ordering the same manoeuvre that was to prove so disastrous three years later. In 1890, however, he had the good fortune to be disobeyed

time Sir George himself was some thousands of miles away on the doomed *Victoria*.

No doubt the author imagines that he is on safe ground in recounting this story, for in various forms it has been cited by many other authors. Indeed the late James Wentworth Day, a writer on the supernatural, even described it as 'one of the best-authenticated ghost stories in living London history'.

But for all that, Richard Winer's confidence is misplaced. A careful comparison of the different versions shows that the story has the same mythical quality as the widely accepted Lord Dufferin tale.

For a start, there is conflict over even the most basic claims. One account has it that Tryon walked through the reception room of his home and then disappeared. Another states that he walked through the crowded ballroom and was seen by some 300 guests. Another claims that he appeared at a party in the drawing room at the time of his death – that is, at about 3.40 p.m. But the most detailed account of all gives the time of his appearance as 11.30 p.m. – that is, some eight hours *after* his death. And according to this last account Sir George walked across the ballroom floor and was recognised by some 50 or so guests.

So here we have complete discord over the time, the exact place and the number of witnesses. There is one point of close accord, though, for they all agree that Lady Tryon saw nothing of the apparition. Richard Winer claims that she did see it, and thus adds his own special variation.

Now these disagreements are significant enough; but even more significant is the complete absence of contemporary references by witnesses. For a short while during this author's search for such references, however, two leads looked promising.

The first was found in an account by Ian Fellowes-Gordon, in which he quotes from an alleged eyewitness. He introduces the quotation by saying: 'Months later Sir Jasper

'true ghost stories'. And oddly enough, among them is one that turns out to be the genesis of the Tryon legend!

It is entitled 'A ghost in a ballroom'. It tells how a Mr W. walked through a ballroom without speaking to any of the people present, including the lady he was due to partner. On the following day, the witnesses learned that Mr W. had been found drowned. Remarkably, 'his watch had stopped at 10.15', the exact time at which he had been seen in the ballroom.

So the tale of the ballroom apparition of a drowned man was circulating at least six months *before* the *Victoria* met her end. But that disaster was so spectacular and puzzling that it invited rumour, speculation and fantasy. A new slant was given to an old story, and the shadowy Mr W. became the beefy Sir

Hoad was to explain what had happened. And his account, verified by every other guest present in the ballroom at 11.25 that evening, would go down in history.' There follows a reconstructed version of a conversation between Sir Jasper and Lady Tryon.

Unfortunately, though, Ian Fellowes-Gordon is no longer able to remember where the information in the conversation came from. In the event this proved unimportant. For the peerage lists for 1893 and later years show that *there never was* a Sir Jasper Hoad. The 'testimony' of a man who never existed counts as nothing.

The second lead was found in the most bizarre account of the Tryon case in print. It is included in Will Eisner's *Spirit casebook of true haunted houses and ghosts*. And this time Sir George is said to have appeared in the library of his London house in 'Bristol Square', where guests found him standing behind his desk. His eyes were riveted on his globe, 'his finger pointing to Tripoli . . . on the Mediterranean [in what was then Syria]. They greeted him. He nodded absently . . . trance-like in his movements.' They told the glad news of Sir George's presence to Lady Tryon but when she reached the library it was empty. But on the globe was a still-moist fingerprint, and the clock had stopped at 3.44 – the time of his death. And the 'most startling of all: a damp footprint – the Admiral's size – on the floor.'

Bizarre as it is, this version does at least give a source: the August 1893 issue of *The Review of Reviews*. This reference, however, turns out to be bogus. The account in that issue of *The Review of Reviews* is nothing but a straightforward report of the collision at sea with no mention of the ghostly portent in London. What is more, there is no mention of the apparition in *any* issue of the *Review* from 1893 to 1895 – and that in itself is most revealing. For the magazine's editor was W.T. Stead, an ardent Spiritualist who went out of his way to collect and print any good story that had a supernatural slant. In fact his Christmas 1892 issues were crammed full of

Top: the *Victoria* settles in the water and begins to heel over to the starboard side. Hundreds of sailors drowned when she sank: one was Admiral Tryon, who did not attempt to save himself

Above: W.T. Stead, editor of *The Review of Reviews*. The Christmas before the sinking of the *Victoria* he had published a report of a man who, at the very moment he was drowning, was 'seen' attending a ball. Did this tale attach itself to the tragedy of Admiral Tryon?

Right: the Tryons' Belgravia home, where the Admiral's apparition was allegedly seen. It ignored the guests and left wet footprints on the carpet – strange behaviour for a well-bred man, but fitting for the ghost of someone who had drowned in the eastern Mediterranean that same day

George – complete with wet boots.

But how about that curse? Does *that* stand up to scrutiny? Not for one moment. As Admiral Colomb subsequently testified, Sir George acted 'with a strong and frequently expressed impatience of all mathematical calculations and mechanical certainties'. He also had a mathematical blind spot. For he occasionally confused the radius of a ship's turning circle with its diameter. This confusion had almost led to a disaster some three years earlier. He then had signalled precisely the same fatal manoeuvre during the 1890 naval exercises off Plymouth. But Rear-Admiral Tracey had refused to comply.

As for Tryon's 'trance state', it must be remembered that at the time he was plagued by a painful ulcer on the leg, which refused to heal. The medication and pain killers he was using were more than probably laced with laudanum and other opium derivatives, like so many medical remedies in those days. These were enough to slow anyone's reflexes and bring a glazed, vacant look to the eyes!

Mayfair's haunted house

For decades the elegant house in the heart of London's West End was plagued by ghosts, but each haunting seemed to take a new and different form. The story is fascinating – as are the possible explanations

IN 1884 the *National Observer* magazine published a poem by Rudyard Kipling. Entitled *Tomlinson*, it told the story of a London society 'waster' whose soul was rejected by the Devil on the grounds of mediocrity. But it was the setting of the poem that was calculated to interest the general public. It began:

> Now Tomlinson gave up the ghost in
> his house in Berkeley Square,
> And a spirit came to his bedside and
> gripped him by the hair . . .

For the previous four decades, Berkeley Square had been synonymous with ghosts (as it was with nightingales 60 years later).

According to popular rumour the focus of the trouble was No 50, a four-storey town house of brick and stone, built in the mid 18th century. For some years it had been the

Above: 50 Berkeley Square as it appears today

Right: the front door, from behind which startled neighbours heard curious thumps, bumps and the ringing of bells

London home of Prime Minister George Canning (1770–1827), but it seemed unlikely that the supernatural disturbances in the house had any connection with his restless spirit. Canning was not particularly ethereal in life and in any case had breathed his last at Chiswick, some miles away.

The general consensus seemed to be that the 'thing' that haunted No 50 was 'too horrible to describe' – it seemed to be more a demon or terrible elemental than an ordinary ghost. Even before Bulwer Lytton used the house as a setting for his famous ghost story *The haunters and the haunted*, stories abounded of a 'nameless, slimy thing' that slithered up and down the stairs, leaving a foul-smelling, snail-like trail in its wake.

One tale, not unlike Bulwer Lytton's, told of two sailors who had broken into the empty house to shelter for the night. On the morrow, one was found dead, impaled on the railings in the street below, having leapt from the top storey in a frenzy of fear, while his companion was discovered white-haired and mad in the house itself.

No matter that no documentary evidence for such a remarkable incident existed. The story was firmly believed by society dandies and East End costermongers alike, and for several decades was kept alive by poems, newspapers and music hall songs.

Charles Harper, writing in 1907, remarked that 'the famous "haunted house" in Berkeley Square was long one of those things that no country cousin coming up from the provinces to London on sightseeing bent ever willingly missed.'

Harry Price investigated the mystery in the 1920s, two decades before his mishandling – or worse – of the Borley Rectory case made him an object of suspicion in psychical research circles. In the Berkeley Square investigation he seems to have done a

reasonably objective job: without, however, reaching any firm conclusions. On the one hand, he said, he had discovered some evidence that in the late 18th century – presumably before Prime Minister Canning's tenancy – the house had been the headquarters of a gang of forgers and coin clippers, who actively encouraged tales of the supernatural in order to disguise the true nature of the 'bumps in the night' that neighbours heard from time to time.

On the other hand he pointed out that the house had been empty for remarkably long periods and, while empty houses often tend to father ghost stories around themselves, 50 Berkeley Square was one of the most desirable addresses in London – so why had

Left: Rudyard Kipling, from a portrait by Burne-Jones. Kipling's poem *Tomlinson* exploited the notoriety of the house in Berkeley Square – and helped sell out the magazine in which it appeared

it been deserted for so long? Perhaps the rumours had some truth after all?

Price's final surmise was that No 50 may well have been a target for poltergeist activity. In 1840, he discovered that several of the neighbours had heard a variety of noises coming from the empty premises, including bumps on the stairs, dragging noises as if heavy furniture were being moved about, tramping footsteps and, fairly regularly, the jangling of the signal bells below stairs.

One of the more headstrong neighbours, weary of the commotion, obtained a key and, as soon as he heard the bells tinkling, dashed into the house and down to the kitchen. He found the bells still bouncing on their curled springs, but no other sign of life in the locked house. All this, pointed out Price, fitted exactly with the type of phenomenon described by the Society for Psychical Research as poltergeist activity: the one difference being that poltergeists – in practically all known cases – centre themselves on people.

In the course of his investigation Price had

had to wade through a great deal of speculative data that rarely gave dates or names. For instance, in the 1870s the magazine *Notes and Queries* had launched an investigation into the case, culminating in a long series by the writer W. E. Howlett.

The mystery of Berkeley Square still remains a mystery [he wrote]. We are in hopes that during the last fortnight a full, final, and satisfactory answer would have been given to our questions: but we have been disappointed. The story of the haunted house in the heart of Mayfair can be recapitulated in a few words. . . . The house in Berkeley Square contains at least one room of which the atmosphere is supernaturally fatal to body and mind. A girl saw, heard, or felt such horror in it that she went mad, and never recovered sanity enough to tell how or why.

A gentleman, a disbeliever in ghosts, dared to sleep in it and was found a corpse in the middle of the floor after frantically ringing for help in vain. Rumour suggests other cases of the same kind, all ending in death, madness or both as a result of sleeping, or trying to sleep in that room. The very party walls of the house, when touched, are found saturated with electric horror. It is uninhabited save by an elderly man and his wife who act as caretakers; but even these have no access to *the* room. This is kept locked, the key being in the hands of a mysterious and seemingly nameless person who comes to the house once every six months, locks up the elderly couple in the basement, and then unlocks *the* room and occupies himself in it for hours.

In 1881, an anonymous writer, again in *Notes and Queries*, testified to the truth of the

Right: Edward Bulwer Lytton, who used 50 Berkeley Square as a setting for a gruesome short story

'electric party walls' story, though he too failed to name names, possibly because the witnesses were 'society people'.

The incident in question had taken place at a ball given in 49 Berkeley Square early in the season of 1880. 'A lady and her partner,' said the writer, 'were sitting against the party wall of number fifty when on a sudden she moved from her place and looked around. The gentleman was just going to ask the reason when he felt impelled to do the same. On comparing their impressions, both had felt very cold and had fancied that someone was looking over their shoulders from the wall behind! From this it would appear that "stone walls do not a prison make" for these uncomfortable ghosts, who can project themselves right through them to the great discomfort of the next door neighbours.'

The most likely explanation of the origins of No 50's sinister reputation was printed shortly after this account appeared, and differed from most in that it could be verified, at least in part: doubtless because the parties mentioned were dead. According to the writer, in *Pall Mall* magazine, the house had been bought after George Canning's death by an Hon. Miss Curzon, who lived there from time to time until her death in 1859 at the age of 90. It was then leased by her executors to a Mr Myers, a well-to-do man about town who was engaged to be married and who spent the next few months of his tenancy redecorating and furnishing, only to have his bride jilt him on the eve of her wedding day. The unfortunate Myers became a recluse in his new home, developing a curiously Dickensian character, part Scrooge, part Miss Haversham.

In 1873 he was prosecuted by Westminster council for non-payment of rates, and refused to answer the summons in person. Despite this, the magistrate gave him time to pay, and was surprisingly lenient with him in his summing up: 'The house in question is known as "the haunted house" and has occasioned a good deal of speculation among the neighbours. Mr Myers' failure to pay his rates had arisen from eccentricity.'

The *Pall Mall* author went on: 'The disappointment [of his rejection] is said to have broken his heart and turned his brain. He became morose and solitary, and would never allow a woman to come near him. The miserable man locked himself away in the ill-fated top room of the house, only opening the door for meals to be brought to him occasionally by a manservant. Generally speaking he slept during the day and, at night, would emerge from his self-imposed exile to wander, candle in hand, around the house that was to have been the scene of his happiness.'

Possibly Myers was the 'mysterious and nameless person' alluded to by W. E. Howlett, for he died, apparently, towards the end of the 1870s.

'Thus,' said the writer in *Pall Mall*, 'upon the melancholy wanderings of this poor lunatic, was founded that story of the

Below: Berkeley Square in the 1860s. The macabre goings-on at No 50 sorted ill with its gentility and refinement

ghost . . . those whom so many persons insist on calling "mad doctors" could tell of hundreds of cases of minds diseased and conduct similar to that of poor Myers. His sister was, it was said, his only relative, and she was too old or great an invalid to interfere.'

New twists to the tale

There the story should have ended, but did not. In 1912, Jessie A. Middleton, a popular author on the occult, wrote in her *Grey ghost book* that her own research had shown that the ghost was that of a little girl in a Scots kilt. She claimed that the child had been either frightened or starved to death in the fourth-floor room and had been seen there from time to time ever since, weeping and wringing her hands in dismay. But Miss Middleton added that another version of the story – echoing the 'falling sailor' tale – held that the girl had not been so young, that her name was Adeline, and that rather than submit to a 'fate worse than death' at the hands of her wicked guardian, she had leapt from the window and been spiked to death on the area railings.

As late as 1969 another strand was added to the already tangled skein of the Berkeley Square affair. Mrs Mary Balfour, an oc-togenarian lady of noble Scottish family, whose letters from society names attested to her apparently remarkable powers of clair-voyance, told a reporter of the only actual ghost that she had seen. Early in 1937 she had moved with her maid into a flat in Charles Street, which is adjacent to Berkeley Square, having lived previously in the Highlands of Scotland.

'It was about the time of New Year,' she recalled, 'and I had come in late when my maid summoned me to the kitchen at the

Above: reputedly the seat of all the disturbances – the haunted room at No 50, now quiet and tranquil as part of a modern office

Left: George Canning, sometime Prime Minister, who owned – but apparently did not return to haunt – the house in Berkeley Square

back of the flat. We could see into the back windows of a house diagonally opposite and in one of them stood a man in a silver-coloured coat and breeches of eighteenth-century cut, wearing a periwig and with a drawn, pale face. He was looking out sadly, not moving. I thought perhaps that he had been to some New Year party in fancy dress, and either had a hangover or some personal trouble, I rebuked the girl for staring at him so. It was only afterwards that I discovered that the house was number fifty. Believe it or not, I had not until that time heard of the reputation of the house.'

If Mrs Balfour had not, many people had, and stories about No 50 Berkeley Square continue to circulate even today. In the early years of the Second World War the house was taken over by antiquarian book sellers Maggs Brothers Ltd. According to a spokes-man, in late 1981 they were still getting three or four calls a month from tourists seeking the ghosts: 'Unfortunately we can tell them nothing. The so-called "haunted room" is next to the accounts department; none of us has ever seen, or heard, or felt anything out of the ordinary there. During the war members of the staff used the room as a dormitory while firewatching without any discomfort apart from draughts. I can only regretfully suppose that the ghost was ex-orcised long before our arrival.'

Borley: a haunting tale

Was Borley Rectory really 'the most haunted house in England' – or was its fame built on a great publicity stunt by ghost hunter Harry Price? Indeed, was Price a headline-seeking fraud?

BORLEY PARISH CHURCH stands on a hillside overlooking the valley of the river Stour, which marks the boundary between the counties of Essex and Suffolk in England. Borley can hardly even be called a village: the hundred or so inhabitants of this Essex parish, mainly agricultural workers and weekend cottagers, do their shopping and socialising in Long Melford or Sudbury, the two nearest small towns on the Suffolk side; for more important business they travel from Borley Green to Bury St Edmunds, about 25 miles (40 kilometres) away.

But in 1940 the publication of a book entitled *The most haunted house in England* made the community world famous, and in 1946 a further volume, *The end of Borley Rectory*, set the seal on its fame. Both were written by the flamboyant ghost hunter Harry Price, who made psychical research headlines in his day. The two books claimed that Borley Rectory, a gloomy Victorian house that had burned down in 1939, was the centre of remarkably varied paranormal

Borley Church, whose vicars lived in the reputedly haunted Borley Rectory not far away. Harry Price, ghost hunter, psychical researcher and author, put the parish of Borley 'on the map' when he wrote a book about the rectory hauntings in 1940

phenomena. These included a phantom coach, a headless monk, a ghostly nun who may or may not have been the monk's lover, the spirit of a former vicar, eerie lights, water that turned into ink, mysterious bells, and a multifarious cascade of things that went bump in the night.

'One of the events of the year 1940' was how the first book was described by *Time and Tide* in its glowing review, while the *Church Times* said that it would 'remain among the most remarkable contributions ever made to the study of the paranormal'. Price, who professed to have devoted 10 years to his study of Borley's ghosts, continued to lecture, broadcast and write on the subject until his death on 29 March 1948. An obituary in *The Times* the following day summed him up as a psychical researcher with 'a singularly honest and clear mind on a subject that by its very nature lends itself to all manner of trickery and chicanery'.

Not everyone who knew or worked with Price agreed with this glowing testimonial, however. Some months after his death, and with the danger of libel safely out of the way, an article by Charles Sutton of the *Daily Mail* appeared in the *Inky way annual*, a World's Press News publication. Writing of a visit he had paid to Borley in 1929, in the

middle of Price's first investigation with another colleague, Sutton said that he had discovered what might be fraud on Price's part. After a large pebble had hit Sutton on the head, he found that Price had 'bricks and pebbles' in his pockets.

On a more careful investigation, two members of the Society for Psychical Research (SPR) – Lord Charles Hope and Major the Hon. Henry Douglas-Home – had had serious doubts about 'phenomena' they had witnessed at the rectory in the late 1920s. Both of them filed testimony with the SPR stating that they had grave suspicions. Douglas-Home went as far as to accuse Price of having a 'complete disregard for the truth in this matter'. He told how, on one occasion, he was accompanying Price around the rectory in the darkness when they heard a rustling that reminded him of cellophane being crumpled. Later, he sneaked a look into Price's suitcase and found a roll of cellophane with a torn edge.

It was as a result of this testimony that the Council of the SPR invited three of their members, Dr Eric J. Dingwall, Mrs K. M. Goldney and Mr Trevor H. Hall, to undertake a new survey of the evidence. The three were given access to Price's private papers and correspondence by his literary executor, Dr Paul Tabori. They also had access to documents in the Harry Price Collection, which Price had placed on permanent loan to the University of London in 1938 and bequeathed to that institution on his death. This survey took five years to prepare and was published in 1956 under the title *The haunting of Borley rectory*.

The reviews of this book were as enthusiastic as those of Price's two volumes in the 1940s, although for diametrically different reasons. The *Sunday Times* said that the Borley legend had been demolished 'with clinical thoroughness and aseptic objectivity', while Professor A.G.N. Flew in the *Spectator* commented that the 'shattering

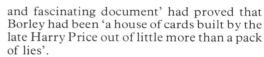

Price in action: on the radio direct from a haunted house in Meopham, Kent, in 1936 (above) and on a much-publicised trip to Germany with C.E.M. Joad to re-create a magical scene on the Brocken in the Harz mountains in 1932 (below)

and fascinating document' had proved that Borley had been 'a house of cards built by the late Harry Price out of little more than a pack of lies'.

There, perhaps, the matter should have rested, but due to a combination of factors it did not. The principal reason may have been that Borley had made sensational copy for the world's popular newspapers for over a quarter of a century, and even the most objective of reporters dislikes seeing a good source dry up. Newspapers and television programmes glossed over the painstaking evidence of Dingwall, Goldney and Hall, one referring to them as 'the scoffers who accused Harry Price, the greatest of ghost seekers, of rigging the whole legend'. And once more, the events described by Price were said to be 'puzzling, frightening, and inexplicable'. Peter Underwood, the president of the Ghost Club, and the late Dr Tabori returned to Price's defence in 1973 with a book entitled *The ghosts of Borley: annals of the haunted rectory*. They dedicated it to 'the memory of Harry Price, the man who put Borley on the map'.

In his book *The occult*, published in 1971, Colin Wilson made a fair and scrupulously unbiased summing up of the evidence for and against the Borley case. His conclusion was that 'a hundred other similar cases could be

extracted [from SPR records]. . . . Unless someone can produce a book proving that Price was a pathological liar with a craving for publicity, it is necessary to suspend judgement.'

And, indeed, in 1978 SPR investigator Trevor H. Hall set out to prove Price 'a pathological liar with a craving for publicity'. The title of his book, *Search for Harry Price*, was a pun based on Price's own autobiography *Search for truth* (1942).

Had it been less carefully documented, Hall's book could have been fairly described as a piece of muckraking. He revealed, for instance, that Price's father was a London grocer who had seduced and married Price's mother when she was 14 and he was over 40. Price himself, in his autobiography, had claimed to be the son of a wealthy paper manufacturer who came of 'an old Shropshire family'.

Price stated that his childhood had been spent between the London stockbroker suburb of Brockley and the family's country home in an unnamed part of Shropshire. He said that he usually 'broke his journey' there on the way to and from school, implying that he was educated at a boarding school in the country. Hall's researches clearly showed the family home to have been in New Cross, not far from, but far less salubrious than, Brockley. Price, said Hall, attended a local secondary school, Haberdasher's Aske's Hatcham Boys' School, a perfectly respectable lower middle class establishment, but not a public boarding school. The only family connection

Above: Peter Underwood, the president of the Ghost Club, who came down on the side of Price in the controversy over the latter's integrity

Below: the ruins of Borley Rectory four years after it was completely destroyed by a mysterious fire. This did not end the speculation over its haunting

with Shropshire was that Price's grandfather had once been landlord of the Bull's Head at Rodington.

According to Price, he had held a directorship in his father's paper manufacturing company after leaving school, spending the 10 years between the end of his schooldays and his marriage in 1908 pleasantly as an amateur coin collector and archaeologist. In fact, according to Hall, Price earned his living in New Cross in a variety of odd ways. He took photographs of local shopfronts for advertising purposes; hired out his portable gramophone and records for dances, parties and other functions; performed conjuring tricks at concerts – a skill that he was later accused of using during his Borley investigation – and peddled glue, paste and a cure for footrot in sheep from door to door in the Kent countryside. Price had an indubitable flair for writing, as the impressive sales of his books – some 17 in all – testify.

In 1902 Price wrote an article for his old school magazine, *The Askean*, about the excavation of a Roman villa in Greenwich Park, quoting as his source a book written by the director of the project. By 1942, in *Search for truth*, he was claiming that he had actually helped to excavate the site. He also contributed a series of articles to the *Kentish Mercury* on coins and tokens of the county, following this up with another series for Shropshire's *Wellington Journal* on 'Shropshire tokens and mints'.

Hall asked the Reverend Charles Ellison, Archdeacon of Leeds and a leading authority

Left: Haberdasher's Aske's Hatcham Boys School, where Price had his education, as it looks today. According to Price's detractor, Trevor H. Hall, Price hinted in his autobiography that he had attended a public school

Below: the Harry Price Library in the Senate House at London University. Price bequeathed to the university his outstanding collection of thousands of books on magic and the occult – which Hall characterises as Price's 'most useful achievement'. Price also tried to get the university to establish a psychical research department, but failed. Some say that the institution was scared off by his flamboyant approach to scientific investigation

Green-Price unequivocally stated that she had never heard of Robert Ditcher-Price and that she was 'quite certain that he never resided at Norton Manor'.

In his first book on Borley Rectory in 1940 Price used a version of the 'nun's tale' supplied by the Glanville family – father Sydney, son Roger and daughter Helen. While holding a seance with a planchette at their home, Helen Glanville elicited the information that a nun had indeed been murdered at Borley and that she was a Frenchwoman called Marie Lairre. On the subject of this and subsequent seances he held, Sydney Glanville was almost apologetic to SPR researchers Dingwall, Goldney and Hall, admitting that suggestion had played a part: all three Glanvilles had studied the history of the Borley hauntings.

After the story of the French nun's ghost appeared in *The most haunted house in England*, Price received an elaborate theory from Dr W. J. Phythian-Adams, Canon of Carlisle, to the effect that Marie Lairre had been induced to leave her convent and marry one of the local landowners. She had been strangled by her husband and buried in a

on numismatics, to examine Price's writings on coins. The archdeacon found them to be straight plagiarisms from two obscure works on the subject. 'It is unsafe to rely on any statement made by Harry Price which lacks independent confirmation,' he concluded.

Hall reported that Price's financial independence came from his marriage to Constance Knight, who inherited a comfortable fortune from her father. It was her means, and not family wealth as claimed, that gave him the leisure to put his days of door-to-door peddling behind him and embark on his career as psychical researcher and book collector. The assembling of a library of occult and magical books running into several thousand volumes was, said Hall, 'Price's most useful achievement during his life'.

Even the library seemed to offer opportunities for chicanery, however. In the collection Hall found several valuable books clearly marked with the imprint of the SPR. Price had catalogued them as his own, even attaching his own book plate.

Price's book plates were a source of interest and amusement for Hall, as well as another example of Price's covertness. Price used two crested plates. One featured a lion rampant and proved on investigation to be the family crest of Sir Charles Rugge-Price of Richmond, with whom Harry Price had no connection. The other, bearing a crest and coat of arms, carried the name 'Robert Ditcher-Price' and the address 'Norton Manor, Radnor'. Hall's investigations revealed that the crest and arms were those of Parr of Parr, Lancashire, and that Norton Manor belonged to Sir Robert Green-Price, Baronet, whose family had lived there since the 17th century. A letter from Lady Jean

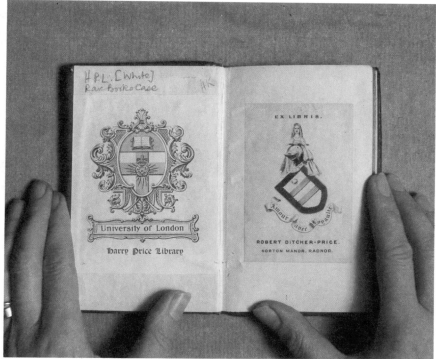

Three of Harry Price's book plates. The one on the far right, bearing the name of 'Robert Ditcher-Price' and the address 'Norton Manor, Radnor', was investigated by Hall. He says that the titled family residing at Norton Hall, the Green-Prices, had never heard of a Robert Ditcher-Price

well on the site of the rectory. The canon suggested that the ghost of the former nun stole a French dictionary from the residents of Borley Rectory in the 19th century so that she could brush up on her English in order to communicate with them.

Despite some other preposterous twists in the canon's theory, Price seized on it eagerly. Hall accuses him of manufacturing and planting evidence to back it up. Part of this evidence was two French medals that Price claimed had appeared as 'apports' during his first visit to the rectory in 1929. One was a Roman Catholic confirmation medal and the other a badge or pass issued to members of the National Assembly after the revolution. Yet previously, Price had said that there was one apported medal and that it was a 'Loyola' medal. Price's faithful secretary stated that the Loyola medal was the only one she had ever seen.

Puzzling finds

Further to this case, Hall recounts how Price had excavated what he called a well in the ruined cellars of Borley Rectory in 1943, discovering a human jawbone in the soft earth. The excavation was made by lamplight. The well turned out to be a modern concrete basin. And during the demolition of the ruins, a switch and lengths of wire were found in the cellar, though the house had never been supplied with electricity. Had Price used this equipment with a portable battery to light the cellars as he secretly buried the jawbone for later discovery?

And so Trevor Hall's book goes on, each damning fact backed by documentary evidence, much of which is from Price's own unpublished notes and correspondence.

Price's accounts of psychical research projects are shown time and again to be inaccurate, or almost entirely invented, or presented over the years in different versions with contradictory details. *Search for Harry Price* certainly fulfills Colin Wilson's criterion: it shows Price as a confirmed liar and publicity seeker. The absurd experiment in which Price and Professor C. E. M. Joad conducted a magical ceremony in the Harz mountains in Germany for a regiment of press photographers more than proves the latter. But even more, the revelations indicate that he was a fraud.

But does the tarnishing of Price's character necessarily mean that the haunting of Borley Rectory was fraudulent? From the year the rectory was built in 1863 until 1929, when Price first became interested in it, stories circulating in the area had seemed to suggest paranormal happenings. Furthermore, from 1930 to 1937 Price visited Borley only once, and yet at least 2000 allegedly paranormal incidents were recorded during that time. In a year straddling 1937 and 1938, when Price rented the empty rectory and recruited a team of independent witnesses through an advertisement in *The Times* to live there with him, several incidents were reported in Price's absence. Finally, between Price's residency and 27 February 1939, when the rectory was 'mysteriously' destroyed by fire at midnight, odd events occurred.

So, regardless of Price's role, was Borley Rectory in fact the 'most haunted house in England?'

Large, dark and ugly, Borley Rectory seemed to invite haunting. And with the arrival of ghost hunter Harry Price, it became a hive of paranormal activity. Was someone helping things along? The Borley case clearly required careful examination

ALTHOUGH IT SERVED as rectory to the 12th-century Borley church, which stood amid ancient gravestones on the opposite side of the Sudbury road, the ' most haunted house in England' was only 76 years old when it burned to the ground in the winter of 1939. Borley Rectory was an ugly two-storey building of red brick, its grounds dotted with tall trees that cast gloom on many of its 23 rooms. It was built in 1863 by the Reverend Henry D. E. Bull, who was both a local landowner and rector of Borley church, to house his wife and 14 children.

Immediately behind and to one side of the house lay a farmyard bounded by a cottage, stabling and farm buildings. When an extra wing was added to the house in 1875, a small central courtyard resulted. The dining-room fireplace was carved with figures of monks, a decoration suggesting that the Rev. Bull may have believed a local legend that a 13th-century monastery had once occupied the

Presented to The Rev⁰ Henry Foyster Bull on his Marriage by the
Choir and Organist of Borley Church. September 12. 1911.

Above: the Reverend Henry (Harry) Bull and the choir of Borley church. Like his father before him, Harry Bull perpetuated the story of the haunting of the rectory by a nun

Below: the gloomy 23-room rectory as seen from the tower of the church

spot. One of the monks from this monastery gave rise to the first ghost story about the site. He was said to have eloped with a nun from a convent at Bures, some 8 miles (13 kilometres) away. But the couple were caught and executed, he being beheaded and she walled up in the convent. And their ghosts haunted the area. The roots of this picturesque tale were cut away in 1938 by a letter from the Essex Archaeological Society to Sidney Glanville, one of the most diligent and

Borley: the tension mounts

honest volunteer investigators for the ghost hunter and author Harry Price. It stated that neither the monastery nor the nunnery had ever existed.

However, there is evidence that both the Rev. Henry Bull and his son and successor as rector, the Rev. Harry Bull, enjoyed telling the story. It gained currency particularly among Sunday school children, many of whom presumably grew up believing it – in view of its source – to be 'gospel'.

Before this first 'nun's tale' was replaced by a later version, reports grew that various members of the Bull family – notably two of the sisters, Millie and Ethel – had seen a shadowy figure in the long rectory garden moving across what then became known as the 'nun's walk'. This route followed the path of an underground stream, along which clouds of gnats were inclined to drift on warm summer evenings. The two sisters told Price that they had seen the nun in July 1900, adding only that it was 'evening' and 'sunlit' – so no one can be sure it was not a formation of gnats. A later rector, the Rev. G. Eric Smith, told of being startled by a 'white figure' that turned out to be the smoke from a bonfire, while V. C. Wall, a *Daily Mirror* reporter, saw a similar apparition that proved to be the maid.

The Bull family lived at Borley Rectory in basic discomfort – without gas, electricity or mains water – for almost 65 years. When his father died in 1892, Harry took over as rector and continued to live in the house with his numerous siblings. At least three of the family remained in occupation until Harry's

Above: the summerhouse in which Harry Bull dozed away his last years. He claimed that he saw the ghostly nun and other apparitions while he rested here

Below: the place where the ghost of the nun disappears after her walk in the rectory garden. Up to this point – and where she walks – the stream is underground

death in June 1927. He himself moved across the road to Borley Place when he married in 1911, but returned to the rectory in 1920, presumably after his wife's death.

Despite the architectural gloom of their surroundings, the younger Bulls seem to have been a lively crowd, according to the testimony of friends and acquaintances who contacted researchers in the late 1940s and early 1950s. The house had curious acoustics that lent themselves to practical jokes. According to Major the Hon. Henry Douglas-Home of the Society for Psychical Research, footsteps in the courtyard at the rear of the house and voices in the adjoining cottage could clearly be heard in the rectory, along with the noise made by the hand pump in the stable yard. These provided plenty of thumps and groans, he said. Another source told researchers that the young Bull sisters took a delight in telling maids that the house was 'haunted', and one old servant mentioned that after being primed in this way by Edith Bull, she had heard 'shuffling' noises outside her room.

As he grew older, Harry Bull added his own contributions to the village gossip. He appears to have had narcolepsy, a condition in which the sufferer is always drowsy, and took to sleeping for most of the day in a summerhouse. After his snoozes, he claimed he had seen the nun, heard the phantom coach in which she had eloped with the monk, and spoken to an old family retainer named Amos, who had been dead for years. By 1927, when Bull died and the family finally left the rectory, it had become a 'haunted house' in local imagination. This reputation was probably enhanced as the house lay empty and dilapidated for over a year.

On 2 October 1928, the new rector of Borley arrived with his wife. The Rev. G. Eric Smith had spent his early married life in India, but following his wife's serious illness there, he decided to return home, take holy orders, and seek a living. Desperation may have been setting in when he accepted Borley, for he took it on trust and both he and his wife were dismayed when they discovered the condition of the rectory.

To add to their troubles during the first winter, the Smiths soon heard that the house was 'haunted'. The 'ghosts' themselves did not trouble them, however. As Mrs Smith was to write in a letter to the *Church Times* in 1945, neither of them thought the house haunted by anything but 'rats and local superstition'.

Smith's main worry was that the more nervous of his parishioners were unwilling to come to the rectory for evening meetings. When he failed to talk them out of their fears, he took what was perhaps the fatal step of writing to the editor of the *Daily Mirror* to ask for the address of a psychical research society. He hoped that trained investigators could solve the mystery in a rational way and allay the fears of the locals.

Instead, the editor sent a reporter, V. C.

Below: the spectral nun and the phantom coach haunting the site of Borley Rectory (seen on the left). In some versions of the story, the drivers of the coach were beheaded – which accounts for the headless figures in this picture. The nun was eloping with a monk, who was hanged when the two were caught. She was bricked up into a wall, we are told

Bottom: pointing out the place where the apparitional coach vanishes

during the weeks that followed, each visit being accompanied by strange phenomena that were duly reported in the *Daily Mirror* by Wall.

The results were predictable: far from quelling his parishioners' fears, the Rev. Smith had not only unwittingly increased them but added another dimension to his catalogue of woes. The district was invaded by sightseers night and day. Coach parties were organised by commercial companies and the Smiths found themselves virtually under siege. On 14 July, distressed by the ramshackle house and its unwelcome visitors, they moved to Long Melford. Smith ran the parish from there before taking another living in Norfolk in April 1930.

Price must have been made uneasy on at least two occasions at Borley. One of these was when some coins and a Roman Catholic medallion featuring St Ignatius Loyola 'materialised' and fell to the ground at about the same time as some sugar lumps flew through

Wall, and on Monday, 10 June 1929, he filed the first sensational newspaper account about Borley Rectory. His story talked of 'Ghostly figures of headless coachmen and a nun, an old-time coach, drawn by two bay horses, which appears and vanishes mysteriously, and dragging footsteps in empty rooms. . . .'

The *Mirror* editor also telephoned Price, who made his first visit two days later. With Price's arrival, 'objective phenomena' began for the first time. Almost as soon as he set foot on the premises, a flying stone smashed a window, an ornament shattered in the hallway, showers of apports – pebbles, coins, a medal and a slate – rattled down the main stairs. The servants' bells jangled of their own accord and keys flew out of their locks. During a seance held in the Blue Room – a bedroom overlooking the garden with its 'nun's walk' – rappings on a wall mirror supposedly made by the late Harry Bull were heard by Price and his secretary, Wall, the Smiths, and two of the Bull sisters who were visiting the house.

Price made several trips to the house

the air. When they were picked up, they were, recalled Mrs Smith, strangely warm to the touch, as if from a human hand. Her maid Mary Pearson, a known prankster, gave her the solution: 'That man threw that coin,' she explained, 'so I threw some sugar.' An even more farcical incident marked the second near-miss for Price during a further seance in the Blue Room. Heavy footsteps were heard outside, accompanied by the slow rumble of shutters being drawn back. In the doubtless stunned hush that followed, Price asked aloud if it were the spirit of the Rev. Harry Bull. A guttural voice, clearly recognisable as that of a local handyman, replied: 'He's dead, and you're daft.'

Rats, Mrs Smith later averred, lay behind the bell ringing – the bell wires ran along rafters under the roof. As for a mysterious light that 'appeared' in an upstairs window, it was well-known locally as a trick reflection of light from the railway carriages that passed along the valley.

For six months after the Smiths left Borley parish, the rectory was unoccupied once more. Then on 16 October 1930 the Rev. Harry Bull's cousin, Lionel A. Foyster, moved in as the new rector. The Rev. Foyster, a man in his early fifties, had moved back home from his previous post as rector of Sackville, Nova Scotia, which he had held between 1928 and 1930. He suffered from rheumatism but, despite his painful illness, he was a kindly and well-liked man. He was deeply devoted to his attractive wife Marianne, who was 31, and their adopted daughter Adelaide, a child of about two and a half.

During the five years that the Foysters lived at Borley, an estimated 2000 separate 'incidents' occurred, most of them within a period of about 14 months. These included

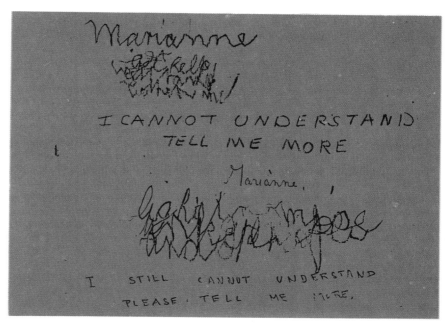

Top: an example of the 'spirit' writing on the wall of the rectory, addressed to Marianne Foyster. Paranormal phenomena increased when the Foysters came to live at Borley

Above: Harry Price at work in his own laboratory. His investigation of the Borley haunting is one of the most controversial of his career

Left: the foot of the main stairs of the rectory, scene of a rain of apports – coins, pebbles and other materialised objects. This happened almost immediately after Price arrived

voices, footsteps, objects being thrown, apparitions and messages scribbled in pencil on walls. It is probably true to say that with one possible exception, none of these could be attributable to Harry Price, who visited the rectory only once while the Foysters were there. The day after his visit, on 15 October 1931, he wrote one of the few straightforward statements he was ever to make on the Borley mystery in a letter to a colleague: '... although psychologically, the case is of great value, psychically speaking there is nothing in it.'

Six months had elapsed since the Smiths' departure and the Foysters' arrival, and in that time Borley Rectory had become more dilapidated than ever. According to her husband's cousins, the Bulls, Mrs Foyster hated the place from the moment she saw it. She made no friends locally, and her only companion, apart from Lionel, was a family friend, François D'Arles, a French-Canadian much nearer her own age. He rented the cottage at the rear of the house, and SPR investigators got the impression that he dominated the household. By 1932 Marianne Foyster and D'Arles had opened a flower shop together in London and returned to Borley only at weekends, the implication being that they had become lovers. Mrs Foyster often behaved oddly, if not hysterically, fainting when frustrated. Once she flung herself on her knees before assembled investigators to pray to St Anthony for 'vindication' when no manifestations were forthcoming – as though she expected to be able to produce them.

When the 'hauntings' of Borley Rectory began again shortly after the Foysters' arrival, the villagers accused Marianne Foyster – to her face – of being behind them.

Borley in ruins?

Writing on the walls, bells that ring themselves, apparitions and mysterious fires – such were the non-stop paranormal phenomena that occurred after the Foyster family moved into Borley Rectory. The cause of these manifestations remained in doubt

IN 1878 A YOUNG WOMAN named Esther Cox became the centre of 'mysterious manifestations' at her sister's home in Amherst, Nova Scotia. Esther saw apparitions visible to no one else. Objects were thrown, furniture was upset, small fires broke out in the house and messages addressed to the girl were found scribbled on the walls. The 'hauntings' became the subject of a book, *The haunted house: a true ghost story . . . the great Amherst mystery* (1879) by Walter Hubbell. The book was a huge success, running through 10 editions and selling over 55,000 copies. But in 1919 the American Society for Psychical Research printed a 'critical study' by Dr Walter F. Prince, suggesting that the Amherst case was not in fact a poltergeist manifestation. Prince said it was all trickery by Esther Cox while in a state of dissociation, or conversion hysteria.

The township of Amherst is about 5 miles (8 kilometres) from the equally small community of Sackville, where another of Esther Cox's married sisters lived and where, 50 years afterwards, the Reverend Lionel Foyster and his wife Marianne lived. The Foysters would have heard of the Amherst case as surely as anyone living in, say, Sudbury today would have heard of the Borley mystery. The fact that Foyster used the pseudonym 'Teed' when writing of the happenings at Borley Rectory during his stay

Above: Borley Rectory, which seemed to reach the peak of its haunting when Marianne Foyster lived there. It is still an open question as to whether she created the events herself. If so, was it because she suffered from an hysteric disorder she could not control – like Esther Cox in the similar Amherst case? Or did she produce the phenomena through PK?

Below: the cottage that was once part of the Borley Rectory property and in which François D'Arles lived

there offers what is tantamount to proof that he not only knew of the Amherst case but was familiar with its details: the unusual name 'Teed' was the married name of Esther Cox's sister. It seems likely, therefore, that his wife also knew of the case, though whether she made deliberate – if unconscious – use of it for her own behaviour is a matter for conjecture. The resemblance between both cases is, in fact, striking; Dingwall, Goldney and Hall in *The haunting of Borley Rectory* offer no less than 19 points of general concurrence, including the ringing of bells, throwing of objects, setting of small fires, and mysterious messages written on walls.

For example, a short time after Marianne Foyster arrived at Borley and took such a dislike to the place, she began to 'see apparitions'. No one else did. Shortly afterwards

the manifestations, so similar to the Amherst case, began. Her husband, loyal and devoted, answered villagers who accused her of faking that he could not see the visions because 'he wasn't psychic', but in her 'defence' he began to keep a rough record of events. This was not perhaps as helpful as he hoped it might be because, as he admitted, much of it was written later and many things were confused.

In October 1931, in answer to a plea from the Bull sisters, Harry Price returned to Borley once more. It is interesting to speculate on the motives behind the Bulls' concern: perhaps because they knew the source of the pranks and hoaxes during their own tenancy, they suspected the genuineness of the new 'haunting'. The same could be said of Harry Price, for he returned from his visit convinced that Mrs Foyster was directly responsible for fraud.

In their examination of the alleged phenomena, Dingwall, Goldney and Hall analysed

Below: the ghost hunter Harry Price (left) and Mrs K. M. Goldney of the Society for Psychical Research (right) pose with the Foyster family at Borley Rectory. The Foysters' adopted child Adelaide and an unidentified playmate complete the picture

Bottom: one of several messages that appeared on the walls of the rectory. All of them were scribbled in pencil in a childish hand and were mostly addressed to Marianne Foyster

caught on at least one occasion trying to set fire to bedclothes.

In 1933 when the Foysters went on leave for six months, they left Canon H. Lawton as locum. Nothing untoward happened though the canon, like Major Douglas-Home of the Society for Psychical Research, noted the curious acoustics of the house and surroundings. In any case, by that time Mrs Foyster was spending most of her time in London with François D'Arles at their flower shop. An exorcism by a group of Spiritualists the previous year, when Marianne and François first left to open their shop, seemed to have put paid to what the Foysters cosily called 'the goblins'. Or was it that Marianne Foyster was no longer on the premises?

In October 1935 the Foysters left Borley. When the Reverend A.C. Henning was appointed five months later, he chose to live elsewhere, and since his time the rectors of Borley have lived at Liston or Foxearth

the incidents described in Foyster's first record, which he later elaborated upon. Treating the constant bell ringing as a single phenomenon, they isolated 103 different instances. Of these, 99 depended totally on Mrs Foyster's sincerity, three were readily attributable to natural causes, and only one was in any way 'inexplicable'.

Among the most suspicious incidents was the appearance of pencilled writings on the walls. About seven messages appeared during the Foysters' tenancy, most of them addressed to Marianne and appealing for 'light, mass, prayers'. Another, not noted by Price in his Borley books, spelled 'Adelaide', the name of the Foysters' adopted daughter. All the messages were in a childish scribble. Little Adelaide may have been responsible for one or both of the 'mysterious' small fires that broke out in the rectory, for she was

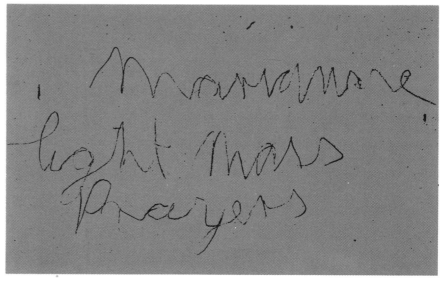

rectories, parishes amalgamated with Borley since the 1930s.

But the battered, drama-ridden old house had still another four years of life to run. On 19 May 1937 Harry Price rented the rectory, and a week later inserted an advertisement in *The Times* asking for 'responsible persons of leisure and intelligence, intrepid, critical and unbiased' to form a rota of observers at the house. If, he later stated, they 'knew nothing about psychical research, so much the better'.

As has been pointed out by Price's critics, ignorance of psychical research is a curious requirement for a team of ghost hunters, but could make it easier to use their 'experiences' to build a good story.

If Harry Price and Marianne Foyster had used fraud for their own personal ends, another trickster who came on the scene in November 1938 was working for purely financial gain. He was Captain William Hart Gregson, who bought Borley Rectory six months after Price's tenancy expired. He immediately asked Price's advice about organising coach trips to see his new property and broadcast on the radio, recounting several minor 'phenomena'. But his coach tour plans were brought to an abrupt end at midnight on 27 February 1939 when fire gutted the building, leaving only a few walls, charred beams, and chimney stacks standing.

Sidney Glanville, one of Price's volunteer researchers of impeccable reputation, said that at a seance at the Glanville home, an

One of Price's 48 volunteer investigators takes a break from his duties at the rectory. Price rented Borley for a year and gathered a team of 'observers' through an advertisement in *The Times* to work with him there. He did not ask for experience in psychical research, but required his volunteers to have 'leisure and intelligence' and to be 'critical and unbiased'

entity named 'Sunex Amures' had threatened to burn down Borley Rectory. But the real cause was flatly stated by Sir William Crocker in his autobiography *Far from humdrum: a lawyer's life* (1967). Crocker, a distinguished barrister, and Colonel Cuthbert Buckle, an insurance adjuster, investigated the claim made by Gregson on behalf of the insurers. Crocker states: 'We repudiated his impudent claim for "accidental loss by fire" . . . pleading that he had fired the place himself.'

'Bare-faced hocus pocus'

The ruins of Borley Rectory were finally demolished in the spring of 1944 and the site levelled. An orchard and three modern bungalows now occupy the spot. During the demolition, Price took a *Life* magazine photographer and researcher Cynthia Ledsham to Borley, and by sheer fluke, the photographer captured on film a brick that was apparently 'levitated' by unseen forces – but was in fact thrown by a worker. *Life* published the photograph over a jokey caption, but Price, in his book *The end of Borley Rectory* (1946), claimed it as a final 'phenomenon'. Cynthia Ledsham was astounded, calling it 'the most bare-faced hocus pocus on the part of . . . Harry Price.'

The truth is that the haunting of Borley Rectory was the most bare-faced hocus pocus from start to finish, with Price feeding his craving for personal publicity from it in the most short sighted way. For, as was shown after his death, his shallow frauds could not hope to withstand investigation.

In a letter to Mr C.G. Glover in 1938, Price wrote: 'As regards your various criticisms, the alleged haunting of the rectory stands or falls not by the reports of our recent observers, but by the extraordinary happenings there of the last 50 years.'

But he wrote to Dr Dingwall in 1946 in reference to the occasion when a glass of water was 'changed' into ink: 'I agree that Mrs Foyster's wine [*sic*] trick was rather crude, but if you cut out the Foysters, the Bulls, the Smiths, etc., something still remains.' It is then logically left that the 'something' is the 'reports of our recent observers'.

As Dingwall, Goldney and Hall said: 'If one wished to dispose of the Borley hauntings on one small piece of paper merely by reference to Price's privately expressed opinions of the evidence', it would be necessary only to quote the two letter extracts in juxtaposition. However, one great irony remains. Despite the demolition of Price's pack of lies, ghost hunters of the 1960s and 1970s doggedly persisted in investigating the area. And they may just have stumbled on something truly paranormal – not at the rectory site, but in Borley church itself.

No end to Borley

Were Harry Price, his detractors and his defenders, chasing ghosts in the wrong place by concentrating on Borley Rectory? A strong case can be made for a genuine haunting across the road at Borley church, under investigation since the 1970s

IN ALL HIS BORLEY investigations and writings, Harry Price paid scant attention to the 12th-century church itself. He was aware of a story, told to him by Ethel Bull in 1929, that coffins in the Waldegrave family vault under the church had been mysteriously moved at some time during the 19th century, but he made little attempt to follow up the matter. Price may have missed his real chance to confront the paranormal. For, since the early 1970s, unexplained events in and around the church – many of them recorded on tape – have proved to be far more baffling than anything that happened in the old rectory.

The manor of 'Barlea' – the Anglo-Saxon for 'boar's pasture' – was mentioned in Domesday Book, when a wooden church served the locality. The south wall of the present church contains remnants of the flint and rubble building erected in the 12th century. The chancel, the north wall of the

Below: Borley church, the major part of which was constructed in the 15th century. Should the many who investigated the Borley Rectory hauntings have looked here instead?

nave, and the west tower were added in the 15th century, followed a hundred years later by the red brick south porch.

In the little churchyard itself, planted around with clipped yews and horse chestnut trees, lie the graves of the Bull family. Vandals have broken the stone cross on that of the Rev. Harry Bull, the Victorian rector who drowsed away his last days in the

summerhouse and reported seeing a ghostly nun and phantom coach. Geoffrey Croom-Hollingsworth, who runs a small psychical research group at Harlow, Essex, believes from his investigations that the cause of the rector's death in 1927 was syphilis. Advanced syphilis is accompanied by narcolepsy, a constant drowsiness, during which the sufferer hallucinates – a fact that would seem to explain the rector's 'visions' neatly. But Croom-Hollingsworth does not think this is the whole answer, for he and an assistant, Roy Potter, claim to have observed the phantom nun themselves for a period of about 12 minutes.

Croom-Hollingsworth came upon the Borley controversy in the 1960s and decided to examine the facts himself. He and his group began a series of vigils at Borley. Like subsequent investigators, they chose to keep watch at night to avoid interruption. Over a period of years, in differing weather conditions and at different times of year, they heard an assortment of noises: raps, heavy panting and the sound of furniture being moved. On one occasion while in the orchard, something huge and dark, 'like an animal', approached them between the fruit trees and banged loudly on the fence.

On another night, at about 3 a.m., the group heard 'laughter and merriment . . . which seemed to be coming up the road towards Borley church'. The night was misty, but there was sufficient light to see that nobody was in the roadway. Assuming that the voices were those of late-night

Previous page: the Enfield Parapsychical Research Group at Borley church. Ronald R. Russell (far right), a founding member, leans towards Price's side in the controversy over Borley's hauntings. But the group have found the church itself of most interest and have done many tests with cameras and sound equipment (right)

Above right: the vandalised grave of the Reverend Harry Bull in Borley churchyard. Harry's father built the nearby rectory that became famous as 'the most haunted house in England', so drawing attention away from the church

revellers, but puzzled by the direction of the sound, Roy Potter got into his car and coasted down the road towards Long Melford with his engine off. He met nobody. Using his walkie-talkie link with Croom-Hollingsworth, he arranged the experiment of shouting at various points along the Long Melford road to see if the sound carried. The listeners in the churchyard heard nothing. In an attempt to record similar noises, a tape recorder was set up in the porch of the church, while the group kept watch from a distance. Nobody was seen to enter the porch, but the group heard a loud crash and found the tape recorder 'pretty well battered'. The tape had been torn from its reels and lay in a tangle.

But it was the sighting of the nun that convinced the Harlow group that something was indeed strange about Borley. One clear night, Croom-Hollingsworth was standing in the orchard, looking towards the 'nun's walk':

Suddenly I saw her quite clearly, in a grey habit and cowl as she moved across the garden and through a hedge. I thought 'is somebody pulling my leg?' Roy was out in the roadway, the nearest of the group, and I shouted to him. The figure had disappeared into a modern garage, and I thought that was that, but

BBC as a basis for a television programme, are, Densham says, 'quite baffling'.

The first taping began at midnight during the winter months. After the church was carefully examined and searched, a cassette player was placed by the altar and the investigators sat at the other end of the church. The tape picked up a series of bumps and raps. Next, two tape recorders were locked up in the church, one by the altar and the other halfway down the aisle. Both picked up the unmistakable sound of a heavy door being opened and slammed shut, complete with the squeaking of a bolt. Neither the porch door nor the smaller chancel door had been opened – the researchers had kept watch on the church from outside – and examination showed that the chancel door bolt did not squeak.

The following week Densham and his team started their vigil at 12.30 a.m. They set up a sophisticated stereo tape with two high quality microphones, again placing one near the altar and the other halfway down the aisle; an additional cassette machine was positioned in front of the altar. Then half the team were locked into the church and the other half kept watch in the churchyard.

'Suddenly there was a curious change in the atmosphere,' said Densham. 'One of the team felt as if he was being watched, and we all felt very cold.' During the next few minutes the tapes picked up a clatter, as if something had been thrown down the aisle. There were also knockings, rappings, the sound of the door opening again – although both doors remained locked and bolted – and, chillingly, the sound of a human sigh. Afterwards, the team found that the small cassette recorder had jammed, and the tape

as Roy joined me we both saw her come out of the other side. She approached to about 12 feet [3 metres] from us, and we both saw her face, that of an elderly woman in her sixties, perhaps. We followed her as she seemed to glide over a dry ditch as if it wasn't there, before she disappeared into a pile of building bricks. Neither of us was frightened. It was an odd sensation, but peaceful and tranquil.

Not surprisingly in view of his experiences, Croom-Hollingsworth has little time for the critics who point to the discrepancies in Price's account of the haunting. On the other hand, he says,

I don't give a damn if Price invented things or not. The basic question is – is the place haunted? And you can take it from me it is. I have invented nothing. Roy and I saw the nun quite clearly for a period of about 12 minutes. . . .

Croom-Hollingsworth's determination impressed Denny Densham, a film director and cameraman. In 1974 he got permission to experiment with tape recorders in the church. The results, which were used by the

Above: the Waldegrave tomb, memorial to an old and influential Borley family. Local gossip had it that the Waldegrave coffins in the vault under the church were 'mysteriously moved' in the 19th century

Right: one of the stained glass windows of the church, dedicated to the Reverend Henry Bull. His retelling of the story of the ghostly nun of Borley Rectory gave a boost to the reputation of his family home as a haunted house

had been extracted and tangled up, as the Croom-Hollingsworth tape had been.

In July, the party visited Borley again. At 1.45 a.m., they felt a change in the atmosphere.

> We all felt watched, and a curious tingling sensation was felt; oddly enough the machines seemed to pick up a lot of static at this point. We recorded stealthy sounds near the altar, the sound of the door shutting again, a crash as of something being knocked over, and then the sound of hollow, heavy footsteps, like those of a very large man walking by the altar rail. We could not reproduce them normally: the floor there is of stone, heavily carpeted.

The observers then saw a glow of light near the chancel door, followed by a terrifying grunt. On this, their final visit, the team saw pinpoints of light in the curtains by one door, and heard the sound of a heavy crash. Densham said:

> Frankly, I am at a loss to explain what goes on at Borley. We made every effort to ensure that our legs weren't being pulled, and the tapes were new and untampered with. No theory I have tried to put forward seems to pan out. We tried leaving pencil and paper in the church, asked the thing to rap and so on, but it doesn't seem to be trying to communicate, unless the damage to the tapes and the throwing of invisible objects in our direction meant that it resented our presence. One's left with the feeling that whatever causes the phenomena is indifferent to or perhaps unaware of observers.

'Ectoplasm' in the churchyard

Since that summer of 1974, one of the most regular researchers at Borley has been Ronald R. Russell, a member of the Enfield Parapsychical Research Group and professional photographer. Frank Parry, an electrical engineer, and John Fay, a mechanical engineer, usually work with him. Russell has achieved odd results while taking photographs of the area with an Agfa CC2 I camera, in which the film is contained in a cassette and processed in the Agfa laboratory.

> Sandwiched between perfectly normal frames we got 'ectoplasmic' stuff in the churchyard, shadows where no shadows should be, and a thin light near the north door. As a photographer I'm at a loss to explain this as camera or film malfunction.

Parry has used a graphic analyser, an eight-channel recording machine with slider controls that adjust pitch and level, cut out interference, and enable its operator to 'pinpoint' sounds. As Russell said:

> We have recorded hundreds of extraordinary noises, footsteps, crashes and so on. On one occasion we located a

The altar in Borley church. In 1974 some strange sounds – including raps, crashes and mysterious footsteps – were picked up here on a cassette recorder

centre of disturbance near the Waldegrave tomb; it was tangible, like a swirling column of energy. When you passed your hand through it you felt a sort of crackle, like static electricity. On another occasion we heard a deep, grunting voice, which reminded me irresistibly of Lee Marvin singing *Wandering Star*.

Russell is inclined to side with the Price faction on Borley, though he concedes that Price may have embellished facts.

> I think there may be three basic factors at work here. First, the nun. There would be nothing odd about a nun in the household of a Catholic family like the Waldegraves. Perhaps the apparition which Mr Croom-Hollingsworth saw is simply a psychic record of some such person. Secondly, there seems to be some sort of power concentrated in the church itself. It is on the intersection of two ley lines, and when you try dowsing in the church the rod practically twists from your hands. Thirdly, I would suggest that the power is boosted by the presence of observers, and also that it waxes and wanes with the seasons; in January phenomena are sporadic, while in August they seem to be at full flood.

The church authorities are non-committal, preferring to avoid discussion of the topic. But in the parish guidebook, under the heading 'ghosts', is a footnote:

> There are, of course, those who suggest the church itself is haunted. Many old churches and buildings have noises and chill areas which some would classify as ghostly, but those who have lived long in the village and we who worship in the church have not experienced anything which would support such thoughts. . . . Visitors should please remember that this is God's house and treat it with reverence.

Enfield: the trouble begins

In the late 1970s a family in north London became the focus of a poltergeist attack – and a great deal of publicity. One of the investigators, GUY LYON PLAYFAIR, tells the story of the Enfield poltergeist

THE ENFIELD POLTERGEIST first made itself known at about 9.30 p.m. on 31 August 1977. Mrs Harper, a divorcee in her mid forties, was putting two of her four children to bed in one of the three upstairs bedrooms of her semi-detached council house in Enfield, north London, when Janet, aged 11, and one of her brothers, aged 10, complained that something was making a 'shuffling noise'. Shortly afterwards, Mrs Harper was astonished to see a heavy chest of drawers moving about 18 inches (46 centimetres) along the floor, well beyond the reach of either child's feet. She pushed it back into place, but it moved again, as before, and this time it refused to budge when she tried to move it. At about the same time, there were

As objects fly about the room the Harper children show obvious signs of distress (below), with the exception of Janet (centre), who merely smiles. She seemed to be the focus of the poltergeist activity – the very existence of which was hotly disputed even among the psychical researchers who investigated the case. But whatever really took place in that council house in Enfield, in north London, the world's press seized on the story with avidity (bottom)

four loud knocks that seemed to come from the party wall.

Mrs Harper, as she recalled about a week later, began literally to shake with fear. She was convinced, as were her usually exuberant children, that something was going on that did not have a normal explanation. Her immediate reaction was just to get out of the house. She thought of calling on her brother John Burcombe, who lived six doors up the road. But her immediate neighbours, Vic and Peggy Nottingham, still had their lights on, so it was to them she first turned for help.

The knocking sounds began again as Vic and his son were making a thorough search of the house. As Vic walked down the stairs, the noise seemed to come from the wall right beside him. He immediately searched both front and back gardens, but saw no sign of anybody.

They called the police at about 11 p.m., and in the presence of one of the two constables who were soon on the scene, a chair in the living room slid along the floor more or less as the chest of drawers had done a couple of hours earlier. WPC Carolyn Heeps later signed a written statement to this effect, thereby testifying to at least one genuine phenomenon on the very first day of the case.

The following day, marbles and pieces of toy brick began to fly around the house at great speed. Some, when picked up, were found to be unusually hot. This aerial bombardment went on for three days, and by

THE ENFIELD POLTERGEIST

GHOST STORY

GHOST HUNTERS CLASH OVER MYSTERY OF SPOOK OR SPOOF KIDS

esotera

Der Spuk von Enfield: Poltergeist-Phänomene wie nie zuvor

GEHEIMZINNIGE KLOPGEEST Mensen en meubelen vliegen door de kamer

BUMPS THAT HAVE BOFFINS BAFFLED

Boffins baffled by poltergeist

DAILY Mirror

Sunday 4 September both the Harpers and the Nottinghams were at their wits' end. By then, they had called the police again, sought help from the local vicar and from a local lady who claimed to be a medium, but all to no avail. The Harpers had never heard of the Society for Psychical Research (SPR), and the only course of action they could think of was to call the *Daily Mirror*. They were not seeking publicity; they just wanted somebody to tell them what on earth was going on.

Reporter Douglas Bence and photographer Graham Morris spent Sunday evening with the Harpers. Nothing happened until just after they left at about 2.30 on Monday morning, when the toy brick blitz promptly restarted. Peggy Nottingham's father called them back just as they were driving off.

A violent reaction

Morris, a veteran Fleet Street freelancer with experience of several violent street demonstrations, had always managed to dodge flying bricks while working. But not this time. As he stood in the living-room doorway, with everybody visible through his wide-angle lens, a sharp-cornered toy brick hit him hard on the forehead at the moment he pressed his shutter. (When I met him a week later, he still had a large bruise.)

Senior reporter George Fallows was sufficiently impressed by his colleagues' experience to follow up the story himself. It was he who explained to the Harpers that what was happening was something known as poltergeist activity, and he suggested calling in the SPR. He also asked Mrs Harper if she wanted to move house, knowing that some council tenants have, in fact, created 'haunted houses' in the hope of jumping the rehousing queue. Her reply was 'definitely not!'

The SPR became involved in the case as the result of a series of coincidences. Maurice

The Harper family and their neighbours await the next attack by flying objects. Left to right are: neighbours Mrs Nottingham and her son Gary, Mrs Harper and her children – John, Rose and Janet

Below and below right: a settee flies, ending in a disastrous heap at the other side of the room

Grosse, a businessman and inventor, had been a member for barely a year despite a life-long interest in the paranormal. He had joined after what seemed to him an unusual string of inexplicable events that followed the death of his youngest daughter Janet after a road accident in 1976, and he had repeatedly asked the SPR secretary to give him a case of his own to investigate, preferably within reach of his north London home. Therefore, when George Fallows telephoned from Enfield, secretary Eleanor O'Keeffe lost no time in calling Grosse, who in turn went at once to the scene, arriving within a couple of hours of Fallows's call.

He witnessed nothing paranormal on his first visit. He was certain of one thing, however: the atmosphere of fear in the Harpers' home was real. That, he reckoned, could not be faked.

It was on 8 September that he had his first close encounter with a poltergeist. On that day, the SPR met to hear a lecture, arranged several months previously, by its librarian Mr Nicholas Clark-Lowes. His subject – poltergeists. At discussion time, Grosse leapt to his feet to announce that he was investigating one right now, and would appreciate some help.

Enter Maurice Grosse

There was not a single volunteer. I happened to be sitting next to Grosse, but did not even volunteer myself. I had seen plenty of poltergeist activity during the years I lived in Brazil, but I had written up and published all my cases and moved on to other interests.

'Let me know if you get really stuck,' I said, without much enthusiasm, as I headed for the local pub with some friends. But Grosse went straight to Enfield, and between 10 and 11 p.m. he witnessed more paranormal activity than most SPR members have seen in a lifetime. It was just three days after his début as an investigator of such matters.

First, a marble whizzed through the air towards him; it was definitely not thrown by any of the children. Next, the chimes on the living-room wall began to sway to and fro, which, he found, they did not normally do even when the doorbell connected to them was rung. He then saw a door open and close by itself with nobody anywhere near it – and not just once, but three or four times. This was followed by an incident identical to one I later witnessed myself, in which a shirt hopped off a pile of clothing on the kitchen table and fell to the floor. Finally, Grosse experienced one of the most frequently reported of poltergeist symptoms: a sudden cold breeze that seemed to move up from his feet to his head.

Janet Harper always seemed to be near the site of the action – although she was not always near enough to have caused the incidents by normal means – and Grosse therefore kept a close eye on her at all times. She had certainly not opened or closed the door, levitated the shirt, moved the chimes or, presumably, produced the cold breeze. However, she certainly played a few tricks of her own later in the case, as any experienced psychical researcher would expect since children are, after all, accustomed to imitating what they observe. In a French radio interview in 1982, Janet readily admitted to having done this. She wanted to see, she said, if the investigators would catch her out. And she added: 'And they always did.'

On 10 September 1977, the Enfield case made the front page of the *Daily Mirror*. The story was picked up by LBC radio (a London-based station), and that evening Grosse, Mrs Harper and Mrs Nottingham took part in a two-and-a-half-hour *Night Line* programme devoted to it. The following day, there was a detailed account in BBC Radio 4's lunchtime news broadcast by reporter Rosalind Morris, who gave her own first-hand impressions of a night in what the *Daily Mirror* had justifiably

When informed about the strange goings-on at Enfield the Society for Psychical Research suggested that businessman Maurice Grosse (right) take up the case. It seemed that no one else was interested at that stage. Shortly afterwards, media reports convinced author Guy Lyon Playfair (below) that what was happening was genuine – and he joined Grosse in what was to prove a lengthy and controversial investigation. Playfair's book *This house is haunted* (1980) is a sympathetic view of the Harpers' nightmare

called 'The House of Strange Happenings'.

It became clear to me that the Enfield case could prove to be an exceptional one. It was already one of the very few to have been witnessed by an SPR member on the spot and within days of its inception. So I telephoned Maurice Grosse and offered my help, which was readily accepted. We agreed that since poltergeist cases seldom lasted more than a few weeks, we should take this opportunity to see a case through to its end. Had we known it would last for 14 months, we might have thought otherwise.

Playing the rapping game

I witnessed a relatively minor incident on my first visit, on 11 September. As Graham Morris and I stood outside Janet's bedroom, frequently looking through the open door, a marble hit the linoleum floor right in front of my feet. It did not roll or bounce. The sound it made could be repeated only by deliberately *placing* it on the floor, which the two of us could clearly see that nobody had done.

Subsequent events were far more dramatic. The knocking on the walls and floors became an almost nightly occurrence, and its source seemed to have intelligence of a kind, since it would rap out answers to simple questions: one rap for no and two for yes. One evening, during a lengthy 'rap session', Grosse asked how many years ago the supposed entity had lived in the house, as it had previously claimed to have done. There followed no less than 53 raps, heard and recorded on tape by both of us while everybody was in full view. Shortly afterwards, however, the rapper began to beat out non-sensical rhythms, whereupon Grosse exclaimed: 'Are you having a game with me?'

Exactly two seconds later, a cardboard box full of soft toys and cushions took off from a corner of the bedroom, flew over the

bed and hit Grosse squarely on the forehead. It had travelled about 8 feet (2.5 metres), in his full view, and I was able to witness at least the end of its inexplicable flight. A BBC television team failed to replicate this.

On another occasion, I witnessed a large armchair slide along the floor after Janet – who had just got up from it and was walking towards me – and then crash over backwards. This, together with about 30 other incidents witnessed by either Grosse or myself, was recorded on tape at the time. (We indirectly witnessed several more, and reckon, at a very conservative estimate, that around 2000 inexplicable incidents were observed during the case, by about 30 different people.)

Photographer Graham Morris spent much of his spare time attempting to photograph something paranormal as it actually took place, which he eventually did; I believe him to be the first professional photographer to have done this.

He soon found, however, that poltergeists are camera-shy. Moreover, they are skilled saboteurs. On one occasion, when he had fitted three separate cameras with flashguns so that they could be fired together by remote control, all three flashes were apparently drained of power shortly after being recharged. Eventually, after much patience, he managed to take two sequences on his motor-driven camera, with high-speed flash recharger, which still await satisfactory explanation.

Morris was not the only professional to suffer mechanical failure of his equipment. A team of enthusiastic ghost hunters from the electrical firm Pye of Cambridge brought along a Newvicon infra-red-sensitive television camera, with which we hoped to do some remote monitoring of the bedroom. The company's chief demonstrator carefully checked all his equipment before entering the house, but when he began filming his

Above: for four days two *Daily Mirror* reporters and two of its photographers joined Grosse and Playfair's vigil in the Harper household. On one occasion reporter Douglas Bence and photographer David Thorpe were standing just outside an empty bedroom when they heard 'an almighty bang'. They investigated and found that a metal-framed chair had apparently flung itself 4 feet (1.2 metres) from its original position. Shortly after they left the room they heard another crash and discovered that the chair had moved to yet another position

videotape deck behaved very oddly. All the lights on the machine went on at once, and the tape became jammed so firmly that the entire deck had to be dismantled to free it. And almost the same thing happened later to one of Rosalind Morris's BBC reel-tape recorders.

Grosse and I lost count of the number of times our cassette tapes were found to be mysteriously broken, or wiped wholly or partially clean. I also discovered that one of my recorders had a metal part bent inside it, to the complete bewilderment of the repairman, while on one memorable evening the machine disappeared altogether for about an hour, reappearing underneath a heavy dressing-table that had fallen forwards, landing on Janet's bed and nearly squashing her.

The activity soon became so regular and intense that Grosse and I were faced with a

dilemma: were we encouraging it just by being there? Should we go away and hope it would stop? We did this twice, and were urgently asked to come back on both occasions. It has been suggested that a poltergeist outbreak is a form, conscious or unconscious, of seeking attention. This may be so, yet the Harpers – who gained the attention of the world's press, radio and television – gave the impression at all times that they just wanted a return to normal life. For the researcher, another dilemma is that one cannot learn more about poltergeists – and find ways of helping families afflicted by them – without investigating them on the spot.

Grosse and I did what Mrs Harper and her brother John Burcombe repeatedly asked us to do: stay with them and try to end the phenomena. We sought the help of several mediums, all of whom achieved a degree of reduction in the activity. Indeed one of them, a young Dutchman named Dono Gmelig-Meyling, may have been responsible for the

Although ostensibly paranormal phenomena took place in almost every part of the Harper household, the girls' bedroom seemed to be favoured most often. Both girls were said to be pulled out of bed by an invisible force (below and bottom, far left), while furniture seemed to take on a life of its own, such as the dressing table that nearly squashed Janet flat (bottom left). Bedclothes were often flung back or twisted (bottom right) as if by a very strong hand

eventual ending of the case, in October 1978. We also were able to stop the phenomena, although only temporarily, by separating members of the family.

While the furniture continued to fly around, we felt that it would be in the interests of science to record as much data as possible to enable others to expand their knowledge of mental states, physical systems, and the now evident connection between the two that poltergeist phenomena indicate. We had no luck with psychologists, several of whom came to Enfield (and left without making any useful suggestions), or with local doctors and psychiatrists. We did manage to have Janet spend six weeks in the Maudsley Hospital in south London, where she underwent extensive tests for any signs of physical or mental abnormality – but none were found.

We were luckier with physicists, and Professor J. B. Hasted, head of the physics department at Birkbeck College, University of London, responded at once to our appeal for technical help by assigning his assistant David Robertson to the case for a whole week.

In psychical research, one tends to find what one seeks. The sceptic is confronted with evidence that only adds to his scepticism, whereas the mind of the open-minded tends to be opened even wider. This was certainly the case with Robertson, who already had considerable experience of paranormal physical phenomena in the form of metal bending, a field in which Professor Hasted had been working in a serious and thorough way since 1974.

A few days after David Robertson had moved into the Harpers' home, an exceptionally bizarre series of events took place, in front of several witnesses.

When a north London family seemed to be at the centre of a poltergeist attack, several experts were called in to assess the authenticity of the phenomena, but it quickly became obvious that the case posed more questions than it answered

POLTERGEIST ACTIVITY is a syndrome – a coming together of separate events to form one collective manifestation. We have not yet identified all the symptoms, but the syndrome has been with us for a long time. In the first century AD, Suetonius described an occupant of a former home of the Emperor Augustus as being thrown out of bed, clothes and all, by 'a sudden occult force'. Exactly the same thing happened nearly 2000 years later to Janet Harper in Enfield. In fact, it happened several times, once even including the mattress.

The Enfield case included examples of every major form of poltergeist symptom previously recorded. The most frequently observed or reported were: knocking sounds, movement of objects large or small, interference with bedclothes, appearance of water on floors, outbreaks of fire (followed by their inexplicable extinguishing), human levitation, interference with electrical systems, and a variety of altered states of consciousness suggestive of trance or 'possession'.

A full account of this activity would fill several books, even if it were limited to testimony from reliable witnesses. But the events of one day – 15 December 1977 – stand out from the rest.

It is often suggested that poltergeist activity is associated with young children close to the age of puberty. This is not always true; cases are on record in which no children were involved. But it was certainly true of the Enfield case, for 15 December was the day of Janet's first menstruation.

For some days prior to this, an extraordinary raucous male voice had been making itself heard, apparently emitting from her throat, over which Janet herself repeatedly stated she had no conscious control. The voice claimed several identities, all of them male and none of them verifiable, with two notable exceptions. Whether it was a manifestation of a secondary personality or an independent entity cannot be established. At times, its conversation closely resembled that of Janet in her normal state. But occasionally it provided true information not known to her. It gave an account of the manner and place of death of the former occupant of the house, who had died before Janet was born, the details subsequently being verified.

Whatever the true origin of the information provided by Janet's bass voice, it gave the investigators the chance to address the presumed source of the poltergeist disturbances directly. As soon as physicist David

Enfield: whatever next?

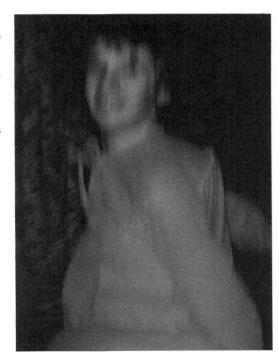

Above: kitchen furniture was thrown about by the invisible agency at Enfield. Here (left to right) Rose, John and Janet Harper pose beside the havoc – but only Janet can raise a smile for the photographer. Her frequent equanimity has led to various speculations: was she insensitive to the apparent horrors that surrounded her family; was she the focus of it all – or was she the trickster who kept investigators and the media on the hop? Whatever the truth of the matter, Janet was certainly at the centre of much of the phenomena – such as being apparently whirled about by invisible forces (right)

Robertson joined the team, he lost no time in attempting some practical experiments. Hoping to be able to observe human levitation, he asked Janet to bounce up and down on her bed and attempt to take off. He was then ordered out of the room by the 'voice', and when he heard Janet call out that she was being 'levitated', he found he could not open the door. A bed had apparently been pushed against it.

Rose, Janet's elder sister, became alarmed and went to fetch her neighbour Peggy Nottingham. Janet then attempted another levitation, again with the door closed, and subsequently claimed that not only had she risen into the air, but had passed through the wall of her semi-detached house into Peggy's

have seen them. (I myself subsequently tried to repeat this incident, and found it possible, though very difficult and quite perilous!)

This was not all the tradesman saw. When he arrived outside the house, he could see Janet through the upper bedroom window, as he put it: 'floating horizontally across the room', accompanied by books, dolls and cushions that seemed as if they were being whirled around on pieces of elastic. The tradesman's evidence is of interest since he did not know the Harpers and did not believe a word of what neighbours had told him concerning their poltergeist. What he saw that day made him change his mind, and left a profound and lasting impression on him.

Much of his testimony was supported by

bedroom on the other side of it.

Nobody believed her. Mrs Nottingham had already witnessed a good deal of strange activity since the first day of the case, in August 1977 – some of it in her own house. But this was a bit too much. She calmly told Janet to try it again, then went back to her house, where – she later admitted – she half expected to find Janet.

Janet was not there, but on the carpet beside her bed Mrs Nottingham found a book (entitled *Fun and games for children*) belonging to Janet. It had certainly not been there when she had made her bed, and Janet had not been in her house.

Robertson then handed Janet a large and heavy plastic-covered sofa cushion and asked her to make it 'disappear'. He was hoping to obtain direct evidence for one of the most controversial of all alleged paranormal phenomena – teleportation, the passage of solid matter through solid matter.

A local tradesman later testified that at this time he was walking along the road towards the Harpers' house when he suddenly saw a large red cushion appear on its roof, in his direct line of vision. Had anybody opened the bedroom window and leaned out to place it on the roof, he would certainly

Poltergeists – whether they be 'unruly spirits' as used to be believed, or some powerful subconscious exertion from a human mind – turn the rational, everyday world upside down. Bedframes may appear at the bottom of a flight of stairs, as at Enfield (above left), or drawers may be wrenched out of a bureau (above) by an invisible agency. The 'normal' response to such phenomena is that someone in the household is deliberately faking the ostensibly paranormal effects. But research has frequently indicated that many poltergeist cases are genuinely inexplicable in normal terms

another eyewitness, school-crossing supervisor Mrs Hazel Short, who was on duty right across the road from the Harpers' house. She too insisted that she had seen Janet 'definitely horizontal' in the air, and from her description the investigators later calculated that Janet must have been about 28 inches (70 centimetres) above her bed, the mattress of which was hard and firm.

A further witness, contacted several weeks later, was apparently still too confused and frightened by what she had seen to make a statement. Whatever really happened in Enfield on 15 December 1977, several witnesses undoubtedly saw a good deal they could not explain.

Several other members of the Society for Psychical Research (SPR), in addition to chief investigator Maurice Grosse, David Robertson and myself, made visits to the Enfield house during the case, but almost none of them witnessed anything they considered paranormal. This inevitably led some of them to cast doubts on the evidence presented by Grosse and myself at the 1978 SPR international conference in Cambridge, and subsequently led to considerable controversy about the case.

How good is the evidence for the reality of

the Enfield poltergeist? Whatever its quality, which ranges from unverifiable subjective reports of 'apparitions' to signed written statements by a number of responsible people, it cannot be denied that more documentary evidence was gathered on this case than on any previous one of its type. About 200 hours of tape recording were made, and a special committee of the SPR carried out a lengthy follow-up investigation, during which most of the principal witnesses were re-questioned.

In camera and on film

The photographic evidence has tended to add to the controversy surrounding the case, although much of it is not quite up to professional standards. Freelance photographer Graham Morris spent much of his spare time in the house, over a period of several weeks, hoping to record paranormal activity as it happened, and two of the many sequences he obtained on his remote-controlled motor-driven camera are of special interest. One shows two pillows, one of which is in mid-air and the other on the floor, but still, apparently, in motion. The other shows Janet's bedclothes seemingly being pulled off her, while at the same time the curtain beside her bed twists into a tight spiral and seems to blow into the room – although the window behind it was closed.

This curtain-twisting phenomenon was observed several times by Janet – who claimed that it once wrapped itself around her neck as if trying to strangle her – and also by her mother. She, it must be emphasised, was ready at all times to denounce her daughter if she were caught playing tricks, as she occasionally was later in the case.

While gathering the evidence (and doing their best to stop the activity for the family's sake), the investigators made what attempts they could to obtain evidence of some scientific value. With the co-operation of one of Britain's leading phoneticians, Maurice Grosse managed to record Janet's deep voice on a laryngograph, an instrument that registers patterns made by radio-frequency waves as they pass through the larynx. The results confirmed what a speech therapist had

Poltergeists are famous arsonists – and also conscientious extinguishers of the fires they start. At Enfield there were several fiery occurrences, such as the severe burning of two pound notes (right) and a fire that flared up between kitchen fittings and then mysteriously died out, leaving a noticeable scorch mark (far right).

already deduced: that the deep voice was not produced by Janet's normal vocal equipment, but by the so-called false vocal folds. Actors can learn to speak with these (to produce a gravelly voice, for instance), but for most people it is a painful process. Yet Janet, or the poltergeist, could keep it up for three hours without her normal voice being affected at all. It is also worth noting that abnormally deep voices coming from young girls are a recognised symptom of poltergeist cases. Numerous examples are given in T. K. Oesterreich's book *Possession, demoniacal and other* (1966), such as that of 11-year-old Dinah Dagg through whom 'a deep gruff voice, as of an old man . . . instantly replied in a language which cannot be repeated here.'

At Enfield the closest we came to a properly controlled scientific experiment was David Robertson's paranormal metal bending test. He attached a piece of metal to a strain gauge and a chart recorder, so that any strain on the metal would be recorded on paper. During the two-hour session, while Janet was under continuous observation and not touching the metal, several sharp deflections appeared on the chart; Robertson saw

Right: an invisible force apparently hurls a pillow from one of the girls' beds to join another on the floor. However, critics have pointed out that this sequence does not prove the existence of a poltergeist – the pillows could, they say, have been thrown by one of the girls

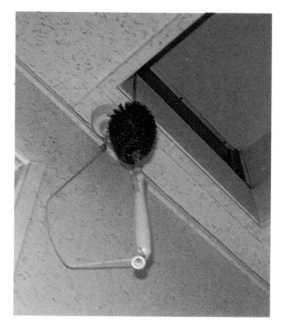

Right: investigator Maurice Grosse found the Harpers' lavatory brush securely knotted up with the light flex. Certainly the brush had been in its usual place the last time any of the adults had been in the toilet and, as far as they knew, none of the children had been there after that. Is this evidence of paranormality – or, as one SPR critic suggests, had one of the children sneaked in and tied up the brush by standing on the toilet seat?

the metal bend through about 15° before it finally snapped in half.

In 1982, four years after the Enfield poltergeist disturbances had ended, Janet took part in a strictly controlled laboratory experiment at Birkbeck College, London, supervised by Professor J. B. Hasted, head of the physics department, and observed by four others including Robertson and Grosse. The purpose of the experiment, which was one of a series using several different subjects, was to examine the possibility that certain people can lose weight paranormally – a phenomenon that, if genuine, is clearly related to that of levitation. And since Janet had already been reported as having levitated, she seemed a natural choice as subject.

She sat on a chair placed on a specially constructed platform that functioned as a weighing scale. This was connected to a computer and a chart recorder, which monitored any change in weight. If someone stands on this platform and jumps into the air, the chart will show a peak above the stable 'baseline' trace, and this will be followed at once by a downward deflection on the chart when the body lands. However, the

apparatus began to behave abnormally very shortly after Janet sat on it.

The observers were surprised to find that, although Janet had sat perfectly still on the chair, the pen of the chart recorder had moved steadily upwards for about 30 seconds, and during this time it had also recorded several sharp peaks. Two of these surges were so strong that the pen had run off the top of the paper. According to the chart, Janet had lost about 2 pounds (1 kilogram) in weight for about 30 seconds. 'I cannot explain this in normal terms,' said Hasted.

Professor Hasted points out that the experiments he conducted with Janet are not proof of levitation (and although she apparently lost weight paranormally she did not rise from the chair into the air). He thinks it possible, however, that in view of her record as a metal bender (sometimes without touching the metal), she may have been exerting a psychokinetic influence on the piano wires on which the platform was suspended. Indeed, the brief bursts on the chart were similar to those recorded during successful metal bending sessions with other subjects.

Whatever the explanation, Janet seems to have had a paranormal effect on the weighing machine. It is gratifying that some positive results have emerged from the destructive chaos of the Enfield poltergeist case, which put a severe strain on both the Harper family and the SPR investigators who stayed with them until the disturbances ended in October 1978. If future poltergeist victims are as co-operative as the Harpers, and scientists follow the lead of the likes of Professor Hasted, we shall surely learn more about how the human mind can, in certain states, apparently influence solid objects.

Enfield on trial

The saga of the Enfield poltergeist may have begun with genuinely paranormal phenomena, but was it kept 'alive' by the very presence of its investigators? Several of the case's many critics believe this was so; one of them, ANITA GREGORY, sums up

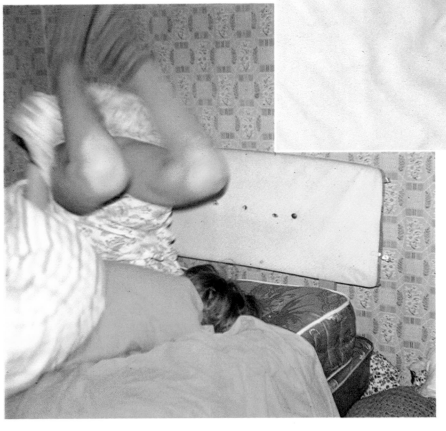

GUY LYON PLAYFAIR, in his book *This house is haunted* (1980), has written an interesting and lively account of mysterious happenings in the house of the unfortunate Harper family, giving his impressions of what he and his co-investigator Maurice Grosse felt went on there. It is my opinion that Guy Playfair and Maurice Grosse may perhaps have experienced genuine paranormal happenings, particularly towards the beginning of the case. However, neither anything I saw, or experienced, when I visited the house, nor the content of either Mr Playfair's book or Mr Grosse's defence of it suggests to me that there is evidence here for anything other than a chaotic – and at times distressing – state of affairs.

Top: Janet in a trance. As she was the focus for the alleged poltergeist activity, a certain amount of dissociation might have been expected; but perhaps the attention of the investigators helped create ideal conditions for such a state

Above: Janet being flung out of bed by the 'entity'. Critics have observed, however, that she was an extremely athletic girl and could have jumped from her bed to the floor

To begin with, like all the other researchers, I was excluded from the children's bedroom where the phenomena were supposed to occur. We would all stand or sit on the landing or in adjoining rooms, waiting: then there would be a thump and a squeal, everyone would dash in and see Janet sitting on the floor, the claim being that the 'entity' had thrown her out of bed. By way of evidence we were assured that Janet could not possibly have jumped that far; however, not only were the bedroom walls decorated with certificates testifying to Janet's athletic prowess, but of course there was no need for her to jump at all: a thump on the floor would have sufficed.

Nor was my impression that the girls were play-acting lessened in the least when, as a special favour, I was eventually allowed in the girls' bedroom when phenomena were supposed to be actually happening. I had to stand facing the door, covering my head with the girls' quilted dressing gowns and other garments hanging there – while, amid much giggling, slippers were shied at my head. I made it more than clear that I did not regard the incidents as anything other than a game, and I felt convinced that the girls were rather relieved that I, at least, was treating this as a joke. My lighter approach – I told the girls that all good poltergeists go to bed at 11 p.m., for example – was never held against me by the family, who always welcomed me most cordially, nor by the 'voices' themselves, who allowed me into the sanctuary when 'true believers' were excluded.

I found the 'voices' wholly unconvincing

Left, below and below right: a sequence of photographs taken by a remote controlled camera at intervals of less than a second apparently shows Janet's bedclothes being pulled off her while a curtain blows – in a tight spiral – into the room, although the window was shut. However, sceptic Melvin Harris points out that the curtain is not blowing – it was merely hit by the bedclothes, which could have been easily thrown to one side by Janet. But how was the curtain twisted so quickly?

of voice production to patients who, for example, have lost their vocal cords as a result of operations. She laughed at the notion that Janet's gruff voice was anything remotely paranormal, and suggested that a child could quite easily teach herself to talk like that. I am not an expert in this field myself, but I have yet to be convinced that there is even a case to answer. Moreover, so far as I know, these voices never said anything that was at all paranormal, in the sense of being true but unknown to the children.

The way Mr Playfair presents his data is, as I have pointed out, somewhat chaotic, and the absence of an index in his book makes it hard to trace any particular theme or person. At times the writing is positively confusing. Just by reading the book it is impossible to form an accurate picture of the precise course of the investigation. For instance, I took physicist Dave Robertson of Birkbeck College, University of London, and some video equipment (by arrangement with Professor Hasted, head of the physics department at Birkbeck) up to Enfield on 15 January 1978. Yet *This house is haunted* gives no clear picture of what was or was not achieved that night, using the monitoring equipment. Towards the end of his book Mr Playfair tells his readers that it was decided to set up video equipment so that the bedroom could be

as anything other than childish play-acting. Almost invariably the children would cover their mouths with blankets or sheets, or simply avert their faces while producing this 'phenomenon'. Maurice Grosse actually believed that the expletives uttered (which, when addressed to me, at least, were punctuated by giggles) were proof of supernatural origin. Where, I was asked, would nicely brought up girls get such words from?

The deep, hoarse voices were originally elicited in response to exceedingly leading questions by Maurice Grosse, who asked the 'entity' to speak to him – and the first voice 'was produced within minutes of being requested.' Moreover, no evidence has been offered that the 'voices' were continuous for two or three hours on end as was frequently claimed. To demonstrate such continuity would require a great deal of scientific work, showing the proportions of 'voices' to 'silence' over prolonged periods, which could then be duly analysed by qualified physiologists.

I must say that I never heard the voices in anything other than quite short snatches. I described what I had heard to a senior hospital consultant who has extensive experience of teaching the various techniques

Below: psychical researcher and lecturer Anita Gregory. As a council member of the SPR, she visited Enfield – and was not impressed with what she saw, believing the children to be enjoying themselves fooling the investigators – although the case may indeed have had paranormal origins

viewed without the girls' knowledge. He then goes on to say:

It seemed like a great idea at the time, but it was a total flop. No sooner were Maurice [Grosse] and David [Robertson] out of the house than Janet hopped out of bed for no apparent reason and peered through the keyhole of the back bedroom, and by a particularly unfortunate coincidence the TV monitor and revolving recorder reel happened to be in direct line with the keyhole. Janet saw them and . . . realised we were playing a trick on her. So nothing happened. Janet later told me she had suspected our trick at once.

We finally decided that Janet had to

get out of the house. . . . She left home on 16 June 1978. . . .

Did they really wait until June 1978 before trying to monitor the bedroom where most of the poltergeist activity was supposed to take place? And what of the video recording that Dave Robertson took *before* Janet knew he was doing so, and in which she can be seen bending a spoon and trying to bend a thick metal bar in a thoroughly normal manner – by force – and then bouncing up and down on the bed making little flapping movements with both hands?

Mr John Burcombe, Mrs Harper's brother, and Mrs Nottingham, a neighbour, with both of whom I frequently had long talks, seemed to me to be sensible and reliable witnesses. On 23 December 1977 Mr Burcombe told me that he thought that Janet had taught herself how to talk in a deep voice,

Right: the word 'ghosts' and some numbers written by Janet 'in her sleep'. Automatic, or dissociated, writing is not in itself proof that the writer is psychic, and this, say some critics, is not even proof that Janet was asleep as claimed

Below: Matthew Manning – himself once a poltergeist victim – visits the Harpers. He gave them sympathy but, as something of a 'psychic superstar', his interest might have encouraged the children to prolong their case by faking the phenomena

and that she thoroughly enjoyed misleading strangers (like most mischievous children). On 15 January 1978 I had a talk with Mrs Nottingham, who told me that she thought that what was going on at that time was 'pure nonsense', and only being kept going by the interest of the investigators. But she stressed over and over again Maurice Grosse's great kindness towards the family, to which I myself can also testify. He was almost like a father to them, taking an interest in the children's homework, helping with holidays, for example. I made notes of these conversations at the time and, within a few days, circulated them in reports to various colleagues to ensure that there would be a contemporary record of them. Mr Grosse now says that in 1981 Mr Burcombe and Mrs Nottingham denied that they ever said these things to me. I am afraid we will just have to leave this as a clash of testimony.

Mr Grosse also claimed that Mr Playfair had presented 'abundant evidence' for paranormal happenings in the Enfield case. As I see it, he has done nothing of the kind. What he has done is to produce a readable and

entertaining book containing assorted claims (of varying degrees of persuasiveness), but it is, as I wrote in my review of it in the SPR's *Journal*, 'far too sketchy, impressionistic, unsystematic, imprecise, ambiguous, and confusing, to be seen as a contribution to *research*'.

In challenging my views of the Enfield case in a letter to the SPR's *Journal*, Mr Grosse even went so far as to suggest that I was not prepared to admit the very existence of the phenomena that the SPR was founded to study. Now I believe that this is a total and important misunderstanding, of both my own position and that of the society.

To start with the lesser of these two: I personally have been one of the earliest and most persistent exponents of the view that many members, even including the founders, of the SPR have been at fault in belittling – to an unreasonable degree – some very sound evidence for physical phenomena. I have made no secret of this view, and have frequently expressed this in print. Specifically, as regards Mr Playfair's book, I wrote that it 'does provide testimony which I personally accept as being sincere, and some of which it is reasonable to accept as competent, for paranormal movement of objects, particularly in the earlier phases of the case'. Mr Grosse does not improve his case by attributing to me views contrary to those I have often expressed. In fact, I do consider that there is, on record, good evidence for the existence of physical phenomena – but not in the Enfield case. It is precisely because the matter is of some importance, particularly to those who think that there is a good case for physical paranormality to be made, that poor cases should not be paraded as good ones.

There is, as regards the Enfield case, a certain amount of testimony – some of it quite impressive and reassuring – but there is no real *evidence*. And, above all, there is no convincing analysis of the alleged phenomena that would be acceptable to a critical and careful psychical researcher.

Haunted
Scotland

Turning in his grave

Why does the ghost of the wretched Alexander Gillan linger at the site of his execution on a lonely Scottish moor? Was he innocent of the murder for which he was ignominiously hanged?

THE LOW-LYING COAST of Morayshire, around the mouth of the River Spey in Scotland, has always been a bleak and desolate place, a natural breeding ground for stories of the supernatural. There is a black dog with 'eyes like cogies' (whisky tumblers) that prowls through the local forests; the Red Fisherman who foretells death; and the 'Auld Guidman', once the local landlord, who still guards the Bog of Gight with a medieval claymore (two-edged broadsword).

The best known story, as convincing now as it was 170 years ago, is of the ghost of Alexander Gillan that is said to stalk the Muir of Stynie. Apparently, even Crown Forestry workers and gamekeepers avoid this area at night for fear of meeting his ghost on a cart track known as 'Gillan's Way'.

Alexander Gillan was a farm labourer who lived alone in the hamlet of Lhanbryde. One story has it that he was an Irish immigrant, disliked and distrusted by his neighbours,

The Muir of Stynie, the lonely moor shunned by locals for fear of the ghost of murderer Alexander Gillan. Charles Hope, Lord Justice Clerk to the Scottish Sessions (right), was the judge who convicted Gillan. A man of imposing presence, with a magnificent voice and a gift for declamation, he had the reputation for being brutally harsh to felons

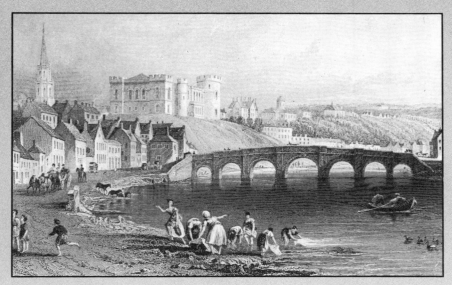

another that he was a half-witted orphan. One misty night in August 1810, a 10-year-old girl named Elspet Lamb disappeared while walking from her father's croft at Lhanbryde to the hamlet of Urquhart, 2 miles (3 kilometres) away. The next morning the men-at-arms from Elgin searched the surrounding moors and forests while prayers were offered in the local kirk for her safety. Alexander Gillan was present in the congregation. The hunters used tracker dogs and soon found the girl's body in a thicket on the

The town of Inverness, where Alexander Gillan stood trial. After being convicted he was kept in its pestilential Tolbooth jail on a diet of bread and water until, on the day of his execution, he was cast into a tumbril and taken to the scene of his crime to be hanged

Muir of Stynie, 'her head battered open'.

A pair of blood-stained trousers was found in a nearby trench, which locals quickly identified as belonging to Alexander Gillan. He was arrested just as the kirk service finished, wearing his 'best breeks' (trousers). He was charged with 'molesting' and murdering Elspet Lamb and taken to Inverness to be tried. The date for the trial was fixed for 29 September 1810.

Gillan, unfortunately, appeared before Charles Hope, Lord Justice Clerk to the Scottish Sessions. Hope was a self-made man, who had risen from being a poor law student to Member of Parliament for Edinburgh. He was a high Tory, thought by many to be a disciplinarian and a snob, who nevertheless endeared himself to the Scottish gentry by his 'integrity, kindness and gentleman-like manners'. However, when sitting as a judge he seemed to abandon these qualities and could be brutally harsh with those appearing before him. His judicial contemporary Lord Cockburn described him as being 'greatly wanting in tact and judgement'.

According to the Inverness records, the case against Gillan was considered water-tight even though the trousers were not positively identified as being his, and though he was not questioned as to his whereabouts on the night of the crime.

At the trial he clutched a crumpled piece

of paper from which he attempted to read, but he was not given any opportunity to speak in his own defence. Instead, with the black cap lying beside him, Hope launched into a 10-minute declamation that must be one of the most spine-chilling judgements ever handed out:

I look upon any punishment you can receive in this world as mercy. Did you flatter yourself that if you escaped detection and conviction, you could have lived and taken your place amongst the decent-living and industrious, amidst the daily avocations [occupations] of your fellow men?

The mangled corpse of this innocent child would have unceasingly haunted you. Her departed spirit would have drawn aside your curtain at midnight, and horror and remorse and despair would surely have driven you, at length, to take vengeance upon yourself.

Even God found crimes such as Gillan's hard to forgive, said the judge, particularly as

. . . it was no small aggravation of your foul deed that you went reeking with the blood of your victim to The Temple of the Lord, impiously to mix with God-fearing people while they offered up their prayers. You thought that by going to Church, assuming the solemn appearance and devout conduct of Christian people, you would be able to conceal your guilt . . . but . . . you lost that composure which a conscience at ease bestows . . . so the House of God to which you had impiously fled to cover your wickedness became a means of bringing your guilt to the light of day.'

Bereft of burial

The Lord Justice Clerk ordered pastors to attend Gillan during his last days in order that he might prepare himself for death.

But it is decreed that a criminal such as you shall be bereft of all burial and that his body shall not be permitted to descend into its Mother Earth like those of Christians. I have resolved to make you a lasting and memorable example of the fate which awaits the commission of such deeds as yours.

The situation of the countryside in which your crime was committed, its vast woods, its uninhabited moors, and the solitude which reigns over it are but too well calculated for outrages such as yours. I am therefore anxious that these extensive wilds may be traversed by every person of both sexes at all times, even in the hours of darkness, with confidence and security. It is my duty to make them as safe as the streets of this town.

I have therefore determined that after your execution you shall be hung suspended in chains until the birds of

The 'red kirk' of Lhanbryde, where men-at-arms arrested Gillan as he was leaving after the service

Henry Gordon, seventh Duke of Richmond (1845–1928), who agreed in 1911 that Gillan's gibbet was a public nuisance and should be taken down and buried where it stood. When a hole was dug, the remains of a human skeleton were discovered

the air pick the flesh off your body, and your bones bleach and moulder in the winds of heaven, thereby to afford a continuing warning of the consequences of doing as you did and operating, I hope, as an example for the prevention of such crimes, and for procuring the safety of all people proceeding around the region. Therefore . . . you . . . shall be taken from the prison and on some convenient part of the moor near to the place where the crime was committed be hanged by the neck until you are dead. This I pronounce for doom. And may God almighty have mercy on your soul.

On the morning of Wednesday, 14 November, Alexander Gillan, weak from a diet of bread and water only, was driven the 40 miles (64 kilometres) south to the Muir of Stynie in a cart. There, in the dying winter light, a 12-foot (3.6-metre) high oaken gallows had been erected; beside it on the ground lay what the *Huntly Express* described as 'an ingenious device, a cage of bands and chains and swivels'.

Bundled off without a word

Gillan had had no opportunity to speak out at his trial, nor did he have one now. Still clutching a piece of paper, he was bundled up the ladder by a hangman and, 'the noose being tightened around his neck he was swung off into eternity with . . . the piece of paper from which he had intended to read the statement of his sorrow and repentance.'

As soon as he was dead the body was taken down and shackled into the iron cage, and then this was hoisted up and hung from the gallows. The officials then withdrew down a rutted track, which quickly became known as 'Gillan's Way'.

However, at dawn the following morning the body had gone, though the cage was still there. The men-at-arms questioned local villagers at Lhanbryde, Urquhart and

Garmouth but nobody divulged anything.

In spite of this, the gallows and the cage were left where they were. Charles Hope died 41 years later in 1851, but the gallows were to outlast him by 60 years. The solid oak, swivels and rusting chains withstood the corrosive sea mists 'becoming', according to the *Northern Scot* newspaper, 'a nuisance to those living nearby. In the gentlest breezes the ironwork rattled and groaned, but in a gale the swivels spun and squealed and were heard for miles downwind.'

Quite soon, people reported a different kind of nuisance. Those who had been down Gillan's Way said they had seen the shadowy figure of Alexander Gillan lurking beneath the pine trees. For weeks after his death people said that the scrap of paper that he had been clutching had been seen blowing about beneath the gallows. But no one dared pick it up and read it.

The cross that marks Gillan's grave. Made, it is said, from an arm of the gallows on which he was hanged, it has weathered the years remarkably well. A strong iron rivet was driven through its centre, presumably in accordance with the tradition that iron stakes keep the unhallowed dead from 'walking'. But the locals still avoid the area of 'Gillan's Way', especially after dark

One hundred and one years after the hanging, the then Duke of Richmond agreed that 'Gillan's gibbet' was a public nuisance and he ordered it to be taken down and buried at that very spot. While a trench was being dug human bones were unearthed. The Duke was immediately told and he went, with a local doctor, to investigate. The doctor identified one of the bones as a man's thigh bone. The remaining bones were left where they were. Obviously, someone had lowered the cage, taken Gillan out and buried him there and then. The Duke had the bones replaced, the gallows laid on top of them and the trench filled in. Later, a cross (reputedly made from the arm of the gallows, presumably by a local) was erected on the spot.

A cross marks the spot

The cross is still there, though very few people, even locals, know its exact location. It is made of rock-hard, weathered oak, and has a great iron rivet driven through its centre.

A local person who knew the site well said:

> My grandmother was one of the folks who petitioned the Duke to pull the gallows down. Our family was closest to the site and never a day nor a night went by without the sound of the gibbet stirring. I remember, as a child, myself and some friends tried to put flowers on the grave in the summer, and a keeper caught us at it. He was angry; he said that it was unhallowed ground, and no good would come of laying flowers there as you would on a Christian grave. And what do I feel about it? I rarely come here. I'll drive my tractor along Gillan's Way to the pub at dinner time, but at night I take the long way round. It depresses you. The area carries a black depression about it, especially at dusk.

The Muir of Stynie is now Crown Land, looked after by the Forestry Commission. But land officers treat the story with respect; one of them stating clearly, 'I'm not a local but the place worries me simply because you never see deer or a bird there: a hundred yards [30 metres] away, yes, but that place is always deserted.'

One interesting point about this ghost story is that most accounts tally in almost every respect. One version, however, goes further than the rest:

> He got the wrong lassie. He was no' a bad man, by all accounts, but he'd fallen for Elspet's elder sister and she'd jilted him. So he waited for her by the forest side there, and he got the wrong one in the mist. That's what was written on the scrap of paper, and some around here knew it. So they took him down and they buried him, in spite of the high judge.

The horror of Glamis

For centuries Glamis Castle has had a reputation as a place of strange and awful happenings – events that strike terror at the hearts of all who witness them. The story of this famous haunted mansion may be based on fact

GLAMIS CASTLE stands in the great vale of Strathmore in Tayside, Scotland. For hundreds of years the vast fortified house with its battlements and pointed towers – looking like the setting for a fairy tale – has been the ancestral home of the Earls of Strathmore. Their family secret is reputedly hidden within the walls of Glamis, famous as one of the most haunted houses on earth.

That there was unpleasantness within the castle's walls is an undoubted historical fact. And that the castle is today the centre of a triangle formed by three biblically named villages – Jericho, Zoar, and Pandanaram – may indicate the terror felt by its minions, for, according to a Scottish National Trust guidebook, the men who built and named them 'had at least some knowledge of the Scriptures and regard for the wrath of God'. That wrath, claim locals even today, was called down on Glamis for the sins of the first dozen or so Lairds. The present, 17th Earl of Strathmore, Fergus Michael Claude Bowes-Lyon, is well-liked by his tenants, and there is no evidence that his immediate forbears

Below: Glamis Castle, picturesque home of the Earl of Strathmore and Kinghorne, was a wedding gift from King Robert II upon the marriage of his daughter to Sir John Lyon in the 14th century. From the time Sir John moved to Glamis, the family seemed to be dogged by misfortune

Right: the painting of the third Earl, Patrick, with his children and greyhounds dominates the far wall of the drawing room at Glamis. It is around Patrick that two of the strangest stories revolve

Above: Malcolm II, who reigned as King of Scotland from 1005 until his death at Glamis in 1034 at the hands of an army of rebels. Tradition holds that he was slain in what is now known as King Malcolm's Room (top right), and that his brutal murder saw the start of the 'horror' at the castle

were any less affable; but the conduct of at least one of their ancestors called into being what is still known as the 'horror' of Glamis.

It is the nature of the horror that makes it one of the great mysteries. No recent Earl has ever spoken of it to an outsider, except in enigmatic terms. No woman has ever been let in on the secret. It is passed on only to the Strathmore heir on his 21st birthday.

The historical record of horror at Glamis Castle goes back to 1034, when King Malcolm II was cut down by a gang of rebellious subjects armed with claymores, the large broadswords peculiar to Scotland. It was said that every drop of Malcolm's blood seeped from his body into the floorboards, causing a stain that is still pointed out today, in what is called King Malcolm's Room. That the stain was made by Malcolm's blood is disputable, however, for records seem to show that the flooring has since been replaced. Nevertheless, Malcolm's killers added to the death toll of Glamis by trying to escape across a frozen loch, but the ice cracked and they were drowned.

Curse of the chalice

The Lyon family inherited Glamis from King Robert II, who gave it to his son-in-law, Sir John Lyon, in 1372. Until then the Lyon family home had been at Forteviot, where a great chalice, the family 'luck', was kept. Tradition held that if the chalice were removed from Forteviot House a curse would fall on the family; despite this, Sir John took the cup with him to Glamis. The curse seemed to have a time lapse, for though Sir John was killed in a duel, this did not occur until 1383; nevertheless, the family misfortunes are usually dated from this time.

The 'poisoned' chalice may well have influenced events 150 years later when James V had Janet Douglas, Lady Glamis, burned at the stake in Edinburgh on a charge of witchcraft. The castle reverted to the Crown, but after the falsity of the charge was proved, it was restored to her son. The spectre of Lady Glamis – the 'Grey Lady' as she is known – is said to walk the long corridors even today.

It was Patrick, the third Earl of Strathmore, who made the idea of a Glamis 'curse' widespread in the late 17th century; indeed, to many people he seemed the very embodiment of it. A notorious rake and gambler, his drunken debauches were well-known in London and Edinburgh as well as throughout his home territory. The facts of his career and his character are festooned with folklore, but he must have been something of an enigma, for despite his wild ways he was philanthropic towards his tenants at least. The Glamis Book of Record, for instance, details his plans for building a group of lodges on the estate for the use of retired workers. Now known as Kirkwynd Cottages, they were given to the Scottish National Trust by the 16th Earl of Strathmore in 1957 to house the Angus Folk Collection.

Two principal stories endure about Patrick. The first is that he was the father of a deformed child who was kept hidden somewhere in the castle, out of sight of prying eyes. The second is that he played cards with the Devil for his soul – and lost.

The first is fed by a picture of the third Earl that now hangs in the drawing room. It shows Patrick seated, wearing a classical bronze breastplate, and pointing with his left hand towards a distant, romanticised vista of Glamis. Standing at his left knee is a small, strange-looking green-clad child; to the child's left is an upright young man in scarlet doublet and hose. The three main figures are placed centrally, but two greyhounds in the picture are shown staring steadfastly at a figure, positioned at the Earl's right elbow. Like the Earl this figure wears a classical breastplate apparently shaped to the muscles of the torso – but if it is a human torso it is definitely deformed. The left arm is strangely foreshortened. Did the artist paint from life – and if so does the picture show the real horror of Glamis?

The second story goes like this. Patrick and his friend the Earl of Crawford were playing cards together one Saturday night. A servant reminded them that the Sabbath was approaching, to which Patrick replied that he would play on, Sabbath or no Sabbath, and that the Devil himself might join them for a hand if he so wished. At midnight, accompanied by a roll of thunder, the Devil appeared and told the card-playing Earls that they had forfeited their souls and were doomed to play cards in that room until Judgement Day.

The pact presumably came into operation only after Patrick's death, for there is some evidence that he revelled in the tale: but did he tell it merely as a joke or as some sort of elaborate cover up, to scare intruders forever from the castle? If the latter was his intention, it was strikingly successful. In 1957 a servant at the castle, Florence Foster, complained in a newspaper article that she had heard the Earls at their play in the dead of night, 'rattling dice, stamping and swearing. Often I lay in bed and shook with fright,' she said. She resigned rather than risk hearing the phantom gamblers again. The story persists of a 'secret room' known only to the Earls themselves, and it is true that no one knows for certain which of the hundred-odd rooms at Glamis was used by Patrick for his diabolical game of cards.

Grisly tales

One story tells – with curious precision – of a grey-bearded man, shackled and left to starve in 1486. A later one, which probably dates from before Patrick's time also, is gruesome in the extreme. A party of Ogilvies from a neighbouring district came to Glamis and begged protection from their enemies the Lindsays, who were pursuing them. The Earl of Strathmore led them into a chamber deep in the castle and left them there to starve. Unlike the unfortunate grey-bearded man, however, they had each other to eat and began to turn cannibal, some, according to legend, even gnawing the flesh from their own arms.

One or other of these tales may account for the ghost of a skeletally thin spectre known as Jack the Runner. And the ghost of a Negro pageboy, also seen in the castle, would seem to date from the 17th or 18th century, when young slaves were imported from the West Indies. A 'white' lady haunts the castle clock

Below: Lady Elizabeth Bowes-Lyon, the future Queen Mother, grew up at Glamis. She is said to have felt the presence of the horror in the Blue Room

tower, while the grey-bearded man of 1486 appeared, at least once, to two guests simultaneously, one of whom was Mrs MacLagan, wife of the Archbishop of York at the turn of the 20th century. Mrs MacLagan told how, during her stay at the castle, one of the guests came down to breakfast and mentioned casually that she had been awakened by the banging and hammering of carpenters at 4 a.m. A brief silence followed her remarks, and then Lord Strathmore spoke and assured her that there were no workmen in the castle. According to another story, as a young girl Queen Elizabeth the Queen Mother (daughter of the 14th Earl, Claude George Bowes-Lyon) once had to move out of the Blue Room because her sleep was being disturbed by rappings, thumps, and footsteps.

Fascinating as all these run-of-the-mill ghosts and their distinguished observers are, however, it is the horror that remains the great mystery of Glamis. All the principal rumours – cannibal Ogilvies notwithstanding – involve a deformed child born to the

The 13th Earl of Strathmore, Claude Bowes-Lyon (left), was deeply troubled by the tales of strange events at Glamis. The wife of the Archbishop of York wrote that for many years, after the revelation of the secret, Claude was quite a changed man, silent and moody, with an anxious scared look on his face. So evident was the effect on him that his son, Glamis, when he came of age in 1876, absolutely refused to be enlightened'

The 14th Earl (below) and Mr Gavin Ralston, the estate factor (below right). When told the secret by the Earl, Mr Ralston was so appalled he vowed never to sleep at the castle again

embargo on the secret by telling it to his estate factor, Mr Gavin Ralston, who subsequently refused to stay overnight at the castle again.

When the 14th Earl's daughter-in-law, the next Lady Strathmore, asked Ralston the secret, Ralston is said to have replied: 'It is lucky that you do not know and can never know it, for if you did you would not be a happy woman.'

That statement, surely, is the clue to the horror of Glamis. Old Patrick's deformed offspring did not alarm the father because nothing like it had been seen in the family before. Possibly the 'wicked' Earl rather delighted in him. But if the same deformity appeared even once in a later generation, the head of an ancient, noble and hereditary house would certainly have been reluctant to broadcast the fact. Perhaps Claude, 13th Earl of Strathmore, knew of such a second, deformed child in the Bowes-Lyon line, and passed the secret and the fear of its recurrence on to his successors?

family and kept in a secret chamber who lived, according to 19th-century versions of the story, to a preternaturally old age. In view of the portrait openly displayed in the Glamis drawing room, and always supposing that the mysterious child is actually portrayed, the subsequent secrecy seems rather pointless. If Patrick himself was prepared to have his 'secret' portrayed in oils, why should his successors have discouraged open discussion of the matter?

An unmentionable horror

Despite the secrecy, at the turn of the 19th century the stories were still flying thick and fast. Claude Bowes-Lyon, the 13th Earl who died in 1904 in his 80th year, seems to have been positively obsessed by the horror, and it is around him that most of the 19th-century stories revolved. It was he, for instance, who told an inquisitive friend: 'If you could guess the nature of the secret, you would go down on your knees and thank God it were not yours.' Claude, too, it was who paid the passage of a workman and his family to Australia, after the workman had inadvertently stumbled upon a 'secret room' at Glamis and been overcome with horror. Claude questioned him, swore the man to secrecy, and bundled him off to the colonies shortly afterwards. To a great extent the obsession seems to have visited itself upon his son, Claude George, the 14th Earl, who died in 1944.

In the 1920s, a party of 'gay young things' staying at Glamis decided to track down the 'secret chamber' by hanging a piece of linen out of every window they could find. When they finished they saw there were several windows they had not been able to locate. When the Earl learned what they had done he flew into an uncharacteristic fury. Unlike his forbears, however, Claude George broke the

Left: the chapel at Glamis where a secret room was discovered in the late 19th century. A workman came upon the door by chance and, finding that it led into a long passage, decided to investigate – but he emerged soon after, shaking with fright. He reported his experience to the Earl who, anxious to preserve the family secret, persuaded the man to emigrate

After an 18th-century English sergeant disappeared from a lonely Scottish village, his ghost appeared to a local shepherd and named two men who were subsequently arrested for his murder.

A CURIOUS DOCUMENT dated 11 June 1754 lies in the archives of General Register House, the repository of Scottish High Court Records in Princes Street, Edinburgh. It forms part of the Court Record Book for the years 1752 to 1754, and is unique in both legal history and the history of the paranormal – for it tells of the only occasion on which the 'testimony' of a ghost was tacitly admitted as evidence for the prosecution in a British murder trial. The document includes a report of the statement of a 'fervent country lad' named Alexander MacPherson:

a few nights before, when he was in bed, a Vision appeared to him, as of a Man clad in blue who told the Deponent I am Serjeant Davies but that before he told him so the Deponent had taken the said Vision at first Appearance to be a real living Man. . . . That the Deponent rose from his Bed and followed him to the Door and then it was as has been told that he said he was Serjeant Davies who had been murdered in the hill of Christie aboute near a year before and desired the Deponent to go to the place he pointed ate where he would find his Bones. . . .

The story that emerged when Alexander

MacDonald, a forester, and Duncan Clerk, a deer-stalker, stood trial for the murder of Sergeant Arthur Davies of General Guise's 6th Regiment of Foot was a tangled one, reeking of the acrimony that troubled the Highlands in the aftermath of the last great Jacobite rising in 1745. But one clear fact emerged: if it had not been for the persistence of Alexander MacPherson, who saw the vision of the man in blue, the murder might never have come to light.

After the breaking of the clans at Culloden in April 1746, the revenge of the Hanoverian army under 'Butcher Billy', the Duke of Cumberland, on sympathisers with Prince Charles Edward Stuart was immediate and totally ruthless. Wounded men were burned alive or hacked to pieces where they lay, women were raped and murdered, children spitted on bayonets. When the first welter of bloodletting was over, slightly saner counsels prevailed, and although the horror could not be erased, the English 'army of occupation' belatedly began to use the rule of law rather than the sword to keep down possible insurgents. Acts were passed prohibiting the wearing of the kilt and any tartan garment, and the keeping or carrying of any weapon except under licence. One of the men assigned to enforce these laws in the area of Aberdeenshire around Braemar and the Linn of Dee was Sergeant Arthur Davies.

In the circumstances it was a perilous task, and one that called for the utmost tact – and, judging by the records, Sergeant Davies was good at it. His regiment, Guise's, had not been present at Culloden, nor had it been particularly active in the area of the Dee during the violent reprisals that followed. In order to cause the least resentment possible, Davies did not wear the hated redcoat uniform but went about his duties in civilian dress most of the time, and cultivated the friendship of the local people. At Christmas

Following the defeat of the Jacobites at the battle of Culloden in 1746, the revenge of the English Hanoverian army on the Scottish rebels was brutal and bloody. Sergeant Arthur Davies was one of many officers of the English army of occupation stationed in villages throughout Scotland to root out Jacobite sympathisers (above: *After Culloden: rebel hunting*, from a painting by Seymour Lucas)

Dead men tell no tales

1748 he took the ultimate step of marrying a Scots woman, Jean, and taking her to live with him in the village of Dubrach, where he was billeted with the family of a farmer named Donald Farquharson, who had become his friend.

According to the evidence of his wife, the sergeant was liked well enough by the children of the village, whatever their parents may have felt about him. A 'canny' man who drank rarely, he had managed to accumulate about 15 golden guineas from his army pay, and he would show these to the local bairns, taking the coins from the green silk bag inside the leather pouch that he carried with him at all times. He also dangled his silver watch and chain, and flashed his two gold rings, one of which bore an unusual seal. It was, perhaps, incautious behaviour in view of the hostility and poverty of the people among whom he and his colleagues lived, but Davies liked to cut a dash. Although he did not powder his hair, after the fashion of the military at that time, he wore his long dark locks tied with a black silk ribbon, surmounted by a black hat and silver buckle. His hand-made brogues were also decorated with silver, his well-cut breeches and dark blue coat were silver-buttoned, and his shirt, on the day he disappeared, was of silk.

The 30-year-old sergeant's duties were to supervise two platoons of eight men, one at his own village of Dubrach, the other 12 miles (20 kilometres) away at Glenshee, where his immediate subordinate was a corporal. Twice weekly the two platoons marched to a point midway between the villages for a council between the non-commissioned officers. Their main duty, of course, was to root out Jacobite sympathisers, but even in this Davies seemed eager to follow a *laissez faire* policy. The penalty for wearing tartan was a statutory six months' imprisonment, with transportation for life on a second offence. The sergeant's only punitive act in two years at Dubrach was to 'admonish' a John Growar for wearing a plaid jacket.

At dawn on 28 September 1749, the

Below: the scattered remains of the isolated village of Dubrach, where Sergeant Davies was billeted with the family of a local farmer

Dubrach patrol set out with the sergeant at their head to meet the corporal and his men from Glenshee. Davies was carrying a musket, lead ball and powder flask, and told the corporal when they met that he intended to stalk deer in the hills, leaving his men to return to base alone. He had made similar trips before, and although the corporal warned him to be careful he laughed off the caution, pointing out that he was an old campaigner and fully armed. His patrol saw him set off up the braeside, and later reported that he exchanged nods with John Growar, the man he had admonished. As they marched away they heard three clear shots in the distance, and assumed that their sergeant had sighted some game.

Search party

Davies was never seen alive again. During the next few days a search of the area by his two patrols failed to find any sign of him, and when a larger detachment of Guise's under a Captain Molesworth marched down from their station at Strathglass, further north, they fared no better. The terrain was full of natural hazards: crags, treacherous bog, burns that ran swift and deep. It was assumed that the sergeant had fallen prey to one of these, and the search was called off.

The time sequence of subsequent events became somewhat tangled in the accounts of the witnesses, but it seems that it was in June 1750, 10 months after Davies's ill-fated hunting trip, that his friend and former host Donald Farquharson received an agitated visit from a 'fervent country lad' named Alexander MacPherson. He was a young shepherd who lived in a lonely shieling – a single-roomed hut – 2 miles (3 kilometres) south of Dubrach on the slopes of Christie Hill. Eight days previously he had, as he was later to testify to the High Court, had a 'vision as of a man clad in blue' as he lay in bed. At first he took the apparition to be a 'real living man' whom he knew – a brother of Donald Farquharson – but as he rose and moved closer to the shadowy figure by the

door he recognised the pale face of the dead sergeant.

The ghostly visitor addressed MacPherson in Gaelic – a fact that later surprised the court, for the English soldier knew nothing of the language. Pointing to a place on the side of the hill of Christie, he asked the young shepherd to 'go to the place he pointed ate where he would find his Bones and that he might go to Donald Farquharson and take his Assistance to the burying of him'.

At first light MacPherson scrambled up the hillside to the spot indicated, and there, half buried under a peat stack, found skeletal remains. The shepherd left everything as he found it and made his way back down to his hut, 'much troubled in his mind'. Later that day he met John Growar, the man whom Davies had warned about wearing tartan, and asked him what to do. Growar bluntly told him to do nothing. But MacPherson approached a local laird, John Shaw of Daldownie, and poured out his tale. Although Shaw was, of course, not a Jacobite – for he still held his lands – he, too, advised silence.

The next part of MacPherson's evidence held a strong indication of the truth of what he said, for to make it public could have had unfortunate consequences for him: when the apparition appeared again, he was sharing his shieling with Isobel McHardie, the wife of his employer.

When Isobel McHardie saw the ghost, she was so frightened that she hid under the blanket and refused to come out until daylight. She heard the ghost tell MacPherson that he must seek out Donald Farquharson

and give the body a decent burial. He also named his murderers: Alexander MacDonald and Duncan Clerk. The following morning the shepherd went straight to Donald Farquharson and told him the whole story.

Farquharson later testified that he was sceptical of the 'spirit' evidence, but dutifully followed the lad up the hill of Christie. There, under the peat stack, lay a skeleton with a few scraps of dried flesh clinging to it. Hair of the same colour as Sergeant Davies's clung to the scalp, and the tattered blue coat and cracked brogues seemed identical to his, although the silver buckles and buttons had gone. Like Growar and the Laird of Daldownie, Farquharson decided that silence was the best course, but he fulfilled the spirit's request and buried the remains on the hillside. The ghost never appeared to MacPherson again – although there are local reports that the hill is still haunted.

A few months after the burial, the young shepherd was dismissed by farmer McHardie – perhaps because of the liaison with Isobel – and was forced to take employment with Duncan Clerk, one of the men accused by the phantom. Like several local people, MacPherson noticed that Clerk's

Left: the terrain where Sergeant Davies disappeared was craggy and treacherous, with many bogs and deep streams. The murdered man's bones were found on the hill of Christie, to be seen in the background

Below: the mill stream at Inverey, where the miller found a black hat with a silver buckle, similar to the one worn by the missing sergeant

mistress, Elizabeth Downie, wore two large gold rings, one of them bearing an unusual seal. One day during a row, the shepherd accused Clerk of killing the sergeant. Clerk immediately backed down, pleading with MacPherson to hold his tongue, and giving him a note of hand for 20 pounds Scots, which was later produced in evidence. MacPherson was to state that Clerk also had a green silk purse with gold coins in it.

By now, the story of the ghost and its accusations had circulated among the locals in the area, though it had not reached the authorities. But when a black hat with a silver buckle on it floated into the mill stream at Inverey the miller, perhaps recognising it as similar to the one worn by Davies, took it to

Left: Braemar Castle, where the Hanoverian troops were garrisoned, was where Alexander MacDonald and Duncan Clerk were first imprisoned after their arrest. They were probably held in the Laird's Pit (below), a wretched hole in the ground 12 by 6 feet (3.5 by 1.75 metres) reserved for suspected murderers. The pair were eventually transferred to the grim Tolbooth prison in Edinburgh (bottom) to await trial

and owned guns, and both had records of theft; MacDonald had stolen money, and Clerk had stolen sheep. Furthermore, according to the evidence of crofter John Grant, they had both left to go deer-hunting on the hill of Christie on the morning of 28 September, the day that Davies disappeared. Apart from MacPherson's ghost story, there was also the tangible evidence of the money given him by Clerk as the price of his silence.

Ensign Small also produced a witness, Angus Cameron, a stranger from Pitlochry, who claimed to have seen two men shoot a man in a blue coat twice while he and his friend Duncan Cameron were visiting the Christie area. He claimed to recognise the defendants as the murderers, but the eyewitness account was slightly marred when it was announced that Duncan Cameron had since been hanged for committing a felony.

Interfering with witnesses

It was on this point that the defence advocate, Alexander Lockhart, seized. He claimed that Ensign Small had been seen in Edinburgh threatening Angus Cameron and two of his colleagues with a sword shortly before the trial, and presented a formal petition to the court that Small should be charged with intimidating witnesses.

At 6 p.m. on 12 June 1754, the jury returned with the astonishing verdict of not guilty. In reply to Lockhart's charge of intimidation, Ensign Small pointed out that he had absolutely nothing to gain from such an action, that his military record was impeccable, and that he had wished only to clear up the mystery. He was given a token sentence, being bound over to keep the peace for a year in the sum of £50.

But there is no doubt that the shepherd, Alexander MacPherson, impressed the court with his straightforward, almost naïve account of what had occurred, an account corroborated by Mrs McHardie. Neither of them had any previous connection with the dead sergeant, and there was no reason why either of them should 'frame' MacDonald or Clerk as the murderers. Indeed, none of the locals had attempted to do so, despite the rumours that circulated, until authority, in the person of Ensign Small, stepped in.

The charge of intimidation against Small in the sense that he 'rigged' Cameron's evidence seems ludicrous, for the very reasons he himself gave to the court. But Ensign Small evidently took his military duties more seriously than did Sergeant Davies, and any questioning by a uniformed officer of the Hanoverian army in those tragic years must have seemed like intimidation to the native Scots. There, indeed, most probably lies the answer to the strange verdict; whatever their faults, MacDonald and Clerk were Scotsmen, and whatever his virtues, Sergeant Davies was a hated English soldier. So, despite the testimony of his ghost, his murderers left the court acquitted.

the military commander of the area, Ensign James Small, who was acting as factor of the forfeited estates of Robertson of Struan. Sharp enquiries by the ensign uncovered the local suspicions, and he arrested Alexander MacDonald and Duncan Clerk, taking them first to Braemar Castle and then to the Tolbooth at Edinburgh to await trial.

There was no apparent reason why MacDonald and Clerk should have borne a political grudge against the sergeant, for the fact that both of them were in relatively privileged positions indicated that they had not been involved in the rising. MacDonald was Lord Braco's head forester, and Clerk ran his own sizeable croft as well as being a deer-stalker. But both had firearm warrants

The curse of Fyvie Castle

An ancient curse laid on Fyvie Castle in Scotland is said to be still effective today. This macabre legend includes the melancholy ghost of a 'Green Lady' that haunts the great staircase, portending death

ALEXANDER FORBES-LEITH bought Fyvie Castle in 1889. With it, he acquired both a curse and perhaps the only ghost that has ever signed its name in stone for later generations to see.

The castle, which stands some 30 miles (50 kilometres) north-west of Aberdeen, has been described as the 'crowning glory of Scottish baronial architecture'. Its foundations were laid before the Norman Conquest and, since the 14th century, it has been held by only five great families.

Like many a blight on old Scottish families, the 'Fyvie curse' was the work of the ubiquitous Thomas the Rhymer. Although he was shrouded in legend and superstition, Thomas of Erceldoune seems certain to have been a real person. He was born in 1220 and mentioned as witness to a deed at the Abbey of Melrose around 1240; in Peter Langtoft's early 14th-century *Chronicle* he is stated to have been a poet.

In his own day Thomas the Rhymer was widely credited as being the lover of the Queen of Elfland. It was she who had given him the power of prophecy, and when he vanished without trace it was presumed that she had carried him off. It is more likely that he entered a monastery or, as Sir Walter Scott believed, was murdered by robbers.

The magnificent south front of Fyvie Castle (above) was extensively rebuilt in the early 16th century by Alexander Seton, Lord Fyvie (right). According to legend, three 'weeping stones' of ill omen had been built into the earlier fabric of the castle; as long as they remained there, no heir would be born within the castle's walls

When he was alive, however, his travels were well-recorded both in local lore and in contemporary documents. He cannot have been a welcome guest, since his prophecies invariably foretold disaster; bloodshed and general mayhem were his stock in trade. Nevertheless, few of the lairds Thomas the Rhymer visited cared to turn him away in case even worse befell them.

According to James Murray, the 19th-century editor of the five ancient manuscripts that tell Thomas's story, the gates of Fyvie Castle had stood 'wall-wide' for seven years and a day, awaiting his inevitable arrival. When he finally turned up it was in a typically ostentatious style:

> He suddenly appeared before the fair building, accompanied by a violent storm of wind and rain, which stripped the surrounding trees of their leaves and shut the Castle gates with a loud crash. But while the tempest was raging on all sides, it was observed that, close to the spot where the Tammas stood, there was not wind enough to shake a pile of grass or a hair of his beard.

Not surprisingly, after such a dramatic entry Thomas had to deliver an equally blood-curdling prophecy:

> Fyvie, Fyvie, thou's never thrive
> As lang's there's in thee stanis [stones] three.
> There's ane intill [one in] the oldest tower,
> There's ane intill the ladye's bower,
> There's ane intill the water-yett [water gate]
> And thir three stanes ye's never get.

This somewhat obscure pronouncement was

Above right: the Seton tower over the main gate, which was being rebuilt by Lord Fyvie when he married his second wife in 1601. Because the new apartments in it were not ready for occupation, the couple spent their wedding night in a room in the older part of the castle

Above: the panelled charter room, decorated with crescents, cinquefoils and the arms of the Seton family, was another of Lord Fyvie's improvements to the castle. The only one of the three 'weeping stones' that has been located is reputedly kept in a wooden bowl in this room

taken to mean that three stones, known as the weeping stones, which had originally been taken from a nearby church property, would act as evil omens to Fyvie as long as they remained part of the building. Only one of the stones, the one originally in 'the ladye's bower', has been found. Today it stands in a wooden bowl in the charter room; at times it is bone dry and at others 'exuding sufficient water to fill the bowl'. The stone purported to be beneath the 'water-yett' has never been located; the third one may have been built into what is now the Preston Tower since once, records an ancient document at the castle, 'when the rightful but dispossessed

heir to the property approached the water gushed forth in mournful salutation.'

Although Thomas the Rhymer was far from specific, the actual nature of the curse was interpreted as meaning that no heir would ever be born in the castle, and this is said to have been true since 1433. Furthermore, the castle would never pass from a father to his eldest son; again this claim has held good. Indeed, the tradition looks set to continue since the present owner put Fyvie on the market in 1982.

But there is another mystery surrounding Fyvie. It too concerns a stone, one that is situated immediately above the charter room; it forms a window sill three storeys up the sheer face of the castle wall. The puzzle, which dates from the night of 27 October 1601, has so far defied any rational explanation. At that time the laird was Alexander Seton, Lord Fyvie, afterwards first Earl of Dunfermline, and Lord President of the Scottish sessions.

In 1592 Seton married Dame Lilias (or Lilies) Drummond, daughter of Lord

Left: the stone window sill with the name of Lord Fyvie's first wife, D. LILIES DRUMMOND, carved upside down in characters nearly 3 inches (7 centimetres) high. The room is said to be the one occupied by Lord Fyvie and his second wife on their wedding night; during the night they heard deep sighs, and in the morning they discovered Dame Lilias's name incised outside the window

Patrick Drummond, another peer connected to the ruling house of Stuart. Dame Lilias was a handsome, happy woman and for nine years she and her husband were contented together. In that time she bore five daughters, four of whom survived to marry influential noblemen. However, Lilias was not as strong as her appearance suggested; on 8 May 1601 she died at her husband's house in Fife and was buried there.

The merry widower

Dame Lilias was not quite 30 when she died. According to the historical record, Seton seems to have mourned her death, and the fact that he remained on good terms with his brother-in-law seems to bear this out. Tradition, on the other hand, asserts something quite different: tired of waiting for the son and heir who never came, Seton had begun an affair with the beautiful Lady Grizel Leslie, young daughter of the Master of Rothes, whose home was 20 miles (32 kilometres) from Fyvie; Dame Lilias died of a broken heart.

Although history and hearsay would appear to part company in their accounts of Seton's behaviour immediately after his wife's death, there can be no doubt that he lost little time in wooing Lady Grizel Leslie. Within six months they were married.

On the night of 27 October they retired to their temporary bedchamber, a small room at the top of the spiral staircase in the older part of the castle, as their new quarters in what is now Seton tower were not yet finished.

That night they both heard heavy sighs coming from outside their room, and even

though Seton went out to investigate and roused a servant, no intruder was found. With the dawn, however, they discovered a startling indication of the intruder's identity. Carved upside down on the window sill in neat 3-inch (7-centimetre) high letters was the name D. LILIES DRUMMOND.

The carving, still clear and quite unworn, is over 50 feet (15 metres) from the ground in the old defensive wall of the castle, which had deliberately been built without any footholds.

Various suggestions have been put forward ever since as to a natural origin for the carving; none seems tenable. The precision of the work, the perfection of the lettering shows that however it was done it took great skill, so that any 'hoax' on the part of Seton or one of his ordinary household must be ruled out. Besides, why should the laird do something so calculated to terrify the young wife with whom he was obviously in love? And if he or someone in the castle did it, why write it upside down?

Seton was the great architect of Fyvie as it stands today, and work was probably under way at the time of his second marriage. It has been suggested that one of his masons inscribed the name out of respect for the dead mistress, but again, why do it upside down on a window sill where it could be seen only from the interior of the room? Normal commemorative plaques, usually consisting of initials and coat of arms, were carved on stone let into the surface of the wall where they could be seen. Again, the room was normally disused, far from the sumptuous new apartments Seton was then building,

Another of Lord Fyvie's additions to the castle was the great stone wheel staircase (below). It is on this staircase that the Green Lady, the ghost of the unhappy Dame Lilias, is sometimes seen. She is dressed in a shimmering green gown, and her appearance often heralds a death in the family. A portrait (right) that hangs in the castle is said to be of the Green Lady ghost rather than of Dame Lilias: it is dated 1676, 75 years after Dame Lilias died

and was chosen at literally the last moment. To reach the window sill, scaffolding would have to be erected – a lengthy process – and then the mason would have to climb the scaffolding and hammer out the deeply incised lettering – a noisy one. All the newly married couple heard were 'deep sighs'.

Whether natural or supernatural, the mysterious 'topsy turvy' writing marked the beginning of the haunting of the staircase, and the corridors leading from it, by a luminous 'Green Ladye', as 17th-century documents call her. Naturally, it was presumed that she was Dame Lilias, although a portrait dated 1676 that hangs in the castle and is reputed to be that of the ghost bears only a slight resemblance to the portrait of Seton's first wife. It is clad in a blue-green dress, and a faint bluish iridescence seems to radiate from the enigmatic features.

The 'Green Lady' and her nocturnal rambles up and down the great wheel staircase were periodically documented over the years; each account tells of the greenish-glow that surrounded her; sometimes, indeed, she was seen simply as a flicker of light at the end of a dark corridor. Colonel Cosmo Gordon, fifth Laird of Gordon of Fyvie, who had the castle from 1847 to 1879, recorded that on one occasion he was shaken out of bed by unseen hands, and on another night a wind arose inside the castle – when all outside was quiet – and blew the bedclothes off him and his various guests: presumably Dame Lilias in a boisterous mood.

The Gordons came to Fyvie in 1733, and the apparition was seen so many times that they came to adopt the Green Lady as their own, believing that her existence was personal to them. One story told by Colonel Cosmo Gordon seems to bear this out. A lady and her maid, named Thompson, were staying for a weekend. At breakfast one morning the visitor remarked that her maid had seen a lady she did not know in a green sacque-dress going up the principal staircase.

'It must have been the Green Lady,' said the Colonel, adding rather possessively, 'though she only appears to a Gordon.'

'Oh,' exclaimed the visitor, 'I always call my maids "Thompson" as a matter of course. Her real name is Gordon!'

Just before he died, Cosmo Gordon himself saw a figure beckoning him from the shadows of a room. He took the apparition to be an omen of his own impending death. A few days later his younger brother saw the Green Lady walking towards him in the gloomy December light that shone through the inscribed window. As she reached him, she dropped him a slow curtsey. The following morning Cosmo died.

During the First World War a Canadian army officer, a Captain A., left an account of his brush with supernatural forces at Fyvie, which was one of the most impressive in the castle's annals. A mining engineer by profession, he was a complete sceptic: 'If anyone had told me before I came here that there were such things as ghosts or anything supernatural I should have looked upon that man as an arrant fool,' he said.

Illuminated pictures

On the first night of his stay he had retired to bed and fallen asleep. Some time later he woke up to find the light on, or so he thought, and got up to switch it off:

> But so doing, to my amazement I found that I had switched it on. I extinguished it once more, but the light remained. The room was illuminated from some other cause, and as I watched, the light got gradually brighter. It was like little flames playing around the pictures, and I could see the colours of the pictures quite distinctly.

The same phenomenon occurred every night until the end of his stay, and although no apparition apart from the strange light appeared, there was, said the Canadian, a feeling of 'someone or something in the room – something I wanted to hit.'

Lord Leith of Fyvie, who bought the castle in 1889 and died in 1925, had not only seen the same phenomenon but had 'had it investigated scientifically', at the same time having the 'weeping stone' examined. The latter proved to be a form of porous sandstone, which absorbed and exuded moisture by a natural process; but no 'scientific explanation' for the carving on the window sill, or the wanderings of the Green Lady and her luminescence, was forthcoming.

Since Lord Leith's death, the Green Lady has been glimpsed only periodically by visitors – the castle is not open to the public – but the enigmatic carving remains. Whatever the truth behind the stories of Fyvie Castle, Lord Leith's motto on the subject seems to have been a sound one: 'Never combat the supernatural,' he told a guest. 'Meet it without fear, and it will not trouble you.'

Burning with guilt

Left: Frendraught House, the family seat of the powerful Crichton clan for many years. Because of the tragedy that took place there in the 17th century, it is said to be haunted – and the wife of the present owner is one of the witnesses to the haunting

Below: the scene of a modern-day haunting – part of the original old tower staircase at Frendraught. At the time of the fire, the rest of the tower staircases were wooden – and, burning fiercely, cut off the doomed guests

When a major feud between two great Scottish clans ended in a fire that killed several members of one faction, the local populace laid the blame on the lady of the manor. It is said that her guilt-ridden ghost still haunts the scene of the crime

ONE OF THE CLASSIC THEMES of supernatural lore is the unhappy ghost doomed to haunt the scene of its earthly wrongdoing until its sins are expiated. Is Frendraught House in Aberdeenshire just such a scene of a 'penitential' haunting? There are folklorists and witnesses who think that it is.

Frendraught House lies about 6 miles (9 kilometres) to the east of Huntly in the centre of the extensive Bognie estates. Its foundations date from 1203, though additions were made to it as recently as the 1840s. Its main bulk – containing inner walls up to 9 feet (2.7 metres) thick – was built between the 14th and 17th centuries when it was both home and fortress to the powerful Crichton family. During those three centuries the Crichtons, along with their cousins and neighbours the Gordons and Leslies, controlled the northeast of Scotland. They were often embroiled in bloody feuds.

In the spring of 1630 Frendraught was occupied by Sir James Crichton. He had made a good political marriage to Lady Elizabeth Gordon, eldest daughter of the

Earl of Sutherland, and she took an active part in her husband's continual disputes. As one Victorian commentator put it, she played a role somewhere between that of Medusa and Lady Macbeth.

The 1630 dispute over boundary lands was between Sir James Crichton and Gordon, Laird of Rothiemay. Sir James settled it in typical fashion by shooting Gordon dead. The Marquis of Huntly, the local High Sheriff who was himself a Gordon closely related to both sides, fined Sir James heavily. This 'blood money' was paid to young John Gordon, the new Laird of Rothiemay, and honour seemed satisfied.

By midsummer, however, Sir James was fighting again, this time with Leslie of Pitcaple. Matters came to a head when a Crichton shot Leslie through the arm with an arrow. Again the Marquis of Huntly heard the case, this time ruling in favour of Sir James. The wounded Leslie rode off in a fury, openly swearing revenge on the house of Crichton: Sir James therefore took the precaution of assembling an armed party to escort him back to Frendraught. Surprisingly, it included young John Gordon of Rothiemay as well as the Marquis of Huntly's son, John Melgum Viscount Aboyne. The party arrived in the dusk of an October afternoon. Lady Crichton, perhaps relieved to see her husband home safe, pressed even the unloved Gordon kin to stay the night. The guests were put in the old tower.

Lord Melgum was given a room separated

Right and below: Sir James and Lady Elizabeth Crichton. Their guests, among them some clan rivals, met death by fire at Frendraught House. Lady Crichton was known to be a strong support to Sir James in his many feuds, which may be why people thought her guilty of causing the fire

Below right: the Marquis of Huntly, the local High Sheriff, was closely involved in the events at Frendraught House – and not just as an official. His son, Lord Melgum, was one of those who burned to death in the old tower while trying to help the others

When he stood at the wire window
Most doleful to be seen
He did espy the Lady Frendraught
Who stood upon the green.
And mercy, mercy Lady Frendraught
Will ye not sink with sin
For first your husband kilt my father
And now ye burn his son.
Oh, then it spake Lady Frendraught
And loudly did she cry
It was great pity for good Lord John
But none for Rothiemay
But the keys are sunk in the deep
　　draw well
Ye cannot get away.

To the Marquis of Huntly there was only one way to avenge his dead son. Laying aside his High Sheriff's impartiality, he recruited a small army of highlanders and raided Frendraught, carrying off 60 cattle and several dozen sheep.

Crichton appealed to Edinburgh, and the Privy Council came down in his favour. Huntly was fined and Sir James received damages.

Despite their vindication by the Privy Council, both Sir James and his Lady seemed changed by the terrible fire. Three years afterwards he gave a silver chalice, said to have been one of 11 brought north by Mary Queen of Scots, to the nearby kirk at Forgue. Today the chalice, the oldest known

from the upper storeys by a wooden staircase. John Gordon of Rothiemay was on the second floor, and the other guests and servants above him. Spalding, a contemporary chronicler, tells what happened: 'About midnight that dolorous tower took fire in so sudden and furious a manner, and in ane clap, that the noble Viscount, the Laird of Rothiemay, English Will, Colonel Ivat and others, servants, were cruelly burned and tormented to death.'

Lord Melgum, it is said, ran to help the others, but the wooden stair caught fire and he was trapped with them. According to Spalding: 'They hurried to the window looking out into the close, piteously calling for help, but none was or could be rendered them.' Altogether about a dozen people lost their lives.

Death by design

An event of this magnitude cast shadows far beyond north-east Scotland, and the Privy Council in Edinburgh became involved, setting up a commission of bishops and neutral peers to investigate. The commission sat at Frendraught on 13 April 1631. The bishops merely declared that 'the fire could not have happened accidentally but designedly.' There the mystery of the fire rests, unsolved to this day. However, local opinion of the time laid the blame squarely on Lady Frendraught. An anonymous ballad written a few months after the event said of Rothiemay's final moments:

piece of hallmarked silver in Scotland, lies in a bank vault in Huntly.

Lady Frendraught took her three daughters and went to live as a recluse at Kinnairdy on the River Deveron. Born a Catholic, she was excommunicated when she signed the Solemn League and Covenant supporting Presbyterianism. Turning back to her old faith, she was rebuffed. 'I refused absolutely to see her,' wrote Father Blackhall, 'because

'According to local opinion and the direct testimony of tenants, guests, and my wife,' says Mr Morison, 'Frendraught is haunted by Lady Elizabeth Crichton, who is bound there because of her guilt. I have never felt or seen anything myself, but according to legend the Laird never does anyway.' Mr Morison believes in Lady Crichton's guilt. He cites documents showing that, when the 'deep draw well' in the courtyard was cleaned out during alterations in the 1840s, massive keys were found. This supports the allegations of the old ballad.

The recorded sightings of a 'dark woman in a white dress' at Frendraught go back at least to the early 18th century when a Victorian clergyman-writer claimed that she was seen both in the house and among the great beeches around it. The first modern sighting on record occurred in 1938 when the house stood empty and locked. The late William Thomas, former manager of Glendronough Distillery on the borders of the Bognie estate, was in his early teens at the time. One autumn afternoon he was out shooting crows behind the house. Looking up, he saw a pale face surrounded by dark hair, watching him from a window overlooking the courtyard. He called a keeper who also saw the 'intruder'. Armed with their shotguns, the two broke in through a kitchen door and searched the house from top to bottom. There was nobody there, and no sign of forcible entry but their own.

Nearly 10 years later, Mrs Yvonne Morison encountered the ghost.

It was 28 October. I remember the date because my husband had gone away with the Canadian Army reserve the day before. I was completely alone in the kitchens in the basement – the oldest part. Suddenly in the silence I heard footsteps coming down the staircase from the top of the house. I was

she was suspected to be guilty of the death of my Lord Aboyne. . . .' When she died, it was without benefit of clergy, on an unrecorded date. She was buried, like her husband, in an unmarked grave.

Sir James's eldest son was the last of his line. He was created Viscount Frendraught by his cousin Charles I for services rendered during the Civil War. After his death, his widow married George Morison of that Ilk, Chief of the Morison Clan and Laird of Bognie. His descendant, Alexander Gordon Morison, became Laird of Bognie and Mountblairy and owner of Frendraught House in 1942. He was born in Canada and inherited the chieftainship and family estates from his uncle. Immediately after the Second World War he and his young family lived at Frendraught House, but later moved to Mountblairy – not, he insists, for fear of ghosts, but for practical reasons. After several years of being leased, Frendraught House now stands empty.

Opposite: the main staircase at Frendraught House. The ghost of Lady Frendraught in a white-and-gold dress has been seen here and on the back stairs, as well as in the grounds of the estate

Opposite below: the silver chalice presented to Forgue Kirk by Sir James three years after the fire. It is said to have been brought to Scotland by Mary Queen of Scots and is the oldest piece of hallmarked silver in the country. Did Sir James give it to the church to ease a guilty conscience?

terrified, but something made me go to the bottom of the stairs where they eventually entered the kitchen. I peered up into the darkness and remember thinking very strongly – I may even have spoken aloud – 'Well, come on then. If you exist, show yourself.' Perhaps fortunately, the footfalls stopped at the top of the kitchen stairs, and I saw and heard nothing else.

The footsteps were too heavy and clear to be made by mice, she said, and rats had never

Above and left: the present owners of Frendraught House, Yvonne and Alexander Gordon Morison. The Morisons lived at Frendraught for a time after the Second World War, having inherited it in 1942. Mrs Morison had a personal encounter with the ghost of Lady Crichton – as did guests and later tenants

been seen in the building. 'I knew all the "natural" creaks and groans of the old place. It was none of these.'

Twice the Morisons had guests who cut short their visits because of mysterious disturbances. On both occasions the guests were level-headed people. One was an old army colleague who had been in the thick of the fighting with Mr Morison during the Italian campaign. In both cases their stories matched in every detail, though they had never met. Mrs Morison explained:

It was quite funny at first. They were a bit embarrassed and it became clear that they thought my husband and I had had a furious fight during the night. When we pointed out that the wall between our bedroom and theirs was 8 feet [2.4 metres] thick and totally soundproof, they became alarmed. They said that they had heard the most dreadful cries for help, with the sound of crashing, like heavy furniture being thrown about, and screams. They had been too terrified to investigate.

Curse of the chalice

Several guests and subsequent tenants at Frendraught had described seeing a dark lady in a white dress edged and decorated in gold. She was usually standing or walking on the main staircase or the back stairs.

Mr Cryle Shand, genealogist, lawyer, and tenant of Yonder Bognie Farm, has an open mind on the subject of the ghost, but feels that Lady Crichton was more to be pitied than blamed. According to his own theory, she may have been impelled to whatever action she took by a curse – the curse of the chalice that Sir James gave to Forgue Kirk three years after the fire.

From my research I am almost certain that the cup was one of those brought north by Mary Queen of Scots in the middle of the 16th century: although it is hallmarked 1663 its base is typically pre-Reformation. The Bible says that 'he that eateth and drinketh unworthily, eateth and drinketh damnation unto himself.' Although the Crichtons were nominally a Catholic family, they were a fairly ungodly lot. I believe that Sir James used the sacred chalice for profane purposes – probably for drinking his dram out of – and that the troubles of his family and that of the Gordons who were so closely related to them were brought about by that Biblical damnation. That is why Crichton so piously repented and gave the cup back to the church. That is why it is treated with such respect by the elders of Forgue Kirk to this day. And that is why Dr Arthur Johnson, an 18th-century Scottish Latinist, describes Frendraught as *Tristis et infelix et semper inhospita turris* ('O sad and unhappy and ever inhospitable tower').

Shrieks, groans, heavy footsteps and the uncanny sound of something being dragged along the floor made nights at a lonely Scottish castle a terrifying experience for the occupants. The noises continued, although no rational explanation for the phenomena has ever been found

ON A WINDY WEEKEND in March 1946 a party of students gathered at Penkaet Castle in Scotland to rehearse a play they intended to perform at Edinburgh College of Art. After the first day of rehearsal on Saturday, supper was served and the party retired to bed. Two of the girls, Susan Hart and Carol Johnstone, were put in the King Charles room, so called because it contained a massive carved four-poster bed, reputedly slept in by Charles II.

On either side of the bed a candle burned, throwing long shadows in the cavernous room. Although there was an oil heater, it was extremely cold, so cold that the girls found it impossible to get to sleep.

About midnight both girls heard a sound, which they said was like 'something trundling across the floor above', or 'something going down a slope'. The strange sound was

A sense of something strange

Left: a 17th-century painting (from the studio of John Michael Wright) of King Charles II, now in the National Portrait Gallery, London. Because a massive carved bed had reputedly been slept in by Charles II, the room containing it was known as the King Charles room. Many of the paranormal happenings at Penkaet Castle (right) were connected with this room

repeated from time to time, and they also heard footsteps.

About 2 a.m. a new phenomenon was presented to them. On the wall opposite the bed they noticed a large, dark brown stain. It was on the right-hand side of the fireplace, giving the impression that part of the paper had come away from the wall and was now hanging down. The following night, to their surprise, the patch had disappeared. Although the girls experimented with the candles in an attempt to produce a shadow of the same shape and position, they were unsuccessful.

This was not the first time that Penkaet Castle had been the scene of inexplicable manifestations. Dating from the beginning of the 16th century, the castle stands near Haddington, Lothian. It is virtually unmodernised and retains many of its historic furnishings. There is a legend that a former owner, John Cockburn, killed his relative John Seton, and his troubled conscience causes his ghost to haunt the place. Another former owner, Sir Andrew Dick Lauder, had, as a boy of nine, seen a ghost standing before the fireplace in one of the rooms.

In the early 1920s the castle was bought by Professor and Mrs Holbourn, who soon began to experience strange phenomena. 'When we first came here in 1923,' Mrs Holbourn was reported as saying in the *Journal* of the American Society for Psychical Research,

> we were often disturbed by the sounds of heavy footsteps going about the house, and the sound of something heavy and soft being dragged along. Various people who occupied the house [in our absence] complained of hearing shrieks and groans, and that doors which were shut and even locked at night were found open in the morning. One girl was so terrified that she refused to sleep alone.

Sometimes, when Professor and Mrs Holbourn found the noises too persistent and annoying, the professor would admonish 'John', telling him he was behaving childishly and asking him to stop. The sounds would cease at once.

Music and movement

While carols were being sung in the music room at Christmas 1923, a piece of wood carved with the family crest was seen to lean forward from the wall, 'hesitate' and then return to its former position. Two years later, a friend occupied the room containing the King Charles bed, and heard someone moving about on the ground floor during the night. She and the professor searched downstairs but could find no one. On their return to the first floor, they heard from the room above the sound of someone turning over in the bed the girl had left.

Ten years later when a Mrs Carstairs, recuperating from an illness, was sleeping in the King Charles bed, Mrs Holbourn's brother, who was in the room below, was wakened by urgent knocks apparently coming from overhead. Thinking that Mrs Carstairs had fallen out of bed and was knocking for help, he woke Mrs Holbourn; she found the lady sleeping soundly in her bed.

Other people (including Professor and Mrs Holbourn) spending the night in the bedroom below the King Charles room heard the sounds of movement from the room above when it was supposed to be empty. Sometimes it sounded as if the furniture was being moved around, and at other times it sounded as if someone was 'stumbling and groping about the room'.

In 1924 a cousin was staying in the house while the Holbourns were away. One day he took a visitor up to see the King Charles bed and, when they entered the room, they found the bedclothes ruffled as if the bed had not been made. The cousin mentioned this to the gardener's daughter Mrs Anderson (whose job it was to make the beds), and she expressed surprise, maintaining that she had in fact made the King Charles bed that very

Left: the four-poster bed in the main bedroom of Penkaet Castle had been a present from students to Professor Holbourn, who bought the castle in 1923. The masks on either side of the bottom of the bed were said to be replicas of the death mask of Charles I, and the bed had been used by his son Charles II. On several occasions the bedclothes were found rumpled as if the bed had been slept in, even though no one had been in the room

morning. The incident was dismissed – until it happened again. The cousin took another visitor up to the room, this time someone who wanted to photograph the bed. Again the bedclothes were found to be disarranged, and again Mrs Anderson had to remake the bed. The visitor took his photograph and left; he returned a day or so later to say that the photograph had been under-exposed. When he and the Holbourns' cousin went up to the bedroom so that he could re-photograph the bed, they found that once again the bedclothes had been pulled about. This time, after Mrs Anderson had put the bedclothes straight, the cousin took the precaution of locking the two doors leading into the room and checking that the windows were secure. He also placed two bricks against the main door. The following day the bricks had been moved and the bedclothes were again disarranged. At the time these strange occurrences took place, the cousin was the only person living in the house.

Another incident that took place in the same room concerned a massive antique cabinet, which was very difficult to move. This was found 6 inches (15 centimetres) away from the wall. In addition, a brass jug and basin had been placed on top of the cabinet, and the jug was lying on its side.

In the summer of 1935 Professor Holbourn's son was working late one evening in the workshop on the ground floor. Although it was about 11 p.m. it was only just getting dark, and Mr Holbourn took the job he was working on outside to look at it in the fading light. While he was outside the housekeeper, Betta Leadbetter, came to the window to tell him that someone was taking a bath. She had heard the taps running, some-

one splashing about in the bath, and later the water running out. As his wife had been in bed since 9 p.m., Mr Holbourn decided to investigate. When he entered the bathroom he found it full of steam and the mirror and windows completely misted over, although the bath itself was quite dry. No one in the house admitted to having used the bath. The most bizarre feature of this incident concerned the soap. At the time it was customary for large houses to order soap by the half hundredweight (25 kilograms). The Penkaet Castle soap was all of one colour. What was found in the bathroom, however, was a square piece of white soap totally unlike the other soap in the house.

It is well known that domestic animals are acutely sensitive to paranormal phenomena, and another incident at Penkaet Castle bears this out. On the night of her husband's

Legend has it that a former owner of Penkaet Castle (above), one John Cockcroft, killed a relative, and that his troubled spirit haunts the place and is responsible for the strange noises and other unaccountable happenings that are so often reported there. At Christmas 1923, for instance, a piece of wood in the music room, carved with the family crest, was seen by several witnesses to lean forward from the wall, 'hesitate' perceptibly, and then return to its proper place

funeral, Mrs Holbourn senior said that she had heard footsteps coming down the path outside the house; she also heard the front door open and shut. When her eldest son investigated he could find nothing to account for the sounds. When he returned, the cat preceded him, showing every sign of being terrified. It took refuge under the table, lashing its tail from side to side.

On another occasion, Mr Holbourn heard a scratching sound at one of the two doors leading into the Middle Room. As the household possessed a Siamese cat at the time, Mr Holbourn went to open the door for it. To his astonishment, when he was about 3 feet (1 metre) from the door it suddenly swung wide open, and the door at the opposite end of the room did likewise. A curtain blew outwards, although there was no wind. As Mr Holbourn stood there, footsteps were heard down the passage.

Among the students who had come to Penkaet Castle to rehearse their play that weekend in March 1946 was Mrs Holbourn's son. Most members of the party arrived on the Saturday and after a rehearsal and supper they all retired to bed.

Because the house was so crowded, Mrs Holbourn senior occupied the music room that night; she heard, from somewhere above her, loud noises that continued until nearly 3 a.m. Her son and his wife spent the night in the dining room, and they too heard disturbing noises, so severe that they hardly slept at all. It sounded as if the other members of the group were rehearsing the play again, behaviour that seemed quite extraordinary at that time of night.

In the morning the two girls who had occupied the room above the music room were asked how they had slept. They had, they complained, been much disturbed by peculiar noises, but had tried to ignore them, thinking that perhaps someone was playing a trick on them.

When Carol and Susan, who had occupied the King Charles room, came down they told the others about the noises they had heard, and the ghastly stain they had seen on the wall. They wondered if William Brown (who had been in the room above theirs) had been playing a trick on them, but when he at last came down he said he had slept soundly.

Another member of the party, Margaret Stewart, had slept in the Long Room on the same floor as the King Charles room, sharing it with Carolyn Smith. She had also heard the trundling noise. She said that the room was very cold, and that she had the feeling that they were never quite alone.

The clock that would not go

Susan Hart had encountered another puzzling phenomenon. She had brought with her a clock, which had been in her possession ever since her schooldays and had never been known to go wrong. At Penkaet she wound it up, but found that it would not go for more than five minutes continuously during her stay at the castle, even though she tried to get it going several times. Mr Holbourn said that he had discovered that any clock placed on the wall between the dining room and the next room would not go. He had also tried hanging a watch on that wall, and it stopped.

Two of the girls, Carol Johnstone and Margaret Stewart, said that they had felt ill throughout their visit to the castle. All in all, it seemed that the weekend produced a number of strange and inexplicable events.

On 6 October 1946 a trustee of the Edinburgh Psychic College took a statement from Mrs Holbourn; he also interviewed most of the members of the rehearsal party in Edinburgh on 4 December the same year. William Brown sent a statement from his army camp on 28 January 1947 in which he said that on the Saturday night in question all he did after the party retired to bed was to go to the library to look for something to read, go to his room, undress, and lie in bed reading. He said he was asleep long before midnight.

On 29 July 1946 public attention was drawn to the 'entity' that had disturbed the party of young people in March the same year. It was the day that about 100 members of the East Lothian Antiquarian and Field Naturalists Society had an outing to the castle. In an upper gallery, used as a library, there was a glass dome that covered and protected a model of the house. The dome was about 2 feet (60 centimetres) high, and stood on an oval base about 20 inches (50 centimetres) long. Suddenly, for no apparent reason, and with no one anywhere near it, the glass dome shattered. Could this have been a hint from 'John Cockburn' that he was getting a bit tired of so many visitors?

With the arrival of a new housekeeper at a remote Scottish shooting lodge, the tranquillity of the house was violently disrupted by inexplicable nocturnal noises and a bizarre phantom.

ON A BLEAK, BITTER DAY in 1968 an army team drove past the little cemetery just south of Fort Augustus in Scotland, and turned on to a narrow road that led to a gaunt, rambling house not far from the icy waters of Loch Ness. Ardachie Lodge was ringed with black cypresses, and screened from the loch by a jungle of rhododendrons. It had been some years since any living tenants had inhabited Ardachie, and the old house had been condemned as a dangerous ruin. The soldiers packed charges of dynamite around the walls and lit the fuses: the empty windows of the old shooting lodge looked out across the Scottish landscape for the last time.

When the explosions were over and the dust had settled, the local people wondered if that would be the end of the ghost. As if he shared their fears, the landowner ordered the debris to be bulldozed and removed from the site. The demolition of the house marked the end of a story that had begun back in 1953, when three days in August transformed a year of happiness for Ardachie's owners into a nightmare.

In December 1952 a young couple, Peter and Dorothy McEwan, moved into Ardachie. They had been living in London since their marriage two years earlier, but Dorothy McEwan had been advised that country life would improve her health. They planned to breed pedigree pigs, and the old shooting lodge with its outhouses seemed ideal for the purpose. Soon after moving in, they found a

The case of the crippled phantom

local girl to act as nanny to their toddler and new baby, and a gardener-handyman to help on the land. The McEwans added chickens and sheep to the pedigree pigs, and by the summer they were sufficiently established to be able to employ a live-in couple – the wife as housekeeper and the husband to help with the livestock.

Situations vacant

The job of finding a suitable couple was undertaken by Peter McEwan's parents in London. An advertisement in a newsagent's window attracted the McDonalds, a couple in their forties. They were interviewed, and accepted the post even though they were not told the identity of the family they were to serve, or the location of the house. Within a week, they were aboard a sleeper on their 400-mile [650-kilometre] journey north. At Spean Bridge they were met by Peter McEwan's father (who owned a cottage in the locality) and he drove them to Ardachie.

Their arrival at the house on 17 August 1953 marked the end of the McEwans'

Highland idyll. The events of the next three days were recorded at the time by Peter McEwan, who was a member of the Society for Psychical Research (SPR), and a report based on his account was subsequently published in the SPR's *Journal* in December 1955.

The McDonalds were determined that their month's trial period at Ardachie should be a success. As Peter McEwan observed, they had burned their boats. McDonald had been employed as a postman in London, and by giving up his job he had lost his pension. His wife was a strong-willed woman and had made up her mind to settle down with the McEwans. They made a careful inspection of the house and grounds, and enquired about their duties. As it was obvious that they were both tired after their long journey (Mrs McDonald had been unable to sleep on the train) Dorothy McEwan bade them goodnight early, and joined her husband and father-in-law for supper.

The family were gathered in the sitting room at about 10.30 when the McDonalds

Below: Dr Peter McEwan and his wife Dorothy standing on the site of their former home, Ardachie Lodge, which was demolished in 1968. The isolated house, near Loch Ness (left), was more than a mile from the nearest village and half a mile from a public road. Fort Augustus (right) was the nearest town

burst in. They apologised for the interruption, and asked whether there was anything 'wrong' with their room. Soon after going to bed, Mrs McDonald had heard footsteps that disturbed her twice. As the corridor appeared to be deserted, she had woken her husband, who had slept through the noises. The footsteps had returned, said Mr McDonald, and he had heard them, but they seemed to come from the wall, not the corridor. To reassure the couple, the McEwans explained the layout of the old house, and suggested various sounds that the visitors might have heard. All their suggestions were rejected by the McDonalds: the cat's movements were too quiet, the dog had been locked away in a shed, and the hum of

here. There's a woman in this room.'

She turned away from the wall, and suddenly stiffened in horror. Dorothy McEwan said, 'Don't look like that, Mrs McDonald,' and glanced at the men to urge them to bring her back to the door. But everyone in the room seemed frozen in a bizarre tableau. Mrs McDonald seemed to be in a state of trance; she was staring fixedly into a corner of the room and beckoning something towards her. Yet the others could see nothing.

After a moment or two the spell was broken by Mrs McDonald appearing to awake from a kind of dream. She looked around her and seemed puzzled; she asked the others what they had seen. She said she had seen 'an old lady with a cap on her head, a shawl around her shouders and . . . beckoning me to follow her.' Mrs McDonald also said that the old lady had 'straggling grey hair' and that the experience had been preceded by 'a noise like a rush of wings'.

The household set off to find yet another bedroom where the couple could sleep. Peter McEwan was privately resolving to question his neighbours the following morning to learn more about the previous owners of the house. Would any of them fit Mrs McDonald's description of the old woman? Meanwhile, he asked Mrs McDonald whether she had felt anything else strange about the house in the short time she had been there. She told him that during a walk round the grounds that afternoon she had been

the generator (which produced electricity for the isolated house) was nothing like the sound of footsteps. Dorothy McEwan retraced her own movements about the house earlier in the evening, but these could not be heard in the McDonalds' bedroom. Mrs McDonald insisted, however, that the steps she had heard had been human.

By this time it was late in the evening, and everyone retired to bed. An hour after their first appearance, the McDonalds roused the household. They were both plainly terrified, and said that something 'supernatural' had happened. After going back to bed they had heard rapping: three or four blows at a time on the wall. As soon as McDonald switched on the light the rapping stopped.

The McEwans and the McDonalds went downstairs to the kitchen. Peter McEwan suggested that the two men should return to the bedroom, where they sat in the dark for 10 minutes, listening – but heard nothing. At midnight it was decided that since Mrs McDonald was obviously not going to be able to get a night's rest in that room, the couple should be moved to the guest room. This was some distance away, separated from the first room by two flights of stairs and another corridor.

As soon as she entered the guest room Mrs McDonald crossed to the far wall and pressed her ear against the fireplace, as if listening for something. Then she said, 'She's in

In scenes from the BBC television series *Leap in the dark* (1977), a dramatic reconstruction of events at Ardachie, Mr and Mrs McDonald (played by Neil McCarthy and Wendy Williams) arrive at the house (top) to be employed as handyman and housekeeper by the McEwans (above, played by David Buck and Jacqueline Pearce)

overcome with a distinct feeling of unease in a little overgrown garden just outside the sitting room window.

It was clear that Mrs McDonald was in a distressed state. She said she felt 'as if all the strength has been washed out of my body.' Dorothy McEwan suggested that the couple should sleep in the empty room opposite the McEwans' own bedroom, which was far away from the scene of the earlier alarms. They would leave both doors open and the lights on, and then surely Mrs McDonald would have nothing to fear. This plan was carried out, but within minutes the McDonalds heard faint tapping on the bedhead; Mr McDonald was adamant that it was not the movement of the bed against the wall.

The party gathered again on the landing at the top of the main staircase. Suddenly Mrs McDonald froze, and showed signs of fear. 'There she is again,' she said. 'Can't you see her? Now she is crawling on her hands and knees with what looks like a candlestick in one hand.' McEwan urged his housekeeper to speak to the apparition. 'What's troubling you?' she managed to murmur, but was unable to continue. None of the others could

see anything unusual.

Mrs McDonald began an hysterical running commentary on the crawling woman. At first the figure moved away round a corner; then it returned and began crawling with difficulty towards the terrified Mrs McDonald. The housekeeper was so frightened that the others had to bundle her downstairs to the safety of the kitchen.

Another conference was held, and the four of them agreed to abandon the house for the rest of the night and sleep in Peter McEwan's father's cottage near by.

The next morning, after feeding the animals and breakfasting, Peter McEwan paid a visit to his neighbour, Mrs Beckett of Cullachy House. He knew that she had been a close friend of the previous owners, the Bruens, and he hoped that she would be able to tell him something about the history of the house. It seemed that Ardachie had been built in 1840 as a large shooting lodge for one Charles Gillespie. Although essentially a Georgian-style country house, it incorporated some older farm buildings. Many local people still had vivid memories of the busy months of the year when shooting parties were in residence.

Between the two World Wars a Colonel Campbell was master of Ardachie, and it was after his death that the estate was sold to the Bruens, who had previously owned property in Ireland. Old Mrs Bruen and her sister

In further scenes from the television reconstruction *Leap in the dark* the McDonalds, who had retired early after an overnight journey from London, are awakened (above) by footsteps apparently coming down an empty corridor. Alarmed, they go to find Peter and Dorothy McEwan, who join them in the kitchen (top) to discuss their next move

Lady Hare had been very popular in the neighbourhood. McEwan asked Mrs Beckett to describe old Mrs Bruen carefully. Would the description match his housekeeper's description of the apparition?

Yes, agreed his neighbour, Mrs Bruen wore a kind of shawl and a small hat, and her hair might well have looked as Mrs McDonald had described it. Had she died at Ardachie? McEwan asked. No, replied his neighbour. Although she had lived at Ardachie until a few months before her death, she had eventually been taken to a nursing home in Inverness. It seemed that Mrs Bruen had suffered from a crippling form of arthritis, and had had a stroke so that it was very difficult for her to move in the last months of her life; she had been in the habit of crawling on her hands and knees.

As he made his way home, McEwan wondered whether his housekeeper could really have seen a ghost invisible to the rest of them. The remainder of the day passed without incident. The McDonalds moved their beds downstairs to their own small kitchen, and they retired to bed early at 9.30 p.m. Fifteen minutes later Mrs McDonald got up again, having remembered that she had forgotten to bring in the milk, which was left outside the back door by the shepherd each evening. As she went towards the kitchen door the rapping started, and when she opened the door she saw the old woman waiting at the foot of the stairs. She could not discern any clear features, and the wraith seemed, she said later, barely human. She rushed back into the kitchen and slammed the door.

After this experience, the McEwans and the McDonalds hesitated no longer. Taking the two children with them, they abandoned the Lodge for that night.

The crippled phantom of Ardachie Lodge could be seen only by the new housekeeper – but it could be heard by many people. Eventually its activities made the house intolerable for its living occupants and the Ardachie affair was brought to an end

WHEN THE NEW HOUSEKEEPER and her husband arrived at Ardachie Lodge, Inverness, Scotland, on 17 August 1953 the peaceful life of the household was shattered. For two nights in succession the family were kept awake by the activities of a noisy phantom that only the housekeeper, Mrs McDonald, could see. She claimed that the ghost was an old lady in a shawl, who crawled along the floor on her hands and knees.

The house's owner was Dr Peter McEwan, a qualified psychologist and a member of the London Society for Psychical Research (SPR). His feelings about the case were mixed. On the one hand he was experiencing for the first time a full-scale haunting with plenty of opportunity for scientific study. On the other hand he wanted to protect his wife and young children from alarming phenomena and sleepless nights. He contacted the SPR to find out if there were any members in the locality who might help him clear up the case.

On the third and fourth nights that Mr and Mrs McDonald spent at the Lodge, they were awakened again by the familiar sounds of knocking and rapping, and, unlike the previous occasions, the noises continued

A desirable residence?

after the lights were put on. Peter McEwan had told them to wake him if they heard anything, but they ignored these instructions; they were becoming increasingly apprehensive that these nocturnal disturbances would jeopardise their employment at the Lodge.

On the fifth night the party at the Lodge was joined by a Mr Ross and a Mr Matheson, both members of the SPR. At 10.30 p.m. the household assembled in the McDonalds' kitchen (where the couple were now sleeping) and settled down for a vigil. With the main light turned off, the room was lit only by the glow from the open kitchen range. Ross and McDonald sat on one bed, Matheson on the other; Mrs McDonald sat between them in an armchair. The McEwans stood near the door. Soon the watchers heard rappings from the window wall, rather like the sound of knuckles tapping on wood. The knockings came in slow tempo, three raps at a time with a short interval between individual raps. Sighs coming from Mrs McDonald seemed to be synchronised with the noises.

Mr Ross was watching Mrs McDonald carefully. He reported in the SPR's *Journal* (December 1955):

> She appeared to become transfixed. A lit cigarette dropped from her right hand on to the carpet. Her two arms hung rigid by her side. Her attention was focussed, glassily, on the open door.

Suddenly Mrs McDonald screamed, and shrank back. Hastily, the lights were put on. The housekeeper recovered herself a little, and told the others she had clearly seen the figure of a woman enter the room.

Most of the party then withdrew, to give

Mrs McDonald a little time to recover. When they returned, she was in bed. As soon as the lights were turned off, her breathing became laboured and the rapping began again. After a time Mrs McDonald sat up, and asked her husband if she had been dreaming. She said something about a 'rose tree' and 'neglect'. Then she said, 'It's coming to me now – someone has moved a rose tree.' She lay back, and the rappings began again.

Was Mrs McDonald producing the noises herself? During one set of knockings, Matheson flashed his torch on the wall from which they emanated. This appeared to distress Mrs McDonald, but none of the watchers saw her hands move. The session was brought to a close, and everyone went to bed. The next day the McDonalds claimed that the rappings had continued until five in the morning. Matheson and McEwan spent the night in the guest room (where the ghost had made its first appearance) and slept soundly without any disturbance.

Left: Dorothy and Peter McEwan (top) revisit the site of Ardachie Lodge. They had spent less than a year in the house when the spate of hauntings disrupted their happiness in August 1953. They sold the house (below) as soon thereafter as they could, and a later owner demolished it in 1968

The roses (top) at Ardachie Lodge were the pride of Mrs Bruen, the former owner. But her favourite rose tree died after Davy Coutts (above) moved it at the McEwans' request. Mrs Bruen's spirit apparently complained of this when Mrs McDonald, the housekeeper, spoke in a trance-like state of a neglected rose tree

The next day the SPR investigators departed, leaving Peter McEwan to think about the riddle of the rose tree. When he and his wife had first arrived at the Lodge, he had instructed the part-time gardener to clear out an old greenhouse in the garden so that they could grow tomatoes in it. The only occupants of the greenhouse had been a peach tree and a large old rose tree. The rose had been transplanted outdoors, and had subsequently died. Could this be the rose tree Mrs McDonald was referring to?

A passion for gardens

The McEwans' neighbour, Mrs Beckett, had already told them about Mrs Bruen, the old lady who had previously owned Ardachie Lodge. She now confirmed that Mrs Bruen had had a passion for her gardens, particularly the little rose garden where Mrs McDonald had felt so uneasy on her first day at the Lodge. Her pride and joy was a rare early-flowering rose tree in the old greenhouse. Peter McEwan could not bring himself to tell his neighbour the rose was dead.

The McEwans were quite certain they had not talked about Mrs Bruen to the McDonalds. How could Mrs McDonald have known what Mrs Bruen looked like, and how could she have known about the rose tree? The two people most likely to have told the McDonalds about the previous owner were the nanny, Jenny Maclean, and the gardener Davy Coutts. When this author investigated the haunting in the 1970s, he took pains to trace them.

Jenny Maclean had gone to school in Fort Augustus, and had first seen Mrs Bruen in church and then got to know her at Ardachie. Could she have met the McDonalds and described Mrs Bruen as she had seen her, cycling through the district in her shawl and little hat? But it seemed that Jenny Maclean was in Inverness when the McDonalds arrived at the Lodge, and she did not rejoin the

Ardachie household until after they had left.

When the author questioned Davy Coutts at his home in Fort Augustus he could recall vividly events at Ardachie Lodge during the 1950s. He remembered losing the prize marrow and a hundredweight (50 kilograms) of best seed potatoes to the pedigree pigs, and could also recall the rose tree incident. He was adamant that he had not spoken to the McDonalds; and his diary confirmed that he was at home in Fort Augustus looking after the children (while his wife was away) when the McDonalds were at the Lodge.

So it seemed impossible for Mrs McDonald to have heard about Mrs Bruen and the rose tree from the local people. What of the rapping noises and the footsteps? Could Mrs McDonald be producing these by fraud? On the night of 22 August the McEwans sat with the McDonalds yet again,

Above: Ross and Matheson, called in by Peter McEwan, a fellow SPR member, take Mrs McDonald's pulse in the BBC-TV reconstruction of the Ardachie case. She had just been terrified by 'seeing' the ghost of a woman, invisible to everyone else

Left: the Abbey School, Fort Augustus, in the rolling pine-clad countryside that was the setting for the nightmare at Ardachie Lodge. The fertile imaginations of the school's pupils provided many of the stories that circulated about events at the Lodge. And Abbot Oswald was said to have carried out an exorcism service at the house

but although sounds were heard it was impossible to determine their origin and the session was inconclusive.

By this time the sense of strain at Ardachie was becoming unbearable. Peter McEwan arranged for his wife and children to go away for a few days; the McDonalds were asked to leave. On 29 August McEwan drove them to the station to catch the Glasgow train en route for London. It was only 12 days since they had arrived, with only three pounds and high hopes of a new life. They left in tears.

With their departure peace returned to Ardachie, but as far as Dorothy McEwan was concerned her home had been ruined. Peter McEwan put the estate on the market, and sold it to a vet, who carried on the farming business successfully. He in his turn sold it to a Major Vernon, a landowner who also bought the adjacent Glen Doe estate. A few years later, in 1968, the empty Lodge was demolished to put an end to the gossip.

Some of the stories that were circulating concerned an exorcism that had reputedly been carried out by the head of a local abbey. During the McDonalds' last days in residence mass had been said at Ardachie by Abbot Oswald, and candles had been lit, it was said, at all the places where Mrs McDonald had seen the crawling woman.

Other stories were told of Mrs Bruen's last days. Tormented with illness and increasingly confused she suffered from the delusion that she had been robbed. She was to be seen, local legend had it, searching along the corridors of the house on her hands and knees, knocking on the floorboards for her missing valuables.

Stories like these convinced Peter McEwan that he had been dealing with authentic paranormal phenomena at Ardachie. The strange thing about the haunting was not that a previous owner of the house should return to her old home, but that she should appear to only one person, the unfortunate Mrs McDonald.

Haunted
Europe

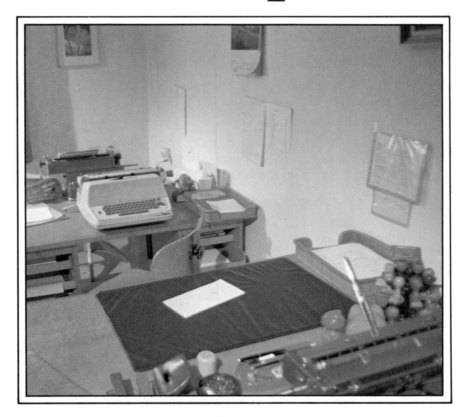

A pinch and a punch

Left: Professor Hans Bender, director of the Freiburg Institute for Border Areas of Psychology and Mental Hygiene, talking to Thierry and Carla on his first visit to the apartment at Mulhouse

A poltergeist that had plagued a young French family for three years with bizarre phenomena proved resistant to all attempts by parapsychologists to dislodge it

ONE DAY IN NOVEMBER 1980 staff at the Freiburg Institute for Border Areas of Psychology and Mental Hygiene, in West Germany, received an urgent telephone call asking them to investigate an unusual and complex poltergeist case. The caller was a Dr Fleur, a physicist, who had been investigating the case but felt in need of expert advice.

The case concerned a couple in their mid-thirties who were living with their young son Jean, aged four, in a ground-floor apartment in Mulhouse, France. Thierry, the husband, was a technical designer and painter; his wife, Carla, was Spanish-born but had been living in Mulhouse since the age of 15. For the past three years they had been plagued by poltergeist activity. The manifestations occurred at least three times a week and included the sound of knocking at the windows (also heard by other witnesses), of cars crashing, babies crying and animals whimpering; a heavy table was seen 'dancing', pillows and sheets were pulled away from the bed during the night, and the bed itself sometimes moved. Abrupt changes of temperature in the apartment were reported, and it was sometimes as hot as 80°F (27°C) when the heating was turned off. To monitor the temperature changes Dr Fleur had installed a chart recorder, which would record the temperature continuously on a graphic read-out – but the resulting print-out was in a form that the machine was not (technically speaking) capable of producing.

These manifestations, together with others that Fleur described, were classic poltergeist phenomena; they were teasing,

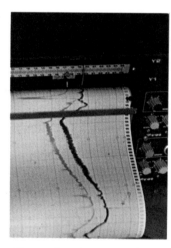

Above: the chart recorder installed by Dr Fleur to record the extraordinary fluctuations in temperature in the poltergeist-stricken apartment. Although designed to produce continuous lines on graph paper, the machine somehow produced broken lines and several 'impossible' horizontal lines

playful, sometimes threatening, and at all times disruptive. The most unusual aspect of the case however was that the activity had been going on for three years. Such a long-lived case was almost unheard of and, as the investigators from the institute were later to discover, this poltergeist was also downright aggressive.

Plan of campaign

The investigators agreed on the following plan. They would interview the family and any other witnesses, and examine the notes Thierry had kept since 1978; they would install a continuously running tape recorder in the apartment for several nights; and they would conduct a hypnosis experiment in the hope of producing observable phenomena. This experiment was planned in two parts. In the first part, Carla would be hypnotised and given the suggestion that something 'observable' would happen later in the evening. For the second part of the experiment, radar equipment (provided by Dr Fleur) was to be placed in a locked room, where it would monitor objects on a table (the objects were to be ones that had already been moved by poltergeist activity, according to the family). If any of the objects moved, the radar equipment would activate a ciné camera, which would then film for 10 seconds. It was hoped that post-hypnotic suggestion might produce psychokinetic movement of the prepared targets.

The couple told the researchers how, at the suggestion of friends, they had begun to practise glass rolling when the poltergeist activity first began (glass rolling is a variation on the ouija board). In the course of these sessions the couple often received words in Spanish, which would seem to indicate a

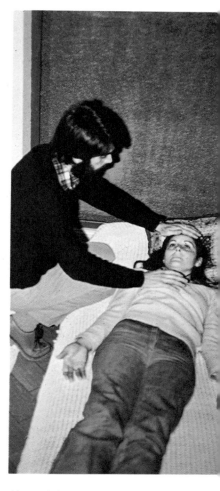

away from where it had stood before.

An outstanding feature of the case was the amount of hostility directed towards Carla by the poltergeist. In his journal for 1978 Thierry wrote: 'Carla sometimes feels punched in the stomach. She has received strong pinches on her leg . . . the black marks are visible the next day.' He also said that scratches had been seen on her face and arms, and cuts on her arms had been discovered when she woke in the morning. She had felt trapped in bed as if held down by 'strong arms' and had twice felt 'cold hands' attempting to strangle her – the marks remained on her neck for two or three days and were seen by other witnesses.

The journal entries for 1979 showed that the aggression towards Carla was becoming less violent and less frequent. Nevertheless, she still endured many unpleasant experiences. She twice found herself trapped in the outhouse (although the door had no lock). Articles of clothing disappeared, to reappear months later in strange places. And one afternoon she saw the small rug from the kitchen move up and down the hall, apparently of its own accord.

After visiting Mulhouse several times, the investigators agreed to proceed with the hypnosis experiment. The hypnotist, named Gaston, suggested to Carla that 'something observable' would happen during the evening, and he added the post-hypnotic suggestion that the 'agent' might be kind enough to do something between 8.30 and 9 p.m.

An unco-operative spirit

When 9 p.m. came, however, nothing out of the ordinary had happened. After dinner Carla, Thierry, M. Gaston and Dr Fleur sat down together at the glass-rolling table, and asked Henri why he was being so unco-operative. The response spelt out 'no . . . no . . . no'. All at once, M. Gaston went into a semi-trance, with deep breathing; he spoke to the others and said that he had heard a message: 'The bed, the bed.' Carla ran to the bedroom, but all was well. However, when the bed was moved, two drawings were found on the floor – a cross inside a circle and a triangle. Five days earlier, similar designs had been found drawn on Carla's thigh.

It was impossible to establish exactly when the drawings on the floor had been made. Carla said that the bed had been moved two days earlier when the room was cleaned, and at that time the floor was unmarked. She said she always made a point of checking under the bed, because the previous year markings had been found on the floor three nights in succession. It was also not clear whether the words heard by M. Gaston had any real connection with the experiment; perhaps he had perceived the markings clairvoyantly before the hypnosis session and the glass rolling.

Above left: a friend of the family in front of the door to the outhouse in which Carla had twice found herself mysteriously imprisoned, although the door had no lock

Above: the hypnosis experiment, in which Carla was hypnotised and given the suggestion that paranormal phenomena would occur after she awoke from her trance

connection with Carla; but her curiosity and genuine surprise at the results seemed to indicate that this was not a case of trickery. They had attempted to communicate with the unknown trickster in the apartment through glass rolling; it appeared that he was called Henri, but the messages they received from him were often silly.

Apart from hearing about Henri, the investigators learned a good deal about Carla's background on their first visit to Mulhouse. She had begun to sleepwalk as a child of three; at the age of five she was known to have an uncanny ability to recognise pregnant women, being able to detect a pregnancy even in its earliest stages. Carla said that she had experienced extra-sensory perception several times since childhood. She had had premonitions of her grandmother's death, and had had a detailed vision of a serious accident involving her brother just before it happened. Carla clearly had some psychic powers. Thierry, however, said that he had never exhibited any paranormal tendencies.

A study of Thierry's journal showed that Carla was the person around whom the activity seemed to centre. She was almost always present when something strange occurred – apart from one occasion. She and Thierry had gone to the cinema, and on their return they found that the drawing-room table had moved; it was quite 3 feet (1 metre)

The investigators from the institute met again in Mulhouse two weeks later to conduct a second hypnosis experiment. This time they hoped they would be able to film PK phenomena produced by post-hypnotic suggestion. Dr Fleur set up his radar equipment and camera to monitor the objects arranged on a table, and the room was locked. If any of the objects on the table were to move, the equipment would trigger the camera and it would film for 10 seconds.

Carla was put into a deep hypnotic trance. She was then given the suggestion that Henri should 'move the table or any of the objects

on it'. Everybody sat down to wait. By 1 a.m. nothing had happened, and the investigators, somewhat disappointed, drove home.

Half an hour later, just as Carla and Thierry were on the point of going to bed, the camera was triggered and started to film. Instead of stopping after 10 seconds it ran and ran, until after three minutes Thierry decided to switch it off at the electric point, which was located outside the room. However, when it was developed, the film did not show any movement of the target objects: it seemed that something else had affected the radar equipment or triggered the camera. After examining all the equipment Dr Fleur reported that the relay that should have cut the electrical current after 10 seconds had got stuck. Was this pure chance? Or another teasing manifestation of the poltergeist?

In the weeks following the experiment the activities of the poltergeist seemed to be on the increase again. Young Jean began to talk in his sleep. He claimed to hear music when others could not (as did Carla at times). Jean also told his parents about 'visitors' who came to his bedside at night, or when he was playing with his toys. At last, in a final desperate bid for help, Carla and Thierry sought the advice of an exorcist, and he made an appointment to visit their home. But Carla cancelled the appointment. She and Thierry had decided to leave Mulhouse.

Above: markings on the floor under Carla and Thierry's bed, similar to ones that had appeared earlier on Carla's thigh

Below: after the first hypnosis experiment, Thierry checked his bookshelves and found several of his books turned upside down

An alarming increase in paranormal activity had led to this decision. One afternoon Carla had gone down to the cellar to get a bottle of wine for the evening meal. Halfway down the stairs, she thought she saw the outline of a dark figure crouched on the landing. Although she was frightened, curiosity prompted her to take a closer look. As she hesitatingly descended a few more steps the figure rose, reached out to her menacingly, and then vanished. Carla screamed and fled back upstairs.

A day or two later the figure appeared again, this time in the apartment. In panic and confusion, Carla ran right through it: it was not seen again.

Naturally enough, after this incident Carla did not feel like going down to the cellar to get the wine for dinner, so she sent Thierry. When he got to the cellar door, he found it was impossible to open. It seemed that the ground level beneath the door had risen. Thierry fetched a shovel and started digging out the earth under the door, half expecting to find a grimacing skeleton. He had got only 8 inches (20 centimetres) down when the shovel broke. Since he was now able to open the door, Thierry decided there was no point in digging any further. The hole under the cellar door looked ridiculous, and became a standing joke among the couple's friends.

Two weeks later, on the evening of 17 April 1981, Carla spontaneously entered a trance-like state. This in itself was no longer an uncommon occurrence, and Thierry had taken to keeping a loaded camera in readiness by his bedside, in case something happened that he wanted to record on film. He had taken the precaution of sealing the body of the camera with masking tape to ensure the film was not tampered with: rolls of film had already disappeared from the camera on several occasions.

When Carla went into a trance and began to mumble, Thierry grabbed the camera but, to his amazement, he could feel a lack of

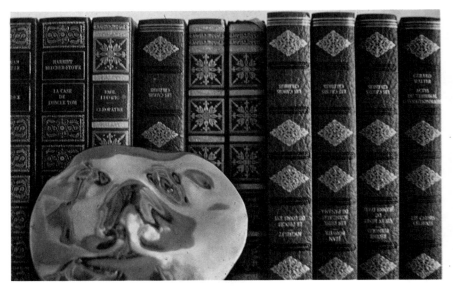

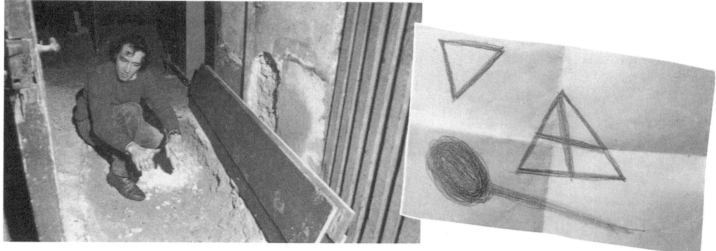

tension in the wind-on lever, which told him the camera was empty. When he broke the seal with a razor blade he found that the film was indeed gone: in its place was a small folded piece of paper. Pencilled on this were three designs – a triangle, a triangle with a cross inside it, and a large dark spot with a protruding line. These designs were very similar to those the investigators had found under the bed, and marked on one of Carla's thighs.

Thierry and Carla decided that they had had enough. They determined to sell their home, and Thierry found a job in the Antilles, on the other side of the world. It was at this point that Carla called the exorcist to cancel their appointment.

The Freiburg investigators believed the phenomena were due to the eruption of some kind of energy or psychic force, which in most instances was focused on Carla. The question was how to subdue this force, or better still put it to constructive use.

A surprising talent

Quite unexpectedly, Carla began to produce automatic drawings. Like many other mediumistic artists she was surprised and delighted with her pictures, which seemed to draw themselves. She never knew what the outcome of her 'efforts' would be, and even the titles of her pictures were written without her conscious participation.

It became obvious that the process of drawing was an outlet that allowed Carla to express and release pent-up conflicts and problems. She said, 'I don't know exactly why I started to draw, but somehow it was a strong urge. I felt as if I had to get things on paper. . . . My work was raw and strong, and sometimes the paper would tear because I was using too much force. I must confess I was shocked at first, although now that my pictures have become softer and less impulsive I can look back at the first ones and see them as the expression of some strong feelings.'

Up to this point everybody concerned with the case, including the family, had

Above: Thierry pointing out the hole in the cellar floor that he was forced to dig in order to open the door. The Freiburg investigators were unable to explain how the ground level beneath the door could have risen. Before the incident occurred Carla had seen a figure crouching nearby

Above right: the drawings found inside Thierry's camera. There seems to be no rational explanation of how the piece of paper got there. The camera had been sealed with tape that had to be cut, using a razor blade, before the contents could be removed. There was no indication that the seal had been tampered with. No one knows whether the symbols were intended to be significant or whether they were the poltergeist's idea of a joke

believed that Carla was either the psi source (that is, she was actually causing the events) or she was an unwitting catalyst setting off poltergeist activity in the apartment. Whichever it was, events were linked to her, and Carla's outbreak of creative activity tended to confirm this view.

However, while Carla and Thierry were strapping up the last boxes to be sent to their new home, they were visited by a neighbour. Surprised to see their preparations, he asked why they were moving. Thierry said something about a change of job and mentioned Carla's 'difficulty in sleeping'. The neighbour then told them that the previous owner of the house, a certain Madame Arricot, had also had trouble falling asleep due to 'unexplained knockings and the mysterious opening and closing of doors' when she was alone in the house. She had sold the house, said the neighbour, because of these disturbances. 'I suppose you don't know,' he added, 'that she recently passed away?' This was news indeed – was the house haunted after all?

But Carla and Thierry had no time to consider this new piece of information. Two days later the Freiburg team met them at the airport where they were anxiously awaiting the departure of their flight to the Antilles. Last goodbyes were said, and the family walked happily to the customs hall. A few minutes later Carla reappeared in tears. All her identity papers were missing.

It took a lot of fast talking and diplomacy, plus the testimony of several witnesses, to get Carla on that aeroplane. But finally they were off. A few weeks later Carla and Thierry wrote from Guadeloupe to say that everything was fine, more or less. Carla had found her papers in the new apartment, underneath the mattress of the bed. And the television had broken down, for no apparent reason, seven times.

Was Carla causing these electrical problems? Or had the mischievous poltergeist taken a transatlantic trip? The Freiburg investigators had to confess themselves baffled, and the riddles remain unanswered.

Beware-PK at work

When a Bavarian lawyer started to have trouble with his telephone, he little suspected that his quiet office was about to be plagued by a massive poltergeist attack

Above: the quiet town of Rosenheim where, at Konigstrasse 13, the increasing ferocity of the poltergeist made work almost impossible

A LAWYER'S OFFICE IN ROSENHEIM, Bavaria, was the unlikely setting for a poltergeist case that completely altered public opinion about poltergeists in Germany. The activities were centred on several rooms at Konigstrasse 13, the offices of a lawyer named Adam.

Herr Adam told investigators that the events that were to become so famous began quietly in the summer of 1967, when telephone malfunctions were reported by office staff. Calls to the office on Rosenheim 1233 had been interrupted by clicks or cut off, and sometimes all four receivers would ring at once although the line was dead. The malfunctions had become too frequent to overlook, and the office manager, Johannes Engelhard, called in repair men from Siemens, the company that had installed the equipment – a junction box and four telephones.

The Siemens engineers worked in the office for several weeks, testing wiring and equipment. Although they found no faults, they replaced the receivers and junction box – but, as this did not improve matters, they called in the post office.

Early in October, the post office replaced the Siemens equipment with official post office telephones. They installed a meter so that, as they were made, calls could be recorded visibly in the office on a counter, with a similar meter at the telephone exchange to provide an official record. At the same time, Herr Adam asked his staff, the office manager Johannes Engelhard, two

Below: trouble with the telephone was the first sign of poltergeist activity in Herr Adam's office. No mechanical or electrical fault could be found with the instrument, but massive bills were run up – and not, it seemed, by any of the employees.

office clerks and a part-time worker, to make a note of their calls.

On 5 October 1967, Adam and Engelhard were amazed to see the meter register a call although no one in the office was using the telephone. On 19 October, the same thing happened while Adam was with accountant Dr Schmidt, who produced an affidavit for Adam to show the post office. Comparing the records from his own meter, the meter at the exchange and the notes of his staff, Adam realised that these two incidents were by no means isolated. Dozens of undialled calls had been registered. The post office insisted that all the calls had been made in the normal way and, even more peculiar, they had all been made to the speaking clock.

A row broke out between the post office and Herr Adam. Adam pointed out that all his staff had watches and could hear the chimes of at least two church clocks, and could therefore keep a record of the timing of their telephone calls. Furthermore, no one was ever alone in the office, and it was ridiculous to suppose that so many calls could have been made unnoticed by anyone. Between 7.42 and 7.57 a.m. on 20 October 1967, 46 telephone calls were registered to the speaking clock. Adam further pointed out that although at least 17 seconds are needed to dial and connect with the speaking clock, even if one does not wait to hear the time, the post office claimed that as many as six calls a minute had been made, and continued to send enormous bills. Nevertheless, on 31 October, they replaced the telephones again. This time, the dials were locked and only Herr Adam had a key.

This step made no difference, and on 8 November Herr Adam was extremely angry to receive another huge bill that did not correspond with the records at all. He issued an accusation – against person or persons unknown – of fraud or embezzlement; it began: 'For several months my telephone installation has been so disturbed that a regular telephone call is impossible.'

Addicted to the time

By the spring of 1975, Adam had gathered a sheaf of statements from the post office in which 0119, the number of the speaking clock, appeared over and over again. 'In five weeks,' he said, 'the speaking clock has been connected between 500 and 600 times. In one day, 80 times. I was very angry with the post office; I even wanted to found an association for the protection of the subscriber.' However, Adam soon had disturbances of a different nature to deal with.

On 20 October 1967, the office lights suddenly went out with a bang. Herr Bauer, an electrician from Stern's, a local firm, was called in to repair them. He examined the lights and found that each fluorescent tube had been turned 90° in its socket and disconnected. He had finished replacing the tubes and put away his ladder when there was another bang. The tubes had twisted and disconnected themselves again. He was even more puzzled when the office staff told him that the automatic fuses in the office ejected themselves for no apparent reason, sometimes on all four circuits at once. Bauer began a full investigation of the office wiring and equipment, all of which he found in excellent order. He confessed to Adam: 'I was faced with a puzzle and called it "witchcraft".'

Since no fault could be found in the office, he concluded that something must be wrong with the electricity supply itself. The *Elektrizitätswerk* – German electricity board – was asked to take over the investigation. Accordingly, Paul Brunner, Auxiliary Works Manager, arrived at Adam's office on 15 November 1967.

Brunner is a small, dynamic man who impressed greatly with his authority and his

Right: Paul Brunner who, on behalf of the German electricity board, began investigations at Herr Adam's office on 15 November 1967

Below: the Unireg recorder (left) on which abnormalities in the electricity supply were detected and traced on a graph (right). At first the investigators thought that these were caused by the local electricity substation – but they found absolutely no faults there

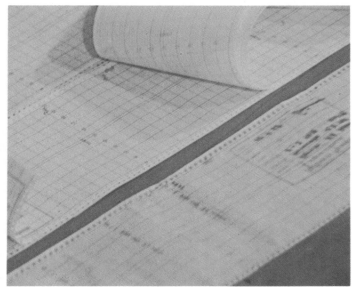

efficiency. He was born in Rosenheim and belonged to the second generation of his family to work at the electricity board. He stated that he had had no interest in the occult, but approached Adam's office with curiosity because of its scientific challenge – yet, ironically, the official report he prepared became one of the most significant documents in paranormal research.

The escalation of the Rosenheim phenomena can be seen when viewed chronologically. On Wednesday, 15 November 1967, extensive checks were run on the wiring and appliances at 13 Königstrasse, especially in Adam's flat. Everything was found to be satisfactory and short circuits were ruled out as a possible cause of the phenomena.

On Thursday, 16 November, a Siemans Unireg – an electrical instrument that shows voltage fluctuations on a single-track pen recorder – was installed at the office. Later a Tektronix plug-in unit with a storage oscilloscope was added, giving two more pen traces that showed fluctuations in the magnetic field and the noise level. A pen recorder gave

a continuous read-out of current and voltage variations at selected points in the office circuitry, and the times at which they happened. The machine was sealed to prevent tampering. Over the next few weeks, it was established that abnormal deflections on the paper record occurred, but only in office hours and never at weekends. The automatic fuses were replaced with screw-in types and, to rule out trickery, these were also sealed.

On Monday, 20 November, after a 'normal' morning of twisting tubes, inexplicable voltage variations and bangs, a fluorescent tube in Adam's private office fell to the floor and shattered. At the same moment, a huge surge in the electric current – 50 amps – was registered, yet the safety fuses did not blow. On examining the read-out, Brunner was puzzled to see loops instead of the expected straight lines. Other tubes fell as the day wore on.

On Tuesday, 21 November, as a safety measure, all the fluorescent tubes in the office were replaced by normal light bulbs. More loud bangs were heard, and the photocopier

began leaking chemicals. It was plugged in but not switched on. Brunner wondered if electricity were being conducted into the building through gas and water mains. The team ran a number of tests – and this possibility, too, was ruled out.

On Wednesday, 22 November, the light bulbs began to explode. The neighbourhood was searched for freak power sources. None was found.

On Thursday, 23 November, the office apartment was disconnected from the electricity mains and was connected directly by cable to the transformer, High Tension Station K11 in Königstrasse.

On Friday, 24 November, Brunner thought the mystery was over. He found full deflections on the paper record, some so savage that the paper had been torn by the pen. As the meter was connected directly to K11, he thought the fault had to be there in the supply itself, and that his team had been correct in pronouncing all the electrical equipment in the office satisfactory. With relief, engineers, equipment and cable were

Above: Herr Adam inspects one of the lamps that began to swing wildly on 27 November 1967. The lamp on the office landing moved as much as 22 inches (55 centimetres) from its normal position

Above right: one of the more violent deflections of the trace on the Unireg recorder. No physical reason could be found for the disturbances in the electricity supply – though they did occur only during office hours, suggesting that someone on the staff was somehow responsible

evacuated from the office and camp was set up at K11, to pinpoint the fault. But no fault was found. Camp was reinstated at the office.

The entire supply grid of Rosenheim was checked and pronounced sound.

On Monday, 27 November, a girl was cut by flying glass from an exploding light bulb. All remaining bulbs were covered by nylon bags to prevent further accidents. Four more exploded that afternoon. Between five and six o'clock, an alarming new development forced Brunner to admit that he was dealing with something outside his experience: the lights began to swing.

The next few days were spent observing swinging lamps and trying to find an explanation for their movement: 'We leapt repeatedly up and down the floor overhead to try to make the lamps swing – without success. The traffic outside was also watched carefully, and tests were made for electrostatic charges, but none was found.'

On Thursday, 30 November, the office was severed from the mains, and power supplied instead by a 7-kilowatt generator-truck parked outside. The generator's meter showed a steady 220-volt output, yet inside the office deflections and crashes continued, lamps swung, bulbs exploded and fuses were ejected erratically.

On Thursday, 7 December, over 90 deflections were registered during the morning. Lamps swung so violently that they smashed against the ceiling, denting the plaster.

Paintings begin to twirl

To vindicate his methods and results, and to safeguard his reputation, Brunner asked the advice of Dr Karger of the Max Planck Institute of Plasma Physics, and Dr Zicha of Munich University, two of Germany's most eminent physicists. Following a suggestion from Karger, Brunner disconnected the office supply from the Unireg and placed an ordinary 1.5-volt battery across the Unireg terminals. To the astonishment of everyone, instead of registering 1.5 volts until the battery exhausted its charge, the pen began its trace at 3 volts and then zig-zagged wildly across the paper. The Unireg (which was in perfect working order) could not be monitoring the battery to which it was connected.

On Monday, 11 December, at 8.45 a.m., Brunner and his assistant, Mayr, were chatting together in the typists' office, when suddenly a painting twisted on its hook. Surprised, Brunner stretched out his hand to straighten the picture. Other paintings in the room started to rotate, some falling to the floor. The typists, who later said they had felt unusually tense that morning, were rooted to their desks with fear, but Mayr and Brunner stationed themselves at vantage points to observe this new phenomenon. They saw the first painting to move turn through 320°, its string wrapping itself round its hook.

At this point, Brunner, realising that he

Herr Adam sits pensively in front of the painting that turned, by itself, through almost a complete circle – to the terror of the watching office staff

was out of his depth, prepared to wind up the experiments and wrote his official report. In it, he was relieved to point out the excellent state of Rosenheim's electricity supply, which had been thoroughly checked – to even Herr Adam's satisfaction; yet inexplicable voltage deflections still occurred in the office:

It became necessary to postulate the existence of a power hitherto unknown to technology, of which neither the nature nor strength nor direction could be defined. It is an energy quite beyond our comprehension.

Alarmed by the thought that there was no apparent way of controlling this mysterious and often harmful energy, Brunner handed over the investigations to the physicists who had been monitoring the experiments.

Like Brunner, Dr Karger and Dr Zicha were fascinated by the scientific challenge of explaining the electrical disturbances in Adam's office, and they carried out an independent investigation using the most sophisticated equipment. They concentrated on finding the cause of the deflections on the

meter, installing probes to examine voltage levels, magnetic fields and sound levels. Their questions and answers can be summarised as follows.

1. Were the deflections accompanied by voltage surges? *No, voltage remained constant.*

2. Were the disturbances caused by high-frequency voltage transmission from outside the office? *None measured and none found.*

3. An electrostatic charge? *No.*

4. A static magnetic field? *None detected.*

5. Loose contact in the measuring equipment's amplifier? *None found. A second machine also showed the same anomalies.*

6. Ultrasonic or infrasonic vibrations? *None found.*

7. Manual interference? *Fraud and trickery impossible.*

While measuring sound levels, they noticed that, although no sound was heard, their monitor showed a huge deflection, so they concluded that there must have been direct pressure on the crystal in the microphone. They speculated that a similar invisible force could be acting on the pen of the Unireg itself, causing the unnatural loops directly, independently of the electric current. They speculated further: the same force could be acting on the tiny springs inside the telephone, bypassing the dial. It was active only for short periods, its nature was complex and it was not electrodynamic. Known physics could not explain it.

A fugitive intelligence

Karger and Zicha also felt that the telephone anomalies suggested that an intelligent force was at work, because it had 'chosen' to focus its attention on the speaking clock. It was clear that the force resisted investigation, and this was another reason to speculate on the existence of an intelligence avoiding scrutiny. They prepared their report and left.

As the physicists left Adam's office, teams of investigators from other scientific fields were eager to take their place, including Professor Hans Bender from the Freiburg Institute, who began his experiments in mid December. He was joined by several policemen who had come as a result of Adam's exasperated accusation 'Against person or persons unknown', and independently these new investigators began gathering evidence. The physicists had left two important clues. First, they had suspected that a rational being was behind the phenomena and second, they confirmed that the 'poltergeist' was active in office hours only. Investigations were now centred on the office staff, Johannes Engelhard, Frau Bielmeier (the part-time assistant) and the two clerks, 17-year-old Gustel Huber and 18-year-old Annemarie Schneider.

A spirit of anger

Left: Annemarie Schneider, centre of the Rosenheim poltergeist phenomenon, photographed with her young son in April 1975

Below: a portion of the Unireg pen trace showing violent deflections beginning around 7.30 a.m. – the hour when Annemarie reported for work

Gesamte Installation am Netzstrom - Aggregat

Teams of investigators were mystified by the weird events at the Rosenheim lawyer's office. At length they began to suspect that the happenings were centred on one of the members of the office staff – but who was responsible? And why?

AS THE PARANORMAL EVENTS in Herr Adam's office continued, work became increasingly difficult. The army of investigators and reporters who were constantly present did not make things any better, and the staff, who felt they were under continuous scrutiny, became tense and nervous. It was bad enough to have to cope with the poltergeist phenomena that continually interrupted their work, but they also had to cope with mutual suspicion each time something happened. A typical event occurred on 12 December, when Johannes Engelhard, the office manager, was opening the morning post with a knife. Frau Adam called to him from the next room, and, as he walked to the door, he heard a picture fall somewhere behind him. He spun round to see the painting lying on the floor. But that was not all. Neatly stacked on it were the letters he had been opening, together with the knife. Although the two clerks were in the office, they could not have touched the letters or the picture in the moment it took for Engelhard to turn round. All the same, he could not help suspecting that they had played a trick on him.

Soon, however, suspicion began to centre on Annemarie Schneider. She appeared to be the most tense of the office staff, and she twitched strangely whenever poltergeist activity took place. The Unireg record, which

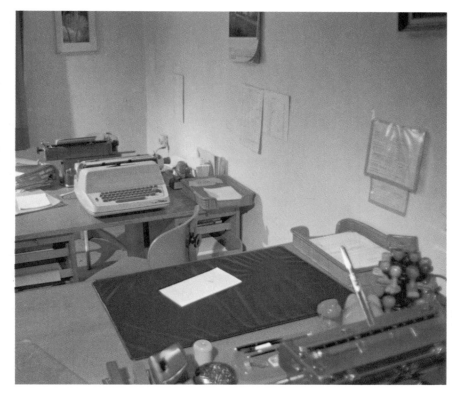

had shown deflections only in office hours, was checked closely, and it was found that events began at 7.30 a.m. – the time that Annemarie reported for work. Hans Bender's team from the Freiburg Institute had discreetly centred investigations on her for some time. One day, one of Bender's assistants noticed a lamp swinging strangely as Annemarie walked along the corridor underneath it. It had already been decided that each of the office staff would take a short holiday, since things had been so trying. This would also enable the research team to check who, if anyone, was responsible for the phenomena. Annemarie was given first leave – and, sure enough, the office was peaceful again.

Screaming and sobbing

When Annemarie returned to work on 18 December, she seemed even more tense than before, and screamed out when a lamp began to swing. The phenomena had returned with her – and with renewed intensity. Pictures swung merrily, dropping to the floor with a force that dismantled their frames, but left their glass intact. Pages flew off the calendar, and light bulbs exploded. Drawers slid out of desks, and Frau Bielmeier had to wedge one shut with a stool weighted by a typewriter. Annemarie grew more tense every day, screaming and sobbing when phenomena occurred close to her. Fortunately, the Christmas holidays arrived.

Work at the office recommenced on 1 January 1968. When everything had been normal for over a week, Adam began to hope that he was no longer Rosenheim's principal consumer of light bulbs and fluorescent tubes

Above: the desks at which the two girl clerks in Herr Adam's office, Gustel Huber and Annemarie Schneider, worked

Below: on the afternoon of 17 January 1967 this oak cabinet, which weighs over 400 pounds (180 kilograms), moved a distance of more than a foot (30 centimetres)

– until 10.30 a.m. on 9 January, when Annemarie returned.

As before, the phenomena returned with Annemarie, and as before, they had grown still more violent. Annemarie received an electric shock in her leg as she picked a picture up off the floor, and Frau Bielmeier had a cracking sensation in her ear.

The climax was reached on 17 January. With only Annemarie and Frau Adam in the office, a number of light bulbs exploded. Annemarie was so frightened that she ran upstairs to the dental surgery, where Herr Geistaller, the dentist, managed to calm her down. Later, the police came to photograph the damage. Annemarie was back at her desk, typing, when the calendar fell from the wall and desk drawers slid out. Suddenly, a metal cash box jumped out of a drawer and clattered to the floor, spilling coins and stamps everywhere. The police, who also believed Annemarie was somehow at the centre of the phenomena, began to keep a closer watch on her.

Officer Wendl was in charge of the police investigation, and he was eager to solve the case. His belief that he would eventually catch Annemarie moving objects physically was shaken that afternoon when a heavy oak cabinet moved a foot (30 centimetres). The cabinet weighed over 400 pounds (180 kilograms), and Wendl realised that, even using levers or with the help of Fräulein Huber, Annemarie could not have moved it. It had been lifted clear over the edge of the linoleum, which would have puckered had the cabinet been shoved, and it took the efforts of two burly policemen to restore it to its place. Had the cabinet episode not occurred, Wendl would have felt sure that he had proved his case, but now he doubted it. He

strange red patches appeared on her skin. That day, she was given further leave of absence. As she left, she noted sadly in a diary she had been asked to keep by Hans Bender: '18 January. As from today, I am on the sicklist. . . . I hope everything will proceed quickly so I can have my rest at last.'

Herr Adam lost no time. Annemarie was dismissed, and never returned to the Königstrasse office – and neither did the strange phenomena. During the poltergeist activity, the cost of the damage had amounted to 15,000 Deutschmarks, which the unfortunate Adam was obliged to pay.

Hans Bender took the opportunity of asking Annemarie to visit his Freiburg Institute so that he could do some laboratory tests and, after initial reluctance to leave home, she agreed to spend from 21 to 26 January 1968 there. A team of scientists duplicated the circuits and equipment of Adam's office, hoping to reproduce the poltergeist effects, but none of the deflections or other phenomena occurred. It seems that Annemarie could produce paranormal events only in certain specific circumstances.

Abandoning the attempt to reproduce psychokinesis, Bender tried testing Annemarie's ESP abilities. Again, nothing significant was discovered – except momentarily, when Annemarie scored highly while upset by an unpleasant memory. This seemed to confirm that stress encouraged paranormal events in her case.

Stress and frustration were seen to play a major role in Annemarie's personality. During her stay at Freiburg, she underwent extensive psychological assessment by a psychologist colleague of Bender, John Mischo. He concluded that she was unstable, irritable and suffering from frustrated rages.

was beginning to think, along with the scientists, that the ordinary laws of physics did not apply in the office, but as an extra check he organised a search for tools. None was found.

At 4.30 the same afternoon, Frau Adam arrived at the police station to inform Wendl that the cabinet had moved again. He and Officer Tischler accompanied her back to the office, which they found in chaos. The girls were almost hysterical because they had been getting electric shocks in their arms and legs all day, and before the second movement of the cabinet, tables and chairs had moved. One table had jerked along with a horrified visitor perched on it. When Frau Bielmeier left the typing room, her chair had risen, and Annemarie and Fräulein Huber's chairs both sunk. The height of the typing chairs is adjusted with a ratchet that, to prevent accidents, cannot be altered when any weight is on the seat – yet that afternoon, Professor Büchel of the Physics Institute at Pulach, near Munich, had watched Annemarie's chair descend while she was still sitting on it. She was shocked; her face blanched, then

She was unable to tolerate denial and was aggressive, although she suppressed her aggression. He believed that her constant frustrations discharged themselves through psychokinesis, via a process yet to be explained. Her own doctor had remarked on the severity of her nervous symptoms, which included hyperaemia (an excess of blood gathering in one place) and cramps. Her cramp attacks always followed the same pattern: she would cry out, and her eyes would glaze as the cramp spread. Her hands and feet would be worst affected, fingers and toes stretched painfully rigid. Muscles in her knees and hips would also flex agonisingly.

Professor Bender looked for psychological motives for the phenomena. He felt that the speaking clock was contacted as a result of

Annemarie continues the story:
We had been engaged for three years and once a week we went bowling. On one occasion, the relays behaved in an eccentric way and the bowling was spoiled. I was told the relays had been put out of action, I don't know what they were talking about. My fiancé took the whole thing much too seriously and said that under the circumstances, marriage would be quite impossible.

This happened in the summer of 1969. Whatever the scientists' belief about Annemarie's subconscious wishes, she took several years to get over her broken engagement. She felt victimised, since there had been nothing to prove that the failure of the bowling mechanism was anything whatsoever to do with her.

Blamed for a death
Finally, a team of investigators went to talk directly to Annemarie. They met with her in April 1975. She turned out to be a stout, plain girl with a sad, prematurely aged face. She told them that after leaving Adam's office, she had been employed by another solicitor, Weinzier. Stories of her ability to move lamps and produce other phenomena followed her. This was the first in a long series of jobs, since the unfortunate Annemarie would always be dismissed if anything odd occurred. 'I never had influence over anything. I was very hurt indeed.' Her Bavarian colleagues still had medieval superstitions and apparently whispered that she was a witch.

She went on: 'I worked in Regenfelchen in a paper factory, and there was an accident there when a man was killed. The workers who knew who I was said, "That woman is responsible for the man's death." They didn't give me the sack from the factory immediately, they just dropped hints, so I left on my own accord. I wasn't even in the factory when it happened.'

Since that highly dubious case, there have been no new reports of paranormal happenings associated with Annemarie. She has moved to Munich where, in the anonymous surroundings of a big city, her reputation for producing psychokinetic effects has not been able to catch up with her to plague her. And perhaps this has something to do with the fact that she apparently no longer produces these effects: for, unlike most paranormal phenomena, these seemed actually to be encouraged by attention from scientists and the media. Hans Bender has pointed out that this most remarkable of cases was observed over a period of several months by more than 40 witnesses from widely ranging walks of life – office workers, electrical engineers, lawyers, scientists, psychologists and the police. For all the documentary evidence, however, *how* Annemarie produced the phenomena remains as much a mystery to scientists as ever it was.

Below: the bowling alley in Raubling, on the outskirts of Rosenheim. Annemarie used to go bowling here with her fiancé – but, after an incident in the summer of 1969 in which she apparently disrupted the electronically controlled bowling system, her fiancé broke off the engagement

Above left: Hans Bender and a colleague inspect the fluorescent light fittings that spontaneously unscrewed themselves while Annemarie Schneider was present in the office

Left: Annemarie inspects a pen trace during tests conducted by Hans Bender at the Freiburg Institute in January 1968. The results of the tests, in the sympathetic surroundings of the Institute, were disappointing: it seems that, to produce paranormal events, Annemarie had to be in a condition of stress

Annemarie's constant desire to know when she could leave the office. Furthermore, it seems as if the damage in the office could have been prompted by aggression towards Herr Adam, as Annemarie had felt particularly tense in his office and had disliked being in his employment. Apparently, early on in the sequence of phenomena, Adam had sarcastically said: 'All we want now is for the paintings to start moving.' Annemarie was within earshot – and, moments later, the first painting started to move.

A subsequent incident confirmed, according to Bender, that Annemarie seemed to instigate psychokinesis in response to emotional problems. She seemed to Bender to be subconsciously trying to rid herself of her fiancé who, appropriately enough, was an electrical engineer. They used to go bowling together in a small alley in Raubling, a suburb on the outskirts of Rosenheim. Bowls are returned automatically, and the pins are attached to cords controlled by a system of relays that replaces them when they are knocked over. Scores are displayed on an illuminated score board.

Faces from another world?

Portraits that appeared mysteriously in the floor of a Spanish kitchen seemed to change and decay over a period of time – attracting thousands of sightseers and baffling psychical investigators.

ON THE MORNING of 23 August 1971 a housewife in the little Spanish village of Bélmez de la Moraleda went into her kitchen and was startled to find the likeness of a face apparently painted on the floor. It was not an apparition, nor was it an hallucination; the housewife – a simple peasant woman named Maria Gómez Pereira – could only assume that a paranormal phenomenon had taken place in her home. The news spread quickly, and soon everyone in the village had heard about the strange happening and flocked to the house in Rodriguez Acosta Street to examine the face. It looked like a portrait in the expressionist style painted on the floor – but no one had painted it there. The features seemed to emerge naturally from the blend of colours in the floor cement.

The Pereira family tried to play down this extraordinary event that threatened to destroy their normally quiet everyday existence. They decided to destroy the 'painting': six days after the appearance of the face the Pereiras' son, Miguel, hacked up the kitchen floor and relaid it with fresh cement.

Nothing more happened for a week. Then, on 8 September, Maria Pereira again entered her kitchen to find a strange likeness of a human face apparently in the process of manifesting itself in the concrete of the floor, in exactly the same place as the first one. This time the delineation of a male face was even clearer.

It was impossible now to keep the crowds of curious spectators at bay. Every day hordes of people queued outside the house in order to look at the 'face from another world'. The face remained on the floor for several weeks: although it did not disappear, the features started to change slowly, as if the face were ageing or undergoing some other degenerative process.

Recognising the importance of the faces, the mayor of Bélmez decided that the second one should not be destroyed, but preserved rather like a valuable work of art. On 2 November 1971 a large crowd watched while the face was cut out of the ground, mounted behind glass and hung on the wall beside the fireplace. By this time the story of the second Bélmez face had spread far beyond the village, and photographs of it had appeared in the local press.

The floor of the kitchen was then dug up to discover if there was anything buried there that might explain the appearance of the faces. At a depth of about 9 feet (2.7 metres)

Doña Maria Gómez Pereira (below) at the door of her house in Rodriguez Acosta Street in Bélmez. When news spread of the paranormal portraits painted on Doña Pereira's kitchen floor, a crowd of spectators became a permanent feature outside the house (right, at the far end of the street). The family's life was so disrupted by the constant stream of visitors that they destroyed the first portrait

the diggers found a number of human bones. This discovery satisfied the Spiritists interested in the Bélmez faces, since Spiritists believe that a restless spirit may haunt the place where its body is buried, or produce poltergeist phenomena there. But to the residents of Bélmez the discovery of the bones was not in the least surprising, since it was well-known that most of the houses in Rodriguez Acosta Street were built on the site of a former graveyard.

The face that had been put behind glass was scrutinised by an art expert, Professor Camón Aznar, who expressed surprise at the

Psychical researchers photographing the second face, after it had been cut out of the floor and mounted on the wall. Over a period of several months the expression on the face changed from awe to irony, and the delicate lines of the features started to degenerate. Witnesses were also able to watch other faces 'growing' in the floor, starting as very crude lines and evolving into intricately drawn portraits

subtlety of the 'painting's' execution. He described it as the portrait of a startled, or astonished, man with slightly open lips. During the ensuing weeks the lines of the face started to decay, and the expression changed to one of irony.

Two weeks after the kitchen floor had been excavated, and then replaced, a third face appeared very near the spot where the first two were discovered; and two weeks after this, yet a fourth face appeared, the first to have female features. After examining these two latest faces, Professor Aznar expressed the opinion that they were examples of paintings in true expressionist style. Other observers, such as the painter Fernando Calderon and the parapsychologist German de Argumosa, considered them masterpieces of art produced paranormally.

Face in a crowd

Around the fourth face a quantity of smaller faces began to appear; Maria Pereira counted nine of them, while Professor Argumosa, who had taken up the case enthusiastically and become its principal investigator, was able to count 18.

At an international conference of parapsychology in Barcelona in 1977, Argumosa told the author that he inclined to the view that the faces were the result of some poltergeist-like activity produced by unquiet spirits. Although his ideas were not very clearly formulated, he admitted to being 'most surprised when I was able to witness the formation of some of the faces from very crude lines to meticulously drawn portraits'.

On 9 April 1972 Argumosa watched the formation of one face over a protracted period of time. Other witnesses present were the journalists Rafael Alcalá from the newspaper *Jaén* and Pedro Sagrario from *Patria*.

It was incredible, Argumosa wrote afterwards, 'how the face slowly assumed contours before our astonished eyes . . . . I must admit my heart was beating faster than usual.' Pedro Sagrario also described what he had seen: the gradual appearance on the brick-built part of the floor of seemingly unconnected lines, which eventually composed themselves into an impressive and attractive 'painting' of a face. This face was photographed several times; it had virtually disappeared again by the end of the day.

Eventually Argumosa invited his fellow parapsychologist Professor Hans Bender, of the Freiburg Institute in Germany, to help with the investigations. Professor Bender arrived in Bélmez in May 1972 to be met by a chaotic situation. Many people, including priests, painters, parapsychologists and journalists, had witnessed the phenomena, and everyone had a different theory as to what was causing them.

After interviewing many of the local witnesses, Bender was convinced that the faces were genuinely paranormal in origin. However, Bender noted another dimension to the faces: that they seemed to be perceived differently by different witnesses. The same face would appear to be that of a young man to one witness, and that of an old man to another. Some of the faces seemed to be constructed like a jig-saw puzzle, or to 'interlock' with other, larger faces. This quality of one line being perceived in different ways is also often observed in the work of mediumistic artists.

Attempts had been made to clean the faces off the floor with detergents, and by scrubbing. But the faces persisted, evolving and decaying in accordance with some strange law of their own.

In an attempt to document the production

months their investigations produced no conclusive results. But the 'haunted house' had become a place of pilgrimage for those interested in the occult, and people came from Spain, France, England and Germany to look at the faces, which they interpreted variously as demonic or sacred. They also brought tape recorders to record sessions with the 'spirits' they expected to find lingering in the house. Quite a number of unusual recordings were obtained, including one made by Argumosa himself. On this can be heard loud cries, the sound of many voices talking all at once, and the sound of people crying. The author was present when this tape was played in the Barcelona home of the psychical researcher Mrs Carole Ramis, and it certainly had an impressively eerie quality. Mrs Ramis was of the opinion that something very bad must have happened centuries ago at the house in Bélmez – perhaps connected with the graveyard beneath.

But no rational explanation for the faces has yet been given; chemists who examined the cement were quite unable to account for the appearance of the phenomena. In 1982 it was reported in the press that the faces had started to appear again, and in early 1983 eyewitnesses told the author in person that the unearthly artists were indeed at work again on the psychic floor in Spain.

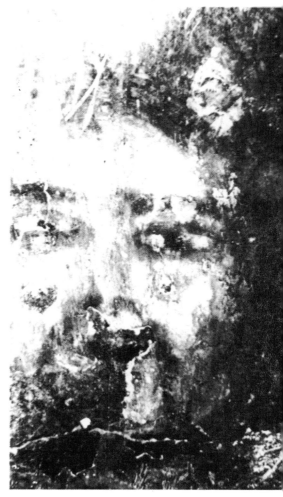

of the faces under experimental conditions, Bender carried out a procedure that Argumosa had already tried without success. He and his team of investigators first photographed the kitchen floor, and then covered it entirely with thick plastic sheeting. The sheeting extended right up to the walls, and was secured at 6-inch (15-centimetre) intervals. The original plan of installing a camera to record the paranormal formation of faces proved impracticable as the light in the room was too dim for filming, and additional lighting produced too many reflections on the plastic sheeting.

This method was intended to ensure that any faces that appeared had not been produced by any outside agency. Unfortunately water started to accumulate beneath the plastic, and the Pereiras decided to remove it before any faces became apparent.

Although Argumosa and Bender paid several visits to Bélmez during the next few

The author photographed the second Bélmez face on two occasions more than six months apart. On 10 September 1971 (above) the features were quite clear; by 10 April 1972 (right) they were starting to decay. Other portraits in the floor appeared, evolved, disintegrated and disappeared within one day – and bore expressions that were differently interpreted by different people. Both scientists and parapsychologists were baffled by the phenomena

Haunted
America

An attractive house in Long Island became first the scene of a series of sadistic murders and subsequently a playground for malevolent paranormal forces. These terrifying and mysterious events turned a dream home into a place of dread

Amityville-horror or hoax?

EARLY IN THE MORNING of 13 November 1974 a young New Yorker, 24-year-old Ronald DeFeo, ran screaming and hysterical into a bar near his home in Ocean Avenue, in Long Island's district of Amityville. Someone, he sobbed, had broken into the DeFeo house and slaughtered the six members of his family. When the police reached the house they discovered his mother, father, two sisters and two brothers shot dead in their beds. DeFeo's claim that the crime had been committed by an intruder was not taken seriously, and he was arrested and charged with the murders.

At his trial the prosecution maintained that DeFeo's motive was a wild attempt to lay his hands on life insurance worth $200,000, plus the considerable funds in the family cash box. Defence attorney William Weber countered with a plea of insanity, backed up by testimony from a string of psychiatrists. But the jury rejected that plea and Ronald DeFeo was sentenced to six consecutive life-terms.

When the trial was over, the DeFeo house was put up for sale. It was an imposing three-storey residence built in the Dutch Colonial style in 1928, and with its garage, boathouse and swimming pool made a substantial property that should have commanded a high figure. Instead, in view of its unhappy history, the house agents offered it at the bargain price of $80,000 but, even so, it remained empty for nearly a year before the Lutz family moved in on 18 December 1975.

Recently married, George Lutz was a 28-year-old ex-marine who ran a land-surveying company; his wife Kathy, a divorcee, was fully occupied looking after her two small sons and five-year-old daughter. The large rambling house seemed the ideal place for a young family. But only a month later the Lutzes were to flee from it – victims, they said, of a relentless, nameless terror.

The full story of their ordeal was told in the book *The Amityville horror* (1978) by Jay Anson, which was based on many interviews with the Lutzes themselves. This book became a best-seller and was acclaimed as 'one of the most terrifying true cases ever of haunting and possession by demons'.

According to the account in the book, the trouble began with overpoweringly foul stenches pervading the house. The bathroom fittings became stained with a black slime, and no household cleaner would remove the stains. Then came the flies – hundreds of them swarming into a second-floor bedroom.

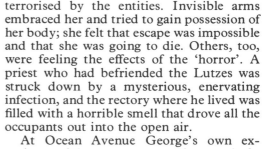

terrorised by the entities. Invisible arms embraced her and tried to gain possession of her body; she felt that escape was impossible and that she was going to die. Others, too, were feeling the effects of the 'horror'. A priest who had befriended the Lutzes was struck down by a mysterious, enervating infection, and the rectory where he lived was filled with a horrible smell that drove all the occupants out into the open air.

At Ocean Avenue George's own experience of the presences was the sound of a marching band parading around the house, boots thumping and horns blaring. Although he was convinced there must be at least 50 musicians not one was ever seen, yet the furniture was found pushed back against the walls as if to make room for the marchers.

Other manifestations of the sadistic forces were the loathsome slime, and hideously

In a scene from the film *The Amityville horror* (1979) the Lutzes' house at 112 Ocean Avenue (far left) assumes a menacing aspect at night when the two top-floor windows seem to stare out like baleful eyes. Another manifestation of the malignant forces in the house is the loathsome slime that Kathy, played by Margot Kidder in the film, finds covering the mirror in her bedroom (above left). Later George (played by James Brolin) and Kathy are awakened in the middle of the night to find the heavy front door wrenched wide open, apparently from the inside, and hanging from its one remaining hinge (left)

The massive front door was discovered wrenched open and hanging from its one remaining hinge. George felt constantly chilled to the bone, despite the huge blazing fire that roared in the living room. It also seemed that a four-feet (1.2-metre) high ceramic lion began moving around the house without human help.

Then the Lutzes spotted cloven-hoof tracks in the snow around the house – they led directly to the garage and stopped dead in front of the door. The door itself had been almost torn off its metal frame, a feat requiring 'strength far beyond that of any human being'. It began to dawn on the new owners that far from being the home of their dreams, 112 Ocean Avenue was a nightmare house, haunted by malignant forces.

Kathy Lutz was the first to be truly

painful red weals that erupted on Kathy's body, as if she had been slashed with a red-hot poker. There were also, according to the book, levitations, drastic personality changes, and demons.

On 14 January 1976 the Lutzes left the house, never to return. But according to the account of their experiences related in *The Amityville horror: part 2* (a sequel to the first book) the evil presences followed them to their new home, where they stayed 'coiled malevolently round them'.

If all this is true, it is a grim and horrifying story. But it is so like fiction that it prompts the reader to ask whether there was ever an authentic horror in the first place. Independent researchers who have investigated the facts have all emphatically answered no.

Dr Stephen Kaplan, the director of the

As told to Jay Anson, author of the book *The Amityville horror* (1978), George Lutz (above) felt continually cold in the house, despite a high level of heating, and was plagued by the sound of a brass band that nobody could see. He began to identify with multiple murderer Ronald DeFeo (above right) whom he imagined he resembled physically. His wife Kathy (right) suffered from painful red weals over her body, as if she had been burned with a red-hot poker

Parapsychology Institute of America, said after months of study and many interviews with those involved in the affair of 'the Amityville horror':

> We found no evidence to support any claim of a 'haunted house'. What we did find is a couple who had purchased a house that they economically could not afford. It is our professional opinion that the story of its haunting is mostly fiction.

After visiting the house Jerry Solfvin, of the Psychical Research Foundation, wrote that the case 'wasn't interesting to us because the reports were confined to subjective responses from the Lutzes, and these were not at all . . . characteristic of these cases.'

The most damning report of all originated with investigators Rick Moran and Peter Jordan who visited Amityville and interviewed people mentioned in the book. Among their startling findings was the fact that the police denied ever investigating the house while the Lutzes were in residence, although the book describes Sergeant Cammaroto touring the house and even inspecting a 'secret room' in the basement.

Father Mancuso (in real life Father Pecorara), the priest who appears throughout the book, flatly denied that he had ever entered the Lutzes' home; so the tale about him blessing the building (and the phantom voice that ordered him out) must be quite bogus. And the pastor of the Sacred Heart rectory dismissed as 'utter nonsense' the Lutzes' yarn about a 'disgusting odour that permeated the rectory' – the alleged 'scent of the devil' – which was supposed to have driven the priests out of their rooms and the building.

In fact, very little in the book stood up under scrutiny. Local handymen and locksmiths knew nothing of the paranormal damages they were supposed to have repaired. And far from being driven out of the house by hauntings, it appeared that the real reasons for the Lutzes leaving their home were much more prosaic: a cash crisis and a near-breakdown.

Defence strategy

Naturally enough, the Lutzes have responded to these revelations with bluff and bluster. But it is worth noting that they have repeatedly avoided a confrontation with their critics on radio or television; and in fact their original accounts were only about things felt and sensed, not about objective phenomena.

Indeed, it was Ronald DeFeo's defence attorney, William Weber, who first pushed the couple into the limelight. DeFeo had spoken of a voice that urged him to kill, and Weber hoped to win a new trial for him by establishing that the house contained some force able to influence the behaviour of the inhabitants. Pinning his hopes on the Lutzes, he won them time on New York's *Ten O'Clock News* television programme.

Although at the outset Weber's involvement seemed to be on a purely professional basis, he later admitted that he had helped to sensationalise the Lutzes' story. In a press release on 27 July 1979 he said, 'We created this horror story over many bottles of wine that George was drinking. We were really playing with each other.'

But the case against the Lutzes does not rest solely on these testimonies by outsiders. The Lutzes themselves have given ample evidence of their unreliability in major interviews recorded before the book was published.

Amityville unlimited

The sensational saga of the alleged entities that possessed a house in Amityville, New York, seems to have undergone a strange transformation at every retelling

Left: Jay Anson, the author of many film and television scripts. He wrote a dramatic account of the hauntings at 112 Ocean Avenue (below), from information supplied by George and Kathy Lutz, in his best-selling book *The Amityville horror* (1978); in a postscript to the book he said he was convinced the Lutzes were telling the truth

THE SINISTER STORY of a house haunted by malignant forces has chilled many people since it was published in Jay Anson's book *The Amityville horror* in 1978. In the preface to the book it is claimed that the story is 'a documentary told by the family and the priest who actually experienced what is reported'; but it has become increasingly evident to independent investigators that the frightening events related are almost entirely fictitious.

Fortunately for the truth, George and Kathy Lutz, who lived at the 'horror' house at 112 Ocean Avenue between 18 December 1975 and 14 January 1976, have left a trail of revealing evidence behind them that does not agree with the account they later gave to author Jay Anson. In an article published in the *Long Island Press* on 17 January 1976, just a few days after the Lutzes had fled from the house, George sets out his experiences; but his story centres around things that were sensed rather than seen and is completely at odds with later accounts of flying objects, moving couches and wailing noises. The only physical phenomenon he mentions is a window that opened of its own accord; later investigations showed that the counterweights were too heavy! At that date the Amityville happenings were purely subjective and scarcely worthy of note.

A year later George produced a new version of events, which journalist Paul Hoffman wrote up for the the April 1977 issue of America's *Good Housekeeping* magazine. This interesting text flatly contradicts the earlier account and conflicts with the Anson story as well.

The *Good Housekeeping* account begins with a Roman Catholic priest blessing the house. When he leaves, the priest warns the Lutzes about one of the bedrooms, saying, 'Don't let anyone sleep in there. Keep the door closed. Spend as little time as possible in there.' But this does not tally with the book. There, the priest's alleged advice about not using the room is given one week after the blessing – and following a whole series of nasty events.

The next person to be affected by the house is Kathy Lutz's aunt, described in the *Good Housekeeping* article as a 'normally placid ex-nun'. When she comes to visit, she behaves quite out of character and becomes hostile towards George, who says she 'sat there and cut me down for three hours'. In the book, this incident seems to have been reshaped to make it more dramatic. The aunt can stand being in the house only for a very short while: she simply inspects it, refuses to enter certain rooms, and leaves. In fact she 'hadn't been in the house for more than half an hour when she decided it was time to go'.

In a scene from the film *The Amityville horror* (1979) George (below), played by James Brolin, is haunted by a vision of killer Ronald DeFeo, with whom he is becoming obsessed. Just before leaving the house for ever, a storm-drenched Kathy (bottom), played by Margot Kidder, returns for the last time to the children's room on the second floor, the scene of some of the most alarming phenomena

A similar re-vamping technique is used on the 'old crone' incident. In *Good Housekeeping* George says that on Saturday, 10 January 1976 he woke at night with 'a compulsion to flee the house'. He yelled at his wife and shook her, but could not wake her. Then, as he watched, his sleeping wife 'turned into a 90-year-old woman'. Her hair became 'old and dirty', she dribbled, and creases and crow's feet appeared on her face; 'it took several hours before she returned to her normal self.'

When this story makes its appearance in Jay Anson's book it has undergone significant changes. First, it is placed some days earlier, on Wednesday, 7 January. George does not wake up wanting to flee the house; on the contrary, he is unable to get to sleep, and in this wide-awake state feels an urge to go out to the local tavern for a beer. When he turns to speak to Kathy, he finds her levitating 'almost a foot [30 centimetres] above him'. He pulls her down onto the bed, where she wakes. And it is then, while awake, that she turns into a 90-year-old woman. In this version, the state lasts only for a minute or two – not several hours.

As described in the book, this levitation is the second of three. The first took place on 4 January, when Kathy floated 'two feet [60 centimetres] above the bed'. And a further levitation takes place after the Lutzes have left the house, when they are staying with Kathy's mother on 15 January; on this occasion both George and Kathy float around at the same time. Yet nothing was ever said about these remarkable levitations in the *Good Housekeeping* account. The only time levitation is mentioned is when George describes waking on the night of Sunday, 11 January, to find 'Kathy sliding across the bed, as if by levitation' – a very different matter from 'floating in the air'.

The ultimate horror however is the series

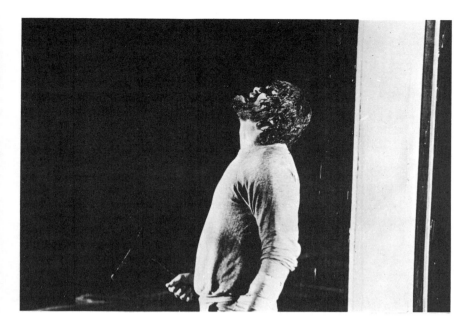

than cutting back on expenditure, George decided to buy a house that was way above his means.

Once the family was settled in the new house, matters fast came to a head. George became apathetic: he didn't wash or shave, and he stopped going to the office. In the book he describes how he lay awake at night, worrying about his difficulties:

> a second marriage with three children, a new house with a big mortgage. The taxes in Amityville were three times higher than in Deer Park. Did he really need that new speedboat? How the hell was he going to pay for all of this? The construction business was lousy on Long Island. . . .

All this worry soon took its toll. George began to blame his inertia, his bad temper and his problems on the house. When he was short with his employees, or when he hit the children, it was the fault of the bad vibrations

of visitations by an entity variously described as a 'gigantic [hooded] figure in white' and a 'demon with horns' with half its face shot away. Yet in *Good Housekeeping* there is not one hint of his visits. There is a passing mention, however, of Kathy seeing 'some eyes at the window', which she described as 'red, beady eyes'. When this story reaches the book, it becomes a point of high drama.

'Two fiery red eyes'
Set in a second-storey bedroom at night, this dramatic episode in the book has the Lutzes' young daughter pointing to a window where George and Kathy see 'two fiery, red eyes. No face, just the mean, little eyes of a pig' looking in. Kathy rushes at the window 'screaming in an unearthly voice'. She smashes the glass with a chair and they hear an 'animal cry of pain, a loud squealing – and the eyes were gone'. The squealing continues for a while outside the house. But George does not go out to look for the flying pig; instead he comforts his wife, who sobs, 'It's been here all the time. I wanted to kill it. I wanted to kill it!'

The story has obviously undergone a remarkable transformation. And similar 'improvements' are apparent throughout the book. Coupled with the equally damning findings of independent investigators, this evidence suggests that the whole bizarre tale is a fabrication.

Without a confession from the Lutzes it will probably never be quite clear what started the whole thing off. But it is known that George Lutz was a man with problems. After his first marriage broke up he tried group therapy, then turned to transcendental meditation. Things seemed to improve for a while after his second marriage, but he was facing a crisis even before he moved to Amityville: Kathy's two sons had tried to run away, his business was in difficulties, and he had problems with the tax people. Rather

In another scene from the film George (above), hatchet in hand, challenges the demonic forces plaguing the house. After visiting the house to bless it, Father Delaney (right), played in the film by Rod Steiger, discovers that his palms are raw and bleeding

from the house, not his own lack of control. In this frame of mind he began to identify with the murderer Ronald DeFeo: he became convinced he was DeFeo's physical double, recording that when he first saw DeFeo's picture, 'the bearded 24-year-old face staring back . . . could have been his own.'

And if he was the physical double of a psychopath, why not the mental double too? There is little doubt that George felt black, murderous thoughts in the house in Ocean Avenue, but they arose from his own plight and frustrations, not from any paranormal forces.

After leaving Amityville, George became more and more enmeshed in his morbid fantasies, and the situation began to spin out of control. The meeting with Anson offered an opportunity to crystallise his sinister imaginings in profitable form. But to become a best-seller, the story had to pose as fact. As fiction, it is debatable whether the book would even have covered its printing costs.

The Bell Witch strikes

The most savage and relentless poltergeist on record must surely be the 'Bell Witch', whose systematic persecution of the Bell family of Robertson County, Tennessee, USA, in the early 19th century stopped only at the murder of one of its members

Slaves on a cotton plantation – similar to the one owned by the Bell family – practise a voodoo ceremony. The Bells may have been influenced by such an atmosphere of belief in the paranormal, giving rise to the 'Bell Witch'

IT HAS BECOME almost axiomatic that ghosts do no physical harm to those who experience them. The fear of ghosts, if it comes at all, is usually retrospective. Apparitions are frequently reported as being solid and 'normal' and it is only when they walk away through the wall or disappear as if switched off that the observer realises what he has seen and becomes alarmed. Even the rumbustious poltergeist, whose activities include such apparently dangerous acts as throwing stones, smashing glass and crockery and starting fires, causes little or no bodily damage to its victims.

But there is one well-attested case of a 'supernatural' power, which not only killed its victim but apparently set out to do so with deliberate intent, and that was the so-called 'Bell Witch'. The late Dr Nandor Fodor, a Freudian psychiatrist and pioneer of modern psychophysical research, termed it 'America's greatest ghost story'; but if his conclusions are correct it must also rank as one of the world's most bizarre murder mysteries.

The malevolent power that laid siege to the homestead of John Bell and his family in Robertson County, Tennessee, USA, during the year 1817 lay totally outside the experience of that rural but rich community. A century and a quarter had elapsed since America's only serious outbreak of witch-craft mania died down at Salem, Massachusetts, and the Fox sisters of Hydesville, New York, founding daughters of modern Spiritualism, lay more than 30 years in the future. The term 'poltergeist' was unknown.

Nevertheless the Bells and their neighbours were Bible-belt Christians with a streak of superstition that paralleled that of their slaves; both black and white consulted a 'village wise woman' named Kate Batt. It was natural that they should call their trouble by an old name. As Dr Fodor put it:

> The 'Witch', as the haunter was called, serves well as a descriptive term . . . modern poltergeists, no matter how much mischief and destruction they wreak, stop short of murder. The Bell Witch did not, and it only ceased its activities after the death by poisoning of John Bell, the head of the household, whom it tortured and persecuted with a fury of unrelenting savagery.

The phenomena began in 1817 and petered out in the late spring of 1821, some months after the death of John Bell, although they did reoccur briefly seven years later, apparently to fulfil a promise to one of the dead man's sons. During its reign the Witch attracted hordes of ghost hunters, most of them anxious to prove it a hoax. But these all met, according to contemporary records,

Above: the late Dr Nandor Fodor, a psychiatrist who believed that the tale of the Bell Witch was 'America's greatest ghost story', but also a case of externalised, repressed guilt on the part of a member of the Bell family

Below: the Bells were known to be on good terms with their black slaves

with 'egregious defeat'.

Richard Williams Bell, a younger son of the family, wrote a record entitled *Our family trouble* in 1846 when he was 36 years old, and although he was only 10 when the Witch ceased its activity, his account tied in well with later, more detailed records. One of these, published in 1867 by a Clarksville newspaper editor, M.V. Ingram, included interviews with all surviving members of the family and some contemporary witnesses, as well as the testimony of the author, who had himself witnessed the outbreak as a child. Another was a document by John Bell Jr as related to his son Dr Joel Thomas Bell. The definitive version was given in 1934 by Dr Charles Bailey Bell, son of Dr Joel, who lectured on neurosurgery at the University of Nashville's Medical Department, was a consultant at Nashville City Hospital, and a prominent member of several national medical bodies. As a young medical student in 1888 Dr Charles had interviewed his great aunt Elizabeth 'Betsy' Bell about her recollections: then 83, she had in her youth been the centre of the phenomena – and perhaps even an unwitting murderess.

John Bell was a prosperous cotton plantation owner, well-liked and respected by his neighbours and friends, who included General Andrew Jackson, later seventh president of the United States and a witness to the Witch's activities. John and his wife Luce lived in a large, two-storey house with their nine children. Their domestic servants and plantation hands were, of course, black slaves but – as far as was possible under such conditions – the Bell children mingled with the hands on terms of easy familiarity and friendliness. One of the most outgoing was Betsy Bell, a robust and apparently contented girl of 12 in 1817.

Disturbing the peace

The manifestations began in the form of knocks and raps on the walls and windows of the house, and increased in power and volume so that by the end of the year they were literally shaking the building to its foundations. Gnawing, scratching and flapping sounds alternated with the rattle of invisible stones on the roof, the clattering of what sounded like heavy chains on the floor, and half-human gulping, choking and 'lip smacking' noises.

Then the force displayed its strength, pulling Richard Bell's hair so violently that it lifted him clear of his bed. He felt 'that the top of his head had been taken off . . . . Immediately, Joel yelled out in great fright, and next Elizabeth was screaming in her room, and after that something was continually pulling at her hair after she retired to bed.'

Up to this point, the family had kept their curious troubles to themselves, but now they let a close friend and neighbour, James Johnson, in on their secret. After witnessing

Above: respectable Puritans arrest a 'witch' during the infamous outbreak of witchcraft mania at Salem, Massachusetts, in 1692, during which 30 people were accused of sorcery and 19 of them hanged. Although most rural areas – as in Europe – had their 'wise women' and natural psychics, from the end of the Salem trials to 1817, when the Bell Witch first made itself known, paranormality in the United States had not been a burning issue. But then, literally as far as the Bells were concerned, all hell broke loose

voice grew in strength, so did the Witch's violence.

'The blows were heard distinctly, like the open palm of a heavy hand, while the sting was keenly felt,' and they were rained indiscriminately on anyone who happened to be around, but particularly on Betsy Bell and her father John.

From the beginning the force seemed to centre on Betsy; as the voice developed, so the formerly robust girl began to suffer fainting fits and breathing difficulties that lasted up to half an hour at a time. During these attacks the Witch remained silent, but as soon as Betsy had recovered it began to talk again. The obvious conclusion was that, somehow, Betsy was producing sounds by ventriloquism, but a doctor who visited the house laid his hands over her mouth at the time the voice was heard, 'and soon satisfied himself that she was in no way connected with these sounds'.

Just a song at twilight . . .

When the voice first developed, its utterances tended to be of a pious nature. It could reproduce, word for word, the Sunday sermons of the two local parsons, imitating their tones exactly. It sang beautifully, and recited tracts from the Bible. Unfortunately this was only a temporary phase. The voice soon began uttering obscenities – which were particularly distressing to a Bible-belt family. It also alarmed them by claiming to be 'Old Kate Batt's witch'.

The Witch's ability to produce disgusting odours was demonstrated on several occasions, once to local witness William Porter when the Witch got into bed with him and twisted his bedclothes off him 'just like a boy would roll himself in a quilt'. Porter leaped out of bed and picked up the roll of bedclothes, intending to throw them into the fire. He said:

I discovered it was very weighty and smelled awful. I had not got halfway across the room before the luggage got so heavy and became so offensive that I was compelled to drop it on the floor and rush out of doors for a breath of fresh air. The odour . . . was the most offensive stench I ever smelled . . . absolutely stifling.

When Porter had recovered, however, he came back into the room and shook out the bedclothes, only to find the mysterious extra weight had vanished – and the stink had evaporated.

Like many other poltergeists, the Witch produced 'apports'. During Luce Bell's Bible study meetings it took to dropping fresh fruit onto the table or into the laps of those present, and once, on Betsy's birthday, produced a large basket of oranges, bananas, grapes and nuts, claiming: 'Those came from the West Indies. I brought them myself.'

But perhaps more in keeping with the Witch's real nature was the scatological

the phenomena for himself, Johnson concluded that some intelligence lay behind them, and performed a brief exorcism that seemed to silence the Bell house for a while.

But the Witch returned – and with renewed vigour, slapping Betsy's cheeks until they were crimson and pulling her hair until she screamed with pain. John Bell and James Johnson called in more neighbours to form an investigating committee, partly to keep the tormented Betsy company, and partly to induce the Witch to speak. Betsy spent a night away from home, but the 'trouble followed her with the same severity, disturbing the family where she went as it did at home, nor were we any wise relieved', wrote Richard Bell later. The committee itself seems to have done more harm than good, inviting the force to 'rap the wall, smack its mouth, etc., and in this way the phenomena were gradually developed'.

In fact, the development of the Witch's voice seems to have come about under the urgings of the committee. At first it was low and inarticulate – a thin whistling sound – but gradually it turned into a weak faltering whisper and towards the end of its career was loud and raucous. Unlike the other physical phenomena, which took place only after dark – although usually in lamplit rooms – the voice began to be heard both day and night, and came from any direction. And as the prank it played on Betsy Bell, when a local quack doctor offered her a potion to rid her of the power that tormented her. It was an unpleasant mixture, and the quack warned her that it would make her very ill. A 'copious evacuation' of the stomach followed, the Witch roaring with laughter at the surprise of the household when Betsy's vomit and excrement were found to be full of pins and needles. Richard Bell wrote:

> They were real brass pins and needles. Mother kept them as long as she lived. I have seen the pins and needles myself. As a matter of course, Betsy could not have lived with such a conglomeration in her stomach, and the only solution to the matter was that the Witch dropped the pins and needles in the excrement unobserved.

A public announcement

As time went on the Witch ceased its physical attacks on Betsy, but began to torment her emotionally. She had become engaged in her early teens to a local man, Joshua Gardner, to whom, apparently, everyone in the family and neighbourhood thought she was ideally suited. But from the moment it developed the power of speech, the Witch derided Joshua and advised against the match, whispering 'Please Betsy Bell, don't have Joshua Gardner, please Betsy Bell, don't marry Joshua Gardner.' Eventually it grew sharper in its remonstrations, making embarrassing revelations about the young couple's relationship in front of friends, and promising that Betsy would never know a moment's peace if she married Joshua. Eventually, 'quite hysterical and worn out in despair', she returned his engagement ring.

But behind all these developments lay the Witch's implacable hatred for John Bell, head of the family. From the start the Witch had sworn that it would 'torment Old Jack Bell' to the end of his life – and it made good its threat.

On 19 December 1820, John Bell was discovered in his bed in a deep stupor and could not be roused. His son John went to the medicine cabinet but instead of the prescribed medicine he found 'a smokey looking vial, which was about one-third full of dark-coloured liquid'.

The doctor arrived in time to hear the Witch crowing: 'It's useless for you to try and relieve Old Jack – I have got him this time; he will never get up from that bed again.' Asked about the strange medicine, it said: 'I put it there, and gave Old Jack a big dose out of it last night while he was fast asleep, which fixed him.'

Neither the doctor nor any member of the household could explain the presence of the mystery bottle, but a rather arbitrary test was made of its contents; the doctor dunked a straw into the mixture and wiped it onto the tongue of the Bells' pet cat. 'The cat jumped and whirled over a few times, stretched out,

Witch on the wagon

When Andrew Jackson (1767–1845), seventh president of the United States, was a general in the army he took a wagon, pulled by a team of army horses, to visit his old friend John Bell and, to his horror and surprise, was treated to a startling demonstration of the Bell Witch's superhuman physical strength.

As Jackson drove up to the house, the wagon suddenly ground to a halt, despite the enormous efforts of driver and horses, straining at the traces. Unable to find any natural cause for the stoppage, the General cried, 'By the eternal boys! It is the Witch!' At this point a sharp, metallic voice – apparently coming from the nearby bushes – said: 'All right, General, let the wagon move.' And the wagon started to roll forward once again towards the Bell house.

kicked, and died very quick.'

The doctor's next action would be unforgivable today, and even in his own time would have drawn suspicion had he done it in Europe, but his scientific training seems to have been overcast by the superstition of rural 19th-century Tennessee. He threw the bottle into the fire, disposing of the Witch's brew for good.

The following morning John Bell was found dead in his bed; the Witch marked his passing by singing ribald songs at his funeral.

After the death of John Bell, the energy of the Witch seemed to dissipate. Its ribaldry

Above: Hollywood's expression of paranormal violence – a scene from *The omen* (1976). The disruption occasioned by real-life poltergeists is often more psychological than physical, but the Bell Witch attacked its victims on all fronts: socially, psychologically and physically

Below: a statue of a Roman house god, or family guardian, known as the *lar familiaris*. Although in many Roman households religion was treated as a mere formality, the household gods were often genuinely revered. Keeping evil out of one's home and family circle has always preoccupied mankind; but the Bell family fell foul of this omnipresent threat. Even in our so-called 'progressive' society exorcists are kept busy ejecting 'evil forces' from family homes

vanished almost totally, and when questioned by John Bell Jr it gave introspective if rather confused answers. Richard Bell, writing years afterwards, surmised that, from the start, it had 'but two purposes, seemingly . . . one was the persecution of Father to the end of his life. The other, the vile purpose of destroying the anticipated happiness that thrilled the heart of Betsy'.

Apparently, having achieved these ends it was content to go. The final phenomenon, which to Dr Fodor was 'highly symbolic of guilt release', took place after supper in the spring of 1821; something like a cannonball rolled down the chimney and burst in a puff of smoke, and a clear voice called out: 'I'm going, and will be gone for seven years.'

This promise was fulfilled. At the time Mrs Bell and her sons Richard and Joel were the only occupants of the homestead – Betsy having married another man.

Scratching sounds were heard, and half-hearted pulling of bedclothes felt. The family agreed to ignore the manifestations, and after a fortnight the Witch vanished for good, pausing only to tell John Jr that it would return again in 'one hundred years and seven' to one of his descendants. As Dr Fodor remarks, this doubtful honour should have fallen to Dr Charles Bailey Bell, but the year of 1935 came and went, and the Bell Witch failed to keep its tryst.

So what actually occurred on the Bell plantation? Even allowing for distortion of some of the details with the passage of time, it seems that the principal events did take

invisible man walking towards the house. The Witch challenged John to take his dead father's boots and match them against those in the snow. When he refused, the Witch said that this was the answer to 'all the foolish people who might think that the dead could come back'.

For his part, 'Old Jack' Bell showed all the signs of what a modern psychiatrist would recognise as symptoms of acute guilt: a nervous tic, an inability to eat and speak, and a general withdrawal from the world. Despite some evidence that an unknown person may have administered the poison that killed him, the strong possibility remains that he killed himself, goaded beyond endurance by

place. In 1849 the *Saturday Evening Post* investigated the case and printed an article alleging that the 12-year-old Betsy had engineered the whole thing. The Bell family lawyers obtained a substantial amount in damages and the magazine printed an apology and a retraction. The hoax theory, then, seems patently absurd.

Dr Fodor pointed out that Betsy's fainting and dizzy spells – immediately followed by the voice of the Witch – are very similar to the symptoms exhibited by a medium going into a trance. On the other hand the Witch, although describing itself as 'a spirit from everywhere' on one occasion, denied all knowledge of life after death. Indeed, after the death of John Bell and towards the end of its career, the Witch frankly told his son, who had asked about the fate of his father's spirit, that it could imitate the dead man's voice to perfection, but had no intention of deceiving the family. People who had died did not talk to those left behind, insisted the Witch. To press home its point it gave a dramatic demonstration. John was asked to look out of the window at the smooth snow outside. As he and the rest of the company watched, footprints appeared, seemingly made by an

Brazil, a country much preoccupied by Spiritism, also suffers from frequent and sometimes severe outbreaks of paranormal vandalism. In one case a pet parrot fell victim to a poltergeist's spite – and had its tail feathers singed (top), and in another a group of people discovered that the settee on which they were sitting was being slashed by an invisible assailant (above). But few people have suffered the indignities and horrors of the Bell family

the disturbances. This might well explain the doctor's arbitrary destruction of the evidence – the poison bottle: by doing so he would remove the strong taint of suicide from a respectable, staunchly Christian family.

Dr Fodor concluded that Betsy Bell suffered from a split personality, that in some mysterious way part of her subconscious mind had taken on a life of its own and literally plagued her father to death. The psychology of such splits is still a mystery, and similar cases are rare – but when they do occur some powerful emotional shock is usually the triggering factor. Dr Fodor made the 'purely speculative' guess that John Bell had interfered with his daughter sexually during her early childhood, and that the onset of puberty and her awakening sexuality stirred the long suppressed memory – bringing into being the Bell Witch.

On the other hand, he admitted that no conventional psychologist would credit split personalities with manifestations, and powers outside the range of the body. Dr Fodor concluded: 'Obviously we are dealing with facts for which we have no adequate theories within normal or abnormal psychology.'

Spook lights over America

Pale, silent, flame-like lights sometimes appear in the night in country districts and to sailors at sea. Many can be explained away as marsh gas or shooting stars, but the United States harbours strange illuminations for which no explanation has been found

THE 'WILL O' THE WISP' or 'Jack O' Lantern' was part of European ghostly lore right up until the advent of gas lighting simply because he indubitably existed. Some said he was a lost soul, treacherously leading travellers onto lonely moorland or dangerous swampland. Others said that he was an essentially benign spirit, and that if you had the courage to dig at the spot indicated by his flickering blue light on Walpurgis Night you would discover buried treasure.

But bad, good or indifferent, he was not, like some ghosts, the product of an overheated imagination: anyone who cared or dared to venture out into certain parts of the countryside after dusk could observe his eerie glow for themselves. With the coming of gas light, even country folk learned the true nature of 'Will' or 'Jack': he was simply iridescent marsh gas, similar to the stuff they now used to light their homes and streets. His mystery, if not his beauty, had vanished.

Over the years science, to the disappointment of romantics, has explained away most of the 'mystery lights' that appear in records down the centuries: aeroplane headlights or UFOs, shooting stars or ball lightning, reflections and refractions from the atmosphere or the surface of the sea. But not all these mysterious phenomena have succumbed to explanation so readily: some refuse to fit neatly into known patterns. Many of these seem peculiar to the United States, and American psychical researchers have jauntily dubbed them 'spook lights' – a tag that is as good as any.

One of the classic American spook light stories has its roots firmly in supernatural tradition. If any completely rational explanation exists, it has yet to be put forward, although several interesting theories have appeared over the years. The story begins in a strictly factual manner with the voyage of the *Palatine*, an elderly ship that set out from Holland in the autumn of 1752 crammed with Dutch families determined to make a

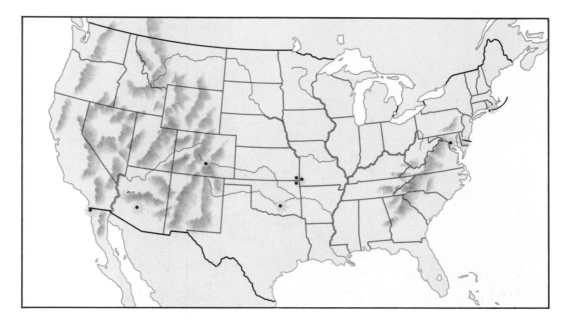

Right: some of the places in the United States where spook lights have been seen repeatedly. Many sightings are associated with rivers or bodies of water, but one is in the Arizona desert

Left: a will o' the wisp glows over the stagnant waters of a marsh, 'like a taper gleaming from some cottage window', in the words of one 19th-century account. The will o' the wisp often led the unwary onto dangerous ground

Below: terrified seamen witness the Flying Dutchman's ship, harbinger of doom. Could ghost ships and spook lights have the same natural explanation?

new life for themselves in the New World.

The vessel's scheduled destination was Philadelphia, but several factors combined to prevent it reaching its port – among them a drunken captain, a surly crew and persistent foul weather, all of which helped to keep the *Palatine* at sea for over two months. As the ship neared the New England coast, there was an argument between the officers as to the ship's exact position, and during the ensuing row the captain either fell or was thrown over the side. Heartlessly, the crew opted to save their own necks and, after robbing the passengers of what cash they could find, they put to sea in the only two lifeboats, leaving the colonists to their fate.

One morning between Christmas and New Year the *Palatine*, with its hapless passengers, grounded on the desolate coast of Block Island, about 11 miles (18 kilometres) off Long Island between Montauk and Gay Head. The local community of fishermen, accustomed to supplementing their poor livings by wrecking, evacuated the passengers but afterwards looted the ship and then set it on fire, allowing it to drift out to sea and sink. This is the story, and tradition adds that one terrified woman had hidden herself below decks. As the burning hulk was swept seaward by the tide, onlookers were horrified to see her standing at the rails screaming for help, but by that time there was nothing they could do.

Ever since then people living on the Rhode Island coast opposite Block Island have sporadically reported seeing the blazing outline of a ship during Christmas week; sometimes it appears luminous white, although in 1969 several people reported to the local newspaper, the *Westerly Sun*, that it was 'a great red fireball on the ocean.'

One of the best reports of a sighting was given by a Long Island fishing-boat owner in *Scientific American* in 1882, though he was hard-headed enough to offer an explanation

that was satisfactory – and he was able to use the incident to his own profit. His boat was out after menhaden – a particularly oily fish related to the herring – with himself on board, when one of the mates said that 'he hoped we were not going off the Point, meaning Montauk. I asked him why. He seemed kind of offish, but at last let out that he had seen sailing ships sailing about in the dead of night in a dead calm.'

The mate was laughed to scorn and the fishing boat eventually made anchor in Gardiner's Bay, a few miles to the west of Block Island. That night the owner was shaken awake by the mate, who pointed anxiously out to sea.

A coaster in the spirit trade
'Sure enough, there was a big schooner about an eighth of a mile [200 metres] away, bearing down on us. There wasn't a breath of wind in the bay, but on she came at a ten-knot [18-km/h] rate, headed right for us. . . . I swung into the rigging and yelled "Schooner ahoy" and shouted to her to bear away, but in a second the white sails were right aboard of us. I shouted to the hands and made ready to jump, when, like a flash, she disappeared, and the skipper came on deck with all hands and wanted to know if we had the jimjams.'

He would have sworn, said the owner, that he had seen the Flying Dutchman's ship but a week later saw the thing again, passing round them and heading back up the bay. Apparently acting on impulse, the owner ordered the skipper to take the fishing boat after the 'phantom', at the same time setting his seine net.

'As sure as you are alive we made the biggest single haul of menhaden on record. The light to my mind was nothing more or less than the phosphorescence that hovered over the big shoal. The oil from so many millions of fish moving along was enough to produce a light; but you will find men all

along the shores of Long Island that believe there is a regular phantom craft that comes in on and off – sort of a coaster in the spirit trade.'

This belief was first investigated in some depth by Professor W. F. Ganong at the turn of the century and his findings were published by the *Bulletin* of the National Historical Society of New Brunswick. After interviewing numerous witnesses and examining all the evidence, he made four positive points on what he called 'The fact basis of the fire (or phantom) ship':

It appears to the author plain that (1) a physical light is frequently seen over the waters, (2) that it appears at all seasons, or at least in winter and summer, (3) that it usually precedes a storm, (4) that its actual form is roughly hemispherical with the flat side to the water, and that at times it simply glows without much change of form, but that at other times it rises into slender moving columns, giving rise to an appearance capable of interpretation as the flaming rigging of a ship.

Professor Ganong inclined to the opinion that the 'phantom' was due to St Elmo's fire, but cautiously added that he was 'not aware of any reports of similar phenomena, of such frequency in one locality, and of such considerable development.'

Only a decade afterwards, however, very similar spook lights were the subject of a Government enquiry. Since about 1850 the people of the Rattlesnake Knob area of North Carolina had observed lights, sometimes red, sometimes yellowish white, appearing over the 2500-foot (760-metre) plateau of Brown Mountain, a blunt outcrop of the Appalachians. Stories grew of spirits on the mountain, though some citizens went in search of brush fires – to no avail.

The Brown Mountain lights continued to

The northern lights, or *aurora borealis*, glow over a lake in Manitoba, Canada. The aurora is caused by electrically charged particles from space, which collide with atoms in the atmosphere high above the Earth and make them glow. The eerie spectacle is seen regularly in the northern latitudes but has often been misinterpreted on its occasional appearances farther south. It may have been responsible for some of the stories of angelic hosts and ghostly armies seen in the sky. Seen low over the horizon, the aurora can look like lights on the ground in the distance, and could have given rise to stories of ghostly activity

be seen for over 60 years, until finally a North Carolina Congressman mentioned the curiosity in Washington, and in 1913 an investigator from the United States Geological Survey was sent down to view it. Examining the mountain, he found that it consisted of ordinary Cranberry granite, which is widespread in the area. There was no marshland on the mountain's slopes, so the 'will o' the wisp' theory was ruled out. Witnesses said that the lights usually appeared at about seven in the evening, stayed for about 30 seconds, and then vanished, often to reappear 'four or five times' before dying out for the night. Others reported a single light that rose from the slopes of the mountain, hovered and then disappeared 'like a bursting skyrocket'.

Investigation renewed

The geologist was perfunctory in his report, ascribing all the lights to locomotive headlights. The Congressman who had instigated the enquiry in the first place was annoyed, and insisted that a second man be sent. The new investigator was more thorough but, after studying maps and geological details of the area, claimed that 47 per cent of the phenomena originated in locomotive headlights, 33 per cent in those of cars, and the remaining 20 per cent in fixed lights and bush fires equally. He added that the countryside at the foot of Brown Mountain was alternately dusty and misty, a combination of conditions that made the air very refractive.

However, a further report in 1925 pointed out several fairly obvious faults in the refraction theory, not the least of which was that the lights had been faithfully recorded for over 70 years – several decades before railroads were built in the area and half a century before the first automobile made its appearance. Furthermore, a season of floods in 1916 had put both railroads and highways out of action for some time, and still the 'phantom' lights appeared. One perhaps significant pointer was given: the lights disappear for long stretches during and for some time after a protracted drought. It may be that water – either the ocean or a river – is in cases such as this conducive to the appearance of ghost lights. (The John River runs by Brown Mountain.) Since 1925, no one has offered any further explanation – but the lights shine on.

In the 'tri-state' area where Kansas, Missouri and Oklahoma meet, spook lights appear so regularly that they have become a tourist industry. This area forms a triangle, the points of which are the towns of Columbus, Joplin, and Miami, about 20 miles (30 kilometres) from each other. Again a river, the Spring, cuts through this triangle, and the nearby US Highway 66 has given rise to the theory that the lights are those of automobiles, refracted by mist rising from the river. In favour of this is that fact that, viewed through binoculars, some of the lights appear in parallel pairs, with both members of each pair either white or red – like the head and tail lights of cars on a motorway.

Against the theory is the objection posed at Brown Mountain – that the lights have a venerable history dating far back beyond the automobile. And, like those of Ada, they occasionally bound up to onlookers; one farmer, ploughing by lamplight, abandoned his tractor and fled in terror when a red globe zoomed at him. So far, however, the lights have done no more than frighten and fascinate – so much so that for the past decade the hoteliers and bar-owners of the three towns have advertised the attractions of 'Spooksville', as they call it, in tourist brochures that they have distributed throughout the country.

There are a number of other 'spook light' sites in the United States. One of the best documented and most intriguing must be that on a hill in the Wet Mountain Valley

Below: the proprietor of 'Spookers' Shanty', near Joplin, Missouri, has managed to make a profit out of the local mystery lights. The lights are visible here beyond the bushes. As the sign indicates, the Moon and planets are alternative attractions when the spook lights do not appear

Bottom: a group of the Joplin spook lights in the far distance, captured in a prize-winning photograph. Spook lights at other locations appear in conditions remarkably similar to these: down tree-lined highways or along railway tracks

Silver Cliff to make an investigation.

Two years later, in an article about Colorado in the *National Geographic*, assistant editor Edward J. Linehan described how he viewed the lights in the company of Westcliffe resident Bill Kleine. It was dark when the two reached the graveyard, and Linehan switched off his headlights. They got out of the car, and Kleine pointed: 'There! See them? And over there!'

Linehan saw them, '. . . dim round spots of blue white light' glowing above each grave. He stepped forward for a better look at one but it vanished, then slowly reappeared. He switched on his flashlight and aimed it at one of the lights. The beam revealed only a headstone. For 15 minutes the men pursued the elusive ghost lights among the graves.

Most people, said Kleine, reckoned that the lights were 'reflections' of the town lights of Westcliffe. Looking back at the tiny cluster far below, Linehan found this impossible to believe, particularly as Kleine went on: 'Both me and my wife have seen them when the fog was so thick you couldn't see the town at all.'

Other theories recounted and discounted by Linehan were that the lights were caused by radioactive ore – but a Geiger counter test of the whole area revealed no trace of radioactivity; that the ghost lights were luminous paint, daubed on the tombs by hoaxers – but no evidence has ever been found to support this charge. Gas from decaying bodies seemed a far-fetched idea, as the last burial took place around the turn of the century. The mercury vapour lights of Westcliffe

area of Colorado, not only because the lights have appeared almost every night for just over 100 years, but also because they focus on that favourite scene of traditional hauntings – a disused cemetery.

In 1880, the township of Silver Cliff grew up in the wake of a sudden 'silver rush' and by the end of its first year's existence the population topped 5000. Due to the usual deaths by violence and mining incidents, a 'Boot Hill' cemetery grew at the same time on the foothills of Wet Mountain. The boom faded as quickly as it came, however, and today only about 100 prospectors live among the dilapidated buildings.

The strange phenomena that haunt the Silver Cliff graveyard were first reported shortly after its foundation, when a group of drunken miners returning to their diggings reported seeing eerie blue lights hovering over each grave. Nor were these lights just a by-product of whiskey – they appeared on other nights to sober observers. In 1956 an article about the lights in the *Wet Mountain Tribune* excited some comment in the Western United States, but it was not until 1967 that the *New York Times* sent a reporter to

might, it was suggested, have caused 'special effects' on the hill side; but not only were they a late installation but on several occasions when power cuts had blacked out every township for miles around, the graveyard illuminations still shone.

Among the old-timers of Silver Cliff only one explanation holds good, said Linehan: the blue-white spots are the helmet lamps of long-dead miners, still seeking on the deserted hillside for traces of silver.

Phantom phenomena

Old soldiers never die

Phantoms are not always the lonely beings of the traditional ghost story; sometimes, especially in damp weather, they appear in large numbers, re-enacting old battles

THE BATTLE OF NASEBY, in Northamptonshire, England, was fought on 14 June 1645. One of the major engagements of the English Civil War, it ended in the rout of the Royalist forces by the Parliamentary armies. But it seems to have been fought not once, but repeatedly – to have been 'replayed' annually for about a century afterwards. Local villagers would congregate on a nearby hill to witness the re-enactment of the fight. The watchers heard cannonfire and saw men fighting and falling, banners flying and cavalry charging; they even heard the screams and groans of the wounded. Yet all this was enacted in the sky above the battlefield.

We are accustomed to think of ghosts as single apparitions, appearing one at a time to one or two observers. But some records exist of large-scale hauntings – of phantoms appearing *en masse*, engaged in collective

An army sleeps on the eve of battle, while phantom warfare rages in the skies above. The apparition may be an anticipation of the bloodshed to come, or a re-enactment of some past engagement. Stories of 'armies in the sky' seen over battlefields are numerous – suggesting that the strenuous exertion and intense emotion of combat are somehow favourable to psychic phenomena

activity. They are often refighting some historic battle, as in the case above.

Another important engagement of the Civil War, the battle of Marston Moor, near York, is re-enacted from time to time, according to a local legend. The most favourable weather for the occurrence of the apparition is said to be fog, even though the original battle of 1644 was fought in midsummer.

Yet another Civil War battle fought over again by phantoms was the battle of Edgehill (1642). Only a few days after the battle, there were reports of apparitions of soldiers, cavalry and phantom scenery – all appearing in the sky over the battlefield. King Charles sent a number of army officers from Oxford to the site – and they not only witnessed the events, but were willing to swear statements to that effect.

Writer Joan Forman experienced the terror of a long-past battle herself, when travelling in Scotland some years ago. She had chosen to stay in Selkirk, because it is a good centre for touring and because she was interested in the career of James Graham, the first

movement and, in spite of heroic charges by the Royalist leader and his cavalry, had slowly driven them back until they were pinned beneath the mass of Minchmoor.

At this point in the narrative, Forman looked over the edge of the Newark courtyard and without warning was engulfed in a feeling of frantic misery and desperation. There was a sensation of turmoil, of many people struggling to escape and being forced back – not against the far side of the valley but right underneath the walls of the castle itself. She stood there for a few minutes, but the sense of furious and desperate fighting was unbearable. She moved away.

As she did so, she said that she believed Montrose's men had been massacred on this side of the valley and not on the other. The guide shook his head. 'Oh, no,' he said, 'I'm sure you're wrong. It is acknowledged that they died on the farther side.' She did not pursue the matter.

Then, as they walked away from that miserable place above the escarpment, Forman

Marquis of Montrose. This great cavalier leader had been Charles I's chief supporter in Scotland – his Captain-General. He had fought the Covenanting forces, which sided with the English Parliament. He had spectacular gifts as a soldier, and in 1644 led his armies in some brilliant forced marches across the mountains to achieve equally extraordinary victories over the King's enemies.

But towards the end of that year Montrose found that his luck began to run out. In attempting to lead his small army away from a much larger force of the enemy, led by General David Leslie, Montrose headed for Philiphaugh, a small plateau near Selkirk, where the Glen of Yarrow meets that of Ettrick, and camped there.

But Leslie was almost upon them. Leslie's army of 6000 men fell on Montrose's force of 700. The Royalists were driven from one end of the valley to the other before they were penned in and cut down. The *annus mirabilis* of Montrose ended in the massacre of his men.

Local tradition has it that the Royalists were pinned down on the side of the valley that lies beneath Minchmoor. On the opposite side of the valley lay a castle known as Newark, perched on an escarpment above the battlefield. It was also said that, although General Leslie offered quarter to those Royalists who surrendered, many of the men and their camp followers were slaughtered after the battle.

Forman already knew of the battle, but not its details, and so she was glad when a knowledgeable Selkirk historian offered to guide her around the site. They found the ruins of the old Newark keep, isolated in its wild and beautiful valley, and entered the remains of the old courtyard. The guide began to describe the battle to her: how Leslie had caught Montrose's small force in a pincer

Top: a crucial battle of the English Civil War is marked by this monument at Naseby, Northamptonshire. Local people saw phantom re-enactments of it during the following 100 years

Above: Oliver Cromwell at the battle of Marston Moor, in Yorkshire. Apparitions of this battle are alleged to occur even today

Right: James Graham, first Marquis of Montrose, led a small Royalist force that was massacred at Philiphaugh, Scotland. Over 300 years later, the terror of the event was apparently experienced by the author while visiting the site

was again immersed in a wave of terror and anguish, now coming from the courtyard itself. This time the feeling of fear and wretched despair were overwhelming: for a few seconds she was unable to move. The air seemed filled with cries of anguish, though she knew she was hearing nothing with the ear.

'It's here,' she said. 'They killed them here in this very courtyard. Where I am standing, and over there by the wall. They must have executed a whole lot of people in this very place.'

The Selkirk man was silent, visibly upset. Finally he said: 'There were people killed later, I think. Leslie went back on his promise; some of the non-combatants – women and boys – were killed, and afterwards some of the men. But I don't think that it was here.'

She said no more, but the misery of the place was heavy and she was glad to go from it.

The kindly historian telephoned the following day and said that the curious episode had so impressed him that he had further investigated the local records. 'It seems you may be right and tradition wrong,' he said. 'There's a contemporary record that refers to the castle side of the valley as being the scene of the final massacre, and that would make it right under the place where we stood. What's more, there seems to be some justification for thinking executions did take place in the castle bailey after the battle.'

Some of Forman's ancestors belonged to the Graham clan and may have fought at Philiphaugh with their chief, Graham of Montrose. Could this fact have helped to make her a particularly sensitive 'receiver' for this strange experience?

Sounds of clashing metal

A further example of 'participation' in a past battle occurred in Windsor in the early 1970s. A house owned by Mr and Mrs Wakefield-Smith was apparently haunted by a man in a dark cloak, and they felt the atmosphere of the place to be unhappy. The garden, however, proved to be an equally interesting site. On one occasion when the owners had walked to the end of it, they suddenly seemed to be in an area of great heat and noise. Both husband and wife felt they were in the middle of a battle, for all around them were the sounds of clashing metal, like swords striking armour. There was a sensation of frenzied activity on all sides. Yet as suddenly as it began the phenomenon ended, and the garden was its usual tranquil self.

Although the Wakefield-Smiths' description of the ghosts suggests the Civil War period, the only battle referred to by local tradition was of a much earlier date, and was fought between Romans and Britons. It seems likely that this is what the couple encountered.

The great heat associated with the occurrence is interesting. Hauntings are generally associated with a fall in temperature, and this did indeed accompany the appearances of the

Above: Newark Castle, seen across the valley that was the scene of James Graham's defeat. The conventional opinion of historians is that Graham's men were trapped on the opposite side of the valley – behind the camera's viewpoint. But Joan Forman's experience while visiting the castle – apparently a 'replay' of the emotions of the battle – convinced her that the battle ended beneath the castle walls

Left: the keep of Newark Castle, from the courtyard. Here Forman experienced, for the second time, the sensation of being engulfed in the anguish of many people. Her belief that the massacre that followed the battle had taken place in the courtyard proved to be supported by independent historical evidence – as did her intuition about the battle itself

ghost in the house. Was the experience of the battle a haunting, then, or some quite different phenomenon?

Not all large-scale manifestations relate to battles. The eerie night-time activity seen by residents Dr and Mrs White in 1969 on the Isle of Wight did not seem to have anything to do with war. Miss Edith Olivier, a Wiltshire author, was involved in a similar event during the First World War. She was driving towards the great Avebury Ring of standing stones as dusk was falling. As she came within sight of the circle she saw what she thought was an entire fair erected around and among the stones; she could hear music and see the lights of the booths. But as she drew level she found that the circle was empty, and there was no sound but that of the wind sighing among the great monoliths. Later Miss Olivier's enquiries revealed that fairs had been held at this spot in the past, but it had been at least 50 years since the last.

Frequently, communities that have lived

Phantom phenomena

by an inflexible timetable reappear regularly in apparitional form for many years after their earthly disappearance. Thus groups of monks and nuns, accustomed to process and attend prayer at set times of the day and night, may be seen and heard repeating the same pattern centuries later. Such stories are numerous throughout Britain. At Hinxworth Place, near Baldock in Hertfordshire, processions of monks have been seen to come through a wall, apparently on their way to or from their worship through a doorway long bricked up.

Occasionally an entire church congregation is seen, as at Dallington, Northamptonshire, in 1907. Two schoolgirls visited a country church at the end of a walk. One, a local girl, entered the church first but came out again in a great hurry. Her companion, a visitor to the area, was intrigued and went into the building. The place seemed full of kneeling people, though they appeared, she afterwards said, 'to be made of a substance similar to soap bubbles'. There seem to be no other reports of similar apparitions at this site, and there is no indication of the period to which the ghostly worshippers belonged.

Yet another instance of a group apparition was reported from Wiltshire, where a detachment of Roman soldiers was said to march along the old road beyond Oldbury Camp. A shepherd who sighted the band on one occasion gave this description of them: 'Men with beards, wearing skirts and big helmets with hair on the top. And a girt bird on a pole a' front on 'em.' A fair, if somewhat rustic, description of a Roman column, carrying its eagle insignia at its head.

Soldiers, in small groups or whole armies, in war or peace, seem to supply the bulk of

Above: Hinxworth Place, in Hertfordshire, is one of the many places in England where a ghostly religious ritual is said to occur: a procession of monks appears through a wall

Below: a typically English church, at Dallington, in Northamptonshire. The ghostly congregation seen briefly in 1907 was more insubstantial – seemingly made of 'soap bubbles'

mass-phantom phenomena. One of the most interesting cases is that of Major A. D. McDonagh, an officer serving in the Indian Army on the North-West Frontier.

On one occasion the Major rode along a range of hills close to the River Indus. He eventually reached a ridge from which he could see across a wide horseshoe-shaped valley, which was heavily wooded. As he gazed down onto it, he abruptly found himself in a large group of soldiers, apparently from ancient Greek times, busy with the usual duties of a military encampment. He saw three altars, and noticed a group of men beyond them, at the head of the valley, gathered around some object. McDonagh could not see what was holding their attention until he walked across. Then he perceived a dressed stone slab with a newly cut inscription. The language was Greek, of which in ordinary life he had no knowledge. However, he found himself able to read and understand what was written here: the inscription seemed to relate to the death of one of the generals of Alexander the Great. He felt, too, a marked sensation of sorrow among the men with whom he stood.

Evidence in stone

Abruptly, the experience ended. Major McDonagh found himself back on the ridge, looking down into the valley, vividly aware of what he had just experienced.

Later he returned with Indian labourers to explore the area thoroughly. He found the place heavily overgrown with jungle vegetation and the men had to hack their way through to the head of the valley in which he had seen the inscribed rock. When eventually they reached it and cleared away the vegetation, they found a partially dressed rock surface with some traces of Greek lettering upon it, though the inscription was

Left: Oldbury Camp, an Iron Age earthwork in Wiltshire, apparently occupied by the Romans when they subdued Britain. A detachment of Roman soldiers is said still to march along the line of the old Roman road nearby

Below: Alexander the Great, (in a crown) before a Hindu idol, following his crossing of the Indus river in 326 BC. The painting is from a 15th-century Persian manuscript. A British officer, Major McDonagh, who had been riding near the river, suddenly found himself in the midst of this army. For an extended period he watched the men, apparently in mourning for one of their generals

badly eroded and defaced. McDonagh had no doubt, however, that this was the memorial he had seen earlier. The valley proved to be the site of one of the camps of Alexander before he forded the Indus in 326 BC.

This account is a particularly interesting example of a mass-phantom appearance. The distance in time between the original episode and its modern 'repeat' was over 2000 years – an exceptional period in these cases. Furthermore, the subject of the experience participated in the events he witnessed – moving around to get a view of the things he wanted to see, and finding himself able to understand a language normally unknown to him.

The idea of reincarnation suggests itself in cases like these. Was Major McDonagh a solider in Alexander's army in some former life? Or did he merely 'pick up' the sensations of the troop who had stood by the rock with its inscription to the dead general?

Occurrences of this nature are too rare to provide much evidence. However, appearances of phantoms *en masse* are not. There are at least two possible explanations of these. They may involve the *reproduction* of the sights and sounds of the original event – possibly because information stored by the physical surroundings is, in favourable conditions, 'retransmitted' to create the impression in the minds of certain specially sensitive witnesses that they are actually observing the original events. Alternatively, they may be true timeslips, in which past and present, or present and future, coexist temporarily. However, this process too might be triggered by the mind of the witness, interacting with information registered by the physical surroundings.

Ghosts on the march

Sometimes crowds of phantom figures appear, acting out events long past – or, occasionally, in the future. A great many of these mass phantom cases seem to be linked with emotional experiences of some kind

THE OCCASIONAL SIGHTINGS of mass apparitions fall into a shadowy area in which it is difficult to distinguish timeslips from hauntings. The large-scale noise and activity, involving many phantom individuals at one time, and the sense of being overwhelmed by associated emotions, suggest that the subject has been plunged into events in some other era. On the other hand, the co-presence of familiar features of the everyday world suggests that it is the phantoms who have strayed into the wrong time.

A high proportion of mass phantom appearances relate to military activity. If they are a 'recording' of historical events, and if such recording is especially likely to occur in the presence of increased mental and emotional stress – and the evidence points in this direction – then it is not surprising that battles should figure so strongly among apparitions.

Weather conditions also seem to be important. Grey, overcast skies, mist or fog seem to be conducive to paranormal effects. One such case was reported by Mrs E. W. Reeves, of Holme Hale, Norfolk, England.

Mrs Reeves and her husband visited friends some miles away on the evening in question and returned home at about 2.30 a.m. The Moon was shining and there were patches of mist when Mrs Reeves got out of the car to open the garage doors for her husband. She heard shouting in the near distance and she drew her husband's attention to it, saying that she thought someone might be in need of help. Mr Reeves, however, who had not yet heard any sound, considered 2.30 in the morning to be an unlikely time for anyone to be needing assistance.

In the next moment the shouting was taken up by other voices, and now Mr Reeves also heard it. The clamour was accompanied by the sound of many running feet. Mr Reeves remarked that the sound seemed to be coming from the far side of a bridge a few hundred yards away. Disturbed and curious, the couple moved into the roadway for a better view. Nothing was to be seen, but the noises continued, presently augmented by the sounds of galloping horses.

The thought that anything paranormal was happening did not occur to the couple. They assumed that the horses they could hear belonged to a neighbouring farmer and they were concerned about stopping their flight. The galloping and shouting drew nearer, but the village street remained as empty of anything visible as when they had first left the car.

The sounds were now so loud that whatever was causing them appeared to be all around the couple, 'milling around us and

Above: a battle in the sky over Verviers, Belgium, in June 1815 – within a month of the battle of Waterloo, some 70 miles (110 kilometres) away. It was explained away as a mirage – yet mirages occur simultaneously with the events that cause them

Left: the rebellion of Robert Ket in 1549 may have been 'witnessed' over 400 years later. After the defeat of Ket – here seen denouncing a landowner – some of the rebels fled through the village of Holme Hale, where a phantom battle was heard in the 20th century

district was twice pillaged by the Danes in the 11th century; a series of riots against the enclosure of common lands occurred in the 1530s; there was further rioting during Ket's Rebellion in 1549, in which some of the rebels fled from Castle Rising to Watton, pursuing a line of retreat passing directly through Holme Hale. Certainly the rebel forces had a camp at Hingham, a short distance away, which was attacked by the troops of Sir Edmund Knyvett. The battle appears to have been fought with staves on one side and swords on the other, suggesting peasants facing organised troops. Ket's rising would appear to fit the facts of the case.

A well-documented sighting was reported by Dr James McHarg in the *Journal* of the Society for Psychical Research for December 1978. The incident concerned a Miss Smith, to whom the experience occurred in January 1950. She was walking home to the village of Letham in Angus, Scotland, after spending the evening at a friend's house. She had been driving back but her car had skidded on the icy road and into a ditch. She had therefore decided to walk the remaining 8 miles (13 kilometres).

She was about half a mile (800 metres) from her home village when the apparition began. It continued until she reached the houses, the whole experience lasting about 12 minutes. She must have been exceedingly

Below: Viking raiders may have been involved in the event that was acted out in the Holme Hale apparition. Vikings occupied large areas of Britain from the 8th to the 11th century. It was towards the end of this period that Holme Hale was twice pillaged by Danish marauders

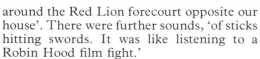

around the Red Lion forecourt opposite our house'. There were further sounds, 'of sticks hitting swords. It was like listening to a Robin Hood film fight.'

By now both husband and wife were bewildered, and shrank against the wall of their house, trying to evade whatever it was that was crashing around them. Presently the commotion shifted away from where they stood, into a field located next to the inn. Finally the noises moved up the hill beyond and faded into the distance. After that, according to Mrs Reeves, all the dogs in the village began to howl simultaneously, and continued to do so for several minutes.

The BBC later investigated this incident for a television programme called *Timeslips*. Their research revealed that, although no pitched battle in the neighbourhood of Holme Hale was on record, there were several likely candidates for the disturbance experienced by Mr and Mrs Reeves. The

'dark tights' and 'a sort of overall with a roll-collar'. There was a roll at the bottom of the tunic. The headgear seemed to be a flattish rolled cap, 'excellent for carrying things on the head with'. The torches were very long and made of a bright red material.

Dr McHarg obtained these details directly from Miss Smith in September 1971 and thoroughly investigated the background to her experience. He found that torches in Scotland were once made from the resinous roots of the Scots fir, which are reddish in colour, and would have been notable for their length. The costume description, too, is borne out by the dress of a figure of a Pictish warrior incised in stone at Golspie.

All in all, this is an impressive apparition. It has marked parallels with that experienced by Dr and Mrs White on the Isle of Wight on an evening in 1969. Both experiences occurred in January, though the weather was different: on the Isle of Wight it was cold, with brilliant moonlight and towering cloud masses, while at Nechtanesmere it was cold and wet after a snowfall that had been followed by rain. In each case the onset of the

tired at this time, for she had been carrying her small dog for the last part of the journey.

The experience began as she crested a rise that in daylight would have given her a view of Dunnichen Hill. Now, with the time nearing 2 a.m., she saw moving torches in the distance ahead of her. As she continued her journey, she followed a left-hand turning that brought the torches onto her right. Still farther down the road on her right, she saw other figures carrying torches. There were figures even closer to her, however, in a field about 50 yards (45 metres) distant. Miss Smith felt that she had stumbled upon some activity that was already in progress when she arrived.

The area that Miss Smith was traversing was the site of an ancient and now vanished loch, known as Nechtanesmere, a name given to it by the English rather than the Scots. It had been the scene of a battle in May 685. The Northumbrians, captained by their king, Egfrith, were defeated here by the Picts under their king Brude mac Beli, and the Northumbrian chief was killed. After falling into an ambush Egfrith's army was apparently routed, and the most desperate fighting seems to have taken place near the shores of the old loch.

This was the area crossed by Miss Smith, and although the loch waters had long been replaced by dry land, she apparently knew that a lake had once existed there, for her account referred to figures 'quite obviously skirting the mere'. She concluded that they were searching for their dead, for she noticed one person in particular turning over body after body and scrutinising each. The corpses also must therefore have been visible.

Miss Smith gave an excellent description of the dress worn by the figures. She saw

Above: the area bordering the site of a vanished loch, Nechtanesmere, which was traversed by phantom figures on a January night in 1950. Miss E.F. Smith watched them for about 12 minutes as the torch-carrying men apparently searched among corpses for their own dead, slain in battle. The battle of Nechtanesmere, fought in 685, resulted in the defeat of Egfrith, king of the Northumbrians, by the Pictish king Brude mac Beli

Right: a Pictish warrior, carved on a stone among animals and fish. His dress resembles that of the figures seen by Miss Smith: a tunic with a rolled hem and collar, and tights

Flight into the future

Phantoms *en masse* are frequently seen in the air – but in one notable case an apparition on the ground was viewed from the air. Air Marshal Sir Victor Goddard told how in 1934 he had been flying a Hawker Hart bomber (left) over Scotland in mist and rain. He flew lower, looking for an abandoned airfield, Drem, as a landmark. He found it – apparently bathed in sunlight, and fully operational. Yellow aircraft were on the tarmac, being serviced by technicians in blue overalls. No one paid any attention to Goddard as he flew low overhead and then resumed his journey. It was only several years later that the meaning of what he had seen became clear to him. In 1938 Drem was put back into service as a flight training station. Trainer aircraft were for the first time painted yellow and ground crew were issued with a new style of uniform – coloured blue. Goddard believed he had glimpsed Drem airfield as it was to be.

vision took place as the parties crested a hill. Both apparitions featured the same type of scene: searching figures carrying lighted torches. It seems likely that they were engaged on the same mission in both cases – a search for the dead after a battle, in order to bury them. The differences in costume in the two cases are explicable by the differences in locality and, presumably, in the dates of the original events.

Action replay

For there seems little doubt that what was seen was in both cases some historical event – a record of a large-scale undertaking in the distant past. The most likely 'source' event is a battle, and the details of the battle of Nechtanesmere are sufficiently well-known to make its correspondence with Miss Smith's vision apparent. The reality behind the Whites' experience must remain speculative, for the Isle of Wight endured many military forays by a series of invaders. Only intensive research could reveal the 'template' for this experience.

And the mechanism that causes this 'replay' of past events? Dr McHarg suggested that memories stored in the collective unconscious of Carl Jung are responsible. But if this is so, something in the physical setting must trigger the recollection, must 'press the button' that causes the brain to respond with its stored knowledge of the place.

It is just as likely that the physical surroundings themselves store the record of the event, the pattern of activity being printed indelibly on the place by the intense emotion generated by mass activity and a temporary unification of purpose. The subsequent presence in the neighbourhood of a person

Football supporters exult as their team scores a goal. The emotions aroused by the mock battle on the field can be almost as intense as those of a real battle. Will gatherings such as this – a phenomenon of the 20th century – provide material for collective apparitions in the future?

whose electrical brain patterns happen to 'resonate' in some way with those of the 'record' might result in a translation of the record into audio-visual experiences.

Perhaps in the future observers with correctly trained and 'tuned' mental equipment will be able to pick up the signals given out by large-scale present-day gatherings. For any crowd gathered together with a common purpose generates a high emotional charge (possibly an enhanced electrical potential) – whether they be football crowds or political demonstrators, carnival celebrators or spectators at royal weddings. Perhaps the global events we record today on videotape will in the future be replayed psychically.

There are skulls that create supernatural disturbances because they want to stay in a favourite place. Can such tales be true? The strange behaviour of screaming skulls that won't stay buried certainly bears investigation

IN THE QUIET VILLAGE CHURCHYARD of Chilton Cantelo in Somerset, England, picturesque in both name and setting, a lichen-covered tombstone dated 1670 marks the last resting place of one Theophilius Broome – or at least the resting place of most of him. For over 300 years his skull, polished like old ivory, has lain in a cupboard at his former home, Chilton Cantelo Manor. This fulfils a deathbed wish that his head should remain in residence. Not unnaturally, his heirs were uneasy about the idea. But they quickly discovered that attempts to bury the skull with the rest of the body only created problems for everyone.

According to the inscription on Theophilius's tombstone, 'horrid noises, portentive of sad displeasure' were heard

Right: the polished skull of Theophilius Broome in its permanent resting place at Chilton Cantelo Manor in Somerset. The skull made 'horrid noises' when anyone tried to bury it

Below: the screaming skull of Bettiscombe Manor in Dorset. As recently as the early 1900s, the skull is said to have taken revenge on someone who tossed it out of the house it loved. Family tradition has it that the relic is the head of a West Indian slave

The skulls that screamed

throughout the village when attempts were made to rebury his head. These ceased only when the bony relic was disinterred and once more returned to its comfortable cupboard.

Another skull, kept at Wardley Hall near Manchester, is said to be that of a Roman Catholic priest executed for treason in 1641. After being displayed on the tower of a Manchester church, it was recovered by a Catholic family and taken to Wardley. Like its Somerset equivalent, it made noises when removed from the premises. More, it was said to have caused violent thunderstorms. Besides all that, it refused to remain buried. In the chilling words of ghost hunter Eric Maple, it 'always managed to find its own way back [to the house] again'.

Burton Agnes Hall, a beautifully restored Elizabethan mansion in Humberside, contains the skull of Anne Griffith. She was the daughter of Sir Henry Griffith, who built

the residence in 1590. Like Theophilius Broome, Anne made the deathbed request that her head be cut off after she died and kept in the house, and the wish was granted. The skull, known locally as 'Owd Nance', was removed on several occasions. Each time it screamed horrifyingly until it was returned to the house. To prevent any further outbreak of such supernatural annoyances, 'Owd Nance' was bricked into the walls of the house itself in 1900 – and Burton Agnes has been mercifully tranquil ever since.

'Screaming skull' legends form a small but curious part of the British folklore tradition. One suggestion is that such stories have their roots in the Romano-British practice of making 'foundation sacrifices' – burying a human or animal victim in the foundations of a house to ensure luck and propitiate the gods. It was perhaps with some knowledge of such practices in mind that Anne Griffith and

Theophilius Broome made their strange requests. Another theory suggests that the stories arose from the rumoured custom of walling up monks and nuns as punishment for breaches of their chastity vows, though in fact such 'executions' were probably rare indeed. A third source could be the Celts. They revered the head in their religion and often preserved severed heads as family treasures or offerings to the gods in sanctuaries. Celtic cult heads of stone have been found in many places in Britain. Whatever their origins, 'screaming skulls' show a uniform objection to being moved from their chosen niches.

One of these 'guardian' skulls has a modern history coming down to the present day. It resides in Bettiscombe Manor near Sherborne in Dorset. Bettiscombe, a fine building of mellow brick and white stone, dates principally from the early 17th century. Parts of it are much older, however, and the land on which it stands has been inhabited since prehistory. The house was built by the Pinney family, who still farm the rich countryside around. Michael Pinney, a noted archaeologist and historian, lives in the manor house itself. His son, Charlie, breeds shire horses for use in film and television

Above: Burton Agnes Hall in Humberside, home of the head of Anne Griffith after her death in the 17th century. The skull was bricked into the walls in 1900 to prevent its ever being touched again – because it screamed terribly when it was moved

Left: Wardley Hall near Manchester. Its resident skull, supposedly that of a Catholic priest, not only screamed but also caused wild thunderstorms when removed from the premises

work. Both the professional Pinney and his practical son treat their guardian skull with deep respect.

The earliest written accounts of the skull date from the early 18th century, but the story itself starts in 1685. At that time Azariah Pinney, the squire of Bettiscombe, took part in the Monmouth rebellion. Being on the losing side, he was exiled to the West Indies. As it turned out, his family flourished there, and his grandson, John Frederick Pinney, was able to return to Dorset in style and move back onto the lands of his ancestors. With him came a black slave who became part of the household and was soon a familiar sight in the village. The Negro had been promised that, on his death, his body would be returned by his master to Africa, from where he had been taken by slavers as a child.

But Pinney died first. When the slave died shortly afterwards, no one kept the promise to him and his body was buried in the local churchyard near that of his master. It did not rest content and a mournful wailing seemed to emanate from the grave. Crop failure, cattle disease and storms accompanied the months of moaning. Finally the body was disinterred and the skull taken back to its adopted home in the manor house. There it has remained. In recent years it has nested in a shoe box in Michael Pinney's study, fulfilling the double role of family heirloom and harbinger of doom to any that remove it. According to Pinney:

> It is said to scream and cause agricultural disaster if taken out of the house, and also causes the death, within a year,

of the person who commits the deed. A photographer once carried it as far as the open doorway to take pictures of it, but my wife snatched it back indoors again without anything untoward occurring.

Local lore has it that the last time the skull was 'interfered with', it took its vengeance just as the legend says it would. At the beginning of the 20th century, a tenant who had leased Bettiscombe prior to moving to Australia had a boisterous Christmas party at the manor. During the party he took the skull and hurled it into a horse pond that lay at the side of the house. The following morning the skull was found not in the pond but on the doorstep. How did it get there, when it had to go up a flight of stairs and across a paved patio? One theory, said Michael Pinney, was that

> it had been blown there by the wind, but it must have been a very strange and powerful wind. In the Thirties, however, I had an unannounced visit from three young Australians. One of them said that he was the son of the former tenant. His father had indeed died suddenly in Australia within a year of the incident, and his mother had always told him that the skull had brought a curse on them.

Kept like an animal

Until alterations were made to the attics of Bettiscombe after the Second World War, the guardian skull had traditionally been kept in a small attic room. The remains of this room can be seen today among the chimney stacks and thick oak rafters under the roof. There is an alternative tale to the black slave legend connected with the attic. This version says that a young girl had been kept prisoner there, bedded on straw like an animal and fed through a grille in the door. Although there is no historical evidence for

this story, as there is for John Frederick and his slave, there is a strong family tradition that the skull's 'place' for many years was under the rafters. In the early 1960s, on the track of the Bettiscombe skull, Eric Maple interviewed an old farm worker who claimed to remember 'hearing the skull screaming like a trapped rat in the attic'. Other locals claimed that during thunderstorms there was a rattling sometimes heard in the upper rooms – a rattling made by 'them' playing ninepins with the ancient relic. Exactly who 'they' were was left to the imagination.

Other snippets of lore about the skull seem to have been added on over the years.

Above: skulls placed in the niches of a French Celtic sanctuary as offerings to the gods. Celtic cult heads have been found in many places in Britain and may be a source for the stories of skulls that scream

A grisly exhibit

Jeremy Bentham, philosopher and political theorist whose reforming zeal helped improve 19th-century life in Britain, shared with the screaming skulls a desire to remain in a favourite place after his death. And he went to elaborate lengths to do so.

Bentham arranged that, when he died, a surgeon friend was to embalm his head and place it upon his skeleton – after the body had been dissected for the teaching of medical students. The skeleton, according to the fun-loving sage's instructions, was dressed in the clothes he had liked best. It was then seated in a glass-fronted upright mahogany box. This was placed in University College,

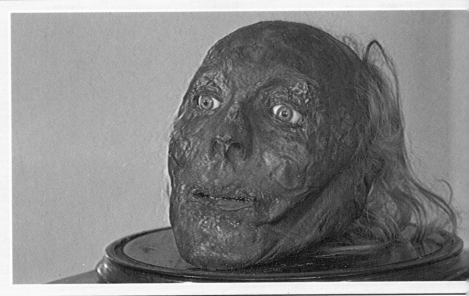

Michael Pinney and his wife were rather startled when a visitor asked if the skull had 'sweated blood in 1939 before the outbreak of the war, as it had in 1914'.

In fact, the 'screaming skull' of Bettiscombe Manor is probably not that of either the slave or the girl of the legend. In the 1950s, at Pinney's request, it was examined by Professor Gilbert Causey of the Royal College of Surgeons. He pronounced it to be much older than anyone had suspected. It was, he said, the skull of a prehistoric woman, a young girl with delicate features who died between 3000 and 4000 years ago.

So how did it come to be kept at Bettiscombe Manor, and why did such weird legends gather around it?

Death by the sword

There is some evidence of a Romano-British settlement on the site, which points back to the idea of a foundation sacrifice. But if Professor Causey's estimate is correct, the skull pre-dates any house that could have been in the settlement by several hundred years. An interesting parallel can be drawn with the screaming *ghosts* of Reculver in Kent. For many years a legend had persisted that screams and cries heard in woodland around this site of an early Roman settlement were made by the ghosts of children who had been murdered there. In 1964 important archaeological excavations were begun, during the course of which a number of children's skulls and bones were unearthed. One of these bore marks indicating that it had died by the sword. The pathetic skeletons were rather older than the Roman site, some dating from between 1000 and 500 BC.

Pinney himself has come up with a plausible if unusual explanation of the skull's arrival at Bettiscombe Manor: it made its own way there.

Behind the manor, the steep slopes of

wooded Pilsdon Pen stretch up far beyond the house's tall chimneys. The tor shows signs of prehistoric fortifications dating from about the same period as Maiden Castle, the great earthworks fortress that lies some miles away to the south-east. Besides containing the remnants of hut circles, the tor is also studded with small burial mounds and cairns. Pinney has excavated some of them through professional interest as an archaeologist. Down from the hilltop trickles a clear stream that travels in an ancient culvert through an outhouse attached to the Bettiscombe kitchens. As Pinney explains:

> I can't prove it, of course, but I rather suspect that the skull was worked loose from the soil at the top of the hill, tumbled into the stream and rolled down the sloping bed of the brook and down into the outhouse here. Such a find would have been traumatic to say the least in a superstitious age. The finder may well have tried to get rid of

London, of which Bentham was a founder and constant supporter. It has remained on a landing of this building near the Gower Street entrance ever since Bentham's death in 1832.

A wax model has replaced the deteriorated head, but the figure still wears the genial philosopher's straw hat and holds his trusty walking stick. A number of witnesses have said that Bentham's ghost, tapping the stone flags with the cane, often walks the corridors near his curious coffin. According to Bill Grundy, the television producer who made a film of Bentham, the ghost 'seems to appear most in times of trouble' – during the 1940 blitz, for example. It is as though the philosopher had appointed himself the 'guardian of University College'.

Top: Professor Gilbert Causey of the Royal College of Surgeons, who was called in to give an expert opinion on the Bettiscombe skull. He said it was that of a young prehistoric woman – a far cry from the slave of the traditional story

Above: the ruins of Reculver church in Kent, which is connected with local legends about children's ghosts that scream pitifully. Skulls dug up on the site proved to be from an earlier time than the stories indicated – suggesting that 'screaming skull' stories have their origins deep in ancient tradition

it, only to feel uneasy about the event – perhaps odd things did occur which convinced him that the skull wished to stay where it had landed. Then the stories began to grow as news of the skull's arrival spread.

The story of the skull at Bettiscombe might easily have reached the ears of old Theophilius Broome at Chilton Cantelo in the adjoining county of Somerset. Perhaps it influenced his decision to arrange that his own head should stay above ground. Whether or not the same idea came to Anne Griffith in what was then Yorkshire from the Bettiscombe tales is anyone's guess.

For their part, Michael Pinney and his family have prospered despite the bizarre relic in the shoe box. So far, however, he has refused to allow the family 'heirloom' to be taken outside the walls of the old manor. 'I'm not superstitious,' he explains with a smile, 'but why risk it?'

A potent mixture of murder, mayhem and a dash of legend enlivens the history of many English pubs and has produced plenty of phantoms to trouble ancient taverns. Many historic inns are haunted by intriguing tales of restless spirits

A large measure of spirits

The infamous Lord Chief Justice Jeffreys (right) was captured on Old Wapping Stairs (above) behind the Town of Ramsgate pub when he was trying to escape to France in 1688. He died in prison before being brought to trial, but it is the stairs that his ghost haunts. It has been seen there by many people, including the Thames river police

THE PUBLIC HOUSE is not only one of the most popular institutions of the English way of life, but also one of the most haunted. In the mid 1970s, when writing *The English pub*, Michael Jackson and writer Frank Smyth carried out a survey among the 'big six' brewery combines and the two dozen or so independent breweries that between them control most of the country's estimated 70,000 pubs. To a question concerning the number of pubs traditionally said to be haunted, the reply was rather surprising: every brewer claimed to have ghosts on his licensed premises. An independent brewer in the north boasted of having three haunted pubs (a quarter of the houses he then owned), while the mighty Bass-Charrington group said that their ghosts were 'too numerous to mention'. A West Country brewery said that 'about one in five' of their pubs had at one time or another been associated with supernatural phenomena. The prevailing tone of all the replies was one of quiet pride; ghosts after all are part of the national heritage and are usually good for business.

The public house is a unique institution found only in England, Wales and parts of Scotland. It is totally unlike the traditional bars and bothies of Scotland and Ireland, or the drinking places of America and Europe. The older pubs are quite as hallowed by time as the churches with which they often stand cheek-by-jowl (and have certainly overtaken them in popularity). It is therefore not surprising that many of them have acquired a reputation for being haunted. Nevertheless it is unwise, for obvious reasons, to take every pub ghost story at face value.

A case in point is the story of Madge Gill, the 'primitive' painter from London's East End, who died in the 1960s. One day in the 1930s she was sitting in a pub in Whitechapel (according to her own testimony) when she became aware of a ghost. This spirit said its name was 'Mirinarest', and urged her to draw pictures under its guidance. She subsequently produced hundreds of finely detailed and elaborate drawings, full of weird patterns and tormented faces. An exhibition of her 'spirit drawings' was held in a gallery in New Bond Street after her death.

'But,' asserted one of her former drinking companions, 'gin was the only spirit that moved her.'

Certainly the combined effects of alcohol and primitive lighting must have contributed to ghostly pub lore in days gone by; with a dash of authentic history the supernatural

Right: the Marsden Grotto pub, near which a gruesome incident occurred in the 18th century. Threatened with exposure by a colleague, a smuggler (who was using a cavern in the cliff as a base) imprisoned the would-be traitor in a tub suspended from the roof of the cavern, where he died. His wails are heard to this day by some who venture down the cliff lift to visit the pub below

cocktail is complete. The tale of the lonely Marsden Grotto pub, on the north-east coast of England, provides an illustration.

The story goes that in 1782 a retired miner, appropriately named Jack the Blaster, widened the natural caverns in the 100-foot (30-metre) high limestone cliffs opposite Marsden Rock in order to use them as a base for smuggling operations. When threatened with betrayal by a colleague, with the equally appropriate name of John the Jibber, Jack rigged a tub on a pulley to the high roof of the caverns and kept John a prisoner in it, lowering him only occasionally for food. The motive behind this arrangement seems to

have been humane: to save murdering the would-be traitor. But he died in the tub, anyway. In 1850 an enterprising gamekeeper named Peter Allan saw the possibilities of the old smuggler's cave as a beer cellar and built the present inn onto it. But the pleasures of drinking were to be spoiled by the ghostly wails and groans coming from the caves, usually late at night. These can still be heard, it is said, and are attributed to the death torments of 'awd John, jibberin away'. But fast tides, a honeycombed cliff face and, perhaps, brown ale may also play a part in the phenomenon.

In rural communities where the inn has been a focal point of life for generations it tends to become a repository of local lore and legend. Tales are told and re-told, polished and embellished. The story of an inn on Dartmoor in Devon illustrates this.

In the late 1960s the novelist Gordon Williams rented a cottage on the edge of Dartmoor to research a novel. His 'local' was the Warren House Inn, high on the moor between Widecombe in the Moor and Moretonhampstead.

The inn, he was told, had once been haunted, but the ghosts had disappeared along with the practice of corpse transportation. Before Widecombe had a consecrated burial ground, bodies had been carried across the moor to the churchyard at Moretonhampstead for burial. Treacherous weather and deep snowfalls are a feature of moorland winters, and when the pall-bearers

were defeated by such conditions they would leave the bodies, pickled in brine, in great cider vats in the inn's cellars to await the coming of spring. One local inhabitant told Williams that all this had happened 'in my grandfather's time' and that the innkeeper was 'fair troubled by the spirits' until a churchyard was opened in Widecombe.

Williams was intrigued by this story and checked it out in the British Library. He found that the tale was indeed based on fact: but the last 'corpse transportation' had taken place in 1134.

Apart from the influence of drink and legend, there remain several potent reasons why a pub should become the scene of a haunting. A phantom seeking the lost comforts of life on earth could do worse than frequent an inn. And if ghosts are merely psychic 'replays' of cataclysmic events, the pub is certainly exposed over the years to a far more varied spectrum of human emotions than, say, the village church. In many instances a pub haunting is a product of murder and mayhem. Two of London's most famous haunted pubs, the Grenadier and the Town of Ramsgate, are cases in point.

An invisible hand

The Grenadier, in Belgravia's Old Barrack Yard, began life in the 18th century as an officers' mess for the Coldstream and Grenadier Guards. In the early 19th century a young subaltern, caught cheating at cards, was reputedly beaten so severely with horse-whips by his fellow officers that he died. Although documentary evidence for the incident is fragmentary, there is good reason to believe that it did take place around 1820, and that the Duke of Wellington himself was involved in the subsequent cover-up.

There is no record of the month in which the manslaughter is supposed to have taken place but, according to reports going back at least to the 1880s, it is always in September that strange happenings occur. These have included an icy coldness in the cellar, the sensation of an invisible body bumping violently into bystanders, and a variety of noises. On one occasion in the early 1970s a barman was struck by an antique military helmet that hurtled from its place on the wall; some years earlier the cellarman had been grabbed by a powerful unseen hand and pulled backwards down the cellar steps. Although admitting to its presence, the Grenadier management are reluctant to advertise their ghost, perhaps fearing that it will deter people from working there.

At the Town of Ramsgate in Wapping High Street beside the river Thames the ghost is said to be that of Lord Chief Justice George Jeffreys, the infamous 'hanging judge' who presided at the Bloody Assizes of 1685, when hundreds of people implicated in the Monmouth rebellion were executed or transported to slavery. The modern frontage of the pub dates from the 1930s, but the main

The Warren House Inn (left) on Dartmoor was reputedly once haunted by spirits of the dead bodies that were left there, pickled in brine, during the winter when the weather was too bad to carry them over the moor for burial in Moretonhampstead churchyard (right)

fabric, the landing stage and Wapping Old Stairs (leading down from the pub to the river) are at least 300 years old.

When James II fled the country in 1688, Jeffreys also tried to escape, disguised as a sailor; he was recognised and arrested on Wapping Old Stairs and taken to the Tower of London, where he died the following year before being brought to trial. Possibly the panic he felt on the steps was so strong that it became 'imprinted' on the place; but his spirit seems to have changed in appearance

The Grenadier pub in Belgravia where a young Guards officer was supposedly whipped to death for cheating at cards. The ghostly legacy from this manslaughter includes bumps, noises and a sensation of icy coldness

over the years. While many witnesses have identified the judge's grim features from contemporary portraits, others have reported seeing a cavalier in a periwig and velvet breeches, or a grey-haired old man in a long white nightshirt. Nevertheless, sightings have been reported over so many years, and by so many witnesses (including the Thames river police) that this tavern phantom deserves to be rated as genuine.

If some people who have encountered the Grenadier ghost have been bruised or buffeted, many of the victims of a pub ghost in North Yorkshire have been even more unfortunate. The Busby Stoop Inn at Kirby Wiske, a village near Thirsk, takes its odd name from an 18th-century owner and his 'stoop', or tall chair. It is the chair that is haunted, or rather cursed. The disreputable Busby appears to have eked out his living by coin-clipping, thieving and receiving stolen goods; he was eventually sentenced to death for the murder of a female relative. As he was dragged from his inn, he swore that anyone who sat in his 'stoop' would die as violently and suddenly as he himself was about to do.

Simon Theakston, whose brewery owned the pub until 1978, told Frank Smyth: 'The legend may be odd and vague, but it is a matter of record that in the last 200 years or so death has struck anyone who dared to sit in the chair within a very short time.' He said that many who sat in the chair were dead within days, or even hours. Eventually the chair was moved out of harm's way.

It has to be said that many of the chair's victims of the last few decades could be categorised as 'high risk' anyway. They included an RAF fighter pilot (killed the following day), a motorist (who crashed the next day and died of his injuries), a motorcyclist

(killed shortly after leaving the pub), a holiday hitch-hiker (knocked down and killed two days later) and a local man in his late thirties (who died of a massive heart attack the following night). But the odds against all of them dying so soon after sitting in the Busby stoop must be high enough to suggest this was no mere coincidence.

Stories of the supernatural and 'real-life' psychical research both emphasise the adverse reactions of some animals to ghostly phenomena. The Star Inn at Ingatestone in

The ferocious bull terrier whose stuffed head (above left) guards the bar in the Star Inn (above) at Ingatestone, Essex, died in 1914. Its ghost is said to haunt the passage leading to the bar

The cursed stoop chair at the Busby Stoop Inn, North Yorkshire. So many people who sat in the stoop died soon afterwards that eventually the brewery moved the chair out of harm's way

Essex, for example, is said to be haunted by a dog that seems to appear only to other dogs. In life it was a bull terrier, which lived in the inn from about 1900 to 1914 and was a notorious fighter: it killed several neighbourhood dogs, and was never defeated. When it died of old age its stuffed head was hung in the bar parlour, and since that day its ferocious spirit has guarded the passageway giving access to the bar from the side of the pub. A former landlord said, 'The moment my dog set foot in the passage she growled, stiffened, and up went her bristles like a hedgehog. She was not only threatening something – but she was being threatened herself. She was dead scared.'

The phantom bull terrier not only continues to 'see off' its earthly kin, but also seems to deter local burglars; although pubs are a prime target in rural Essex, the Star has never had a break-in.

Perhaps the most ironic of pub hauntings is that of the Bull at Long Melford in Suffolk, a few miles from Borley and its` alleged ghosts. The Bull, a 17th-century coaching inn, was used as a base by ghost hunter Harry Price during his lengthy connection with the notorious Borley Rectory 'phenomena'. In 1977 the Enfield Psychical Research Group also adopted the inn as their base when they began making tape recordings in Borley Church. 'One evening,' said a member, 'we had assembled in the bar and I'd just commented that it can't have changed much since Price's time, when a cocktail shaker whizzed off the shelf and clattered to the floor. The barmaid sighed, picked it up and said to me, "Now look what you've done!" Apparently psychokinetic happenings occur there fairly regularly. Perhaps Harry resents his exposure as a fraud and is making a point!'

Ghosts of the air

A Wellington bomber regularly flies along the Towy valley in Dyfed, Wales, and has been seen by many people – but no such aeroplanes are in use now. This is only one of many stories of phantom aircraft and their crews

SOMETIMES IN THE GOLDEN DAYS of late summer, the unmistakable whine of a well-tuned Merlin engine is heard over Biggin Hill airfield in Kent. To older hands at this Royal Air Force training establishment, as well as to pilots at the Biggin Hill Flying Club, the evocative noise means only one thing: a Spitfire fighter. And many of those who glance upwards catch the flash of sunlight on an elliptical wing as the aircraft performs a 'victory' roll over the field before melting into the far haze, its exhausts leaving a rattle of sound in its wake.

In 1940, during the Battle of Britain, RAF Biggin Hill was one of the most famous front line bases. From here, Supermarine Spitfires and Hawker Hurricanes flew out to break German air power and thus deflect the threat of invasion. But the last operational Spitfire left Biggin Hill in the early 1950s. So what is the aircraft seen at Biggin Hill? Can it be the apparition of a wartime pilot flying his spectral aeroplane back home several decades too late? According to an RAF spokesman: 'Too many rational people have reported it for it to

be a hoax, and it's certainly not another make of aeroplane that has been mistaken for a Spitfire.' The craft has been identified as a Mark II which, together with the Mark I, flew from Biggin Hill during the Battle of Britain. Both are now extremely rare.

Significantly the ghost Spitfire is most frequently seen in the late afternoon and early evening, when the wartime squadrons usually came in from their last sortie of the day. And the 'victory' roll may be another significant point, for several inexperienced fliers lost their lives while performing the stunt.

Whatever the story behind the flying

The Spitfire is best known for its heroic role in the Battle of Britain in 1940. The last operational Spitfire flew in the early 1950s – yet a ghostly version still performs the 'victory' roll over Biggin Hill airfield in Kent

Right: a 'gremlin', the creature held responsible by RAF men during the Second World War for 'spooking' – or 'jinxing' – certain aircraft

ghost of Biggin Hill, it is far from unique. Since the infancy of aeronautics, phantom aeroplanes and their pilots have featured in paranormal events. Perhaps this is because airmen have such a special feeling for their aircraft. To them, some are lucky craft, others are jinxed.

It was in the officers' mess of a remote RAF station in India that a name was first put to aerial jinxes. In 1938 a squadron of Wellesley bombers suffered a rash of minor accidents – inexplicably, fuel pipes became clogged, instruments behaved erratically and cables snapped. The mess boasted only one book, Grimm's *Fairy tales*, and the only beer available was Fremlin's ale. From these two sources the pilots coined a name for the power that 'spooked' their craft: the 'gremlin'.

Later, during the war, crews aboard the big four-motor bombers such as the Lancaster and Halifax began to speak of lucky and unlucky gremlins, treating them as guardian spirits of the aircraft. Squadron Leader Bob Grainger of Garmouth in Morayshire, who flew Spitfires in the Battle of Britain, is a keen student of the paranormal and has his own theories on this.

An aircraft is a large but sensitive piece of equipment, and in a fighting aircraft men experience a great deal of violent

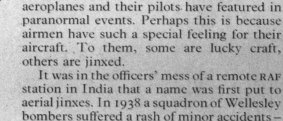

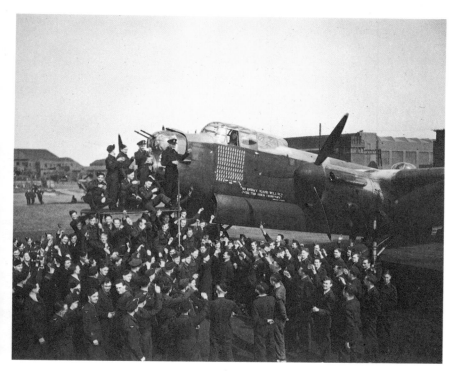

Above: the famous Lancaster bomber *S for Sugar*, with 467 Squadron, after 100 successful missions. Now a major attraction at the RAF museum at Hendon, London, it appears that ghostly airmen have been sitting in the gun turrets. Were 467 Squadron so emotionally bound up with the aircraft that they simply cannot bear to leave it?

Below: an Avro Lincoln that is said to be haunted – which is odd, for that particular aeroplane never saw active service

emotion. Long before the Canadian 'Philip' experiment, where a group of psychical researchers in Toronto deliberately set out to conjure up a table-rapping spirit, I wondered whether something similar could not be created in a particular aeroplane. If a certain Lancaster, for instance, had got you to Berlin and back intact on several occasions, you would begin to feel confidence in it, and that confidence might well affect the crew's performance – the pilot would fly better, the gunners aim more accurately, and so on. But in many instances it seems to have been more than a simple matter of psychology. When a new crew took over a 'lucky' bomber, the unusual luck continued for them, too.

In such cases, suggests Grainger, perhaps man and machine become such an integral whole that in the event of a sudden, fatal crash they continue to exist together on another level.

The most famous flying ghosts of all are centred, appropriately enough, at the Royal Air Force museum at Hendon in north London. Here, in two vast old hangars and one modern building, are Spitfires and their adversaries the Messerschmidt ME 110s, Tempests, Typhoons and many other old and new aircraft. Nearby, in RAF Hendon itself, is the Bomber Command museum containing such rarities as the Mosquito fighter-bomber, the last surviving Wellington and the Avro Lancaster *S for Sugar* with its battle honours emblazoned on its lofty nose.

For years, long before the Hendon museums opened in the 1970s, the sound of an erratic petrol engine had been heard puttering towards the two hangars. Group Captain Bill Randall, a director of the museum since its inception, discovered that a certain Lieutenant Shepherd had crashed and died in his trainer aeroplane here in 1917. Randall comments:

Perhaps Lieutenant Shepherd was responsible for the first 'happening', but I'm frankly at a loss to explain some of the other occurrences here. Of course, in buildings of this size and age, temperature differences, especially when the building is cooling at night, cause odd bumps and cracks. But a whole range of specific noises have been heard, from footsteps to the sound of engine cowlings being lifted off – when, of course, they haven't actually been moved. We've had night watchmen run in panic from the building.

S – for survival?

Most sinister and dramatic of all is the haunting of *S for Sugar*. Built in 1943, the big bomber flew a record 125 missions to Germany in three years, making her one of the most famous fighting aircraft in the world. Now, it seems, her old crew are reluctant to leave her. Says Randall: 'On a number of occasions, people working inside her have reported seeing chaps in World War II flying kit sitting in the gun turrets. One researcher who had wanted to look over her scrambled out immediately and wouldn't go back.'

The ghosts of Hendon have been so insistent that Randall has turned them to good use. A special tape, featuring some of the weird noises, plus interviews with staff who have had 'experiences', can be heard by visitors for a small charge. It seems appropriate that the 'spirit airmen' should help pay for the upkeep of their old aircraft.

Another set of ghosts haunts an Avro Lincoln at RAF Cosford near Wolverhampton in the West Midlands, which is rather strange because, as Randall points out, the

Left: Martin Green, a writer who was amazed to see a Wellington bomber flying down the Towy valley in Dyfed, Wales, in 1979. He could see it quite clearly: its propellers were spinning, and its slipstream bent the tops of trees as it passed by – but it made no sound at all. Green then realised that it was highly unlikely that Wellington bombers were still flying and later discovered that the only one left in Britain is in the RAF museum at Hendon (below). Some weeks after this experience, Green and another writer, Judith Cook, saw the Wellington again in the same valley. Another couple stopped to watch it; all four witnesses noted the complete silence of its flight. Aircraft of this type flew training missions in that area during the Second World War – and it seems that this one, at least, is still doing so

Lincoln never saw active service. Cosford houses the RAF's reserve aircraft, under the curatorship of former Flight Lieutenant Derek 'Clint' Eastwood. But, unlike Randall, Eastwood is reluctant to talk about a possible haunting. 'Extra' crew members have been seen in the Lincoln, he admits, but beyond this he will not go. 'I don't pretend to understand these things, and I'd prefer to leave them be,' he says. 'Let me just say that when people have pried into them, unpleasant things have happened here. On one occasion we did allow a television crew to film the aeroplane. They were being a little humorous about it when their camera was picked up and hurled across the hangar – no one was near it at the time. They packed up and left. Now I'd prefer that Cosford was simply known as an aircraft museum, not a centre for ghosts.'

Many people have seen the phantom Wellington that flies along the Towy valley between Llandeilo and Llandovery in Dyfed, Wales. Martin Green, a writer and former London publisher who lives in the area, first saw the Wellington while out walking along the A40 valley road in 1979.

It flew down the valley towards me at tree top level, but although the propellers were spinning it made no sound. I could clearly see the wind bending the trees in its slipstream. I thought it rather odd that a Wellington should still be flying around. . . . I mentioned the sighting in my local pub, and two or three people said they'd seen it. But I made further enquiries and discovered, of course, that the only Wellington still intact in Britain is in the RAF museum, Hendon.

Some weeks after his first sighting, Green was driving up the valley with journalist Judith Cook when they saw the mystery craft flying silently towards them. They stopped the car and got out, just as a couple on the opposite side of the road pulled up to watch too. 'All four of us saw the aircraft,' said Green. 'The other driver, a middle-aged man, remarked that it was a Wellington bomber. But when it had flown off around a bend in the valley, he suddenly realised that it couldn't be, as there were no flying Wellingtons left. I think he was shocked by the idea of seeing a ghost.'

Wellington bombers did train over the Brecon Beacons and the Black Mountain area around the Towy valley during the Second World War. But it is quite certain that there are no Wellingtons there now – at least, no physical ones.

Index

'A., Captain' 135
Abbey Crescent 76–7
Adam, S. 156–9, 160, 161, 162; *158, 159*
aircraft, haunted 46; phantom 202–4; *203*
airfield, haunted 202–3; phantom 193
Airlie, Earls of 73–4; *74*
Alais 28
Albert Victor, Prince, Duke of Clarence 69; *68*
Aldrich, Rev. Stephen 82
Alexander the Great 188–9; *189*
aliens, extraterrestrial 66
Ambrosius the cellarer 61–2
Amherst 45, 100
Amityville 168–73
Amityville horror, The 45, 168, 169; *168–73*
anaemia 15
Annals of the exploits of *Alfred* (Asser) 57
Anson, J. 45, 168, 170, 171; *171*
Apparitions (Tyrrell) 36, 41
apports 95, 99, 176
Archer, J.W. 83
Ardachie Lodge 144–50; *144–5, 148*
Argumosa, Professor Germán de 165, 166
Arles, Francois d' 99, 101; *100*
Arthur, King 51, 60; *54, 59*
Arundel, Sussex 43; *40*
Athenaeum Library 27–8
aurora borealis 182
Avalon 51, 61
Avebury 187
Avignon, France 28, 29
Aznar, Prof. Camón 164–5

Baccante, HMS 69
Bailey, Norman 69
Balfour, Frederick 77
Balfour, Mrs Mary 90
Ball, Father Peter 23
banshee 71–4; *71, 73*
Barrett, John 34
Barrett, Sir William 60, 61
Bartlett, John A. 53, 56, 61
bath 142
battles, phantom 29–30, 185–7; *185, 190–91*
Beardsley, Richard K. 64–5
Belgravia 85; *86*
Bell family 174–9
bells 44, 88, 91, 100, 101
Bell Witch 174–9
Bélmez 164; *164*
Bender, Professor Hans 16–17, 159, 161–3, 165, 166; *152, 162*
Bentham, Jeremy 196; *196*

Bere, Abbot Richard 52, 53, 57, 62
Berkeley Square 87–90; *87, 89, 90*
Bettiscombe Manor 39, 195–7; *194*
Biggin Hill 202
Bisson, Juliette 20
Block Island 70, 181
Blue Bell Hill 66; *66*
Bond, Frederick Bligh 52–62; *51*
bones 57, 95, 164; *see also* skeletons
Borley Church 96, 103–6; *91, 103–6*
Borley Rectory 44–5, 87, 91–102, 103, 201; *44, 93, 96–102*
Boston, Mass., U.S.A. 27–8, 37–8; *27*
Bowes-Lyon family 124–7; *124–7*
Braemar Castle 131; *131*
Branden, Victoria 35
Brazil 17; *179*
Brolin, James 169, 172, 173
Bromley, Kent 16
Broome, Theophilius 194, 197; *194*
'Brown Lady' 43; *40*
Brown Mountain 182–3
Buck, David 146, 147
Buddhism 51
Bull family 96–7, 98, 102, 103; *96, 97, 104, 105*
Burton Agnes Hall 194; *195*
bus, phantom 31–2, 36
Busby Stoop Inn 200–201; *201*

Cambridge 15
Camperdown, HMS 84, 85; *84*
Canada 64
cannibalism 126
Canning, Elizabeth 78–9
Canning, Geo. 87, 88, 89; *90*
Capet, Louis 12
Carla (focus of poltergeist activity) 152–155; *152, 153*
Carlisle, Esther ('Carrots') 79, 82
Caroe, W.D. 52, 54, 56
Carrick, Mary 20
carving, mysterious 134; *134*
cats 10, 34, 41, 143
Causey, Dr Gilbert 197; *197*
Celts 51, 195; *196*
ceremonies, magical 95; religious 22–5, 28, 188; *22–5; see also* exorcism
Ceylon 12
chair, cursed 200–201; *201*
chalices 125, 139; *138*
Charles I 29, 30; *140*
Charles II 140; *141*
Chevalerie, Marquis de la 61
children, focus of phenomena 11, 14–17, 81, 83, 112, 116–8; *12, 14–17, 112, 116–8*
Chilton Cantelo 194, 197
Christie Hill 129, 130, 131; *130*

Christmas carol, A (Dickens) 28
Churches, Christian 23, 25, 51, 54, 60
Churchill, Charles 78, 83
Civil War, English 185–6
Clerk, Duncan 130, 131
coaches, phantom 34, 44, 98; *98*
Cock Lane 78–83; *78–9, 80, 81*
Cockburn, John 141, 143
cold, supernatural 16, 18, 19, 42, 89, 105, 109, 169, 170, 187, 199
Collins, General Michael 72
Combermere Abbey *35*
Combermere, Lord *35*
'Company of Avalon' 55–60, 62
Cook, Florence 47
Corbett, Sybell *35*
Cornell, Anthony D. 45; *45*
Cortachy Castle 73–4; *74*
Cosford, W. Midlands 203–4
'cosmic force' 21
Court, Anne 64
Coutts, Davy 149; *149*
Cox, Esther 100
Crichton family 136–9; *137*
'crisis' apparitions 35, 41
Crookes, Sir William 49; *47*
Croom-Hollingsworth, Geoffrey 104–5
cross *123*
'cross-correspondences' 52
Culloden, Battle of 128, 129
curses 85–6, 125, 132–5, 139, 196, 200–201
cylinder, apparition of 32

dagger 32
Daily Mail 44
Daily Mirror 98, 108, 109
Dallington 188; *188*
Dalrymple, Miss Margaret 74
danger, phantom warning of 32; *see also* prophecy
Dartmoor 199; *200*
Davies, Sergeant 128–31
death, moment of 35, 41, 71–4, 77, 85, 135
DeFeo, Ronald 168, 170, 172, 173; *170*
Delaney, Father *173*
demons, 9, 22, 25, 87, 168, 169, 173
Densham, Denny 105
Devil, the 9, 29, 68, 125, 126, 170; *22*
devils 15, 22–5; *25*
Diaz, Bartholomes 68
Dingwall, Dr Eric J. 92, 100, 101, 102
disappearance of real people and objects 41, 43, 113, 122–3
dogs 34, 41, 191, *201*; phantom 33, 34, 120, 201
Domrémy, France *42*
'Donald' (poltergeist) 12
Dönitz, Karl 70
Douglas-Home, The Hon. Henry 92, 97, 101
dowsing 60–61
drawings, spirit 12, 153–4, 198; *153, 154*
dreams 10
drugs 23, 25, 86

Druids 51
drumming 11–12, 73–4; *11*
Dubrach 129; *128–9*
Dunstable 63, 64
Dutchman, Flying 67–70, 181; *67–70, 180–1*
dwarf 24

Eawulf, Earl of Edgarley (Eanulf, Eanwulf) 56, 57
ectoplasm 19, 20, 41, 106; *20*
Edgar Chapel 52, 54, 60, 61; *53, 54*
Edgehill 29–30, 38, 185; *29*
electricity 19, 21, 88, 89, 106, 110, 157–9, 163
elementals 10, 87
Elizabeth, Queen, The Queen Mother *126*
Ellison, Rev. Charles 95
English Pub, The (Jackson) 198
End of Borley Rectory, The (Price) 91, 102
Enfield 10–11, 14–15, 19, 20, 78, 107–18; *10–11, 16, 107–18*
Enfield Parapsychical Research Group 106, 201; *103*
epicentre (of poltergeist) *see* focus
epilepsy 17
ESP 162
evil spirits 24; *see also* demons, devils etc.
Ewans of Mull 73
execution 29, 44, 51, 122–3
exorcism 22–5, 49, 101, 150, 152, 153, 176; *22–25*
experimentally induced apparition 41

faces, appearance of 16, 164–6; *165, 166*
fakery 19, 20, 29, 42, 44–5, 49, 78, 92–5, 99, 101, 102, 109, 112, 116–8, 159, 170, 171–3, 179; *21*
false sightings 42, 47–9, 76–7, 85, 86; *see also* fakery
Farquharson, D. 129, 130
Fellowes-Gordon, Ian 85, 86
'F.G., Mr' 37–8
Fielding, Henry 78, 83
Fielding, John 83
fires, mysterious 11, 12, 17, 93, 95, 100, 101, 102, 112, 137; *11, 114, 115*
Fleur, Dr 152, 153, 154
Florida 46; *46*
Fodor, Dr Nandor 174, 178, 179; *175*
Fokke, Bernard 68
Folkestone, Kent 13; *13*
folklore 64–6, 71–4, 136
footman, giant 43
footprints 86, 169, 179
footsteps 10, 41, 44, 88, 98, 106, 139, 141, 143, 145–6, 150, 169
Forman, Joan 47; *48*
Fox case 12, 14; *15*
Foyster family 99, 100–101, 102
Franklin, Benjamin 78
Franzen, James 79, 80
Frendraught House 136–9; *136–8*

frog 21
From the Devil's Triangle to the Devil's Jaw (Winer) 85
Fuller, John G. 46
Fulton, Roy 63, 64, 65; *64*
Fyvie Castle 132–5; *132–5*

gallows 122–3; *123*
Ganong, Professor W.F. 182
Gardner, Ava *69*
gate of remembrance, The (Bond) 58, 60, 61
gematria 58
George, Prince of Wales (George V) 69; *68*
Gerald of Wales (Giraldus Cambrensis) 9, 51
Ghost hunting, a practical guide (Green) 38, 47
ghosts, nature of 35–41; *see also* 'person-centred' and 'place-centred' apparitions, 'recording' theory
Gill, Madge 198
Gillan, Alexander 120–23
Giraldus Cambrensis *see* Gerald of Wales
Glamis Castle 124–7; *124–6*
Glanvill, Rev. Joseph 11, 12
Glanville, Sidney 94, 96, 102
Glasgow, Scotland 15
Glastonbury 51–62; *51–62*
Gmelig-Meyling, Dono 111
Goblin (ship) 70
Goby, Brother John 28–9
God, appearance of 67
god, household *178*
Goddard, Sir Victor 193
Goldney, Mrs K.M. 92, 100, 101, 102; *101*
Gordon, Colonel Cosmo 135
Graham, James, Marquis of Montrose 185–7; *186*
graveyards, haunted 106, 164, 183
Green, Andrew 38, 46, 47; *48*
'Green Lady' 135; *135*
Green, Martin 204; *204*
Gregory, Anita *117*
Gregson, Captain William Hart 102
Grenadier, the (pub) 199; *200*
Grosse, Maurice 10, 19–20, 108–9, 110, 113, 114, 116, 117, 118; *11, 109*
Gurney, Edmund 77

Hall, Trevor H. 45, 92, 100, 101, 102
hallucinations 19, 24, 35, 36, 42, 69, 104
hand, appearance of 19, 41; mark on 38
Hankey, Rosalie 65
Hanks, Harry *12*
Harper family 107–18; *16, 107, 108, 111, 112, 116*
Harris, Alec 49; *49*
Harris, Melvin 45
Harris, Rev. Dr 27–8, 38
Harz Mountains 95; *92*
Hasted, Professor J.B. 111, 115, 117
haunters and the haunted, The (Lytton) 87
haunting of Borley Rectory, The (Dingwall et al.) 100

Hawaii 64
Hawthorne, Nathaniel 27–8; *27*
Haylock, Bill 10
Hayter, Gladys 41, 43; *41*
heat, supernatural 99, 107, 187
Hell Fire Club *78*
Hendon 203–4; *204*
Henry VIII 51, 52, 56, 61, 62
Hindus 51
Hinxworth Place 188; *188*
hitch-hiker, phantom 63–6
Hitching, Shirley 12, 15, 16, 20
Hoad, Sir Jasper 86
Hoe Benham 33
Holbourn family 141–3
Holme Hale 190
Holy Ghost 67
Holy Grail 52, 60
Holy Thorn *60*
Home, Daniel Douglas 15, 32
Hope, Lord Charles 92, 121, 122; *120*
Hornby, Judge Sir Edmund 76–7
horses, phantom 33, 73, 98, 190; *33, 98, 190*
'Howard, Wicked Lady' 34
Howlett, W.E. 88, 89
Huntly, Marquis of 136, 137; *137*
hyperventilation 19
hypnosis 35, 36

Inconstant, HMS 69
infra-red 21; *38, 41*
invented ghosts 13, 19, 37, 45; *19*
Inverness 121; *121*

Jack the Blaster 198
Jackson, Andrew 175, 177; *177*
Jackson, Michael 198
Jackson, Thomas 29–30
Jacobites 128, 129, 130; *128–9*
Janet (focus of poltergeist) 11; *10*
Jeffreys, Judge 199–200; *198*
Jenkins, Stephen 51
Jesus Christ 52, 65
Joad, C.E.M. 95; *92*
Job, Book of 39
Johannes Bryant 54, 62
Johnson, Samuel 82, 83
Joplin, Missouri, U.S.A. *183*
Joseph of Arimathea 52, 55
Journal (of SPR) 21, 45, 47, 118, 145, 191
Jung, Carl 74

Karger, Dr 158, 159
Kenawell, William 56
Kennedy, Pres. J. F. 73; *72*
Kensington 31–2
Kent, William and Fanny 79–83
Ket's Rebellion 191; *190*
Kidder, Margot *169, 172*
Kipling, Rudyard 87, 88
Kirk, Colonel Sir Lewis 30
Korea 64
Kulagina, Nina 20–21; *20*

Lady Chapel *55*
Lairre, Marie 94–5
Lamb, Elspet 121

Lang, Andrew 64, 65
langsuyar 64; *64*
lar familiaris 178
leap in the dark, A 37, 150; *146–7*
Ledsham, Cynthia 45, 102
Legge, William Earl of Carlisle 82
Leith of Fyvie, Lord 135
Leslie family 136
Lethbridge, T.C. 62
Lett, Charles and Mrs 36–7
levitation 18, 19, 102, 112, 113, 115, 169, 172; *19, 21*
Lewes, Bishop of 23
Lhanbryde Church 121; *122*
Life magazine 45
light bulbs and tubes 13, 156, 157, 158, 161
lights, strange 44, 91, 99, 135, 180–3; *180, 183*
Lilias, Dame 133–5
Linehan, Edward J. 183
Loch Scuabain Castle 73
Loft, Bob 46
Lord Mayor of London 78, 82
Lord, Rev. K.F. 42, 43
Loretto Chapel 52, 53, 57; *52–3, 60*
Lund, Rev. 12
Lutz, George and Kathy 168–73; *170*
Lynes, Francis ('Scratching Fanny') 79–83
Lytton, Bulwer 87; *88*

Macbeth 32
McCarthy, Neil 146, 147
McCormack, Irene 71
McDonagh, Major 188–9
McDonald, Mrs 145–50
McEwan, Peter and Dorothy 144–50; *144–5, 148*
McHardie, Isobel 130, 131
McHarg, Dr James 191, 192, 193
Mackenzie, Andrew 47
MacLaine, The 73
MacPherson, Alexander 129–30, 131
magnetism 21, 62, 159
Malaysia 64
Malcolm II, King of Scotland 125; *125*
'Man in Grey' 30; *30*
Manning, Matthew 15; *118*
Markham, Rear-Admiral 84
marks on body 15, 169; *15*
Marlborough 68
Marryat, Captain 42
Marsden Grotto 198
Marston Moor 185; *186*
Mary Celeste 68
Mason, James *69*
mass hysteria 79
material objects, ghosts of 32–4
Mather, Dr Cotton 31, 69
medal apported 95, 98–9
mediums 19, 20, 24, 49, 108, 111, 153, 154, 179
Medlycott, Sir Hubert 43
Melgum, John 136, 137
menopause 16, 23
Mesmer, Anton 21
metal bending 11, 16, 111, 114–5, 118

Michel, Annaliese *23*
Middleton, Jessie A. 90
migraine 17
Miles, Miss Clarissa 33, 34
mirages 69
mirror, reflection in 32, 36, 41
Missiter, Mr 83
monks 43, 44, 51, 53–7, 59, 61, 62, 91, 96, 188; *40*
Montrose, Marquis of *see* Graham James
Moore, Rev. John 80
Morison family 138, 139; *139*
Morley Old Hall 45; *45*
Mormonism 65
Morris, Graham 108, 109, 110, 114
Morris, Dr Robert 34
Morris, Rosalind 109, 110
Morton, Miss R.C. 40–41
most haunted house in England, The (Price) 91, 94
Mount St Helens 66; *66*
Moy Castle 73
multiple personalities 62, 112
murder 30, 34, 81, 94, 121, 122, 129–31, 136–7, 141, 168, 174
music, phantom 43, 74, 169
muslin 19, 20
Myers, F.W.H. 37, 40
Myers, Mr (Berkeley Square) 89–90

Naseby, Northants 185; *186*
Nechtanesmere 192; *192*
Neil-Smith, Rev. J. Christopher 25; *25*
Nephites 65
Newark Castle 186; *187*
Newby, Yorks. 43; *42*
Newton, Sir Isaac 78
night side of nature, The (Crowe) 52
Normans 57
Notes and Queries 88
Notes for investigators of spontaneous cases (SPR) 47
numbers, science of 58
nuns 44, 45, 65, 66, 91, 94, 96, 97, 104–5, 106, 188; *98*

Oakes, Mrs 82
'O'Barry, James' (pseudonym) 72–3
Okehampton Castle 34
Oldbury Camp 188; *189*
'out-of-body' experiences 10, 41
'Owd Nance' 194
Owen, Professor A.R.G. 20

paintings 125–6, 127, 135, 153, 159, 160, 161, 165; *124, 135, 159*
Palatine 70, 180
Pall Mall magazine 89
Palladino, Eusapio 18; *19*
Palmer, Lady, 43; *42*
Pakistan 64
Paracelsus 21
Parapsychology Institute of America 170
Paris, France *12*
Parry, Frank 106

Parsons, Richard and Elizabeth 79–83
Pearce, Jacqueline *146, 147*
Pearce-Higgins, Canon J.D. 49
Pelé 64, *63*
Penkaet Castle 140–43; *140–43*
'person-centred' apparitions 31, 41, 43
Petitpierre, Dom Robert 25
Phénomènes dits de matérialisation (Bisson) 20
Philby, John 37
'Philip' (invented ghost) 13, 19; *19*
Philiphaugh, Scotland 186–7
photography 20, 38, 42–3, 106, 142, 152–3, 165, 166; *35, 38, 40–2*
pigs, phantom 33, 173
Pinney family 195–7
Pittman, Oswald 33, 34
'place-centred' apparitions 41, 43; *36, see also* 'recording' theory
Playfair, Guy Lyon 10, 116, 117, 118; *109*
Poe, Edgar Allan 28; *28*
poison 81, 83, 174, 177, 179
police 17, 47, 63, 71, 107, 159, 161–2, 163, 170
poltergeists 9–25, 42, 45, 65, 79, 88, 100, 107–18, 152–5, 156–63, 174, 201; *9–18, 107–18, 178, 179*
Pope, W.J. McQueen 30, *30*
popes 25, 28, 29, 61; *29*
Porthcurno Cove 70; *70*
possession 112, 168
post-mortem apparitions 41
Potter, Roy 104
prayer 25, 49, 62, 99, 101, 187
Price, Harry 14, 44–5, 87–8, 91–5, 98, 99, 101, 102, 201, 205; *92, 101*
priests 22–5, 27–8, 37, 43, 91, 108, 165, 170, 171, 172, 194; *22–5, 36, 41, 173*
Proceedings (of SPR) 45, 47
prophecy 64, 65, 66, 78, 120, 135
Psychic News 47
psychokinesis *see* poltergeists
psychology 35, 49, 111, 163, 179
puberty 14–16, 112, 179
public houses, haunted 198–201; *198–201*

qabalistic science 58

rabbits 78
Radulphus Cancellarius (Ralph) 56, 57
Ralston, Gavin 127; *127*
Randall, Gr. Capt. Bill 203
rapping 11, 12, 13, 15, 16, 19, 20, 41, 48, 79, 80, 81, 82, 83, 98, 104, 105, 106, 107, 109, 146, 148–9, 150, 154, 175, 176
rats 34, 45, 99, 139
Ratcliffe Wharf 37

rattlesnake 34
Raynham Hall 43; *40*
'recording' theory 28, 62, 189, 190, 193, 199; *30, 33, 36*
Reculver, Kent 197; *197*
Reeves, Mr and Mrs 190–91
Repo, Don *46*
review of reviews, The 86
Rhodes, Alan *14*
Richet, Charles 20
Richmond, Duke of 123; *122*
Ricks, Christopher 30
Rio, Martin del 9
Rituale 25
Robertson, David 111, 112, 113, 114, 115, 117
Robinson, Dean J.A. 56, 58
Robson, Michael 45
Rogo, Scott 21, 65
Roll, W.G. 10
roses 149, 150; *149*
Rosenheim 156–9; *156*
RSPK (recurrent spontaneous psychokinesis) 9, 11, 16, 17; *see also* poltergeists
Rupert, Prince 29–30; *29*
Russell, Ronald R. 106; *103*

St André, Nathanael 78
St Clair, Sheila 71, 72, 74
St Elmo's fire 182
St John's Church 82; *83*
Sandford Orcas 43; *43*
Sarsina, Italy 24
Saxons 57
Schaberl *see* Schneider
Schneider, Anne-Marie 17, 159, 160–63, *16, 160, 162*
'Scratching Fanny' 79–83
seances 13, 19, 21, 24, 46, 59, 98; *19*
Search for Harry Price (Hall) 45, 93, 95
Search for truth (Price) 93
second sight 61
Seton, Alexander, Lord Fyvie 133–4; *132*
Shambala 51
Shanghai 76–7; *76*
ships, phantom 67–70, 181; *67–70, 181*
Sicily 64
Silver Cliff 183
skeletons 56, 61, 68, 130; *58*
skulls 39, 44, 56, 194–7; *58, 194*
slaves 39, 174, 175, 195; *174, 175*
sleepwalking 20
Small, Ensign 131
Smith, Miss E.F. 191–2
Smith, Rev. G. Eric and Mrs 97–9, 102
Smithfield 79, 80; *79*
Smyth, Frank 37; *37*
snail 24
Society for Psychical Research (SPR) 33, 35, 36, 37, 40, 44, 45, 47, 49, 60, 76, 77, 78, 92, 94, 97, 99, 108, 109, 113, 114, 117, 145, 148; *48, 150*
soldiers, phantom 29–30, 35–6, 185–7, 188–9, 192; *185, 190–1*

solidity of ghosts 36, 38, 41
sounds, mysterious 10, 11, 12, 13, 15, 20, 38, 41, 48, 81, 88, 91, 92, 97, 99, 104, 105, 106, 107, 139, 140, 141, 142, 146, 175, 176, 178, 187, 194, 199; *see also* drumming, footsteps, rapping, voices etc.
South Africa 64; *65*
Soviet Union 20–21
speaking clock 16–17, 156
spirit raising 49
Spiritualism 12, 19, 24, 54, 60, 86, 101, 164, 179
Squires, Mary 78–9
Stanbridge, Beds. 63, 64
Star Inn 201; *201*
Stead, W.T. 86; *86*
Steiger, Rod *173*
stones 11, 12–13, 16, 44, 98, 132, 133, 135, 175; *12*
Stote 68
Strathmore, Earls of 124–7; *124–5, 127*
stress 16, 20, 21, 22, 24, 35, 162
subnormality, mental 15
suicide 33–4, 48; *43*
Sunday Times 37
superstition 45, 174
Supernature (Watson) 32
Sutton, Charles 44, 91–2
Sweden 64
Swifte, Edmund L. 32, 33

tables, moving 13, 18; *19, 21*
Tabori, Dr 92
tape recording 104, 105–6, 109, 110, 166
telepathy 15, 35, 36, 37
telephone 16–17, 155–6
teleportation 113
television programmes 37, 45, 150, 155, 191; *146–7*
Theatre Royal, Drury Lane 30; *30*
Thierry (focus of poltergeist activity) 152–5; *152–5*
This house is haunted (Playfair) 109, 116, 117
Thomas of Erceldoune (the Rhymer) 132–3
Thorne, Albert 34
Thurstan, Abbot 57
Tibet 51
Tidworth 11; *11*
Times, The 91, 95, 102
Tofts, Mary 78; *78*
Tolbooth prison 131; *131*
Tomczyk, Stanislawa 21
Tor, Glastonbury 51; *59*
Torno, Guy de 28–9
Tourette, Gilles de la 12
Tower of London 32; *33*
Town of Ramsgate (pub) 199, 200; *198–9*
Towns, Captain 36–7
Townsend, Miss 43; *42*
Townshend, Marquis of 43
Towy Valley 204
trance 18, 41, 84, 86, 112, 152, 153, 179; *116*
treasure, buried 60, 61
tree, prophetic 78
Tryon, Vice-Admiral Sir George and Lady 84–6; *84, 85*
tumour 15
Tyrrell, G.N.M. 36, 41

UFOs 181
Understanding ghosts (Branden) 35
unconscious mind 60, 61, 62, 74, 179, 193
Underwood, Peter 47, 92; *93*
Uniondale 66; *65*
USA legend 64–5, 70, 180–3

vampire 64
Vanderdecken 67, 69
Victor, St 61
Victoria, HMS 84–6; *84*
video recording 110, 117, 118
Vikings 71, 191
voices, supernatural 10, 11, 12, 28–9, 35, 97, 99, 104, 105, 106, 112, 114, 116–7, 118, 135, 141, 143, 166, 171, 176, 177, 178, 188, 195, 197, 199
voodoo *174*

'W., Mr' 86
Walpole, Horace, 82, 83
Wagner, Richard 67, 69
Wakefield-Smith, Mr and Mrs 37
Waldegrave family 106; *105*
walking stick 15, 78; *14*
Wall, V.C. 98
walls, ability to pass through 42, 112
'watchers' *see* Company of Avalon
Wapping Old Stairs 200; *198*
water, mysterious behaviour of 86, 91, 102, 112
Watson, Lyall 32
Waud, Reginald 33, 34
Webber, Jack *21*
weight loss 18, 20, 21, 115; *19*
wells 95, 138
Wells Cathedral *62*
Wells, Mother 79–80
Wesley family 81; *82*
Whyting, Abbot Richard 51, 53, 62
Wilkes, John 78
Will o' the wisp 180–3; *180*
William the Conqueror 57
William the Monk (Gulielmus Monachus) 53, 56
Williams, Gordon 199
Williams, Wendy *146, 147, 150*
Wilson, Colin 92–3, 95
Winer, Richard 85
witchcraft 29, 174–9; *176*
Wonders of the invisible world (Mather) 31
Woodford 43; *41*
writing, spirit 11, 44, 51, 53, 99, 100, 101, 106, 118, 134; *57, 99, 134*

York 16

Zicha, Dr 158, 159
Zugun, Eleonora 15; *15*